Black Radio/Black Resistance

Black Radio/Black Resistance

THE LIFE & TIMES OF THE *TOM JOYNER MORNING SHOW*

MICAELA DI LEONARDO

OXFORD
UNIVERSITY PRESS

Oxford University Press is a department of the University of Oxford. It furthers
the University's objective of excellence in research, scholarship, and education
by publishing worldwide. Oxford is a registered trade mark of Oxford University
Press in the UK and certain other countries.

Published in the United States of America by Oxford University Press
198 Madison Avenue, New York, NY 10016, United States of America.

© Oxford University Press 2019

Library of Congress Cataloging-in-Publication Data
Names: Di Leonardo, Micaela, 1949– author.
Title: Black radio/black resistance : the life & times of The Tom Joyner
morning show / Micaela di Leonardo.
Description: New York : Oxford University Press, 2019. |
Includes bibliographical references and index.
Identifiers: LCCN 2018053833 (print) | LCCN 2019000755 (ebook) |
ISBN 9780190870201 (updf) | ISBN 9780190870218 (epub) |
ISBN 9780190870225 (Online Content) | ISBN 9780190870188 (pbk. : alk. paper) |
ISBN 9780190870195 (cloth : alk. paper)
Subjects: LCSH: Tom Joyner morning show (Radio program) |
Joyner, Tom, 1949– | Radio broadcasting—Social aspects—United States.
Classification: LCC PN1991.77.T66 (ebook) | LCC PN1991.77.T66 D53 2019(print) |
DDC 791.44/72—dc23
LC record available at https://lccn.loc.gov/2018053833

9 8 7 6 5 4 3 2 1

Paperback printed by Sheridan Books, Inc., United States of America
Hardback printed by Bridgeport National Bindery, Inc., United States of America

To the progressive Resistance everywhere

Contents

Acknowledgments

Anyone who engages in a fourteen-year book project inevitably racks up vast piles of intellectual and other debts. I must first thank the *Tom Joyner Morning Show* for its very existence, and offer my profound gratitude to the entire crew, past and present, and its millions-strong, multifarious, witty audience. I am also in debt to the many dozens of black Americans all over the country, listeners and non-listeners, who allowed me to interview them over the last decades about their *TJMS* opinions and experiences. Much gratitude to the institutions that kindly helped fund the research—the American Council of Learned Societies (ACLS), the School for Advanced Research, and the Institute for Policy Research at Northwestern. I would also like to acknowledge the institutions that invited me to give talks about the *TJMS*, or published my pieces about it: various venues at Northwestern, the University of Chicago, the Institute for Policy Research, the Mellon Foundation/ Kaplan Center's 2014 "Global Work and Working-Class Communities" conference, multiple American Anthropological Association panels, the American Studies Association, *Cultural Studies, American Ethnologist, SOULS: A Critical Journal of Black Politics, Culture, and Society,* and *Cultural Anthropology.*

A number of colleagues were key to publishing my ongoing research on the *TJMS,* helping me advance the project. Professors Jeff Maskovsky and Ida Susser convened the Wenner-Gren "Rethinking America" conference in 2004, and published my first piece using *TJMS* materials in the resultant anthology. Professor Della Pollock was wonderfully enthusiastic about my first full *TJMS* article, which she published in *Cultural Studies.* Professor Angelique Haugerud was unfailingly helpful with my *American Ethnologist* piece on the *TJMS* and Obama's first election, and generously gave me extra space in which to treat the topics she pushed me to cover. Professor Jane Rhodes, director of African American Studies at the University of Illinois at Chicago, was appreciative of my contribution to the *SOULS* special issue on respectability politics she co-organized, offered excellent advice on revisions, and solved my final title conundrum. And Professors Lucas Bessire and David Bond invited me to write for a special section on Trumpism in *Cultural Anthropology* right after the 2016 election.

Research librarians and IT (information technology) experts are the unheralded wizards of our research. Profound thanks to all the librarians who helped me locate documents, recordings, and books. Kathleen Bethel, the magnificently skilled African American Studies librarian for Northwestern Libraries, started me on the road and has been helpful throughout. Laura Holt did life-saving inter-library loan work for me during my year at the School for Advanced Research. Multiple Indiana University librarians arranged for me to rent streaming access to the only available copy of the key twelve-part NPR series, "Black Radio." And Professor Zat Jamil of the Pratt Institute, formerly my Northwestern graduate student, offered extraordinary help with powerpoints and embedded audio and video as I was preparing my first illustrated *TJMS* talk. As a native Singaporean, she was hilariously knowledgeable and enthusiastic about soul music, and our conversations also aided me. And she is *still* helping me with tech!

Then there is a very long list of friends, students and former students, and colleagues who have aided, encouraged, and advised me over the lengthy years of research and writing *Black Radio/Black Resistance*. Professor Jane Collins's role has been huge. For decades now, we have shared our work and writing in wonderful comradeship, and she served as sounding board, adviser, and critic of the final manuscript—as well as appreciating dozens upon dozens of my enthusiastic *TJMS* emails over the decades. Professor D. Soyini Madison's early *TJMS* fandom led to many of our most hilarious and enlightening conversations about race, gender, politics, performance, and media. Her work on engaged ethnography has inspired me, and she has been a *Black Radio* cheerleader throughout. The invitation to speak at her Cultural Studies Summer Institute at Northwestern also helped me to kick-start my analyses. Also in Performance Studies, Professor E. Patrick Johnson, director of African American Studies at Northwestern, galvanized me with his own engaged race/gender/LBGTQ (lesbian/bisexual/gay/transgender/queer) research, kindly invited me to speak multiple times to his classes about the project, and used his vast musical expertise to identify a "murdered hit's" source for me when Soundhound and Shazam, and my own knowledge, failed me.

Professor Stephen Steinberg, the well-known CUNY (City University of New York) sociologist of race, and I have been talking about and reading and reviewing one another's work on U.S. racism and its academic enablers for close to four decades, and I have treasured our robust colleagueship. My former students Professors Ana Croegaert and Almita Miranda were both profoundly engaged in the project. Almita generously shared with me her research on Spanish-language U.S. radio, and our discussions of comparative minority political radio broadcasting and of the *TJMS*'s consistent cross-racial solidarity were of enormous help. Ana, a scholar of race, deeply understood the political stakes of my study as well as sharing my soul-music obsessions, and looked over many passages for me. She graciously allowed me to include an embarrassing Chicago race relations vignette in which we both appear. Former grad student Craig Tower, a radio scholar, offered inestimable help on the literature of the field as I began research. Similarly, Tamara Roberts, now a professor of music at the University of California at Berkeley, but then a performance studies Ph.D. student, offered very helpful race/ethnomusicology thoughts as I was first framing the project. Colleague Chris Kuzawa, an excellent writer as well as biological anthropology hotshot, edited my very first *TJMS* piece and gave me helpful positive feedback on one of my *TJMS* talks. My friend and colleague in French, Professor Jane Winston, was unfailingly supportive of the project, and provided helpful direction at key points. Professors Cory Kratz, Madhu Dubey, and Roger Lancaster wrote fellowship letters for me, a thankless task for which I am thanking them.

Music scholar Professor Sumanth Gopinath and his partner, my former student, Professor Beth Hartman, also a music/performance scholar, read several chapters for me using their expertise, and rescued me from many errors. As well, Sumanth's own *The Ringtone Dialectic*, with its race and political economy focus, was of great use. And he took the time to advise me on the complex legalities of song lyric quotations. Sociologist Roberta Spalter-Roth's stalwart friendship encouraged me as I despaired of finishing, and then of *ever* getting the photo array set up, and then of ever seeing the physical book published.

Professor Judith Hamera of Princeton arrived late in the process but was of inestimable help in cheering me on, reacting with great appreciation to the post-Trump election vignettes I shared with her as I felt forced to write an extra chapter on that disastrous political phenomenon and the *TJMS*'s brilliant and furious reactions to it. And Hamera's own political-economy-infused study of Michael Jackson and Detroit in historical context, *Unfinished Business*, has been an inspiration since I heard her speak about it some years ago. Valued archaeology colleague Mark Hauser read and commented with skill on chapters, although I didn't take all of his advice. His brilliant cultural anthropologist partner, Professor Kalyani Menon of DePaul University, gave very helpful feedback on chapters as well. They both have been deeply appreciated good friends in hard times. As have former Northwestern students, and now professors at Colgate College, Santiago Juarez and Kristin De Lucia. Wonderful newish colleague Katie Amato listened with great interest to my narrative of the project and insightfully connected it to her own local adolescent black radio experiences. My old undergraduate student Anneeth Kaur Hundle, now a professor at the University of California, Irvine, shared my deep passion for local black radio and its music, and we spent much time enjoying, singing, and discussing it and the *TJMS*. Professor Brett Gadsden, former graduate student and now African American historian at Northwestern, and his wife Natasha Tretheway, former Poet Laureate, now professor of English and Creative Writing at Northwestern, both threw themselves into solving my end-of-project problems like the good friends they are becoming. As has brilliant African American historian Leslie Harris, new colleague and friend. As did my wonderful new anthropological colleague Emrah Yildiz. Northwestern Screen Cultures Professor Miriam Petty provided inspiring analysis of the Tyler Perry phenomenon and some key citations. And Northwestern media relations specialist Hilary Hurd Anyaso kindly attempted to help with the complex photo permission process.

I must also note my gratitude to the many scholars who have trod the media/politics/race/music ground before me, and on whose work I have thus been able to build. "Anthropology of media" pioneers like Lila Abu-Lughod, Faye Ginsburg, Richard Wilk, Kelly Askew, and others; interdisciplinary communications scholars Robert Entman and Andrew Rojecki, William Greider, Susan Douglas and Robert McChesney, Dolores Inés Casillas; black radio scholars William Barlow, Gilbert Williams, Catherine Squires, John A. Jackson, Craig Werner, E. Riley Snorton, and others; African American popular culture scholars Tricia Rose, Mark Anthony Neal, Melissa Harris-Perry, Marla Frederick, John L. Jackson, Jr, Farah Jasmine Griffin, and many others; everyone involved in the NPR "Black Radio" project; and a wide group of U.S. historians—the late Michael Katz, Eric Foner, Allan J. Lichtman, Stephanie Coontz, John Demos, the late Herbert Gutmann, Jacqueline Jones, Isabel Wilkerson, James Grossman, and so many others. Then there is the indispensable range of black feminist writing across the disciplines: Dorothy Roberts, Evelyn Brooks Higginbotham, Brittney Cooper, Darlene Clark Hine, E. Frances White, Evelynn M. Hammonds, for example. Finally, the study has benefited from the excellent political journalism and race scholarship and activism of many: Bryan Stevenson, Charles Blow, Ta-Nehisi Coates, Gary Younge, Jelani Cobb, Susan Faludi, David Corn, Ian Haney-López, Eduardo Bonilla Silva, John Nichols, David Corn, Richard Rothstein, Nikole Hannah-Jones, Rebecca Solnit, George Lipsitz, Michelle Alexander, and so many others.

Certain friends, colleagues, former students, and family were not specifically involved in helping me with this project, but their own intellectual/political work and their warm support were of enormous use: Professors Ellen Berrey, Niko Besnier, Beth Derderian, Niki Fabricant, Amal Hassan Fadlalla, Christine Gailey, Alana Glaser, Anna Guevarra, Conn (Ringo) Hallinan, Susan Hyatt, Amanda Logan, Nancy MacLean, Gina Pérez, Gayatri Reddy, Dorothy Roberts, Cynthia Robin, Dario Valles; friends Robin Wells and Cary Zeitlin. Then there is my wild, wonderful, and loving family—Kevin McRae, Ja-Ae [Oranit] Jinaphen, Orchid Kwei, Kelly Eve Vanderlan McRae, Ian Kwei McRae, Julie Chaves, and Aaron Oran McRae.

While they did not help me specifically with *Black Radio*, the Northwestern Department of Anthropology staff's extraordinary competence and helpfulness definitely played a role in my ability to finish the book. Thanks to Kulsum Virmani, Will Voltz, Tracy Tohtz, and Nancy Hickey. I also thank the staff and other patrons at my local Starbucks, where (ironically, because the *TJMS* dogged Starbucks unmercifully) much of this book was written. Ungentrified, race- and class-integrated, and with killer soul and jazz music, it provided a wonderful backdrop to my cogitations and efforts, and many regulars expressed great interest in "your black radio project," cheering me immensely.

At Oxford University Press, I am grateful to my insightful anonymous reviewers, to Hannah Doyle, to Alphonsa James, who sympathetically extended herself to help me with software problems during copy editing review, and to excellent copy editor Lori Jacobs, brilliant cover designer Terri Sirma, and particularly to senior editor Norm Hirschy, who arrived very late in the process after my first editor left the press. But he arrived with deep interest in the topic, infectious enthusiasm, and strong opinions, whose rationale he explained with great clarity, and I found myself appreciating his logic and gaining a third wind from his passionate appreciation. He also caught two serious problems while I could still fix them, for which I am extremely grateful.

Toward the end of the project I hired my Ph.D. student Elisa Lanari to work on illustration issues and the index. Always the consummate professional, she trained herself to transform photos and scoured the websites searching for appropriate ones. Lanari, an Italian national but an Americanist anthropologist, showed great sensitivity to the African American materials, throwing herself into the project with infectious enthusiasm. I could not have finished the difficult photo permissions process without her devoted, intelligent, emergency help—although we did also receive late, and crucial, advice from former head of Northwestern's public relations, Pat Tremmel, for which I am also very grateful.

Friend Emmanuel Wilder, despite not being a *TJMS* fan, was extremely supportive of the project, reading passages for accessibility and interest, even attempting to make African American *TJMS* connections for me through his thrift store Classy Closet, a local site of lively interracial amity as well as great bargains. And, while writers rarely mention medical issues in acknowledgements, I suffered several highly painful injuries during the long research and writing process, and my own crack, lively physical therapy team—Stacy Malone, Gloria Gallardo, and Katherine Jackson—returned me to functioning and helped me become relatively pain-free over the many years of writing and revisions.

My beloved late father, Michael di Leonardo, died too young, a decade before the *TJMS* was even founded. But I inherited his musical ear, singing ability, and unashamed theatricality, as well as his own broad musical genre interests—across vocal jazz, blues, pop, soul, and flamenco. I am grateful not only for his warm, unstinting love, but for the ways in which he modeled for me what I later cherished in the *TJMS*: fast, cutting wit, deep appreciation of any clever narrative, profoundly visceral enjoyment of music, and highly emotive, liberal political commentary. I hope that I have honored him with this book.

Finally, my adorable, witty mother-in-law, Clarita MacDonald Reed, was an enormous loving presence in my life for twenty-eight years, until she passed in 2017. My concern for her welfare during Hurricane Katrina, as family evacuated her, spurred my attention to the *TJMS*—they were covering the disaster more fully and angrily than mainstream media, and simultaneously engaging in major charity for victims. Ironically, despite being a New Orleans native, Clarita never listened to any black radio—not even the classic, independent, multiracial local station WWOZ—didn't much care for soul music, or even jazz after the Big Band era. But she understood and practiced, at genius level, a gorgeous musicality of speech, of performance: rapidly code-switching across "standard" English—dropping references to Dag Hammarskjold, the McCarthy era, the murdered and now sanctified archbishop Oscar Romero—and her own New Orleans black idiolect, with its unique terms and references, swooping up and down the intonation contour, throwing the best, nastiest shade, hilariously, fearlessly mimicking the speech of everyone around her across race, nationality, gender, and age, just being herself—an educated, elderly, engaged, angry, extraordinarily lively, hysterically funny, progressive Southern black Catholic woman. I sent her my books and articles as they came out, and she read them all, until macular degeneration felled her. Even then, she would boast about her stuffed bookcase. It is my great sorrow that I will no longer be adding to that bookcase, will not hear that matchless voice again.

1

Introduction

The Best-Kept Secret in America

> The more expansive vision [of civil rights] . . . emphasizes the humanity
> of black people and realizes that black freedom movements encompass
> international and feminist projects.
> —Soyica Diggs Colbert, *Black Movements*, 2017[1]

> The average, struggling, non-morbid Negro is the best-kept secret
> in America.
> —Zora Neale Hurston, 1950[2]

It started out as fan notes.

In the 1990s—the later Clinton into the George W. Bush years—I was in my forties, living in the Chicago area, politically depressed, and hungry for soul music. I happened upon the biggest local adult black FM station, V103 (102.7 FM). Early weekday mornings, they broadcast a show created in 1994 by the Alabama-born, Tuskegee-educated disk jockey Tom Joyner.

The *Tom Joyner Morning Show* (*TJMS*), for four hours Monday through Friday, played the music I identified with and wanted to hear—"the best of the hits and dusties." ("Dusties" is black Chicagoan for oldies.) That translated to a wondrous diet of 1970s and 1980s soul (the Isley Brothers, Aretha, Marvin Gaye, Harold Melvin and the Blue Notes, Atlantic Starr, Earth, Wind & Fire), black pop—Luther Vandross and Anita Baker were still going strong—and funk music, intermixed with some gospel, a little hip-hop—Mary J Blige and the Fugees with Lauryn Hill broke out in this period. And then there were the magnificent rising stars of the neosoul movement: D'Angelo, Angie Stone, Maxwell, Jill Scott, Anthony Hamilton, Erykah Badu, India Arie, Kindred, Gerald Levert, Calvin Richardson, Raheem DeVaughn, Sunshine Anderson, Dwele, Estelle, Rahsaan Patterson. And girl groups like En Vogue, SWV, TLC, Brownstone, Floetry, and Destiny's Child, and boy bands like Toni Tony Tone and Jagged Edge.

I was drawn by the music, *my* music—as Aretha Franklin sang in the 1980s, "with the radio playin our song"—but I stayed for the humor and politics, or, as we will see, frequently the politics *through* the humor.[3] The *TJMS* was a true variety show, incorporating music, hard news and political talk, education—like the regular "Little Known Black History" announcements—with a lot of comedy, celebrity guests and "infotainment," audience call-ins and texts, and philanthropic events like Tuesday's Real Fathers, Real Men, Wednesday's Christmas Wish, and the Thursday Morning Mom. There were also regular activist service provision events like Get Well Wednesdays, with guest medical professionals offering advice and answering listener questions, and frequent tie-ins (pre-Obamacare) to free health screenings in particular cities. And there were the periodic Sky Shows. These were standing-room-only early-morning events, often at HBCU (historically black college and university) campuses, with live musical performances, dance contests, and corporate representatives and local bigwigs presenting scholarship donations.

The show was also extraordinarily popular and lucrative. It grew rapidly over the 1990s, picked up for syndication by black radio stations across the country, achieving a national audience of at least eight million on around one hundred stations by 2004.[4] (I would hear the show in stereo early some mornings, as the guys in the garbage trucks rolling through my back alley blasted the *TJMS*.) In the years since, it has maintained its audience despite fluctuations in syndication, and added first an internet stream—so that fans could listen online from states like Alaska or Colorado that have no black radio stations—and then an iPhone app, making the show available virtually anywhere to millions who could not be near a radio or computer.[5] And listeners did text in from Toronto, Hong Kong, Dubai. Blackamericaweb.com has 15 million page views a month, and more than 1.2 million fans are *TJMS* Facebook followers (the same number as the cable television channel MSNBC). *TJMS* was owned by and syndicated through ABC Radio Network until Tom Joyner bought it through his Reach Media company in 2003, and in 2004 signed a collaboration agreement with the black-owned conglomerate Media One.[6]

The *TJMS*'s huge audience attracted a wide-ranging stable of major corporate sponsors, as well as a host of local business and public-service advertising for individual stations. Among them, at different points, were AT&T, Sprint, ComEd, Allstate, GEICO, ADT, Ford, Toyota, General Motors, Southwest Airlines, Home Depot, Lowes, Staples, Wal-Mart, Sam's Club, Kmart, Target, Kraft, Tyson, McDonalds, Burger King, Buffalo Wild Wings, TBS, TNT, NBC, Wells Fargo, Bank of America, American Express, Proctor & Gamble, Walgreens, CVS, Macys, Old Navy, Budget Rent a Car—even, in recent years, Zip Recruiter.com, *The New York Times*, Universal Pictures, OWN, Amazon, Old Navy, Gap, Capital One, Starbucks, AARP, Blue Apron, Itunes, Audible, Verizon, and Uber. The American business press was always alive to these commercial successes and covered various new sponsor acquisitions and advertising campaigns.[7]

The "crew" (anchors) of the show (see Figure 1.1) all performed particular contemporary middle-aged black characters: Tom Joyner—an out-of-the-box Alabama-born DJ with a lifetime's involvement in the black music scene (he was actually an original member of the Commodores).[8] J Anthony Brown—a Southern

Figure 1.1 From left, Sybil Wilkes, Tom Joyner, and J. Anthony Brown, the heart of the Tom Joyner Morning Show, appear onstage at the Soul Train Awards at Planet Hollywood Resort and Casino on Thursday, November 8, 2012, in Las Vegas. (Photo by Jeff Bottari/Invision/AP) © AP Images.

country-bred clown with a (claimed) taste for white women. Ms. Dupre (the actor Jedda Jones)—an elderly deep New Orleans-born psychic. Sybil Wilkes—a tart-tongued, Chicago-born urban schoolmarm. Myra J—a heterosexual and sassy but respectable single mother. Melvin (the actor Kevin Woodson)—an over-the-top older queeny Southern gay hairdresser.[9] Huggy Lowdown—a languorous DC-based bar habitué. Chris Paul—a younger, openly overweight comic with explicitly progressive politics. And recent younger addition Shaun King, the *New York Daily News* (and then *Young Turks* and *Intercept*) columnist and Black Lives Matter activist. They had, over the years, "bits" on particular mornings, like J Murders Another Hit, "Your Psychic Friend" Ms. Dupre's Lucky Numbers of the Day, Myra J's Tips for the Single Mom, Melvin's Love Line, Huggy's Bamma of the Week, Chris Paul's Morning Minute, the extraordinarily clever audio soap opera "It's Your World," Shaun King's The Scary Truth. I would call (and later email and text) friends—black, white, Latinx, or Asian—just to tell them that Ms. Dupre said your lucky numbers were:

> *Count the number of times you look inside the refrigerator and don't get anything!*
> *Count the number of raggedy drawers you own and don't throw away!*
> *Count the number of triflin family members who offered to bring the PLATES to the Fourth of July picnic!*
> *(June 29, 2005)*[10]

Part of the joy here—the late poet Langston Hughes's "sweet flypaper of life"[11]—arises from Ms. Dupre's send-up of conventional American working-class means of divining lucky lottery numbers through attention to daily life or dreams. The underlying tongue-in-cheek message is—yes, we know that people gamble, and that they make gambling decisions foolishly. Another part of it is Ms. Dupre's witty reference to our shared experiences—our own fidgety behaviors, unsorted wardrobes, annoying freeloading relatives. And finally, there is her clever use of black slang and her extraordinarily fully fleshed and satisfying impersonation—which cannot adequately be described on the page—of a funny, happy, stand-alone older working-class African American woman, all dressed up in the delicious Southern regional nonsense of Marie Laveau the Voodoo Queen. As they would announce Ms. Dupre: "She's got the gift, she's got to *use* it!"

But was the bulk of the *TJMS* audience self-consciously aware of all these points as they are comically embodied? Who was this audience, besides being huge and largely black? And why should we care about this minority radio show anyway?

Of course, the *TJMS* audience never thought consciously about every embedded message of the show, any more than Jon Stewart's or Trevor Noah's Comedy Central *Daily Show* watchers minutely parsed or parse every one of their jokes. That job is left to earnest academics and media critics. The pleasure for ordinary mortals lies in catching references and taking in points on the fly, "getting" pop culture and political references of the immediate present. But here the comparison gains traction: there have been almost no earnest academics and media critics attending to the *TJMS*, even though it has been around for decades (Tom Joyner announced in 2017 that he would end the show in 2019, after twenty-five years' continuous production), and just about as popular (with replacement host Trevor Noah having finally achieved Stewart's ratings numbers again)[12] as the highly visible, constantly referenced and quoted, multiple Emmy Award-winning *Daily Show*.

But I realized over time, as my fandom evolved into serious research, that the *TJMS* audience—unlike Jon Stewart's "advertisers' dream" young, largely white, educated, better-off demographic—comprised a nearly invisible American population: adult to middle-aged working-/middle-class black Americans. Certainly no one would claim, in the era of the two-term Obama White House, Oprah's and Shonda Rhimes' media empires, and the massive commercial success of rap and hip-hop, black sports, film—*Black Panther* breaking box-office records—and television stars, that African Americans are under-represented in the American public sphere. But that representation is highly selective, focusing heavily on younger upper-status/celebrity, and on impoverished or criminal individuals, or those victimized by police (when they do receive attention), while "invisibilizing" the broad adult working/middle class that is the bulk of the nation's black population. That majority—those "average, struggling, non-morbid" African Americans—remain, as Zora Neale Hurston wrote more than a half-century ago, the best-kept secret in America.

This "saints or sinners syndrome," as media scholars Robert Entman and Andrew Rojecki label it, thus publicly erases the comic, musical, and political tastes of the majority of the black American population—of nurses and careworkers, firefighters, bus and taxi drivers, police, schoolteachers, clericals and sales, sanitation, factory, transportation, communication, food service, and postal workers.[13] It is not just a question, though, of mainstream America's deep ignorance of the profound musical gifts and importance of old-school greats like Frankie Beverly and Maze, Gladys Knight, the O'Jays, Minnie Riperton, Teena Marie, Chaka Khan, The Isley Brothers, Geoffrey Osborne, The Dells, Angela Winbush. Or even of the wit and joy involved in the *TJMS* crew's and its audience's hilarious blackening and "working classification" of common American experiences, as we saw with Ms. Dupre. ("Blackening" whites and high-status African Americans for humorous effect is an old black comic practice. It is distinct from minstrelsy in that it is enacted *by* African Americans, *for* a black audience, *with* anti-racist intent.) Or when J Anthony Brown rewrote classic American Christmas songs to illustrate the realities of "jacked-up Christmas"—rarely for any American a Hallmark-card experience, so often characterized by economic stress and family strife:

(To the tune of "Walking in a Winter Wonderland")
I'm walkin cause they repossessed my car!
(December 5, 2009)

(To the tune of "I Saw Mommy Kissing Santa Claus")
I saw Momma kickin Daddy's ass
Underneath the tree outside the house
(December 11, 2009)[14]

(To the tune of "Away in a Manger")
My father's a stranger, not once have we met
All I know about him is his name is Fred
(December 3, 2014)

(To the tune of "I'll Be Home or Christmas")
Lost my home on Christmas,
They foreclosed on me . . .
(December 3, 2014)

It is not just the crew and guests, though, who exhibited stinging wit with a constant undercurrent of class and color consciousness. The *TJMS* audience, phoning and in later years texting in, responded instantly to specific conversations or questions. On July 23, 2013, for example, when the entire American media establishment had as usual gone out of its mind over British royalty, babbling and cooing in saturation coverage over the not-yet-named new baby, first child of England's

Duke and Duchess of Cambridge, Tom Joyner asked his listeners to text him possible royal baby names. He was immediately flooded with witty, sardonic, black-oriented, class-saturated suggestions: Earl Never Lift a Finger, Sir Silverspoon, Prince Work Nevermore, King Bling, The Prince of Balling, Prince Forever Sit on His Royal Assness.

But with the Prince Harry/Meghan Markle nuptials in May 2018, things were a bit different. The *TJMS* and its audience were understandably intrigued by the mixed-race American actor joining the British royal family. They celebrated the deliberate efforts the couple and royal family made to blacken the event—the African American Bishop Curry and his invocation of Martin Luther King, Jr, and the black British gospel choir. Sybil Wilkes related with relish catching the "guys in the barbershop" watching the wedding. ("What!?" they said to her. "But don't tell no one!") She also deeply appreciated Doria Ragland's dignity and refusal to straighten her hair for the royal event: "Meghan's mother . . . struck me as such a class act. Sitting there in her dreads with her nose ring . . . with such grace, as we know she had as a yoga master. . . ." Comic Chris Paul quipped that "the wedding was so black, I'm surprised they didn't say it was directed by Tyler Perry!" When it was revealed that Markle's white father had surreptitiously arranged to be paid for tabloid photos and interviews, the crew expressed disgust that a father would so betray his daughter. But a witty color-conscious texter had the last word:

*(May 14, 2018) Glad that Meghan's dad is the **ratched** side of her family, and he's white!*

And the *TJMS* audience would respond rapidly, as well, with high humor, to a wide range of African American realities. One means of doing so, as we have seen, is to comically "blacken" mainstream American phenomena. Huggy Lowdown, for example, on May 4, 2009, suggested that listeners text in *black* names for Kentucky Derby horses. And they came flooding in: "Nickel Bag," "Win Place or Glue," "Trojan Man," "Oh No You Di'int."

But even then, is the *TJMS* phenomenon so very important? So these millions of African Americans have a particular aesthetic and a humorous optic on American life that isn't filtering into mainstream media. We all know that older, less-well-off people, especially when boringly law abiding, fail in general to capture public interest in youth-, drama-, and celebrity-obsessed America. Just look at all those badly behaved, dysfunctional types on reality television shows! Then add race to the mix. Then add the general unsexiness of "old media" radio in a world captivated by the online universe—as radio scholar Dolores Casillas writes, "the radio set has been largely ignored as a tool of globalization."[15] So there is an overdetermined group of reasons for being ignored. So what?

The answer to the "so what?" question is—politics. And political influence. What really hooked me from the earliest years, what we can see in crew and guest performances, in audience responses, in Democratic politicians', journalists', and movement activists' abundant and consistent appearances on the show—and in actual, real-world political shifts—was an evolving and consequential political perspective, one that has come to be defined by the umbrella term "progressive." That is, with wit and passion, the *TJMS* long articulated and advocated for a synthetic combination of broad pan-racial civil rights—they called out "dog whistle" racist politics long before the label was widely used—anti-war and anti-imperial perspectives, women's and LBGTQ rights, union rights and social-democratic economic policy, and (to a lesser extent) environmentalism.[16]

How did the show accomplish this project? Sometimes through declarative, even angry statements and on-air arguments, sometimes through broad humor, but usually through conversation and debate, frequently linking issues organically to one another.

In the early years of the Iraq and Afghanistan wars, for example, like many Americans, I followed the news obsessively and miserably. Mainstream American news outlets had swallowed whole the false White House and CIA claims that Saddam Hussein, our former ally and protégé, was centrally connected to the 9/11 attacks and had developed weapons of mass destruction. Even after we invaded Iraq and these claims had been thoroughly debunked, aside from left press outlets like *The Nation, The Progressive, Democracy Now, In These Times, The Huffington Post,* or Keith Olbermann's blistering dissents on his then-new MSNBC show *Countdown,* there was still nowhere near enough media criticism of U.S. foreign and domestic policy.

So it was with wonder and great happiness that I would turn on the radio early on weekday mornings, sit with my coffee and newspapers, and hear something very different from what I was reading in *The New York Times* and *Chicago Tribune.* Consider these four conversations over a two-month period in early 2005:

> *(February 1, 2005) Tom talks about a woman who lost both her husband and son in the Iraq war, and Bush's recent advocacy of an increased death benefit and extending troops' stay.*
>
> *J: Now, I went to trade school, and this is not hard to figure out.*
> *Tom: Yeah.*
> *J: Bring 'em home!*
> *Sybil, profoundly sardonic: You'll save more money that way.*
>
> *(March 7, 2005) The crew comment on Martha Stewart's release from prison:*
> *J: Mandela didn't get this much press!*
> *Tom: When he got out of jail, after twenty-seven years ... And it was five months ...*
> *J: You'd think nobody white has ever been in jail, man.*
>
> *(March 21, 2005)*
> *Tom: So this is the second anniversary of the invasion of Iraq.*

Sybil: Almost two thousand deaths later, we're celebrating the second anniversary. (sarcastically, angrily) Mission accomplished!

Tom: (reference to the Terry Schiavo case) And what about the President running back to Washington to save one woman from dying?—when two thousand people have died in Iraq?

J: White people always want to save things. Save the rat, save the gnat, but don't save the n-word.

Sybil: This is also the party that wanted states' rights but now they want to make it a federal issue.

Later in the same show, in a discussion of the high school student who massacred teachers and classmates in Red Lake, Minnesota:

Tom: Do you think they're gonna get the same kind of attention as Columbine?

Sybil and J: No, uh uh!

Tom: Because it's an Indian reservation.

J: And poor.

Tom: I'm just sayin.

(March 30, 2005) Tom reports that the U.S. military is having trouble recruiting blacks into the military.

Ms. Dupre: (sardonically) Wha-a-t?

Sybil: (up and down the intonational contour) Oh, really?

*Tom: Yeah, that's what I said. [pause] (falsetto) Is you **crazy**?*

In these brief segments, we hear angry anti-war dissent, mourning for U.S. military members already killed, and finished contempt for President Bush's prevarications. We also hear pride in black Americans' relative unwillingness to sign up to serve in the unnecessary and failing wars in Iraq and Afghanistan. Finally, we can see the crew multi-tasking their political commentary: they weave into their narrative a critique of mainstream media's obsessive interest in white lives and experiences— Martha Stewart, poor brain-dead Terry Schiavo, the Columbine massacre victims— and lesser concern with the nonwhite and less-well-off—Nelson Mandela and the Indian reservation victims. Sybil Wilkes, house intellectual, manages to insert commentary on the profound Republican inconsistency in fighting passionately for states' rights—until there is an opportunity to call for federal "pro-life" legislation to overturn Florida's law stipulating the mourning husband's legal right to stop extraordinary measures being taken to keep his brain-dead wife alive.

Or, here Tom, Sybil, and J engage in a tour de force Bush-era discussion of the Iraq war, Mexican immigration, and the U.S. role in international political economy:

(May 15, 2006)

Tom: OK, so President Bush has decided that he needs to send National Guard troops to patrol the Mexican border.

Sybil: That's correct.

Tom: So where's he gonna get them? We don't have any left, they're all in Iraq doin two, three, four tours! . . . Not only is the President of Mexico upset but I imagine Latinos are too!

Sybil: So instead of working with Mexico and creating jobs to keep them there, bring out the National Guard . . .

*J: Where's the love? . . . (Sincere question) Who's **left** in the country?*

Sybil: Big Mama and them! The old folks and the children, they're sending money back to support them!

Note how the crew manages to include in this short improvisation a critique of the Bush White House's hyper-exploitation of the U.S. National Guard in the early years of the Iraq war, a reference to the deleterious effects of NAFTA (North American Free Trade Agreement) and other U.S.-sponsored policy shifts on Mexico's economy—a fact that even now we rarely hear outside college seminar rooms and Latinx circles[17]—and sympathy for both the Mexican government and for U.S. Latinx populations. Not only that, but Sybil explains Mexico's post-NAFTA remittance economy, and simultaneously comically "blackens" and thus identifies with Mexican migrants and their families by referring to older women and children left behind with the classic Southern black working-class phrase, Big Mama and them.

The *TJMS* never let up on its dissent from our wars in Iraq and Afghanistan, and worried particularly about the lives of working-class and impoverished black Americans who might be tempted to enlist for financial benefit:

(August 10, 2007) Extended crew discussion of increasingly relaxed army recruiting standards, given the over-stretched military losing wars on two fronts—increased age range, a $2000 signing bonus for getting a friend to sign up.

Tom: Oh they are hurtin! They'll take the blind, crippled, and crazy!

Sybil: Oh, they've been taking the crazy for awhile! . . . Read the fine print, my brothers and sistahs!

Melvin [deeply emotional]: Read the fine print!

Or there is the issue of the long history of overt American racial discrimination. The *TJMS* crew and audience don't shilly-shally around. They are righteously angry, providing catharsis and a spur to further activism—or just some short-term, understandable acting out—for all of us who are beyond aghast at our stalled civil rights revolution:

(January 8, 2015) Audience texter, responding to enthusiastic crew discussion of the new civil-rights film Selma: *"Went to see* Selma *this weekend, went home and broke out my boombox, and played "Fight the Power" so loud my white neighbors could hear it!"*[18]

The *TJMS* also assumes women's equal status, and values hard-pressed single mothers, amidst lots of "war between the sexes" badinage. Here is Sybil on reproductive rights and her prescient Political Science 101 lecture—the Democrats did indeed regain Congress in 2006—in a discussion of the new Supreme Court on the day conservative Justice Samuel Alito began his tenure there:

> (*January 31, 2006*)
> *Sybil: All of these cases are going to change . . . a woman's right to choose.*
> *Tom: When we had the [2004] election . . . everyone was saying Bush will stack the courts.*
> *Sybil: And now this is coming to pass!*
> *Tom: And you think they stole the election, you aint seen nuthin yet . . . So what can we do?*
> *Sybil: We can [work on the congressional midterm elections in November] and get Congress back!*

And Sybil and Myra J, of "Tips for the Single Mom" fame, hilariously ganged up on J Anthony Brown in defense of women's sexual freedom:

> (*February 25, 2005*)
> *After an airing of the latest segment of the show's mock-soap opera, "It's Your World," in which a woman character tells her male lover that she is "seeing other people," and refuses to tell him how many. She declares at the closing, "A woman needs a little mystery."*
>
> *J: She's seein other people? They're writin him soft!*
> *Myra J, disgusted: Oh get a tissue out, you little man-person!*
> *Sybil: (falsetto) Ninny ninny ninny!*

From the beginning, *TJMS* extended its civil rights vision to gay and lesbian Americans, decades before the mainstream media, major corporate, Obama White House, and Supreme Court turnaround of recent years. "Same sex, same problems," the crew would intone, responding empathetically to LBGTQ callers, and long-term crew member Melvin was on hand to keep up the pressure:

> Crew discusses their upcoming Family Reunion extravaganza:
>
> (*April 21, 2006*)
> *Tom: We've got lots of single people comin, and boyfriend and girlfriend . . .*
> *Melvin: And boyfriend and boyfriend, and girlfriend and girlfriend!*
> *Tom: That's right, it's all good, family is **family**.*

Finally, while the *TJMS* crew rarely use the term "working class," they know their audience and play to their passions, self-understandings, and conceptions of the social universe, performing and thus affirming the hard-working black working class and the tensions and contradictions of achieving social mobility. Consider this back-and-forth with a post-Hurricane Katrina caller and its witty commentary on blue-versus white-collar status and intra-black disagreements on blaming the victim:

(August 25, 2006)

Male caller from Alabama: I've been married thirteen years, I love my wife, but she got a clerical job, and you know how some black people change when they're makin money ... She done turned Republican, man. [He describes how, when they were watching Spike Lee's When the Levees Broke, *his wife agreed with former First Lady Barbara Bush's callous, off the cuff remark that many of evacuees were experiencing an increased standard of living in the Houston Astrodome].*

Melvin, archly and angrily: And what was your comeback to that ridiculous statement?

Tom: Let me ask you this ... How much money is your wife makin?

Caller: In the five figures.

Tom: And you?

Caller: I'm a bricklayer, I do all right.

Sybil: His money is as green as hers.

J: On the surface, it looks like she makes more. He ain't gonna get no respect til he makes bricks in a suit!

She done turned Republican, man. His money is as green as hers. Til he makes bricks in a suit. I came to look out for and cherish this political street poetry, this creative and insightful banter, this progressive black counter-narrative, among the crew and between crew members and callers.

I also appreciated the crew's consistent attention to shifts in black Americans' economic status, their celebration of all honest work while always pushing higher education as a gateway to professional careers, and their heartfelt support for decent compensation and union activism—as long as the employer was not one of their sponsors. This is, after all, an entirely commercial show:

(November 7, 2005) The crew discuss the Philadelphia transit workers' strike.

Tom, beside himself: It's about benefits! That's what all these strikes are about! Benefits! You hear that? Benefits! We don't need a war in Iraq, we need benefits!

Understandably, given the historic role that public employment has played in allowing a flying wedge of black Americans to achieve working-class/middle-class status in a United States long characterized by private employer discrimination, the *TJMS* has been particularly sensitive to the long-term right-wing attack on public workers, especially teachers[19]:

> (*August 24, 2006*) *J, on the Gary, Indiana strike: "Hats off to the teachers!"*

> (*September 10, 2010*) *Sybil announces the Chicago Teachers' Union strike, articulates their goals and grievances. Tom asks: "You know, I support our teachers, but . . . what if the money just isn't there?"*
> *Sybil—a native Chicagoan—with deep sarcasm: Oh, I think Mayor Emmanuel can find the money!*[20]

Scholars and activists use the phrase "prefigurative politics" to describe the day-to-day living-out, usually within a political movement, of a set of hoped-for polit-ical goals, and thus, as feminist historian Alice Echols explains, a "commitment to build counter-institutions that would foreshadow the desired society."[21] From the European council communists of the nineteenth and early twentieth centuries, to "beloved community" civil rights workers from the early 1960s, to feminist activists in women-only groups and gay community organizations from the 1970s forward, to organic farming and "off the grid" environmental communities, to the "Moral Mondays" North Carolina progressive civil-rights coalition movement of the 2010s, practicing prefigurative politics has been about trying to embody, literally, a dif-ferent and desired social world.[22]

While a radio show is not a political movement, it is certainly the case that the *TJMS*, from the mid-1990s, "prefigured" a synthetic progressive politics that did not fully enter the Democratic Party's official platform until 2012. That is, this radio show was consistently banging the multi-issue progressive drum, to an audience of eight million, for two decades, until the Democratic Party finally fell into line. And, as we will see, its prefiguration both reflected black Americans' long-term generally social-democratic and tolerant political profile and has been a significant element in extending those politics—in pushing the African American public farther along the road.

Thus the *TJMS* built a powerful linguistic-mediatized counterpublic. As Nancy Fraser and Michael Warner originally expanded Jürgen Habermas's "public sphere" concept, a counterpublic is (in Warner's words) constituted "through a conflictual relation to the dominant public," and it "maintains at some level . . . an awareness of its subordinate status."[23] In this case, that awareness is both raced and classed (and gendered!), and as we have seen, the *TJMS* "reads" events from that perspective. Listeners are hyper-aware of this unique take on social reality, of *TJMS*'s clear un-derstanding of and reportage on the daily discrimination African Americans and other nonwhites face, on the widening economic inequalities in American society. As one woman caller exclaimed, chiding the crew for "clownin"—pulling a very suc-cessful April Fool's joke—"Stop clownin, cause I listen to *y'all* for the news!"

This deep horizontal comradeship (as the late political theorist Benedict Anderson described nationalism)[24] across *TJMS* crew and audience was constructed through shared racial-class identity—the crew are, of course, now largely well-off, but they identified with and performed working- to middle-classness—and awareness of ongoing racial discrimination, social-democratic politics, and linguistic stylization.[25] That is, the crew individually represent, and play with, a range of class and regional black American "voices," from Sybil Wilkes's sometime urban "schoolmarm" performance (my phrase: Wilkes is a Northwestern University graduate), to Tom Joyner's code-switching across "correct" and working-class black English—as in "Is you *crazy*?"—to J Anthony Brown's "country" working-class black English (Brown is from rural South Carolina). To use Jennifer Stoever's phrase, they consistently perform *across* the "sonic color line," and they and their audience are highly self-conscious about the intersections of sound/music, race, and politics, power, and powerlessness.[26]

This linguistic stylization, with its attendant African American humor and constant *entre nous* black musical, sports, celebrity, and political references, drew in a huge audience and aided in sedimenting *TJMS*'s overarching activist progressive politics—including its explicit dissent, as Myra J's performances attest, from the neoconservative "family values" frame that dominated the U.S. public sphere over the 1990s.

Here is Myra J expatiating wittily on April 3, 2006—tax season—on "things single moms should be able to deduct." In the process, she attests to single mothers' hard work, ordinary American parental problems, sass, and rights to a (likely disappointing) sex life:

1. *A bad hair day, when you get jacked by your stylist!*
2. *Self-employment because you just worked a job, and another job!*
3. *The "What-the-Tax" [as in WTF] when you can't figure out your kid's homework.*
4. *The Bad Sex Tax—You don't get it that often anyway. You only get to deduct it once a year. Cause if you go back, you just a* fool!

Fear of a Black Planet

So we return to that niggling, annoying question. Adult African Americans are broadly aware of the *TJMS*—I have been asking that question all over the country since the 1990s, and even non-listeners, like Tanya, an older Florida clerical, would say, "I know about it—my kids and people who live in eastern Florida talk about it." Miranda, a Texas call center worker, told me that she likes to be "peaceful" driving to work, so she doesn't listen to the *TJMS* or anything else in the car. But her mother and her fiancé are major *TJMS* fans, and they keep her informed. "I don't watch the news on television, so whatever I get, I get from them!"

And a significant percentage of all black adults listened to the *TJMS* frequently. As Renee, a Chicago clerical, said: "It gets me going in the morning, so that's good . . . it keeps you abreast if you miss something!" And Patricia, a thirty-something upstate New York clerical, exclaimed, "I been listenin to them—Ooooh—for years! Ever since I was old enough to listen!" A twenty-something Apple "genius" consultant from South Carolina, Alliyah, burst into excited chatter when I brought up the show: "They talk about *everything*! . . . I would listen to it on long car trips, or going to school with my mom, . . . They're *everywhere* around here! [the Carolina South]

Politicians and activists appeared on the show with regularity, including Presidents Clinton and Obama when in office. Dozens of major corporations underwrote it, and the U.S. press reported on their sponsorship. So again, why is it that almost no one else, whether in journalistic or scholarly worlds—including media (after a small flurry of stories when the *TJMS* first began) and African American studies—much noticed this giant political and cultural phenomenon—a phenomenon founded five years before *The Daily Show* and boasting the same mix of multiple characters, generally progressive politics, and sharp humor? With the additional injection of constantly shifting, deeply satisfying, soul music playlists. Was it, as Public Enemy rapped in 2008, Fear of a Black Planet?[27]

And thus my fan notes transmogrified into a mystery story. *Why* was this black elephant in the American living room—and kitchen, and car, and office computer, and headphones—so invisible in the larger American public sphere? Why hadn't journalists and scholars who cover media, politics, and African American culture paid it more attention?

If the *TJMS*'s prefigurative politics were too far ahead of the times in the 1990s and early 2000s, why weren't they worthy of attention when the Democratic Party officially caught up with them? What about the show's profound electoral commitment—significant and rising voter registration and get out the vote activism from at least 2004 forward, moving to frenzied, hysterical nail-biting and all-hands-on-deck labor among crew and audience, allied with the Teamsters and the NAACP, over the 2008 and 2012 Obama presidential elections? Why hasn't that labor, those accomplishments, been of interest to scholars and journalists, especially given long-term rightist efforts to suppress the minority, impoverished, and youth vote?

Instead, we saw, up until President Obama's first presidential win—and revived by Herman Cain's 2012 candidacy and by outliers like rightist black surgeon Ben Carson—a media obsession with "man bites dog" stories about conservative, misogynist, homophobic black Americans. Even though such individuals are statistically rare, they capture the spotlight. Then there was and is high interest in neoconservative white talk jocks, even when, and has mostly been the case, their audiences were dwarfed by the *TJMS*'s.

And on the other hand, there is the ongoing, decades-long, and overwhelming black and white scholarly and journalistic obsession with "hip-hop nation," often including hopeful predictions of rap and hip-hop's progressive political potential. But only in recent years, with the rise of the Black Lives Matter movement, the Beyoncé phenomenon, #MeToo, and explicit "hip-hop feminism" statements and analyses, have we begun seeing Soyica Diggs Colbert's "more expansive vision" in my epigraph, the kinds of productive musical/progressive political interconnections that were characteristic of, for example, the Civil Rights Movement of the 1950s and 1960s.[28] As well, only in very recent years have we begun to see explicitly progressive, serious adult black television shows like *Queen Sugar, Insecure, Luke Cage, Atlanta, The Chi.*

And the youthful, transgressive profile of rap/hip-hop and its makers has drawn massive interest among the white chattering classes since the 1980s. (It's long been known that rap's "dirty little secret" is that its main consumers are white teenage boys.)[29] To put it snarkily: many white professional-class people want to be *hip*, and thus follow cutting-edge black youth music. But they often seem unaware of *adult* black media and musical choices, and thus don't actually engage with the daily experiences of employment and other kinds of discrimination, overt white racism, and the common economic struggles of the bulk of the African American population.

Finally, there is an ongoing fascination with the political potential of "blue media"—self-consciously progressive projects like the short-lived *Air America* radio phenomenon, *The Daily Show* and *The Colbert Report* as they moved leftward, Jon Oliver's and Samantha Bee's relatively new and very progressive television shows, and blogosphere phenomena like *MoveOn, Daily Kos,* and others. And yet these blue enthusiasts often fail to notice progressive *minority* shows and projects.[30]

Ironically, both journalists and media scholars have paid considerable attention to the burgeoning American phenomenon of Spanish-language radio, particularly since the well-organized pro-immigrant rights national demonstrations of March 2006. They frame these stations' and their activist DJs' roles as under the radar, seeing Spanish-language radio as an "on-air organizer," functioning in a language and for an audience unknown to and stigmatized by a significant percentage of Americans.[31] But the "invisible" *TJMS* has also long been an on-air organizer, also serving a less-visible and still-stigmatized population. Just as billboards and bus shelters in Latinx neighborhoods advertise Spanish-language radio shows, so have I seen *TJMS* ads in multiple sites in black neighborhoods around the country. And similarly overwhelming percentages of blacks and Latinos regularly listen to radio: 94 and 95–96%, respectively.[32] (Music scholar Sumanth Gopinath also notes that African Americans and Latinos were the most prolific consumers of cell phone ringtones—and were charged higher fees for them—during that industry's relatively short rise and fall.)[33]

And then there's all that endless "lifestyle" reporting over the past several decades on aging baby boomers. I cannot imagine how many articles I've read about how my generation is doing—our cultural, political, medical, sexual, financial statuses. But the *TJMS* crew and their audience were witty, seriously pissed-off, class-sensitive, politically aware *black* baby boomers—why don't mainstream journalists and scholars notice *them*? Watch Tom Joyner, J Anthony Brown, and Ms. Dupre in sardonic boomer action:

> *(October 12, 2005) [Discussion of rapper Eminem's claim of work exhaustion]*
> *Tom: And Eminem is tired? He wants to take a break?*
> *J: Man, the O'Jays are still out there . . . the last time they had a break, they opened*
>   *for Alexander the Great!*
> *Ms. Dupre: They rolled out in a chariot!*

And, given all the recent salacious and not so faintly disgusted mainstream media references to "cougars" and other older women with active sexualities, J and Myra J's repartee, below, simultaneously combines refreshing matter-of-factness about aging with ongoing and pragmatic self-regard:

> *(April 29, 2005, Sky Show in St. Louis) A heavy funk song plays, to loud cheering.*
>   *At the end, it becomes clear the Myra J has been dancing on the stage:*
> *Myra J: I still got it?*
> *J: You still got it, Myra!*
> *Myra J.: It aint as glittery as it was, though.*
> *J: Teach the babies!*

Teach the babies. As I entered into answering the invisible black elephant mystery, entire universes opened up before me. The eighteenth-century English poet William Blake wrote about seeing a "World in a Grain of Sand . . . and Eternity in an hour."[34] I began to realize that the *TJMS* was my grain of sand: through attending to it so closely, over decades, I was simultaneously seeing America anew, and from the "blackside"—newly illuminating race, politics, economics, humor, generation, culture, art, and aesthetics. This project was much more than solving a public-sphere misrepresentation mystery. I was tuning in to an alternative understanding of the black public sphere in the digital age.

I had been writing about the American public sphere vis-à-vis race and ethnicity, class, and gender since the 1970s. I had gauged the effects of that decade's "white ethnicity" media craze on Italian American self-understandings across gender and class status. I had analyzed the *Godfather* phenomenon and ethnic self-mockery—as in my late father's joking title for my dissertation: "How the Day Goes for Dagos." And I had documented the ways in which that white ethnic renaissance of that era encouraged denigrating, racist comparisons to blacks and Latinos. I had followed the poison crumbs of underclass ideology—a rewriting of the 1960s blame-the-victim "culture of poverty"—in public policy and popular culture across the Reagan, Bush the First, and Clinton years. I had even charted popular-cultural readings—and their political implications—from the Roaring Twenties forward, of key, widely read, American ethnographic texts foregrounding the lives of global Southern women of color. And I spent three decades doing deep immersion fieldwork in New Haven, Connecticut, charting shifting public culture and political economy, with a key focus on African American women's lives.[35] But I had not engaged with the specific histories of particular media—like radio or television—nor had I considered media economics in depth. In order to understand the *TJMS*, I needed to see it in the context of the history of radio in the United States, and in terms of the history of all African American media and black politics.

And another autobiographical theme: the issue of aging, of middle-aged status, is key not only to *TJMS* musical choices but to their overall aesthetic. They worked self-consciously inside the long traditions of black American entertainment and politics: barbershop and street banter; specific—and specifically cruel—black comic "bits"; the theatrical conventions of the old showtime at the Apollo; the raucous fun and dancing in the old Southern juke joints; the "audio trickster" traditions of 1950s–70s black radio; and the black-church cadences of serious political talk.[36]

These traditions fit within a certain larger musical and self-presentational aesthetics that the *TJMS* shared not only with its huge working-class, middle-aged audience but also in general with African American "old media." This category includes the magazines *Ebony, Jet,* and *Essence,* the television channels BET, TVONE, and ASPIRE, some Queen Latifah and Ice Cube film vehicles like *Beauty Shop* and *Barbershop* and their many sequels, and most of actor/writer/mogul Tyler Perry's highly lucrative stable of plays, films, and television shows.

This aesthetic amalgam appeals to a largely black, largely middle-aged to elderly audience, and until recent years tended to be "low-resolution"—have low production values—because of lack of resources. It enshrines nostalgia for a past civil rights and musical golden age, tends toward moral uplift and religious piety (and here the *TJMS* departs from the model), and, at least until somewhat recently, articulates a visceral disgust for rap and hip-hop as unmelodious kids' music filled with misogyny, objectionable language, and the celebration of illegality. This aesthetic/political/cultural amalgam is an historical artifact, in that it arose in consonance with the rap/hip-hop explosion of the 1980s.

For decades, black music, black radio had appealed across generations—the politics, the humor, and the shifting music, including various genres of jazz, blues, doo-wop, R&B, pop, deep soul, disco, funk, house, gospel, neosoul. But rap was a bridge too far for a large chunk of the working adult African American population, and the radio industry responded by introducing new stations and formats, splitting their programming for the black audience into age-specific genres. Arbitron, the official monitoring organization, established the "urban adult" radio format, and stations and programming in that category proliferated. In the late 1990s, for example,

Chicago's V103 simply advertised its generational tastes with a promotional clip of an older black man with a Delta-inflected voice saying slowly and deliberately,

I don't like . . . that rap[37]

They replaced it in 2005 with a clip of then-Senator Barack Obama shouting at a promotional event:

Now I have to admit, and I'm makin a confession here, that between the three [black Chicago] stations, I probably listen to V103 a little mo'! Because I'm over forty!

And indeed, the *TJMS* didn't play rap—not even Kendrick Lamar, when they celebrated his 2018 Pulitzer Prize![38]—and would broadcast only some hip-hop, through almost its entire quarter-century run. They would joke about Eminem, 50 Cent, Missy Elliott, Lil Kim, Jay-Z, and the rest—but they never played them.

I also had to come to terms, listening to and documenting the *TJMS*, with the phenomenon of the American culture of celebrity. The show attended to African American sports, film, television, and music stars—and sometimes writers—and often hosted them during publicity tours as new CDs, films, books, or television programs came out. I could hang with the crew on that issue, because it's clear that these black (and Latinx, Asian, Native American, etc.) celebrities represent racial pride and often the promise of social and economic mobility for African Americans as a whole. Mainstream media have recently saturated the public sphere with narratives educating all Americans on these points—for example, the extensive coverage and multiple films about singers Billie Holiday, Ray Charles, James Brown, The Supremes, Whitney Houston. In terms of athletics, we've seen multiple films on boxer Muhammad Ali,[39] *42* (2013) about Jackie Robinson's breakthrough signing to Major League Baseball, *Remember the Titans,* (2000) about the first integrated— and prize-winning—Southern high school football team, *Glory Road* (2006) about the first integrated, and extraordinarily successful, Southern college basketball team. And with the 2012 rise of the hit network drama *Scandal,* the entertainment press has frequently pointed out that the lead actor Kerry Washington was only the second African American woman to headline a network television show—the first being Diahann Carroll in *Julia* back in 1968.

But when it came to conversation and jokes about Paris Hilton, Lindsay Lohan, Britney Spears, or, heaven forefend, Kim Kardashian—who are famous largely for transgressive public behavior rather than talent, I was lost and horrified: how could this beautiful progressive radio show stoop to the level of *TMZ*? Why did they care about the activities of these no-talent white nothings? Here serious scholars of the rise and functions of celebrity culture in the U.S. offered help and insight. As P. David Marshall has pointed out, celebrities are "part of a very elaborate media economy which is connected to audiences and value" and thus serve as "the source of the self and identity" through "various audiences' interpretations."[40]

Thus my eyes were opened, and I began to consider the political implications of how the *TJMS* dealt with celebrity news and drama. Even a tossed-off insult as silly as nightlife habitué Huggy Lowdown's joke that Paris Hilton was so skinny that she "has to wear suspenders to hold up her thong" radiated meaning. Huggy was saying that this rich, white, deliberately hyper-sexual female celebrity lacked a key element of black beauty—a decently sized ass. Sociologist Karen Sternheimer has made compelling feminist points about "female celebrities' lack of self-control cast[ing] them as immoral and unworthy of wealth and fame."[41] But here the *TJMS* doesn't engage with that prudish "family values" morality issue. They were saying, instead, that on her own sexual terms, Hilton literally didn't measure up—wasn't as attractive as a (stereotypically well-endowed) black woman.

And indeed, the *TJMS* regularly rings the changes on white identity, on whiteness. Whites lack style. They (we) are obtuse about black life, thoughtless and thrill-seeking, reckless about their own safety and comfort—unlike black Americans, who, given their daily experience of discrimination and often tough urban living, are assumed to be pragmatic and prudent—streetwise.

Here's the wonderful Ms. Dupre again, brushing up against the topic:

> *(May 18, 2005) Ms. Dupre's lucky numbers: Count the number of white couples you see walkin down the street holdin hands . . . You don't see many black couples . . . the reason is, a black man has to be ready to defend himself at all times!*

But there *was* a white *TJMS* audience, and the crew was aware of them:

> *(February 8, 2005) Tom, with great good humor: To our Caucasian listeners—I feel for you during Black History Month!*

Thus the *TJMS* largely served a particular audience by race, class, and generation. It also existed within a specific American economic-historical era. As I was researching and writing *Black Radio/Black Resistance,* getting caught up in its sweet flypaper of life, I was also writing and teaching about the global rise of neoliberal capitalism—the shift since the 1970s toward free trade, corporate outsourcing of labor, the endemic privatization of public resources, the financialization of the global economy, rollbacks of state regulation of business, and constant cutbacks in governmental social supports. This process of neoliberal globalization has eroded nation-states' middle classes, greatly expanding the divide between rich and poor.[42] The global recession of 2008 exacerbated this trend toward increasing economic inequality, and the Occupy Wall Street movement from 2011 forward helped to expand public awareness of the plight of the 99%.

But neoliberalization has also given rise to a "neoliberal consciousness" that denies these empirical realities. This structure of feeling, this mode of apprehension and affect, includes the celebration of rapid technological change, of individual entrepreneurial initiative, and the denial of the multiple roles of government in the provision of the very infrastructure that allows businesses to run, human daily rounds to continue. It includes the optimistic and counter-empirical notion that globalization can only improve life chances worldwide. And it rests on the allure of an ever growing and newly affordable cornucopia of cheaply globally produced commodities—the iPhone could be the totem of this phenomenon.[43] (The rise of Trump, and associated racist-rightist populisms in Europe, Asia, and Latin America, now partially counter this vision through a crackpot set of claims about how ending free trade and immigration, giving huge tax breaks to the already wealthy, and further shrinking government will magically bring back "good jobs" and social mobility for white working and middle classes.)[44]

Where exactly did the *TJMS* stack up on these issues—widening inequality, the role of government, neoliberal consciousness? The answer is complex, as culture and politics have changed over the years, as did the show. Over the last twenty-four years, *TJMS* responded to and was engaged with five presidential and four midterm elections, and then developed the single nastiest and funniest set of reactions to the Trump phenomenon in all of U.S. media. It protested our wars abroad, reported on and attempted—with extraordinary efficacy, again ignored by national media—to alleviate suffering during national crises like 9/11, Hurricane Katrina in 2005–06, Hurricanes Harvey, Irma, and Maria in 2017, and Florence in 2018. And it worked with African Americans and others nationally in response to racist violence, as in the Jena 6, Trayvon Martin, Michael Brown, Eric Garner, Tamir Rice, and so many other cases. But it also, as we have seen, responded broadly to issues of racial civil rights for all, women's rights, LBGTQ rights. And it covered environmental disasters like the Deepwater Horizon oil spill of 2010.

In terms of structure, the *TJMS* lost some radio station homes and acquired others, some crew members departed, and others arrived, "bits" were discarded—such as Tips for the Single Mom and the uproariously clever soap opera "It's Your World"—and new ones invented, like Huggy Lowdown's Bamma of the Week and younger comedian Chris Paul's Morning Minute, and Shaun King's The Scary Truth. Hip-hop crept onto the playlist as tastes shifted and the *TJMS* moved to attract younger listeners. And as we have seen, the show rolled with the technological tide, adding a website, blogging, texting, and tweeting capacities, and finally the iPhone app. And, of course, the *TJMS*, like other media outlets, was itself adversely affected by the 2008 recession.

The answer is also complex because of black Americans' collective economic vulnerabilities: largely working class and impoverished but with significant but relatively small middle, upper-middle, and upper classes. Still largely discriminated against in the job market, and heavily represented in the public-sector labor market being continuously cut back and under political attack. And subject to last-hired-first-fired corporate policies, and thus disproportionately in need of social supports in an era of extreme cutbacks in social provision.[45] So the old African American aphorism is now even more trenchant: When America catches cold, blacks get pneumonia.

But something funny happened on the way to "blacks catching pneumonia" this time around, with this recession. Barack Obama was elected president that first recession year, and then re-elected in 2012. His original campaign stimulated pre-existing progressive organizations, but aside from the first economic stimulus bill, the Lily Ledbetter Act, the establishment of the Consumer Finance Protection Bureau, and the real achievement of the Affordable Care Act (Obamacare), the president was unable (or in some leftist analyses, unwilling) to bring sufficient succor to the bulk of underwater homeowners and the under-employed and poorly paid. Nor did his Administration personally prosecute the financiers whose actions caused the recession. Nor did he actually manage to end U.S. involvement in George W. Bush's wars in Central Asia, particularly given the disruptions of Arab Spring of 2011 and the rise of ISIS. At the same time, the sheer public optics of the first black president—the wildly enthusiastic mass public celebration of his first inauguration, for example—in concert with the bubbling-up of overt white racist hate his election stimulated, led to highly emotive African American responses to Obama's presidency. And then Donald Trump leveraged that white racist, xenophobic hatred into an electoral-college win in 2016. And the *TJMS* kept reflecting our complex and evolving reality.

So *Black Radio/Black Resistance* grew far beyond my original fan notes.[46]

It expanded through my immersion in more than fourteen years' worth of officially listening to and transcribing the live show, and through my many dozens of conversations with African Americans who do—and do not—listen to it. This process is formally labeled "media ethnography," but I moved as well into historical scholarship, both by simply working on the project for so damned long and through ranging across a number of fields to contextualize the *TJMS* inside political, radio, and black media history.[47]

Ideally, I would have studied not only *TJMS* radio production but also audience reception—would have listened regularly *with* audience members—for example, next to me in a cubicle or in a car pool. (Although most media studies focus on production—very few attempt to analyze audience reception.)[48] Those stratagems were not feasible here, especially as the project extended past a decade, but I have paid careful attention to on-air audience response, and to my interviewees, all over the U.S. In 2016, Tracy, a medical records clerk in Richmond, Virginia, in response to my query, waxed voluble and enthusiastic: "That is *awesome*! I will definitely hunt your book down if you write about this election! I'll tell people, I already knew her!" And about the *TJMS*: "I love that they offer *facts*—they share with each other. They're for the people. It's not just blacks. They're for *everyone*."

And the *TJMS*, indeed, was for everyone. But it also became a major African American institution. As Tony, a thirty-something Chicago-area paint store manager, declared: "Everybody African American knows about it! Man, it would be the first thing you'd hear in the morning. It got you started! My mom would be makin the coffee...."[49] Don, a twenty-something medical technician, remembered being driven to elementary school in the early mornings, strapped into his mother's car, listening with wild delight to the envelope-pushing soap opera "It's Your World." He mimed for me the rigid stance and wide-open eyes of a little kid in a car seat, hoping not to be noticed as he spies on the universe of adult sex and boundary-breaking. He laughed happily when I sang the "It's Your World" theme song for him.

As a white scholar, I have been concerned about possibly misconstruing material, and have made lavish use of friends' and colleagues' readings and responses to my analyses, as well as checking myself through attending to on-air audience reactions, and through interviewing African American listeners and non-listeners. And I have been painfully aware of how my own daily life experiences differ from those of the *TJMS* crew and guests, but most importantly, from their huge audience, the vast majority of whom are not only black but working class. While my own socially mobile middle-class status has very shallow roots, as the reader will soon discover, I have simply never experienced the kinds of discrimination and insults (aside from gender discrimination and sexual harassment and assault)[50] that are still common fare for most black and other nonwhite Americans. My location within structural and institutional racism is obviously utterly different from that of the *TJMS* crew and the bulk of their audience. In the modern parlance, I am a "white ally" against racism, just as there are and have been large numbers of male feminist and straight LBGTQ allies. And while we lack an agreed-upon term for it—part of the mess of contemporary American politics, although "social democracy" comes the closest— I am also one of the large army of scholars and activists arguing and working for a more economically egalitarian country and world, an American and global policy deck considerably less stacked in favor of the well-off.

Working on a scholarly project for fourteen years is a luxury of full professorship. There is no higher rung of promotion waiting in the wings for which the next book needs to be hurriedly finished and published. But it was certainly not an intentional tack—not a shtick like trying to make all of Julia Child's *Mastering the Art of French Cooking* recipes in a year, or following all of Oprah's advice, a gambit to frame a book. (Although my overwork definitely does connect to my self-consciousness as a white scholar working on an African American topic, my desire to demonstrate my seriousness.) Instead, it is, weirdly, a feature of my own intellectual evolution: I have repeatedly juggled multiple projects, each informing and deepening the other, while they simultaneously mutually interfere with one another, like squabbling siblings.

It is also a form of insanity. Listening to the *TJMS* and analyzing it, in the black phrase, "got good to me." Or as my late father used to say of me, sardonically— stealing from Anthony Powell's description of the English poet John Betjeman—I have a "whim of iron." Fun became a job. Listening to and transcribing the *TJMS* for at least several hours each show, at least several mornings a week, for all these years on end, has been grotesquely burdensome. What had begun as entertainment, enjoyment, enlightenment, also became a painful, guilt-ridden, time-sucking slog. I had lost my choice of how I would be spending a significant amount of time weekly. Or, rather, I could not allow myself *not* to spend that time. Of course, I also kept remembering—as I was feeling sorry for myself—how much earlier the *TJMS* crew had to rise each day, five days a week, in order to prepare for the show and to travel to various studios to broadcast it. And I was constantly reminded—through their own communications to the show—of the *TJMS* audience members who were not cozily at home with coffee and newspapers in the very early morning, as I was, but on their way to or already at their often difficult and poorly paid jobs.

I kept attempting to delimit the study, to put paid to it. I had what I thought was a full analysis of the show by 2007—including the 2004 presidential campaign and the responses to the war in Iraq and Hurricane Katrina—but then I couldn't give up, couldn't stop listening and transcribing five days a week, during the frenzy, which I shared, of Barack Obama's 2007–08 presidential campaign and triumph. Then I had to document the *TJMS*'s response to the complexities of Obama's first term, including the extraordinary uprush of racist vituperation to which the first black White House family was subjected, and the spectacle of the fully obstructive, do-nothing Republican Congress after the 2010 midterm elections. Then I couldn't turn away during the ultimately successful but nail-biting 2012 campaign. And then Trayvon Martin's assassination, and then the development, stimulated by the rise and circulation of cell phone videos, of national press coverage of the police abuse and murder of black people that had previously only been covered locally—and by the black press, including the *TJMS*. The rise of the Black Lives Matter movement. And then the disastrous and terrifying Trump phenomenon.

My whim of iron has had a number of payoffs. I have been able to observe a group of human beings respond collectively and creatively, in real time, to both horrifying and transcendently wonderful news events. I have been able to follow a popular-cultural entity as it scrambled to survive in a technologically shifting marketplace. I have watched as individuals *aged*, as I have aged—and changed as they aged. And I have been able to document the *TJMS* developing strategies to avoid losing market share, through cultivating younger audiences, as they and their audience "aged out."

I have also been able to gauge my own shifting reactions to the show over the years. At points—maybe hitting the apex in 2006, with their coverage of and response to the devastation of Hurricane Katrina, or perhaps in 2008, as they were deeply, nearly hysterically involved in Barack Obama's presidential campaign—I was so appreciative of their and their audience's collective wit, political acumen, and sheer rage at ongoing inequities and the Bush Administration's role in exacerbating them, that I was beside myself with crazed enthusiasm. I was fully inside what black scholars label problematic "racial vindicationist" arguments—a knee-jerk cele-bratory stance.[51] Their reaction to the disastrous, appalling Trump phenomenon stimulated me again into a frenzy of appreciation and sharing transcriptions with friends and colleagues.

At other points, I have been sorely disappointed. The *TJMS* crew ignored some stories and political analyses I thought were crucial, brought on commentators I thought were less than insightful, or didn't approach events and issues as I would have wished. In particular, their profoundly commercial status prevented them from accurately reporting on the extraordinarily exploitative labor policies of Wal-Mart and a number of other corporate sponsors, not to mention widespread corpo-rate tax evasion. And aside from sponsorship constraints, the crew was never by any means uniformly social democratic, as we will see.

I also lamented *TJMS*'s switch (probably for economic reasons) from live audi-ence callers to texters. So much spontaneity, improvisatory back-and-forth between crew and audience, so much "radio texture" was lost with that shift.[52] And they often didn't play the edgier, brilliant neosoul—Guordan Banks, Andrea Triana, Leon Bridges, Charles Bradley, Meshell Ndegeocello—that I've found and relished else-where. But the advantage of such lengthy research has been that I have been able to analyze the *TJMS*'s political and aesthetic shifts, to figure out *why* at certain points they weren't articulating the progressive politics I hoped for, and even to analyze po-litical differences among the crew. Thus, in the end, I have been able to avoid falling into the vindicationist trap of "cherry-picking" only the most admirable, most pro-gressive material from the show. I have documented plenty of difficult, contentious moments.

Aesthetics. Radio texture. One communication conundrum I haven't been able to solve is the inevitable reduction solely to text of the rich *aural* experience that is the *TJMS*. How to convey the sensations inspired by the music—and their var-ious political and memorial mixes are an unheralded art form—and by the music of multiple voices, their varying registers, their differing intonation contours? J's raspy "old man" tone and hilarious, deliberately self-mocking singing voice? Tom's carny-barker enthusiasm and frequent glissando swoops into falsetto? Sybil's vocal shifts across straight newsreader, hang-loose homegirl, and justifiably furious black woman personae? Of course, this is not a unique problem. All scholars of every sort of performance, and all music, television, and film critics, inevitably tussle with it. I have done my best here to represent exactly what was said and broadcast, exactly how, and to give the reader a genuine feel for the *TJMS* listening experience, its radio texture, its community of the air, over nearly a decade and a half.[53]

Here, then, I am pulling together the threads of shifting American politics, political economy, the public sphere, and a huge, vital, variegated and yet largely ignored progressive black counterpublic. Through this process, I hope to offer a reset to our ongoing debates about American racism, progressive politics, generational cultures, black arts, the political economy and technology of media, civil society, and the American—and black American—public sphere.

2

Hidden in Plain Sight

Soul Music, Radio History, and the Rise of the TJMS

One of the reasons I wasn't lonely as a child was that I could listen to the
radio. That was my first love, man . . .
—The late Herb Kent, Chicago DJ extraordinaire[1]

This race has the greatest of the gifts of God, laughter . . . It is frankly,
baldly, deliciously human in an artificial and hypocritical land.
—W. E. B. Du Bois, 1940[2]

And when I came up in the business, I had amazing people like Tom
Joyner on radio, and I had amazing formats like the Quiet Storm that
supported me as an artist . . .
—Anita Baker, BET Awards ceremony, June 24, 2018

Beginnings: Do You Know the Way to San Jose?

I have always been a radio girl. In San Jose, California, in the 1950s, my young World War II veteran father, child of Italian migrant farm and cannery workers, told me bedtime stories I later realized had been cribbed and improved upon from 1930s and 1940s radio serials—cowboy tales and mysterious detective dramas. Who knows what evil lurks? *The Shadow Knows.* A few years later, I was given a cheap little AM transistor radio to keep me from crawling out of bed at night to hear fascinating adult conversation. I turned the dial until I found music, and memorized silly pop songs like the Four Preps' 1958 "26 Miles Across the Sea," And Patience and Prudence's version of "Gonna Get Along Without Ya Now."[3] But I also heard Fats Domino, Sam Cooke, Elvis Presley, the Platters, the Coasters, and Nat King Cole.

I was, of course, far from alone in my radio obsession. As communications scholar Susan Douglas notes for both the baby boomer generation and many of their predecessors—like Herb Kent in my epigraph—lying in bed listening to the radio was a "primal experience . . . listeners had a deeply private, personal bond with radio . . . radio has worked most powerfully inside our heads, helping us create internal maps of the world and our place in it . . ."[4] Or as disco queen Donna Summer put it soulfully: "On the radio, whoa, oh oh."[5]

And in those years, in my working-class household, radio was nearly the only source of music. We did have a small box record player, but the only 78 rpm record—remember those, fellow baby boomers?—my family owned then was Frankie Laine's [born Francesco Lo Vecchio] wild, dramatic "Jezebel,"—"Jez-e-be-e-e-el, it was **you**!"—the number two *Billboard* hit in 1951.[6] Sometimes my father's childhood friend Johnny Gutierrez—from a local Andalusian migrant farmworker family—would come over for an evening, with his wife, Josie, and his guitar. I have since read about the "Latin tinge"—the extraordinary influence of Latin American musical genres on U.S. jazz and popular music over the entire twentieth century. But I remember only my intense delight as Johnny and Josie strolled into the bedroom, hamming it up, serenading me not with a mambo or bolero or tango—or even flamenco—but with the blues giant Lead Belly's 1930s rendition of the old folk song (or probably The Weavers' later version of) "Goodnight Irene"[7]:

> Irene, goodnight,
> Irene, goodnight.
> Goodnight Irene, goodnight Irene, I'll see you in my dreams.

By the time I was a young teenager, as my father's GI Bill-funded law degree paid off in the expanding post-war economy, and his law practice did well, my family had moved from our tiny working-class stucco to a larger house in a new Santa Clara Valley suburb. And like nearly all American adolescents since the rise of radio, I was obsessed with youth-station music. Glued to the AM dial, I was profoundly moved, not really knowing why, listening to the Drifters, the incomparable Mary Wells, and the overwhelmingly black girl groups of the late 1950s–early 1960s: the Shirelles, the Chantels, the Marvelettes, the Chiffons, the Dixie Cups, Ruby and the Romantics. Young, untutored in music, and out on the rim in Northern California, I understood nothing of the racial politics of their production. I didn't know about the largely Jewish songwriters—like Carole King—for "Negro" singers in Manhattan's Brill Building, the separate "race music" category in the process of being dissolved.[8] Instead, indexing the unique post-war Northern California Pacific Rim demography, I first heard the magnificent "Please Mr. Postman"—the Marvelettes' 1961 breakout hit for Berry Gordy's new black-owned Detroit Motown label—through tinny speakers at an outdoor Japanese Obon festival in downtown San Jose.[9] And the hugely talented Fats Domino sang to me that he was "Walkin to New Orleans"—his 1960 R&B and Billboard hit—from a jukebox at the scruffy open-air skee-ball joint, in what was then the very white oceanside tourist town of Capitola, near Santa Cruz.[10]

And my father would come home from the office singing the crossover songs he'd heard on his car radio—like the Coasters' swinging, doo-wopish 1959 "Charlie Brown," about a class cutup—"He's a clown, that Charlie Brown." He particularly relished and mimicked Charlie Brown's rakish bass-voiced summary line: "Why's evrah-body always pickin on me?"[11] *Time Magazine* complained in 1961 about radio-obsessed "red-eyed little tykes [who] come to the table snapping their fingers and lisping "Tossin and Turnin" [another doo-wop hit, number one on *Billboard* in the same year]. But clearly, those tykes' parents were snapping and jiving too.[12]

Even when President Kennedy was assassinated in 1963, I remember retreating from my family clustered around the television to the radio in my room, listening to a male disk jockey choke out words about attempting to keep on broadcasting on this tragic day, trying to find appropriately solemn music to fill the dead air for the dead President.

The radio scene shifted dramatically from 1964 on. Motown continued building on success, pumping out hits by the Temptations, the Supremes, Little Stevie Wonder, Marvin Gaye, Gladys Knight and the Pips, The Four Tops, Junior Walker, and Smokey Robinson and the Miracles. But the British Invasion, led by the Beatles, was taking over the radio waves. High school girlfriends were embracing the Beatlemaniac label, running around school corridors squealing about their preferences for John, Paul, George, or Ringo. I read in the *San Francisco Chronicle* that hotel workers had cut up and sold squares from the sheets they claimed the Beatles had slept on during their 1964 San Francisco Cow Palace engagement.[13] Soon the big debate was the Beatles vs. the Rolling Stones, or girls' preference for good vs. bad boys. And soon I was hearing the Stones' "Heart of Stone" on my secret college boyfriend's car radio, having slipped out my bedroom window late at night to meet him. It was many years later that I realized how profoundly reliant the invading Brits had been on black rhythm and blues—reliant to the point of simply covering (re-recording) original songs and riding them to mainstream hitdom. As the Rolling Stones did on their first album.[14]

Ironically, while many white groups have been rightly pilloried for this wholesale appropriation of black music, often without attribution, *black* performers were sometimes happy with the results. Not only did British/Irish invasion groups like the Beatles, the Stones, Eric Clapton, and Van Morrison draw attention to the blues and R&B artists in whom black audiences were losing interest as other genres gained popularity—they often hired these same artists to tour with them, thus aiding them financially and restarting dozens of careers. As the late B. B. King said memorably in 2005: "When you mention the Rolling Stones, I get on my knees . . . and say, 'Thank you, thank you, thank you.' Because before them, we didn't get the [attention] we do now."[15]

Every adolescent generation thinks it's the first to discover sex, and in one sense they are right, because they are always the first to discover sexuality in their own region and historical era. And accompanied by their own specific musical playlists.

My particular pre-hippie mini-generation linked up sexual freedom and interest in psychedelic drugs to the San Francisco Beat literary scene, and more important, to opposition to the Vietnam War and support for racial civil rights. The music that represented those politics to us was the folk music revival—including local Californian Joan Baez, and Bob Dylan in particular—that pioneered that opposition. Anti-war and counterculture sentiments were soon translated into popular radio playlists through folkies Malvina Reynolds ("Little Boxes," which described the cookie-cutter houses in nearby Daly City), Peter, Paul & Mary—who covered Dylan's "Blowin in the Wind"—rock and roll bands like the Byrds, who covered "Turn, Turn, Turn," Pete Seeger's beautiful anti-war rendition of Ecclesiastes, and others.[16]

Pete Seeger's magazine *Sing Out* became our bible, and we vaguely understood the linkages among anti-war and civil rights politics, and the 1930s economic populism represented by Dylan's god, the extraordinary radical songwriter and performer Woody Guthrie.[17] (One boy carved into his guitar Woody's famous slogan carved into his own: "This machine kills fascists"—a sentiment newly relevant since the 2016 election.) So sex, drugs, and rock and roll came a little later: for us it was sex, anti-war left politics, folk music, rock and roll, and blues. On a rare trip outside my suburb to Kepler's Books in Menlo Park, I managed to snag a copy of poet Allen Ginsberg's famous *Howl*, *The New Lost City Ramblers Songbook* (Mike Seeger, Pete Seeger's brother, was a founder of the band), and a tiny black and white metal peace button put out by the British-founded Campaign for Nuclear Disarmament, CND—the symbol was not yet commonly used in the United States.[18]

How did I find the blues? *Sing Out* was blues-crazed. I read there about Memphis Minnie and Mississippi John Hurt, and hoarded my tiny allowance to buy their albums as well as each Baez and Dylan album as they arrived. I read liner notes as if they were holy writ, finding out about the nineteenth-century English Child Ballad collection from which so much contemporary American folk music drew, about 1920s and 1930s Appalachian versions of earlier UK folk songs, about twelve-string guitars and bottleneck slide techniques, about blueswoman Memphis Minnie's hard and peripatetic life—from Algiers, Louisiana to Memphis, to Chicago. Chris Strachwitz of Blues Classics Records wrote on the back of her 1964 and 1967 albums that she was living back in Memphis with relatives, having suffered a stroke, and was partially paralyzed. She would receive fifty cents from the price of each record sold. (She died in 1973.)[19]

I scrutinized lyrics. The romantic longings and inevitably tragic denouements of Baez's ballads—which encouraged my new obsession with nineteenth-century English Romantic poetry—clashed with some of Dylan's bitter relationship kiss-offs. But more important to me, I realize now, were Memphis Minnie's and John Hurt's metaphorical but earthy sexual lyrics. "Going to let my chauffeur drive me around the world, Yes, he will be my little boy, and I'll be his girl." "All heard what Sister Johnson say, She always take a candy stick to bed, It's the candy man."[20] But give me a break, dear reader: I know all about the long white history of love and theft of black American culture, and the white hyper-sexualization of black men and women and even children.[21] But I was fifteen, living in a pre-Second Wave feminist, pre-internet era. This was literally the first time I had been exposed to the notion of the naturalness of female sexual pleasure.

And I am ashamed to admit it, but I am among the millions of baby boomers whose adolescent anti-war stance was framed less by journalism and scholarship than by Dylan's "Masters of War," "Blowin' in the Wind," "Times They Are A-Changing," "With God on Our Side," and "Hard Rain."[22] And again, I am by no means alone among white Americans of my generation in having been informed about the Civil Rights Movement in the early 1960s as much by Baez's interpretation of "Birmingham Sunday" and Dylan's "Lonesome Death of Hattie Carroll" and "Only a Pawn in Their Game," as by contemporary television, newspaper, and weekly newsmagazine coverage, and the Reverend Martin Luther King Jr's *Why We Can't Wait*, a copy of which my liberal father brought home and I devoured.[23] Looking for more, I clicked the radio dial to FM, and discovered Berkeley's Pacifica station, KPFA.

KPFA in the mid-1960s was a pacifist-founded, raffish, very left-political community radio station, filled with erudite talk. Simply through random listening while doing homework in the afternoons and evenings, I found out about the existence of the civil rights organization SNCC (the Student Nonviolent Coordinating Committee), who German playwright Bertolt Brecht was, that there was such a thing as instrumental jazz—up until then I had only heard the vocal variety—and about the current baroque classical music revival movement.[24] These glimpses of rich intellectual and cultural life were all the more precious to me, immured in South Bay suburban purdah, more than three decades pre-internet, with no public transportation and thus little access to libraries or bookstores. But I tuned in particularly faithfully late on the weekends for Gert Chiarito's *Midnight Special* show.

The Midnight Special, named after the iconic Lead Belly's 1934 version of the blues song of that name which served as its lead-in—"Let the Midnight special shine its light on me"—was an alternately open mike and spun records show. My white male high school friends' parents allowed them to hitchhike fifty miles to Berkeley to stand on line just to get into the studio, perchance to be allowed to play and sing their newly learned authentic black Southern blues songs. Mostly they milled around, watching others play and collecting stories to bring back to the dead suburbs. They never brought back the later published and re-published fact that Chiarito, acting as an unpaid talent scout, discovered both Jerry Garcia and Phil Lesh and brought them together on the show. Thus she served as the unsung midwife to The Grateful Dead.[25]

Whatever its role in storied rock history, Chiarito's *Midnight Special* was to its core a political, folky show, with an intense—today we would say nerdy—focus on the provenance of songs and their political import. Thus I heard about New York City's premier then-contemporary folky Dave Van Ronk, about Lightning Hopkins, about Robert Johnson and his crossroads, about Elizabeth Cotten, the left-handed guitar-playing blueswoman rediscovered by the Seeger family, and about the Carter Family, white Southern country musicians and singers known from the 1920s forward for "The Wabash Cannonball," "Wildwood Flower," "Will the Circle Be Unbroken," and much more. And I heard a whole lot of just-written, very bad anti-war blues.

KPFA—and one delirious day's attendance at the annual Berkeley Folk Festival—became my lodestars as I coped with a deteriorating home situation. I was a rebellious, fanatically anti-war teenager with an LBJ Democrat, pro-war father who had answered the call to serve on the local draft board. And I detested my newly well-off parents' conspicuous consumption—luxury cars, jewelry, furs, parties, expensive restaurants—and longed to enter a "more authentic," less materialistic intellectual world I would later realize I had idealized absurdly. I had the idea of applying secretly to the University of California at Berkeley during my junior year in high school. I had taken advanced placement and summer courses, so I had all the requirements already—except home economics and senior year physical education!—and could theoretically skip ahead to college. I simply forged my parents' signatures on the application. When the acceptance letter arrived—oh, what a different historical period *that* was—I presented them with the *fait accompli*, and to my astonishment was allowed to go.

While I was plotting escape, preparing to leave, and in my early years at Berkeley, I discovered other rich sites on the FM dial. I vaguely apprehended what later scholars documented: an "FM revolution" was taking place around the country. Susan Douglas calls this phenomenon "free form radio, the revolutionary format that catapulted FM into serious competition with AM and eventually led to AM's displacement."[26] In the San Francisco Bay Area, KPMX, and then KSAN with the DJ Tom Donohue, pioneered this new music and talk format.

The FM revolution involved "long-play"—queuing up not just three-minute songs but entire albums, or many musical tracks at a time. DJs eschewed "predictable, cynical" top 40 pop music tracks, instead playing the longer cuts that hip younger musicians were putting out on their albums—as did the Beatles as they developed, as did the rock musicians pioneering the San Francisco Sound. (Music historian David Hadju notes that by 1968, long-play albums were for the first time outselling single-play records—thus mirroring and enhancing this radio development.)[27] DJs chose surprising musical segues, jumping genres while, for example, maintaining the same bass line or cluster of instruments. They had fewer ads—mostly from "hip capitalists" like Leopold's Records, for some years a Berkeley institution—and clustered those ads at the ends of long sets, rather than interrupting the music every few minutes. They offered erudite musical and sometimes political commentary with a "mellow"—lowered, slowed, intimate—DJ voice. They often referred obliquely to their own and their audience's marijuana and other drug use, implying (truthfully) that it enhanced musical appreciation.[28]

I well remember "Big Daddy" Tom Donohue's gravelly but mellifluous voice cluing me in to the latest Dylan album, to the Chambers' Brothers' (whom I had seen at a Joan Baez Big Sur concert) gospel-political "Time Has Come Today," to the San Francisco groups Quicksilver Messenger Service and the Steve Miller Band, and to the Berkeley-based psychedelic band Country Joe and the Fish. Their anti-Vietnam War anthem, "I Feel Like I'm Fixin' to Die Rag," was extraordinarily popular in Berkeley. Its lyrics, among other targets, indicted war profiteers—"Come on Wall Street, don't be slow, Why man, this is war a-go-go!" The song ended with the ultimate Dr. Strangelove exclamation—"Whoopee, we're all gonna die!"[29]

Douglas traces the multiple strands of the rise of progressive FM: the post-war development and commercial success of high fidelity technology, a series of FCC rulings that allowed greater use of the FM band, and the rise of the 1960s youth counterculture, with the rich veins of music the baby boomer generation both discovered and began to produce. She also points out that the progressive FM period was cut short by its own success: within a few years, corporations bought up stations and reasserted control over DJ programming choices, relying on market research to produce mandatory formats: "Music, once so sacred to FM DJs, was now called 'product.' "[30] Business boomed, and companies asserted even greater control by contracting with new "automated programming services that sold syndicated formats."[31] DJs were not merely disciplined, but often eliminated.

East Bay Grease

For Douglas, this was the beginning of the end for American radio—the end being the 1970s rise of talk radio, soon dominated by right-wingers like Rush Limbaugh. Media scholar Robert McChesney has a similar analysis and timeline.[32] But I barely noticed the demise of progressive rock FM, entranced as I was with the worlds opening up before me in Berkeley. Two decades before the popularization of the label "world music," there was an explosion of interest in global musical traditions on American college campuses, and a rush to book both international and American performers. From the mid-1960s to early 1970s, all on the Berkeley campus, I saw Ravi Shankar play, attended a Japanese Noh drama, and was deeply moved by a Balinese gamelan production. I learned what an oud, a tabla, and a bouzouki were, and what countertenor singing sounded like. I also saw opera for the first time, in San Francisco. At the Berkeley student center, I saw Ramblin' Jack Elliot, and a wild R&B band whose name I don't remember. On the Berkeley campus Lower Sproul open-air music venue, I ecstatically experienced local bandleader Johnny Otis's integrated R&B band, with Johnny's gangly teenage son Shuggy making an early appearance.[33]

All of this musical broadening was very exciting, but I missed straight-ahead soul music. I had married and then quickly divorced my freshman-year English professor—an upper-class twit who nevertheless usefully insulated me from my dysfunctional and demanding family in that pre-feminist era—and so was free to follow my own musical tastes again. Douglas and other communications scholars, in their unhappiness with the demise of long-form hippie FM radio, have tended to ignore rich and ongoing black radio traditions. I spun the radio dial, and found neighboring Oakland's KDIA, 1310 AM, "Lucky 13, hits keep happenin," as its jingle declared. And they did.

The late 1960s through 1970s were an explosive and boundary-crossing period for black music. Detroit's Motown was still pumping out wildly innovative work: The Temptations, Aretha Franklin, Marvin Gaye, Stevie Wonder, The Jackson 5. Both Marvin Gaye and Stevie Wonder matured into progressive social commentary—Gaye's 1971 concept album, *What's Goin' On?*—which, according to Craig Werner, Barry Gordy warned him not to record—integrated civil rights, anti-war, and nonviolent politics with environmentalism, and was hugely successful across black and white buying markets.[34] Wonder followed with *Talking Book* in 1972, also departing from the Motown musical template, and offering political commentary. But Wonder's real innovations came with *Innervisions* in 1973. "Living for the City" laid out the horrendously exploitative Jim Crow world that "a boy born in hard time Mississippi" experienced, following him as he migrates to find work in New York City, "cause where he lives, they don't use colored people." He is then set up by another black man in Harlem, and thrown into prison. In the last overlaid recitative lines of the song, a white judge sentences him, and a white guard yells "Get in the cell, N——!" as he groans in anguish. Wonder was both politically and musically innovative: "City" was one of the first soul songs to incorporate voices and urban street soundscapes into the music.[35]

KDIA didn't just play the new "message" songs—it announced civil rights news regularly. (Although I don't remember getting information on civil rights, anti-war, anti-Nixon, farmworkers' union, and feminist demonstrations and marches from them, but from flyers, KPFA, *The Daily Californian*, *The Berkeley Barb*, and word of mouth. I well remember a giant Berkeley Greek Theater "reconstruction" demonstration after Nixon bombed Cambodia in 1970, and National Guard troops killed protesting students at Kent State and Jackson State. A furious black former GI warned us honkies that the army had taught him how to kill, and a young white feminist tried to talk about organizing anti-war women but was booed off the stage by scornful white males.)

KDIA was connected through shared ownership to Memphis's famous WDIA, "The Goodwill Station"—sometimes called "the mother station of the Negroes." WDIA pioneered all-black programming in the early post-World War II years and was extraordinarily financially successful, thus disproving the adage that companies sponsoring "Negro" shows would be tainted by association. It gave musicians like B. B. King and Rufus Thomas their starts as DJs, as well as the very successful DJs Martha Jean Steinberg and Nat Williams. It engaged in annual teen talent competitions—which led to college scholarships—widespread charity funded through annual all-star Goodwill Revue and Starlight Review shows, and innovative programming, like the "Goodwill Announcements"—for missing persons, lost and found, and church meetings—and "Aunt Carrie's advice," a show that clearly provided the model for *TJMS*'s Ms. Dupre decades later.[36]

WDIA also provided a "prefigurative" integrated space for its black employees. The late B. B. King recollected it for an interviewer in 1998:

> At that time the South was segregated. But we had a feeling, us blacks did, when we got into the radio station, it was almost like being in a foreign country, and going to your embassy. When you get there, you know this is home . . . So when we got to WDIA we felt like we meant something. We felt that we were citizens. We felt we were appreciated. And we didn't have to say, "Yes, sir" or "Yes, ma'am" or "No, sir" or "No, ma'am," unless we felt that it was an honor that was due to someone, not simply because we were black and they were white. Everybody worked by that, and when you walked back on the streets it was again like leaving the embassy, in that foreign country, until it really changed, and WDIA did a lot to change it.[37]

Thus black radio has experienced a very different and contrapuntal history to its mainstream counterparts. As long-form FM "hippie" radio was in decline, black radio was expanding in multiple ways: stations were newly willing to hire actual black DJs—as opposed to white DJs who specialized in "sounding black." And the stations themselves multiplied nationwide, and often flipped from AM to FM. Black-oriented radio stations nationwide grew from forty-three in number in 1956 to 108 in 1968.[38] And in a sad echo of Jim Crow American institutions, a separate scholarship on black radio arose, a scholarship of which few communications scholars seemed to be aware. Just as they were, and are, by and large unaware of the adult black stations right there on their radio dials, computer streams, and apps.[39]

As a penniless UC Berkeley Ph.D. student, I haunted the basement of Moe's Books and Records, a Telegraph Avenue institution, collecting used Motown and other classic soul albums for seventy-five cents a pop. I remember bringing a boxful of records to a radical grad student party in the late 1970s, and being congratulated all night by wildly happy dancers, who asked in wonder where I'd gotten all that great music.

Meanwhile, Stax Records in Memphis, despite the tragic loss of its huge singing star Otis Redding in a Wisconsin plane crash in 1967, nevertheless continued nurturing Southern-fried soul produced with integrated bands: Booker T and the MGs, Isaac Hayes, Sam and Dave, Rufus and his daughter Carla Thomas, Wilson

Pickett, Albert King.[40] (Sign of the times: I was then working at the UC Berkeley Doe library. After Redding's plane crashed in Lake Monona, the interior elevator sign—"Otis Elevators" in the ancient creaky carriage, used only by library workers, was regularly defaced to read, in memoriam, "Otis Redding.")

In the same era, The O'Jays, The Spinners, The Delfonics, The Stylistics, Harold Melvin and the Blue Notes, and Teddy Pendergrass, working with the songwriters Gamble and Huff and others, forged the sweet Philly Sound (which later influenced contemporary Philadelphia-based artists like Jill Scott, The Roots, Musiq Soulchild, Vivian Green). John A. Jackson defines Philly Soul as "a multilayered, bottom-heavy brand of sophistication and glossy urban rhythm and blues, characterized by crisp, melodious harmonies backed by lush, string-laden orchestrations and a hard-driving rhythm section."[41] When it first came out, I listened to "Ship Ahoy," the Gamble&Huff-written title track of The O'Jays' virtuoso 1973 album, in wonderment and horror, and burst into tears as I took in the superbly skilled Eddie Levert's soulful singing of the lyrics. The song invoked the Middle Passage, including the atmospherics of creaking timbers and wild seas surrounding the slave ship, and explicitly laid out the tragedy for "men, women, and baby slaves" of our very imperfect American union for those considered less than human "coming to the land of liberty, where life's design is already made."[42] Consider that Alex Haley's best-selling account of black slavery in the U.S., *Roots*, was not published until 1976. And the television mini-series based on that book, which was indeed a major national viewing phenomenon, did not appear until 1977.[43] The music was ahead of the literature.

But the San Francisco Bay Area, while best known in this period for psychedelic rock and roll—The Grateful Dead, of course, Jefferson Airplane (later Starship), the Steve Miller Band, Quicksilver Messenger Service, Big Brother and the Holding Company, the syncretic musical genius Carlos Santana—was also a workshop for progressive soul. In particular, KDIA showcased Sly and the Family Stone, a race-integrated funk band celebrated as "rock's first integrated, multigender band [that] became funky Pied Pipers to the Woodstock generation."[44] Sly Stone's songs, which influenced both contemporary jazz and later hip-hop artists, are remembered for their appeals for peace, racial integration and social toleration.[45] "Everyday People" (1968) asserts that we need "different strokes for different folks . . . We got to live together." Craig Werner sums up the group's brilliance and its own extraordinary prefigurative politics: "Certainly, no musical act presented a more exhilarating image of what America might become. Even as the political world re-fragmented along lines of race and ideology, Sly presided over a musical community that obliterated racial designations. . . . The group's visual presence erased boundaries, conjured up something too beautiful to be anything but a dream. The women played instruments and the men sang."[46]

KDIA also introduced me to another local group, Oakland's equally integrated but Latin-funk horn-driven Tower of Power. Oh, Tower of Power. They were not so much a message band—they mostly produced love ballads and funky dance tracks—and they never blew up as big as other Bay Area bands did. But they were self-consciously gritty, not smooth touristified San Francisco but dirty, multira-cial, industrial Oakland—*East Bay Grease* was the title of their 1970 debut album. African American audiences so appreciated them that Tower of Power was the first non-100% black group to appear on Don Cornelius's famed *Soul Train* show, in 1974.[47] And Lenny Williams, their lead singer from 1972 to 1974, who appeared on the memorable "So Very Hard to Go," went on in 1978 to record the most soaring falsetto, melismatic tour de force, begging-ist lovelorn part-recitative soul ballad ever, "Because I Love You."[48] (It has an immediately recognizable bass line, a fine female backup chorus, lush violins, periodic orchestral climaxes, and goes on for a stunning eleven minutes and seven seconds.) Over the decades, I have heard Lenny moan breathlessly on dozens of black radio stations across the country.

Spike Lee's 2000 documentary, *The Original Kings of Comedy*, reflects this wide-spread black audience delight in old-school soul music and with "Cause I Love You" in particular. One segment showcases a much younger, lesser-known Steve Harvey ranting at a vast, rapturous Charlotte, North Carolina, audience on the superiority of soul to rap and hip-hop: "If you don't get into old school, you done *missed* it! . . . We had songs back then, as soon as you hear'em, your ass just *lit up!*" . . . After playing and miming to Earth, Wind, and Fire's "Would You Mind," and The Ohio Players' "I Want to Be Free," Harvey moved to the *piece de resistance:* "The one I'm on give you now is one of the *strongest* love songs ever sung to a woman before . . . this . . . this *motherfucker* (crowd goes wild) has some feelings so *deep* for this woman, this motherfucker *cried* through the whole goddamned record!" Then the first bars of "Because I Love You" play, and the enormous audience jumps to their feet in rapture. Harvey mimes the lyrics—"Girl you know I lo-uh-uh-uh-ove you, no matter what you do," kicks over the stool and mic stand, and angrily strides to the back of the stage. The camera cuts away to the audience, whipped into a frenzy, grabbing their friends and loved ones and singing along. Harvey runs back up front and screams— "See, that's what songs used to be about!" As Lenny Williams croons, "I hope you understand me, every word I say is true," Harvey screams, "Oh SHIT, sing it!" and threatens to leave if the audience doesn't stand up. They're already mostly up, but now they all jump up and down as they scream, and sing, with Harvey, "I'm thinkin of you, tryin to be more of a man for you." When Lenny soars into falsetto on "And I don't have much riches," Harvey interrupts and shouts: "Boy this motherfucker sings this song!"[49]

And that is exactly how I respond to "Cause I Love You," every single time.

I volunteered for two years at Berkeley's Bay Area Women Against Rape (BAWAR), one of the first rape crisis organizations in the U.S. There I found the feminist politics that was only just developing in Berkeley seminar rooms, fulfill-ment in service to other women, and a major case of insomnia—I was on the mid-night to 8 a.m. phone shift, and always worried that a rape victim call was just about to come in. As they did.

I also got an education, not just in cutting-edge feminist thought on violence against women and in developing feminist and gay politics but also on race and class divisions among women. The group was class-mixed, with a number of lesbians, but originally all-white, then we expanded using Jimmy Carter-era CETA (Comprehensive Education and Training Act) funds, hiring minority women. Which then led to arguments, drama, and unwanted publicity. In the wake of the mess, BAWAR asked me, their only "academic" at the time, to create the organization's first race/ethnicity and class training. And we started picking up black and Latina volunteers.

It was also through BAWAR, through my white "big sister"—then a single mother on welfare—who became a good friend, that I realized I didn't really much like the developing genre of feminist "women's music"—except for the little-known and short-lived Berkeley-based band Joy of Cooking. Nor could I share my friend's delight over Bruce Springsteen's mid-1970s emergence and the power rock he represented. "Born to Run" didn't do a damn thing for me, despite Springsteen's overall progressive politics. I realized, as the years rolled on, that I was losing interest in white rock, and was wedded firmly to soul music. I had become a hard-core black radio girl, indifferent to the largely white popular-musical shifts over the decades. I barely noticed the 1980s hair bands, most disco, the rise of punk, metal, and Seattle grunge. Embarrassingly, in the early 1990s, a black graduate student teased me with great relish because, as she had suspected, I had no idea what "smells like teen spirit" meant.[50]

But what was authentic soul music, anyway? I didn't then know that the young Muscle Shoals, Alabama, sessions musicians, "The Swampers," working their magic behind Aretha Franklin's breakout million-selling 1967 album, *I Never Loved a Man*, were mostly white. And they were also behind Percy Sledge's 1966 smash cross-over hit, "When a Man Loves a Woman." And Wilson Pickett's huge 1966 sensation, "Land of a Thousand Dances." Rock critic Peter Guralnick described The Swampers in these early years: "They were all young, they were all crazy, they were all mad about rhythm and blues."[51] As Craig Werner writes of the Stax phenomenon: "It may seem like something of a contradiction that what was almost universally received as the *blackest* of the soul styles had by far the largest amount of white participation."[52]

It's certainly the case that there is a long history of white musicians appropriating black music—from blues to jazz to soul to hip-hop and rap. Craig Werner notes, for example, that the Beach Boys' "Surfin USA," is "[Chuck] Berry's 'Sweet Little Sixteen,' note for note."[53] Not merely pirating whole songs and styles, but doing so in the absence of any anti-racist commitment. As literary critic Gayle Wald writes: "Historically speaking, an attraction to black culture has not necessarily translated into concern for the actual welfare of black people, just as the tremendous popularity of black American popular music on a national and international scale does not portend the disappearance of white supremacy."[54] Werner, in *A Change Is Gonna Come*, angrily sums up the clueless and widespread white appropriation of black creativity in his indictment of the way the popular—and all white—1983 film, *The Big Chill*, used Motown music as décor: They "turned Levi Stubbs' [The Four Tops' lead singer] agony into a condiment for yuppie angst."[55]

And it is certainly the case that black musicians and singers were frequently cheated out of their royalties by overwhelmingly white-run record companies, and that the working conditions black musicians faced were often wildly worse than those of their white bandmates. Being refused access as customers to the very hotels in which they were performing. Making significant money on the Southern fraternity party circuit but having to endure racist jibes and catcalls while doing so, and knowing that the very college audiences appreciating their music objected strenuously to black student admission to their "white spaces."[56] *Country Soul* author Charles L. Hughes's stark comment on the "Muscles Shoals Sound" could stand in for all racially mixed American bands and music companies of the time: They "symbolize[d] the broader tension between southern soul's long history of black-white collaboration and the painful inequality of that partnership."[57]

But it's also the case that working musicians, even in the South during the worst years of white resistance to the Civil Rights movement, often simply responded to one another's talent and dedication, and came together in mixed-race groups to make transcendent music. They did so in New York City, in the Bay Area, in Muscle Shoals, at Stax in Memphis, and even at Motown in Detroit, ground zero of black musical success—as the haunting 2002 documentary film *Standing in the Shadows of Motown*, about its famed mixed-race, jazz-based backing band, The Funk Brothers, demonstrates.[58] And the Academy-Award-winning 2013 documentary, *20 Feet from Stardom*, illustrated the enormous career boost many black backup singers experienced and experience through performing with a variety of white groups and singers—The Rolling Stones, Sting, David Bowie, Bette Midler, Bruce Springsteen, Sheryl Crow.[59]

I vaguely apprehended this phenomenon through appreciating Sly and the Tower of Power. But I also found myself responding to some white California musicians I would later discover were being labeled "blue-eyed soul." The Righteous Brothers originally broke through in this category with their huge 1964 hit "You've Lost That Lovin' Feeling," and then the extraordinary Phil Spector-produced "wall of sound" 1965 "Unchained Melody."[60] In the 1970s, I was mesmerized by the Doobie brothers—from San Jose, my birthplace, after all—despite their silly name, once the talented Michael MacDonald joined as lead singer. As J Anthony Brown would exclaim of MacDonald, several decades later, commenting as a black baby boomer on the generation gap: "He's *our* Eminem! He came *widdit*!"

Similarly, I was drawn to Boz Scaggs, the jazz-pop singer who came out of San Francisco's Steve Miller Band, and worked with mixed-race backing bands. His hit "Lowdown" was first championed by a black DJ, and then took off, hitting the top 5 on the R&B chart and #3 on the Billboard Pop chart in 1976. V103's Herb Kent, Chicago's longest-working black DJ, or probably DJ of any color—who has a street in Hyde Park named after him—often mixed in Boz Scaggs on his weekend dusties shows.[61]

Chocolate City Radio

Finished with my California ethnographic fieldwork in 1979, I married a second time and moved with my young professor husband to Washington, DC, where he had a teaching job. I agonized over writing my Ph.D. dissertation, and for relief and inspiration—and political duty—joined a feminist political organization, the DC Area Feminist Alliance—an umbrella group with connections across all the violence against women/feminist union/anti-racist/populist housing/queer organizations in the area. I was the second non-lesbian to join. I subscribed to the gender-inclusive and leftist Boston-based *Gay Community News*.[62] And I dialed across DC's extraordinarily rich cache of black FM radio stations.

By my third year in DC, there was WUDC, founded at the [public, and majority-black] University of the District of Columbia, which specialized in jazz, helping me on a still-ongoing self-education journey.[63] There I discovered the incomparable, politically astute, deeply troubled jazz/spoken word singer Gil Scott-Heron—"Winter in America," "The Revolution Will Not Be Televised." And, of course, the equally radical, furious, troubled, and extraordinarily talented jazz singer and pianist Nina Simone. [64] Then there was WHUR, Howard University's station, founded in 1971. It had gone through dramatic struggles of which I was then unaware. Radio historian William Barlow calls these the "meltdown in chocolate city." The original radical talk and broad, multinational, jazz-heavy musical lineup were soon squelched by Howard University administrators looking to attract significant commercial advertising—and a black Howard University President "trying to cultivate close ties with the Nixon Administration."[65]

Ironically, this period of duress at WHUR led to an extremely aesthetically pleasing programming innovation—The Quiet Storm. "Quiet Storm" is, of course, Smokey Robinson's famous and very mellow title-track love ballad from his innovative 1975 album: "Soft and warm, a quiet storm, quiet as when flowers talk at break of dawn."[66] In the same year, African American media mogul Cathy Hughes, then Cathy Liggins, was newly appointed as WHUR station manager, having succeeded so well as sales manager that she drew administrative attention. Greeted by the decimated and rebellious staff as an Uncle Tom, Hughes nevertheless reanimated its morning and evening public affairs and news shows.[67] According to her own account, she also invented Quiet Storm programming.

In order to craft an evening playlist that would draw high ratings—as the then-current jazz programming did not—Hughes polled other black professional (white-collar) women on their preferences, chose Smokey's song as her theme, and drafted then-WHUR intern Melvin Lindsey to try out the concept and playlist—a mixture of jazz, soul, and pop with a focus on romantic ballads. Listening to Quiet Storm, Hughes asserted on the 1995 NPR/Smithsonian series "Black Radio," was a profound emotional experience: "Even if you don't have a date, you're gonna be content to stay home by yourself."[68]

The results were spectacular. Barlow notes that "[b]y the end of 1977, *The Quiet Storm* was the top-rated weekend music show in the Washington, DC, market." Hughes was then able to move it into weeknight time slots, and "the format change transformed WHUR into the number-two rated FM outlet in the nation's capital." Quiet Storm programming spread rapidly across the U.S., and is an evening fixture on hundreds of black radio stations four decades later. I still remember my first stunned and wildly happy reaction to gifted three-octave-range crooner Luther Vandross' 1981 breakout hit, "Never Too Much," which HUR gave significant Quiet Storm airplay. I could tell that his backing band was brilliant. What I didn't know at the time was that the jazz musician Nat Adderley, Jr., Cannonball Adderley's nephew, was Luther's musical arranger.[69]

And it was in those years, through Quiet Storm programming, that I became aware of the hypnotic singer Ann Peebles ("I Can't Stand the Rain," "Tear Your Playhouse Down"), and the multi-talented tragic genius Donny Hathaway ("The Ghetto," "More Than You'll Ever Know"), even though they had recorded their hits earlier in the 1970s. And in 1981, every black DC station played on heavy rotation Stevie Wonder's charming and moving "Happy Birthday Martin," part of his contribution to the fight to establish Martin Luther King, Jr Day.[70]

Then there was WPFW, which Pacifica, the parent organization to Berkeley's KPFA, founded in 1977, and which soon became the country's largest black community radio station. It took over the political, multinational, and jazz programming that WHUR had abandoned under university administration duress. While its entire history has been marked by controversy and fierce in-fighting among staff and with the Pacifica board, I knew PFW from the late 1970s to mid-1980s as a progressive refuge, and a political and musical educator.[71]

These were the final years of the single Jimmy Carter presidential term, marred serially by the energy crisis, runaway inflation, and the Iran hostage crises—and hobbled by his own technocratic instincts, and by a mainstream press, egged on by Republicans, turning on the president for his foreign policy "weakness." When I first arrived in DC, I met many twenty- and thirty-something progressives who had flocked to the city either to take low-level positions in the administration or to work for various organizations to pressure the White House from the left.

President Carter was hardly a liberal by 1970s standards: A former governor of Georgia with a segregationist past, he had waffled on fair housing laws during the campaign, notoriously speaking positively of neighborhood "ethnic purity." His commitment to labor, a Democratic Party tradition since Franklin Roosevelt, was less than firm. He, not the Republican Ronald Reagan, was the first American president to support cutbacks to AFDC (Aid to Families with Dependent Children) ("welfare") that hurt poor women. He memorably, horribly riposted to a group of feminist activists meeting with him to protest the unfairness of the Hyde Amendment, which banned federal funds for abortions for poor women: "Some things in life are just unfair."[72]

Nevertheless, President Carter did continue the environmental policies that, ironically, President Nixon had begun—and was pilloried for them. He pioneered the use of human rights language in discussing foreign policy, even if his own policy decisions were inconsistent. He did *not* invade Nicaragua when the Sandinistas won, nor did he take extreme measures to keep U.S. ally the Shah of Iran on the throne—although the U.S. taking in the ailing Shah for medical treatment probably led directly to the hostage crisis. He shepherded the triumph of the Camp David Accords between Israel and Egypt. He managed the SALT (Strategic Arms Limitation Talks) nonproliferation talks with the Soviet Union. He stood firm on returning the Panama Canal to Panama. But he flip-flopped, over time, on United Nations resolutions against South Africa's apartheid regime.[73]

WPFW, along with progressive journals like *The Nation, The Guardian, Monthly Review, The Manchester Guardian, Private Eye,* and others, provided me contemporaneous political analyses of not only the Iranian revolution and then Khoumeni's takeover and the hostage crisis but of shifting situations in South Africa and other African states, all of Latin America and Asia—especially, in those years, El Salvador and the Philippines. I think PFW herded me along to many of the innumerable demonstrations that I attended in my DC years, demos that increased in size and number after Ronald Reagan's 1980 presidential victory—against the Philippines Marcos dictatorship, the apartheid South African government, the Pentagon's horrific pro-dictator role in Latin America, violence against women, and nuclear proliferation—that was the two million-strong 1982 one, in Manhattan—and for women's and gay rights.

But WPFW was also a source of transcendent entertainment. And there I discovered the Bama Man.

Disk jockey Jerry Washington started the weekend *Bama Hour* and *The Other Side of the Bama* on PFW soon after the station's founding, playing hard-core non-crossover blues and R&B. "Bama," short for Alabama, is a deprecating term for a black Southern country yokel, but Washington, who had attended the HBCU Morehouse College and served for decades in the Air Force, deliberately took on the false identity on-air, playing a fascinating character, complete with a fake younger girlfriend named Denise.[74] I learned the artful use of dead air, listening to the Bama Man plead, "And Denise . . . . I'm sorry" at the end of a show.

"Wash" owned the airwaves during his weekend lunchtime shows—WPFW's audience swelled tenfold. Mayor Marion Barry, a huge fan, was among many celebrities who would visit the studio. And while Wash's main audience was DC's working- and middle-class African American majority—and better-off blacks like General Colin Powell—he also had a significant white fan base.[75]

The Bama Man, showcasing "sophisticated nightclub blues on the borderland of soul,"[76] played on heavy rotation blues and jazzmen and women I had already encountered and loved: Bobby Blue Bland, B. B. King, Muddy Waters, Sarah Vaughn, Nancy Wilson. He even included Frank Sinatra—whose Nelson Riddle-era songs my beloved Italian-American father would croon around the house. But he also introduced me to lesser-known chitlin circuit greats like Albert King, Joe Hinton, Toussaint McCall, Dorothy Moore, Jimmy Witherspoon, Esther Phillips (whom I later found out Johnny Otis had discovered and promoted), Latimore, Betty Wright, O. V. Wright, Denise LaSalle, and Z. Z. Hill. I remember hearing "Cheatin in the Next Room" for the first time ("Makin plans to be with him soon, Talkin softly on the telephone")—and Bama Man intoning portentously afterwards: "Z. . . Z. . . . Hill."[77] And I can still feel my profound happiness as Bama Man cued up Albert King's 1972 classic "I'll Play the Blues for You," with its immediately recognizable intro guitar lick, as I was driving down 16th Street to attend yet another lefty-feminist anti-racist meeting.[78]

Elm City Politics and Radio

After significant struggles and failures on the Reagan-era job market after I had finished my Ph.D., I moved to New Haven, Connecticut, in 1985 to teach at Yale University, and lived there through Reagan's second term—during which I participated in anti-apartheid divestment demonstrations on campus—George H. W. Bush's ascendance, and the first Gulf War. I quickly found the Yale-owned but community (and thus black majority)-run FM station WYBC, as well as the local NPR station. I've forgotten most of the programming I heard in my six years there, but I do remember the huge WYBC fight when Yale moved in the late 1980s to "take the station back for the students," which temporarily ejected their long-term and Bama Man-worthy evening DJ, Willie Wright "The Meteorite," who ranged broadly across soul, R&B, and jazz. I was already a huge Dinah Washington fan, but had never heard her extraordinary rendition of the 1950s hit, "Teach Me Tonight," until Willie Wright cued it up.[79]

I also remember turning off the NPR station in complete disgust during the 1991 Gulf War, as they capitulated entirely to the triumphalist White House and Pentagon Desert Storm narrative. We reconstructed the Yale course I was then co-teaching on American cities to incorporate teach-ins on the backstory of the war—on our American government's complicity in bringing Saddam Hussein to power in the first place, and in supporting his autocratic regime. Until we didn't.[80]

Another local FM station, WPKN, broadcasting from nearby Bridgeport, provided counterweight to the mainstream war narrative. I had discovered PKN, a non-Pacifica community station—then still affiliated with the University of Bridgeport—when I first arrived in New Haven.[81] I listened late at night to a warm, whisky-voiced woman DJ who ran their "Behind the Walls" program for regional prison inmates, with dedications and soul music and jazz. It was my first experience with prison radio. (A decade later, I would discover another such program on *Radio Bilingue* in California, with excellent Chicano-taste soul, *radionovelas,* and late-night DJs reading out messages to prisoners from sweethearts and families.)[82] And PKN had for a time a wonderful weekly *Esquina Latina* (Latin Corner) salsa show, DJed by "Edwin."

Windy City Steppin

I moved to the Chicago area in 1991, to teach at Northwestern University. The first time I tried to find Chicago-area black radio, I was sitting in a fusty room in the old, down-at-heels Evanston Orrington Hotel, where I was staying during the job interview. I spun the dial and hit on an unfamiliar, much-too-cheery jingle, then a man declaiming in soaring falsetto that he was the "hardest-workin man in radio." I got the reference to James Brown's trademark claim that he was the hardest-working man in show business, but I wasn't much impressed with the corny-sounding DJ. That was my introduction to Tom Joyner, who was then the self-labeled Fly Jock— literally flying back and forth between Chicago (WGCI FM, now known as the rap station) and Dallas (KDDA FM) three days a week.[83]

But as I settled in to my new home, and as Tom Joyner took on partners and created the *TJMS* in 1994—becoming the first African American to have a major U.S. syndicated radio show—he grew on me.[84] Or they all grew on me. And the show grew extraordinarily rapidly, as we have seen, becoming *the* black voice on American radio. The backstory to this development is not just an interesting piece of black radio history, but also surprisingly little known. An account of Tom Joyner's actual political evolution, of other scholars' and journalists' evaluations of the show's early politics, and a broader narrative of black radio history and the shifting political landscape within which the *TJMS* has operated are now in order.

TJMS and Black American Radio History

Given the show's progressive politics in the 2000s, I was astonished to read in Joyner's self-published 1995 autobiography that he was then a black conservative who had both voted for Reagan and benefited greatly through his friendship with Reagan's Federal Communications Commission Chair Mark Fowler.[85] Joyner's two key intertwining narratives in *Clearing the Air* are a Horatio Alger bootstraps life story—his parents did indeed start out as tenant farmers, and he did indeed work extremely hard to achieve success—and a classic New Right hatred of government bureaucracy as purely incompetent and exploitative of ordinary Americans through the extraction of taxes: "What justification do they give you, the public, every time they take more bread off your table in the form of taxes to fund their pet projects? . . . Congress is parasite and a huge boil on the butt of humanity."[86]

Joyner went so far as to praise Rush Limbaugh—"I can subscribe to about 60 or 70% of the opinions that I hear from Rush"—and to endorse the Reaganite vision of social programs as killing self-reliance: "Generations of people have come to see welfare as a way of life."[87] Even Joyner's visions, then, of criminal justice, freedom of speech, and rap music fit cozily within the Reagan White House mold.[88]

And yet simultaneously Joyner noted ongoing American racism and the need to combat it, and his own early stunts as a black radio disk jockey underlined those realities. While working at KKBA in Dallas in the early 1970s, for example, Joyner responded to local police targeting only black neighborhoods for radar gun speed traps by encouraging listeners to "drop a dime on the man"—to call the radio station with up-to-the-minute news of precisely where police had set up speed traps: "You call me, you tell me where the radar is and whatever I'm doing, I'm stopping . . . And I'm going to announce where the radar is." This, of course, was decades before we began to understand—post Ferguson—the ways in which Southern and other municipalities often deliberately fatten their budgets via their black (and white) working-class populations through excessive and targeted policing and thus tickets, bail and fines.[89] Not to mention the ever-present danger of a police stop ending in the wounding or killing of a black motorist.

In an extension of this early radio activism—but now focusing exclusively on the private sector—in the first handful of years of the *TJMS*, Joyner, with Tavis Smiley, launched a series of campaigns, using the might of their large radio audience, aimed at preventing U.S. businesses from taking black consumers for granted. In 1999, for example, they asked listeners to send in their CompUSA receipts, "charging that the largest U.S. computer retailer failed to sufficiently advertise in the black community."[90] ABC Radio threatened to pull the *TJMS*, but backed down, as did CompUSA: after a ten-week campaign, the corporation's chief executive apologized on-air, and promised to hire a black-owned advertising agency.[91]

This and other campaigns, such as the successful 1997 effort to prevent the auction house Christies from selling American slave memorabilia (chains and shackles), while they had a policy of refusing to sell Holocaust items, took a page from Jesse Jackson's signature protest politics.[92] That is, in a conservatizing, post-civil rights era, instead of working for classic civil rights goals—pressuring the state to provide and enforce equal access and economic opportunity—minority activists tended instead to focus on affecting individual corporations' policies with regard to race. This incremental, consumer-oriented approach has its uses but can have only limited results. At the same time, of course, even this level of race-nationalist activism contradicted Joyner's earlier stated conservative politics.

And meanwhile, over the late 1990s and into the new millennium, the show was gaining listeners and corporate sponsorship at a fast clip, and simultaneously moving rapidly to the left, mirroring the politics of its target audience. (I cannot assess the relative weight of the Clinton presidency and general U.S. political shift from the right to the center in this period, Sybil Wilkes's and other program staffers' political influence, or sheer commercial pragmatism—mimicking the political profile of the bulk of black Americans—in effecting this political sea change.) The *TJMS* engaged in multiple voter registration and get-out-the-vote campaigns and worked actively for the Democrats in both the 2000 and 2004 presidential races. And they were early activists, as we have seen, on the 2006 midterm elections and Democratic congressional triumph.

As the *TJMS* took over multiple regional markets, its capitalist growth process—parallel to the way in which the rise of, say, chain bookstores, coffeehouses, and then Amazon and other internet giants have killed thousands of independent businesses—threatened locally produced black radio programs, many of them already stressed by federal cutbacks in public and college radio funding. Local black press, and even a single *Washington Post* story, covered the subsequent controversies. In Philadelphia, for example, early in the show's growth history, *The Philadelphia Tribune* mourned the loss of the local Kevin Gardner show on WDAS to the *TJMS*, and quoted loyal listeners lamenting that "WDAS has lost its connection to the Black community."[93] The *Post* story, published in the *TJMS's* second year, documented early protests by local black radio directors against the show's imperialist gobbling-up not only of local black shows but of their associated jobs and local political access.[94]

In order to provide a sense of place-based news and commentary, Tom Joyner taped personal "feeds" to local news, traffic, and weather announcers in black stations playing their syndicated show, and also taped announcements of local disk jockeys' shows.[95] In the early years in Chicago, for example, WVAZ listeners would periodically hear Tom Joyner saying, "What's up with that news, Wanda?"—and WVAZ's Wanda Wells would give a quick summary of international, national, and local headlines of particular interest to black Americans. *TJMS's* peripatetic Sky Shows, as well, held all over the United States, with local audiences and local businesses presenting scholarship checks to students attending local black colleges, helped to build place-based allegiance.[96] Finally, the early call-in feature, Express Yourself, played on regional understandings and loyalties, and enhanced what Susan Douglas describes as disk jockeys' sometime role as "privileged conduits within their listeners' imagined communities."[97] And we can see the role here—and everywhere on the show—of Du Bois's "frankly, baldly, deliciously human" black humor.

Consider this crew and audience seminar on working-class Southern black survival in hard times:

> (*March 14, 2005*) *Express Yourself question: What jammin food did your Mama used to make when you were low on food?*
> *Woman caller: Hey Tom, lemme tell you from a Alabama homegirl. Sauerkraut and neckbones!*
> *Another caller: Bread and gravy!*
> *Tom: Don't you need meat for gravy?*
> *Myra J:* **Where** *are you from?*
> *J: I'm gonna take your country card, man.*

Or this hilarious back-and-forth, simultaneously documenting *TJMS*'s popularity in upstate New York and the widespread post-trial black American presumption of OJ Simpson's guilt:

> (*October 18, 2005*) *Express Yourself:*
> *Male caller: This is Jeff from Buffalo, New York. I want to know if J heard what happened to OJ Simpson at the Buffalo Bills game. Two white girls came up and threw beer all over him!*
> *J: They wouldn't have been able to do that in the dark of night!*

Before moving on with *TJMS*'s evolution, let's recapture and reweave some threads of American radio history, and black American radio history in particular, in order to see how the show constructed its own contemporary garment. The *TJMS* built on long traditions of black comedy, music, and political commentary—going back to Showtime at the Apollo, juke joints, and political demonstrations—and specifically built on black American radio history.

Post-1950s radio programming history includes not only commercial and independent public radio, not only the rise, as we have seen, of the FM band, but the growth and then decline of public college radio stations—coincident with the infusion of and then cutbacks in federal funding—affecting stations like WHUR and WUDC—as well as various local programming trends and controversies. With reference to black-oriented programming alone, three civil rights and post-civil rights era shifts are noteworthy.

First, the Joyner crew, along with other black DJs, reanimated the 1950s role that black radio historian William Barlow labels "audio tricksters": "They talked a steady stream of street 'jive,' using strange-sounding words, some of which were of their own making."[98] Then, Barlow documents the late-1960s decline in black radio news and public affairs programming, as part of the capitalist restructuring process of industrial growth (with payola scandals offering the excuse for 'reform')."[99] Station and conglomerate owners wrested control, program by program, from these local audio tricksters and their white brethren, through the invention, as we have seen, of "Top 40 Radio": "The top 40 soul format effectively ended the black disk jockeys' control over the content of their own programs, just as it had ended the white disk jockeys' reign over rock-formatted stations."[100] But, again, this decline and fall narrative is only one element of the larger and complex whole of post-war radio history.

The rise of black-owned stations in the 1970s—in New York, Washington, DC, and Chicago, for example—functioned to curb the top 40 format through reinvigorating the ranks of local black disk jockeys interested in public affairs programming.[101] Often these DJs also developed specific hip vocal stylings, as had earlier black DJs, and white DJs for black stations, whom black listeners often assumed were black. As the NPR/Smithsonian series *Black Radio* put it: "You had to have a *hook*. . . . That began personality radio."[102] Chicago DJ Herb Kent, who began broadcasting in 1944, had struggled to be accepted and had taken college broadcasting courses to master a smooth, grammatical radio voice, had a somewhat different take:

> I have no problem with people sounding black, but you can be black and correct with your English. Some people are just lazy and they're not going to learn those words; they don't care and they just spit them out.[103]

And in fact, to the day of his death, Herb Kent, with a certain amount of cheerful sadism, regularly corrected callers' pronunciation and grammar.

Finally, the Reagan revolution of the 1980s, with its associated deregulation of the airwaves, political witch-hunts, funding cutbacks, and corporate mergers, led to a large-scale depoliticization of progressive black (and all American) radio.

Radical media scholars for some time have been documenting the public-sphere sequelae of the Reagan-era deregulation of American media, and the later Clinton Administration cherry on the poison cake—the Telecommunications Act of 1996. We have more and more concentrated ownership, cross-industry (newspapers, television, radio stations, the internet) empire-building, and the decline of hard news reporting with the rise of infotainment across all media.[104] As William Greider writes: "The corporate concentration of media ownership has put a deadening blanket over the usual cacophony of democracy, with dissenting voices screened for acceptability by young and often witless TV producers."[105] In addition, the FCC's 1987 abandonment of its historical Fairness Doctrine, in conjunction with heavily funded New Right organizing since the late 1970s, led to a national hard-right broadcasting turn as new media barons (such as Rupert Murdoch and the Fox empire) enforced the neoconservative line in the newsroom.[106]

Nevertheless, even with fragile financing, progressive print, radio, television, and the new online media continued to contest for attention and influence. I noted in the late 1990s that this consolidation/fragmentation dynamic had led to a new fissioning of the American public sphere: the sheer multiplication of what were formerly more unified and limited sets of media units, the proliferation of "niche" media marketing, and the simultaneous corporate consolidation of the "new entertainment state." In this new political media divide, outlets were marketed to "true believer," left or right, racist or anti-racist, feminist or anti-feminist consumers.[107] Since the 1990s, this fissioning process has only intensified: witness the 1996–on rise of Fox News, MSNBC's growth and movement to the left since the early 2000s, and the proliferation of progressive online forums like Huffpost, Salon.com, Slate.com, Daily Kos, etc., and their various rightist, racist, misogynist, xenophobic counterparts.

Turning to radio, as we have seen, political-economic scholars narrate a variant of this larger tale of decline and fall.[108] Despite radio's highly commercial-capitalist history, many commentators have appreciated its past vivacity and cultural pluralism. Susan Douglas notes that 1920s stations' relationship to jazz began "radio's century-long role in marrying youthful white rebellion to African-American culture" and interprets 1930s radio as "a site of class tensions and the pull between homogeneity and diversity."[109] Like many other older scholars (including myself), she has a particularly romantic vision of the rise of rock and roll as black crossover music in the 1950s–60s, and of the short-lived "underground, progressive" FM radio movement of the 1960s–70s.[110]

Thus there is little room in these media scholars' historical narratives for an analysis of the phenomenon that bucked all these trends: the rise of the feisty, original, politically progressive, and yet highly commercial *TJMS* from the 1990s to the present. (Communications scholar C. Riley Snorton has pointed out that the media reform movement failed to include race in its analyses.)[111] Nor is there room for the irony that the show's nationwide syndicated success literally was enabled by FCC deregulation.

In an interestingly parallel fashion, some African American music/media scholars envision the invention of Quiet Storm programming as an uncoincidental artifact of the politically retrogressive Reagan years. African American and cultural studies scholar Mark Anthony Neal, for example, sees the Quiet Storm development in interesting and contradictory ways. It offered a "welcome reprieve from disco and funk" but was also the emblematic indicator of middle-class black adult political demobilization. For Neal, Quiet Storm "allowed the black middle class the cultural grounding that suburban life could not afford them, while maintaining a distinct musical subculture that affirmed their middle-class status and distanced them from the sonic rumblings of an urban underclass."[112] (And this was indeed precisely the historical moment in which non-affluent black Americans were beginning to be widely stigmatized as members of the feckless, innately criminal "underclass.")[113] Neal asserts that Quiet Storm allowed or enhanced the careers of Luther Vandross, Anita Baker (just as she noted in my epigraph), The O'Jays, Harold Melvin and the Blue Notes, The Whispers, Frankie Beverly and Maze, Roberta Flack, and Jeffrey Osborne, while also noting that many of these artists also crossed over to mainstream pop success in these years.[114]

Neal also points out that Quiet Storm allowed musicians the freedom to experiment artistically, particularly in terms of song length: "These changes in popular music represented the first opportunities for black artists to experiment with improvisation and arrangement outside of the genre of jazz...."[115] That is, Quiet Storm allowed black artists to exploit the conventions of Album Oriented Rock with the expectation of radio play, just as the FM revolution of the 1960s–70s had done for rock groups in that era. But for Neal, what is ultimately important is that "these [Quiet Storm] recordings were in most cases devoid of any significant political commentary and maintained a strict aesthetic and narrative distance from issues relating to black urban life."[116]

Where Did All the Music Go?

But as we have seen, Quiet Storm, and the black radio-station fracture into two formats—"urban adult" vs. "rap/hip-hop"—that soon followed its inception, was a phenomenon far more about generation than about class or politics. The bulk of the adult black American population in the 1980s and beyond likely wanted to hear progressive talk and song lyrics, but not when they were married to misogyny, profanity, and the celebration of violent crime—and when they experienced little pleasure in listening to the percussion-heavy, often unmelodious music. As neosoul artist Leela James lamented of rap, "Where did all the music go, we don't sang no mo."[117] Thus the ubiquitous "I don't like . . . that rap" station break on Chicago's V103. Thus the large, constantly shifting lineup of younger singers and musicians since the 1990s—among them Goapele, Miguel, Melanie Fiona, Kem, Tamia, Tank, Anthony Hamilton, John Legend, Vivian Greene, Jill Scott, Lalah Hathaway, Jazmine Sullivan, Kelis, Jaheim, Bruno Mars, Charlie Wilson, Ro James, Raheim DeVaughn, Frank Ocean, Childish Gambino—whose neosoul/R&B/pop releases spur live ticket sales among adult black Americans, and receive heavy airplay on "urban adult" black stations. And thus the wild, growing success of the *Tom Joyner Morning Show* from the 1990s through the 2000s.

And yet in African American studies, amidst an avalanche of analyses of black film and television, of rap and hip-hop, and African American popular culture and style, there are just a handful of mentions of this radio giant. William Barlow, writing only a few years after the show's 1994 founding, noted that it had "built up a large and influential audience among black baby boomers throughout the country," but that "the raucous style of comedy that Joyner and his cohorts perform has generated some controversy in black media circles."[118] Indeed, in many of my early interviews with black American listeners, individuals often termed the show "silly," and many times denied listening to it despite, for example, offering details of specific show "bits," or admitting to having gone to a *TJMS* Sky Show. There is a clear class component, in other words, to some hands-off black reactions to the show. Some, understandably, have wished to define themselves as above its working-class raucousness. As a black woman acquaintance in her forties responded to my enthusiastic narrative more than a decade ago: "Tom **Joyner**?! I'm [jokey black slang] edumacated! **I** listen to NPR!"

Early in the show's career, Mark Anthony Neal labeled *TJMS*, in passing, the "digital chitlin circuit," thus noting its wide national popularity, its Southern feel, and its working-class reputation. But he also labeled it "old-school," and thus doing "little to reach out to the youngest segment of the African-American electorate. . . ." (He did go in-depth into Tavis Smiley's early career moves, when he was affiliated with the show, and repeated with great appreciation J Anthony Brown's joke that "Smiley's commentary was often just an opportunity to tell listeners what the next stops were on his book tour.")[119]

Political scientist and former MSNBC news anchor Melissa Harris-Lacewell [now Harris-Perry], in her 2004 *Barbershops, Bibles, and BET*, noted that *TJMS* in that early era was "the single most recognizable forum of black talk in black America today," and celebrated the show's popularity, racial authenticity, and social justice predilections but did not acknowledge its feminist, economic populist, broadly pan-racial, and LGBTQ rights politics.[120] For Harris-Lacewell, *TJMS*'s politics could be summarized simply as "nationalist": "Joyner is a Nationalist, one whose basic social and political organizing principle is that black is good, black people are valuable, and black people should devote time and resources to ensuring quality of life for other black people."[121] But "black nationalism" is a catch-all political label for historically specific formations that can shade left or right.[122] Labeling *TJMS* "black nationalist" erases the ways in which the show treats issues of class, race beyond blackness, gender and sexuality, and international politics. To give Harris-Perry her due, she put her book to bed in 2003, a year before I began transcribing the show. It is conceivable that *TJMS* politics changed significantly in that interim period.

Let us now look more closely at those politics.

3

Here's to All My Baby Mamas

Family Values and TJMS Gender/Sexuality Politics

> The cultural and political discourse on black pathology has been so pervasive that it could be said to constitute the background against which all representations of blacks, blackness, or (the color) black take place.
> —Fred Moten, "The Case of Blackness," 2008[1]

> Black motherhood has borne the weight of centuries of disgrace manufactured in both popular culture and academic circles.
> —Dorothy Roberts, *Killing the Black Body,* 1997[2]

Early one morning in the late 1990s or early 2000s, I was walking through my living room on the way to get dressed for work, when the voices on the radio stopped me dead in my tracks. An older black woman caller to the *TJMS* was fulminating anathemas against abortion, repeating "killing babies, baby-killing." Suddenly Sybil Wilkes, her voice tight with emotion, broke into the caller's harangue. Slowly and deliberately she intoned: "Ma'am—first of all, it is *not* a baby. It is an embryo, or a fetus."

I was shocked by Sybil's terminology correction, because it signaled what I later confirmed: she is a forthright defender of reproductive rights. In those backlash years, outside distinctly feminist organizations and publications, you would have had to look long and hard to find such statements. And I hadn't yet really figured out *TJMS*'s political profile. I'd been listening to the show since its mid-1990s founding, but erratically. I'd range across the dial, sampling Chicago-area stations, sometimes catching the jazz shows the local NPR station, WBEZ, was still airing, sometimes taking in the "kids' stations"—WGCI (rap) and B96 (transracial youth station playing pop and hip-hop—Aaliyah, Cristina Aguilera, and The Fugees were big in those years). And I'd found the various Sunday gospel shows, one of which aired on Northwestern University's student station, WNUR, which also played world music.

And then there was old Herb Kent (The Cool Gent), who, as we have seen, had started DJ-ing in the late 1940s, and had been a fixture on Chicago's legendary station

WVON (Voice of the Negro) in the 1960s. Through the 1990s, Herb still had evening shows on V103. (He had Saturday morning and Sunday afternoon timeslots until his October 2016 passing at age eighty-eight.) Kent's musical taste wasn't quite comparable to Washington, DC's Bama Man or New Haven's Meteorite—he played far less blues, R&B (with the exception of Bobby Blue Bland), and vocal jazz than they had.

But Herb Kent's playlist was far, far more capacious than most black shows', including the *TJMS*'s.[3] The self-named King of the Dusties (he claimed to have coined the word) focused heavily on the breakout black popular music genres of the 1950s through the 1980s.[4] A lot of doo-wop and girl groups of all varieties, far beyond the range of crossover hits I'd heard as a child in the 1950s and early 1960s. Lesser-known Motown and soul stars—Bobby Womack, Barrett Strong, Ruth Brown, Little Willie John, Mable John, Chuck Jackson, Johnnie Taylor, Barbara Mason, David Oliver, The Dramatics, The Isleys, The Emotions, Heatwave, DJ Rogers—as well as widely popular crossover giants like Aretha Franklin, The Four Tops, James Brown, Gladys Knight, The O'Jays, Al Green, The Temptations, The Supremes, The Delfonics, Marvin Gaye, Stevie Wonder, Barry White, Bill Withers. Herb Kent also showcased specifically local Chicago talent, many of whom were personal friends and would appear on his show: Tyrone Davis, The Chi-Lites, Sam Cooke, The Dells, Jerry Butler/Curtis Mayfield and The Impressions, Chaka Khan, Otis Clay, Syl Johnson. He would reach back to 1950s–60s vocal jazz: Dinah Washington, Brook Benton, Roy Hamilton, Arthur Prysock, King Pleasure. And Herb would also spin from his own idiosyncratic list of favored "blue-eyed soul" white musicians—The Righteous Brothers, Boz Scaggs, The Rolling Stones, Average White Band, The Bee Gees, even the occasional Beatles cut.

I would listen to Herb Kent's evening shows while writing and revising the book that obsessed me at the time, periodically scribbling down names and songs that were new to me. I was sometimes struck with wonder at his remarks—like the time he and another V103 DJ, Wali Muhammed, were messing around at show turnover time. Herb queried Wali sincerely about his Black Muslim faith, finally asking him what exactly the Koran was. Muhammed answered with the classic "holy book" explanation. Herb burst out laughing, artlessly confessing his ignorance: "*Man, I thought it was a rug!*"[5]

So I had plenty of radio listening material in the Chicago area, in this pre-internet, pre-live-streaming era. Of course I noticed the *TJMS* crew making civil rights points—what I expected and looked for in all black radio, part of its attraction. Even Herb Kent, for example, who was relentlessly apolitical, would occasionally dip into civil rights outrage—as he did when he informed his audience that the Pentagon had been built in 1940 with twice the usual number of bathrooms—because of Jim Crow segregation.[6] Similarly, back in 1996, I wrote several friends about the *TJMS* crew's witty badinage concerning three then-current, heavily publicized incidents of corporate racism in Florida. They ended with the summarizing joke: "We *don't* try harder! They get their Avis car, fill it up at Texaco, and go for breakfast at Denny's!"[7]

Nevertheless, up until Sybil's feminist outburst, I had been mostly noting *TJMS*'s music and hilarious, in-house, not particularly political humor. In the summer of 1999, amazed at how the crew and their audience wittily sent up two different black stereotypes, adding commentary on "dead rapper" conspiracy theories, I wrote a friend:

> Did I remember to tell you about the Joyner shtick where they ask, What name tells you the person is black? Joyner went on&on about people named after cities, Like Cincinnati and Philadelphia. The one this morning was, if I never see X again in my life, I'll be happy. First a woman called in and said "chicken," and the whole studio exploded in remonstration. They told her how could she say that about the national bird? Then a guy in LA called and said "Tupac." He was really funny, kept saying, "I just saw him again last month, and the dude is dead."

Sybil's intervention alerted me to pay more attention to overall *TJMS* politics. I listened more often, and hyped the show more to my friends and colleagues. And as I did, over the years, the show as a whole seemed to move decisively to the left. By the 2004 election cycle, I had become a wild-eyed fan, was transcribing whole chunks of on-air conversations and performances, and gave my first talk about the show.

That talk was at a global "family values" conference at the University of Chicago. Over the course of the 1990s, that term, a New Right invention, seemed to be on everyone's lips, and became ubiquitous across mainstream media. But our understanding of its meanings, of the constellation of political stances it represents, has so dwindled in the last two decades of tumultuous political and cultural change, that a review of its history in American politics is in order.

"Dan Quayle Was Right" and Other Horrors of the 1990s

In the American context, "family values" refers to the contention that only heterosexual married couples, in which the woman does not work outside the home during children's minority years, are capable of rearing children properly. Frequently, it includes the notion that human personhood begins at conception. It thus incorporates both anti-gay and anti-women's rights stances—including not only opposition to abortion but even to all forms of birth control. Family values thus serves to indict the morality of all (that is, close to all) Americans not living in such households, and thus of not only all working mothers, and all sexual expression taking place outside heterosexual married units but also all women engaged in any form of reproductive choice.

Family values thus functions specifically as an intentional slur against African American women, who were for decades portrayed uniformly, by the racist right and even by self-defined liberals, as promiscuous single mother "welfare queens," presiding over "perverse" "matriarchal" families. Sociologist Stephen Steinberg, in *Turning Back: The Retreat from Racial Justice in American Thought and Policy*, traces the modern history of this specific racial slur back to President Lyndon Johnson's speech at Howard University in 1965. The speech, which was written partly by Johnson aide (and later Massachusetts senator) Daniel Patrick Moynihan, simultaneously called for affirmative action to remedy past discrimination while also subtly making use of Moynihan's now-notorious report on the black family to blame black Americans for their own oppression through referring to "the breakdown of Negro family structure."[8]

What followed was the long march, through both the public sphere and the academy, of the association of African American status with "faulty" female-headed families, and the neat substitution of family structure for endemic structural and economic discrimination as the cause of black poverty—associated with the late anthropologist Oscar Lewis's "culture of poverty." That core counter-empirical claim was joined, from the President Jimmy Carter period forward, by a rising political critique of "big government" and thus a tendency to look to families to perform basic public functions in the wake of governmental abandonment of social responsibility.[9]

With the neoconservative triumph of Ronald Reagan's 1980 presidential win, racist backlash against civil rights and anti-feminist backlash against the second wave of the women's movement found welcome in the White House, and Reagan's delusional claims that black "welfare queens" were draining the public purse through massive fraud actually became reflexive common sense for millions of Americans. (Indeed, "fake news" has a long American pedigree.) The huge social program cutbacks of the Reagan, and later Bush I, years, particularly in social support and public housing, produced skyrocketing minority poverty rates, which were then neatly explained through use of newly refurbished "culture of poverty" ideology.[10]

Thus the stage was set for Vice President Dan Quayle's 1992 election-year attack on the network television show "Murphy Brown," whose eponymous white, professional-class heroine (actor Candice Bergen) became pregnant and gave birth to a baby outside wedlock. Quayle asserted that the character was "mocking the importance of fathers" and that liberal supporters were claiming that single motherhood was "just another lifestyle choice." Quayle, born to a wealthy family, and notorious for his public misspelling of "potato" and other incidents indicating extraordinary mental dullness, lectured impoverished/

minority Americans: "It's time to talk again about the family, hard work, integrity, and personal responsibility."[11] The airwaves and the mainstream and neo-conservative press were bursting with assertions that black American women had "contaminated" white women—Murphy Brown crooning Aretha Franklin's well-known hit version of the ballad "You Make Me Feel Like a Natural Woman" to her newborn did not go unnoticed in the popular press. Thus the modern usage of family values was set.[12]

While Clinton won the election, as sociologist Judith Stacey has shown, he soon assimilated to communitarian elements in the Democratic Party on both women's and gay rights. And as an avatar of neoliberalism, he had never stood strongly for minority economic justice (as opposed to nominal civil rights) in the first place, and moved to "end welfare as we know it" in the draconian 1996 PROWRA (Personal Responsibility and Work Opportunity Act) legislation.[13] In fact, a few months after the Clinton/Gore inauguration, *The Atlantic Monthly* published an article in an issue whose cover blared its title—and its substance: "DAN QUAYLE WAS RIGHT."[14] Stacey analyzed the development of the "new postfeminist familism" of that time among centrist academics and politicians, a set of stances that looked "tediously familiar": "Sounding like card-carrying conservatives in academic drag, they blame family breakdown for everything from child poverty, declining educational standards, substance abuse, homicide rates, AIDS, infertility, and teen pregnancy to narcissism and the Los Angeles riots."[15]

It was only necessary for the religious right, from the 1970s forward, to respond hysterically to the efforts of some LBGTQ Americans to agitate for civil rights, including the right to marry and to bear or adopt children, for the full contemporary flavor of "family values" to be developed. And, as we can see from the evolutionary trajectory of the term, it simultaneously indexes our neoliberal era with its associated evacuation of all non-military governmental responsibilities, and thus the fetishization of "the family" as the institution responsible for the care of those made vulnerable by youth, age, disability, illness, or unemployment. The term was further transmogrified when some pollsters claimed that George W. Bush won reelection in November 2004 because of "moral values" voters—which translates as family values plus overt rightist religiosity.[16]

But the racism and misogyny inherent to family values ideology actually have a much deeper American pedigree, a framing that arose long before the 1960s–70s backlash against civil rights activism and the second wave of American (and global) feminism. As literary theorist Fred Moten notes in my epigraph, blackness has been equated with pathology for so long and so pervasively that it is impossible to disentangle them. This poisoned ideological history is especially apparent in the United States. Historian Allan J. Lichtman demonstrates that "at the core of right-wing politics in the 1920s and beyond was an anti-pluralistic ideal of America as a unified, white Protestant nation." This crisis mentality, the notion of a beleaguered white male America, so sadly familiar to us in the American present, originated a century ago. Lichtman notes the key importance of an amalgam of anti-black—including Ku Klux Klan terrorism—anti-immigrant, and anti-women's rights politics to the rightist consensus of the 1920s. He reminds us that in the 1920s, no less than the 1970s and 1980s, conservatism asserted that "a morally ordered society requires a morally ordered family, with clear lines of divinely ordained masculine authority and the containment within it of women's erotic allure."[17]

Lichtman traces key features of the decades-long development of conservatism to modern American neoconservatism. The first was the jettisoning of "Protestant" from "white Protestant nation" as conservatives engaged in *rapprochement* with the formerly disdained American Catholic Church, absorbing its anti-abortion reaction against the 1973 *Roe v. Wade* Supreme Court ruling legalizing the procedure. Historically, Republicans had frequently taken pro-family planning positions. But as early as 1976, the official Republican Party platform praised "the efforts of those who seek enactment of a constitutional amendment to restore protection of the right to life for unborn children."[18] This shift was part of the larger effort by Republicans to attract "lunchpail Democrats"—working-class white ethnics—to the party through appealing to hostility to civil rights and feminist activism and youth rebellion.[19]

The second key feature was the virulent, widely publicized reaction against early second-wave feminism, as journalist Susan Faludi documented in 1992 in *Backlash: The Undeclared War Against American Women*:

[Backlash] rhetoric charges feminists with all the crimes it perpetrates. The backlash line blames the women's movement for the "feminization of poverty"—while the backlash's own instigators in Washington pushed through the budget cuts that helped impoverish millions of women, fought pay equity proposals, and undermined equal opportunity laws. The backlash line claims the women's movement cares nothing for children's rights—while its own representatives in the capital and state legislatures have blocked one bill after another to improve child care, slashed billions of dollars in federal aid for children, and relaxed state licensing standards for day care centers. The backlash line accuses the women's movement of creating a generation of unhappy single and childless women—but its purveyors in the media are the ones guilty of making single and childless women feel like circus freaks.[20]

As Lichtman points out, activists like Anita Bryant and Phyllis Schlafly then combined anti-feminism with the third key element, homophobia, in vehement protests for newly coined "family values:" "[D]efense of the family meant battling the Equal Rights Amendment (ERA), abortion, pornography, gay rights, and gun control."[21] Finally, in this period,

[t]he right led the left in tapping the resources of corporations and foundations and grassroots fund-raising through direct-mail solicitation. It used appeals to "family values" and "personal responsibility" to recapture the moral high ground that the left had occupied during the era of the civil rights struggle. It advanced the political uses of technology such as radio talk shows, television evangelism, and Internet blogs and websites to circumvent what was perceived to be a liberally biased media establishment.[22]

The most infuriating element of the new center-right family values consensus was its profoundly anti-empirical demonization of black and brown women. Specifically, as legal scholar Dorothy Roberts writes: "From the moment they set foot in this country as slaves, Black women have fallen outside the ideal of American womanhood . . . [they were portrayed as] immoral, careless, domineering, and devious."[23] And with reference to single-mother households, historian Stephanie Coontz wrote in 1992, "[i]n almost every decade, for 200 years, someone has 'discovered' that the black family is falling apart."[24]

The claim that the source of race-minority poverty is black families' departure—in the "perverse matriarchal black family"—from the American nuclear family norm, is based on entirely flawed presumptions. First, the original American colonial households, and later New England and Eastern Seaboard farm families, were often *not* nuclear in form. Rather, households tended to be large and contain many non-kin members—often indentured servants and/or slaves. And the early Puritans frequently "farmed out" their own biological children to work in other households for fear that they would be "too soft" with them otherwise. As Puritan minister Cotton Mather advised parents: "Better whipped than damned."[25]

During the long nineteenth century, given both high mortality rates and waves of immigration, there was a wide variety of non-black American households: from the living-alone or with female companions and settlement-house adaptations of the new, often spinster college graduates of the late nineteenth century to the boarding-house strategy many European immigrant women practiced to make ends meet.[26] So the "nuclear family" was never the key practice of "our ancestors." And as many historians, beginning with the late Herbert Gutman, have documented, at the end of the Civil War, newly freed black slaves made extraordinary, lifelong efforts to reunite with kin sundered by slaveholders' cruel practice of selling off family members far away from one another.[27]

Whatever household forms individuals and groups practiced may have been in part strategic adaptations to changing American economy and demography. But such adaptations had and have little effect against economic crises, mass unemployment, and racial/ethnic discrimination in schooling, housing, criminal justice, and employment. As Coontz firmly states: "Although there may be things to draw on in our past, there is no one family form that has ever protected people from poverty or social disruption, and no traditional arrangement that provides a workable model for how we might organize family relations in the modern world."[28]

In any event, the mythology of the "perverse" impoverished single-mother family with "too many children," of the defrauding black welfare queen, was precisely that—mythology. Most poor Americans historically—specifically those on AFDC rolls—have been white. Prior to the enactment of welfare "reform" in 1996, 40% of welfare mothers worked for pay as well. In fact, numerous studies documented that women enrolled in AFDC in order to gain access to healthcare for themselves and their children, cycling off the rolls as they were able to find jobs with healthcare benefits. And those black women who were on ADFC, as opposed to the mythology of "having babies to increase the welfare check," always had fewer children than American women in general—the average was 1.8.[29] In any event, black women have always had higher labor force participation rates—defined as working for pay—than white women.[30]

The "black teenage pregnancy crisis," as well, was entirely fabricated. Black adolescent childbearing rates began falling *in the 1960s* and continued to fall through the subsequent decades. While it is true that these young women were increasingly less likely to be married to the fathers of their children, that factor was far more due to those fathers being less and less able to contribute to household finances. That is, over the latter decades of the twentieth century, black men faced increasing difficulty in finding remunerative "men's jobs," first because of the mechanization of Southern agriculture; then given the disappearance of Northern factory work with the waves of deindustrialization; and finally, because of black and brown men's specific vulnerability to the criminal justice system and its literal creation of their unemployability.[31]

So, removing layers of racist mythology, we have, since the 1990s, generations of hard-working, disproportionately single, working- and middle-class African American mothers. In every part of the country. Urban, rural, suburban. Whether particularly religiously observant or not. Whether politically active or not. But definitely all subject to the onslaught of mass media denigration of "toxic single mother families." And these women were the key, indeed the majority audience of the *Tom Joyner Morning Show*.[32]

Thus we return to the show. From its 1994 founding forward, the *TJMS* saucily, effectively spoke to and for this crucial element of its base. It dramatically countered the family values mass-media drumbeat for its enormous black audience. As radio scholar Dolores Casillas writes of Spanish-language radio, the *TJMS* operated "transgressively in real time."[33] And yet this and all its other political interventions were and are invisible to mainstream media and to all the scholars who have bemoaned the modern rise of neoconservative media. Let's look at exactly how the *TJMS* articulated its *own* family values. As Myra J's motto put it: It's All about Love.

Myra J: Live. Love. Laugh.

What the *TJMS* represented across its decades-long existence is implicit *dissent* from the entire apparatus of right-wing rollback. The show offered abundantly clear advocacy of racial civil rights, LGBTQ rights, some anti-war and anti-imperial stances, and economic populist issues. But with reference to gender and family, it did not lecture. It simply assumed, normalized all black women's respectability and moral worth: single, married, divorced, widowed; with children or not; gay or straight or something else. Whatever their household forms.

Myra J's (see Figure 3.1) hilarious monologues addressed to "single moms" anchored that normalization of all black women—actually, all women, period. A Chicago native and Los Angeles-based writer/performer, Myra J started out as a social worker. She tried standup comedy on a dare, and was able to give up her day job and move into both comic performance and writing. She worked with the *TJMS* for fourteen years, and then shifted into writing for Tyler Perry's television comedies *Meet the Browns* and *House of Payne* as well as *The Ricky Smiley Show*.[34] (During one of Perry's appearances on the *TJMS*, Sybil, in a brave show of feminist solidarity, pertly asked him when he was going to give Myra J a raise.)[35] Myra J also co-wrote and performed on the *TJMS*'s witty soap opera "It's Your World," which was discontinued in 2008 when it lost its sponsor.

Figure 3.1 Actor and writer Myra J., crew member until 2008. Reprinted with permission from Myra J.

Myra J's Tips for Single Moms cleverly used the advice column genre to provide a tongue-in-cheek, pragmatic vision of a universe of hard-working, smart, respectable, and sexually active black single mothers who good-humoredly deal with the misbehavior of children, exes, and often current male friends. "Cause if you go back," as we have seen she warned about an evening of bad sex, "you just a *fool.*" In Myra J's vision, the issue is not *being* a single mother. The issue is doing the best job possible with your life and for your children *as* a single mother. Perhaps her cleverest and most paradigmatic intervention was not an official Tips monologue, but her extended response to American Idol winner (and single mother) singer Fantasia Barrino:

> *(January 24, 2005) Myra J says she wants to celebrate Fantasia's popular new song, "Here's to All My Baby Mamas" (which includes positive messages about single mothers simultaneously working, paying their bills, and going to school)—"And girl I know it's hard"[36]—and has some suggestions for new song titles for her:*
> *I can do anything, includin forget about you*
> *All my designer bags are filled with diapers*
> *He bought groceries, I think I'm in love*
> *I'm goin to get my tubes tied*
> *The babysitter only stays til midnight, what we gon do?*
> *The only thing you're gettin out of this house is your kids*
> *I go to school, I go to work, I do skwirk. [mashup of school/work, perhaps with a nod to "twerk"]*

What rhetorical work do these seven tongue-in-cheek song titles accomplish? They assert that single mothers have their priorities straight, and children come first: "All my designer bags are filled with diapers." That they aspire to personal and economic betterment, and work even more than double days: "I do skwirk." That they can be pragmatically hard-headed about disappointing romantic partners: "I can forget about you"—"the only thing you're getting is your kids." That nevertheless they continue to try to have satisfying love lives: "What we gon do?," with perhaps rationally low standards: "He bought groceries, I think I'm in love." But with sensible foresight: "I'm goin to get my tubes tied."

Let's delve further into Myra J's Single Mom World. In common with black comic tradition and black baby boomer opinion, she believes in parental strictness and discipline:

> *(May 23, 2005) Single moms, summer's comin, and you need jobs for your kids! Because your clothes fit a whole lot better when your children are not all down in your pockets!" Myra goes on to recommend that kids hustle—mowing lawns,*

lemonade stands, errands for the elderly, plant caretakers—"And single moms, check those plants your children are watering, make sure they're legal!"—delivering papers, tutoring. "But if your child spells tutor T-O-O-T-O-R-E, look back into that cutting grass thing!"

Disciplining children isn't only about putting them to work but also about restricting potentially dangerous activities. Note Myra J schooling Sybil in this wildly funny bit:

(April 25, 2005) This is high school prom time. Single moms, what are you gonna do?
    Your child wants to stay all night at the hotel where the prom is. Is your answer:
A. Can I go?
B. Maybe in your afterlife, or
C. Who's payin?
Sybil: I'm torn between A and B.
Myra J: Sybil, you have obviously not been around kids for awhile. The correct
    answer is B.

Here's another witty Myra J child-discipline list, including a feminist flick of the whip:

(October 10, 2005) If your child wants "gold teef-ees" for his birthday, you should
    buy him a dictionary instead.
If your child is asking for cough medicine but never seems to have a cough or a cold,
    you have a problem.
A smoothie is when you pop your kid upside the head and he didn't see it comin.
If your child refers to a "gold-digger," that would be a miner from the 1840s.

Discipline also means an intelligent sense of who's running the household and what the rights of a household head are. Back in the 1990s, when a *TJMS* caller asked when was it time for children to move out of the house, Myra J shot back, "When they gettin more diggity [sex] than you are!

Discipline goes for men in single moms' lives as well. On November 7, 2005, Myra J laid it out:

Single moms, you shouldn't be with anyone else who's doin less than you. If he has
    children, he should be takin care of them every day ... Single moms, you deserve
    to be taken out ... Single moms, his life should not be yours—you may not like
    all his friends.
And finally, he should have a job. You have a job, he got to have one too.

Then there are the issues of estrangement, divorce, child support, and division of assets. Myra J and J Anthony Brown play an awards season turn on absconding fathers:

(February 28, 2005)
Myra J: For the single mom who endured endless phone calls and finally found out where the kids' father worked . . .
J, delighted, using comic barker voice: And the Oscar goes to . . .
Myra J: Finding Neverland!

And Myra J and Sybil made an effective team up against "the boys" in arguing for mothers' rights. Here are two different occasions:

(February 12, 2008) Crew is discussing an estranged celebrity couple and how the woman has moved another man into the house. Tom and J are bitching about it.
Myra J: Man up, that's all I'm sayin! Man up! (goes into sardonic baby talk) Ooooh, you got your widdle fee-wings hurt cause she got somebody else?
*Sybil: And you've had somebody else for years! . . . It's **her** house!*
Tom: But he paid for it!
*Sybil: It's her house **now**!*

(June 18, 2007) A woman writes in about her ex, who has stopped helping his three children with her because his new girlfriend has a six-month-old baby. Tom Joyner tries to interpret the situation as a "proud new father" focusing on the baby.
Myra J (instantly inventing a beautiful substitute for the censored "don't give a shit"): Most single moms don't give a dead fly mashed against a nasty wall about that!
Later, male listener calls in to support Myra J's position.
Myra J: Radio hug, baby, radio hug!

Finally, Myra J sometimes gave Oprah-like, but working-class-identified advice on single moms' self-improvement and spirituality:

(March 6, 2008) Myra J: In our post-Oscar frenzy, why not talk about a make-over? You know it's time for a change—
If it's 70s night at the club and you wearin the same clothes you wore to work.
If three of your toes are fine, and the last two are kind of crossed.
If you tie your hosiery in a knot at the knee rather than buying knee hose.
If your bra makes your chest look like it's about to launch two torpedoes.

If every man you meet treats you like an Oscar nominee, and says Good Night and
Good Luck!

(January 30, 2006) Myra J on what to keep:
Keep anybody who could watch your kids on speed dial on your phone.
Then keep anything that can go from Tupperware to tummy in five minutes in the
fridge.
Then you must keep some sunglasses, a tube of lipstick, and a baseball cap in your
car. Now mind you, single moms, this does not work if you come out in a terry
cloth robe!
Keep clean linen in your bedroom at all times!

(December 12, 2005) Myra J's wonderfully upbeat but pragmatic Christmas ad-
vice for harried, cash-strapped mothers:
Single moms, this is crunch time! What we need to do now is set the mood so you
can get everything done! First of all, play the Christmas movies. . . . Have you
sent out your Christmas cards? You don't have time? Yes you do! Little kids
can address those cards. . . . Dig out the Christmas decorations, don't matter if
you may have only two Wise Men. Dig out all your black figurines and set'em
around, say they visitin. String popcorn on the tree . . . And get ready to take half
those gifts back, cause you'll be sayin "I aint givin that to him, he aint worth it."

Final spiritual advice—note that, unlike New Age-y women's magazine articles,
no cash outlay is involved:

(March 14, 2005) Myra J: Single moms, it's SMT, Single Mom Time in your
home. Send everyone else's kids home. Your kids can't watch TV or play video
games, only read or play mind games. Throw a cover over the birdcage, and tell
the cat not to meow. You deserve **quiet***.*

Myra J was also the mistress of embedded political critique. Note how, in her list
of what single moms should "dunk or junk" she slyly notes political shifts, the current
economic crisis, President Bush's unpopularity, and the stress of working-class jobs:

(October 12, 2005)
—Any medication you've had since Clinton was in the White House
—If your hairline has receded further than the U.S. economy, let the bangs go. Your
opportunity to wear bangs has expired!
—If your child's grades are lower than Bush's approval ratings, time for them to let
go of fun. Fun for them has expired!
—If your man's excuses are more tired than the end of night shift at 6 a.m., then
you've got to junk him!

Or there were Myra J's sensitive, empathetic anti-war contributions during George W. Bush's second term:

> *(October 29, 2007) Myra J responds to a woman who has written in: Her husband has cancer and has quit his job. She has a job but is thinking of joining the Naval Reserve as well for financial security. . . . "This woman should talk to serving soldiers. Lord knows I love me some soldiers. Howsomeever! We at war. Straight up! She got some other options with an MA. Kids need their parent . . ."*

But Myra J's voice, while magnificent and much missed, was never the sole progressive feminist beacon for the *TJMS*. We have seen Sybil Wilkes argue for reproductive rights and come out swinging with Myra J in women's-rights teamwork. Ms. Dupre, while often politically inconsistent, was gorgeously matter of fact on gay rights, often working in concert with the whole crew:

> *(January 25, 2006) Crew reports that Simon on* American Idol *is nasty to gay contestants.*
> *Tom: Is he gay?*
> *Ms. Dupre: He's a **self-loathing gay homophobe**, and the gay community don't like that!*

> *(September 28, 2005) Question for Your Psychic Friend: female caller asks, "I need a spell to get rid of an ex-lover."*
> *J: Male or female?*
> *All: Laughter*
> *Tom: Got to get it straight so the spell doesn't get crossed!*

One fabulous morning, the crew was discussing the rumor that *American Idol* contestant Anwar, "the one with the dreads," had a "male-friend website."

> *(April 1, 2005)*
> *Tom: Well let me ask you this, Melvin: Does your meter [gaydar] go off? With Anwar?*
> *Melvin: Bwoopbwoopbwoopbwoop! Like a truck in reverse!*

And one day Sybil, Myra J, and Ms. Dupre were left to run the show alone, which they did with extraordinary élan. The Reverend Al Sharpton phoned in, fully prepared to participate accordingly:

> *(February 2, 2006) The all-female jokes are flying fast. Sybil says, "Tom is out, J is out, and there are very few men who could handle this level of estrogen."*
> *Ms. Dupre: "Can you handle it, Reverend Al?"*
> *Reverend Al: "I can handle it, because I just surrender!"*[37]

Sybil's Book Club

Sybil Wilkes on her own, however, is also a formidable presence, always the most well-informed crew member, widely recognized as premier news source and house intellectual. When listeners wrote or called in to say, "I listen to *ya'll* for the news!" they were largely referring to Sybil's contributions. She even ran a book club for the show audience. At some point, several times every week, Tom Joyner would say plaintively, "Syb, I just don't understand X." And Sybil would smoothly enter the conversation with whatever was needed: correct pronunciations and definitions, statistics, historical context, explanatory details. In fact, Sybil's impressive vocabulary and broad knowledge were a constant source of fairly good-natured teasing among the crew—a process that of course underlines the show's working-class-friendly atmosphere. In the show's very early years, they even had a segment titled "Sybil's Big-A Words of the Day." They replayed a 1995 example on September 22, 2018, in which crew members competed to make the most ridiculous possible definition guesses. But while that "bit" died before I really started paying attention to the *TJMS*, Sybil's intellectual reputation, and the resultant kidding, continued apace:

> (*February 22, 2006*) *Sybil reports that (black) speed skater Shani Davis and his rival Winter Olympics teammate have reached a rapprochement. Myra J instantly interjects "WHAT?!" Ms. Dupre shouts encouragement to her intellectual colleague: "Tell her, baby!"*
> *Sybil explains the situation, and the meaning of rapprochement. Myra J muses, "It sounds like something you get in a café—I want my rapprochement with butter!" Which inspires both Myra J and Ms. Dupre to shout in tandem, riffing on the old Mae West line, "Is that a rapprochement in your pocket or are you just happy to see me?" General hilarity ensues.*

> (*September 5, 2012*) *Huggy Lowdown is beside himself over the successful spectacle of the Democratic Presidential Convention: "The First Lady knocked it outta the park! And that hair . . . straight outta the chair! He stutters . . .*
> *Sybil: Huggy, you're verklempt! [Yiddish word meaning "overcome with emotion," heavily used by a character on "Coffee Talk" on* Saturday Night Live *back in the 1990s.]*
> *Huggy: [disbelievingly] What's that word, Sybil?*

> (*June 17, 2015*) *Sybil, in sports news, reports that "there is some animus against [basketball star] LeBron James." J and Tom instantly start clowning, demand to know what the word means. Sybil: "It's about the same as throwing shade." Tom says, "Then why didn't you just say that?" Sybil ripostes: "I have to say I like the looks on your faces when I say* **animus***!"*

(October 26, 2016) Comic Kym Whitley is on, substituting for Sybil: "Does that mean I have to be all polite, readin the news like a white girl?"

(August 20, 2013) Huggy Lowdown greets Sybil as "the woman whose IQ is higher than Bill Gates' credit score!"

(January 31, 2017) Sybil Wilkes, "the woman that Siri asks for help!"

*(July 6, 2017) "Sybil Wilkes, the woman with a tattoo of **Copernicus**!"*

(July 7, 2017) "Sybil Wilkes, my walking encyclopedia!"

*(November 1, 2017) "Sybil Wilkes, the woman who if she doesn't know about it, fo-**git** it!"*

(December 6, 2017) "Sybil Wilkes, my sagacious sistah from another honor society!" (a play on brother from another mother)

Perhaps the hilarious pinnacle of this tease-the-smart-girl genre on the *TJMS* occurred on March 21, 2012:

Sybil was late to the show, and it came out that she had been attending a fundraiser at a Florida art museum. Tom and J insisted, glorying in the absurdity of their contention, that she had really been performing at a strip club. Tom—the line clearly just having occurred to him—shouted in ecstasy, in club barker voice:

"Now appearing, Smarty-Pants! Make it rain with Kindles!"

Ironically, and counter-stereotypically, it was also Sybil who reported sports news and explained to the guys—often with a home-town Chicago brio—the finer points of football, basketball, baseball, soccer, and tennis. Tom and J openly admit that she has far more sports expertise than they do. Here's a bit in which they comment on J's basketball ignorance, combining it with a joke turning on the "white men can't jump" stereotype—that white players can't "get in the paint," can't score at the basket, have to shoot from behind the 3-point line:

(March 30, 2006) March Madness discussion. Tom says that J can bluff his way through seasonal basketball conversations with one simple question: "Did you see that white boy throw that 3?"

And sometimes the crew just showed their appreciation of Sybil's extraordinary grasp of public affairs details:

(November 3, 2014) The day before the midterm elections. Sybil says that "pretty much everything you've heard, you can throw out the window, because turnout has been incredible!" She goes on to explain that Vice President Joe Biden could

come into his own in the Senate should the Democrats achieve *fifty* votes in that chamber—he would then be able to break tied votes.

Tom: *Teach, Sybil!*

J: *We got a smart one here!*

[Alas, Sybil was right about the civics details, but wrong about the outcome. The Democrats lost the Senate in 2014 and were disastrously reduced from fifty-three to forty-six senators.][38]

Sybil is also the most across-the-board politically progressive member of the *TJMS*. She commented throughout each daily show—often tartly checking Tom and J when they strayed—but also reported the news twice each morning, and used that soapbox to stress, among other issues, women's rights: employment—particularly in the entertainment business—reproductive, health, and appearance issues, violence against women—including under-reported cases of missing black girls and women—and women's/LBGTQ sexual rights.

Sybil's employment interventions were always clear and often quite salty:

(June 2, 2008) Sybil reports designer Yves St. Laurent's death, and adds that he was the first designer to put black women on the runway.

(July 8, 2008) Sybil exclaims "Bravissima bella!" (And she pronounced it properly.) "Italian Vogue's *new issue uses only black models, and devotes the entire issue to racism in the fashion business. But American* Vogue *has only one article!"*

(August 2, 2011) Tom Joyner reports on yet another case of a male politician tweeting a photo of his penis [they say "dick"].

*Sybil: Men are **stupid**! Do you see any women politicians tweeting photos of their body parts?*

Tom Joyner: No.

*Sybil: **I rest my case.***

(April 22, 2013) Sybil reports that it is Administrative Professionals Week. Debate ensues:

Tom: They're secretaries!

Sybil: They're administrative professionals! That's what they like to be called now.

J: It's like the garbagemen, they're sanitary engineers now . . .

Tom: On Mad Men, *they're secretaries!*

*Sybil: That's because it's **1960**.*

*Tom: But I **like** those secretaries.*

*Sybil, dripping sarcasm: You **do**, don't you?*

Woman texter, later in the show: Syb, you tell'em! We are administrative professionals, thank you very much!

Tom and J, instantly pick up on the texter "having attitude"—throwing shade—and mimic her tone joyously: Thank you very much!

> *(March 12, 2015) Sybil reports on a new study specifying how much money women at different educational levels lose over a lifetime because of the gender pay gap.*

And Sybil laid out a consistent feminist stance on women's health, reproduction, and appearance:

> *(February 2, 2006) Tom Joyner is upset that Andrea Yates was released [a white Houston mother of five who, in an episode of post-partum psychosis, drowned her children in a bathtub. She was not actually released in 2006, but transferred to a mental hospital.] Sybil expostulates against Tom's argument.*
> *Tom: So this is a sexist thing?*
> *Sybil: Yes it is, that you guys don't understand post-partum depression! It is a hormonal thing.... [goes on to detail the facts]*
> *Tom: This is one of the arguments of the sexes here.*
> *Sybil: It is! But I'm* **right**.

> *(February 5, 2008) Male caller from Mississippi responds to a Sybil health report, "What is that word that Sybil was using? [endometriosis]—Because I love my wife dearly and I think she has it."*

> *(February 17, 2010) CNN Reporter Roland Martin had interviewed a doctor who lectured black women over their low rates of breast-feeding. Show was besieged by black women objecting to his statements. Sybil summarizes them acerbically: that the doctor was condescending and irrational. He blames women who cannot breastfeed because of their work obligations, or because they cannot produce enough milk.*

> *(March 31, 2015) Sybil reports that a new study indicates that black women's breast cancer cases are statistically far more deadly than white women's, and that the difference "is not necessarily connected to poverty.... "Scientists suspect there may be "genetic differences in our own bodies as black women."*

> *(June 23, 2015) Dr. Raegan McDonald-Mosley, medical director of Planned Parenthood of Maryland, is on the show, reporting on increasingly stringent Texas restrictions on abortion clinics. She points out that one in three American women have an abortion in their lifetimes, and that black and Latina women have abortions at twice the rate of white women. Sybil comments tellingly, linking two hot-button right-wing issues, "They don't want to tell people not to have* **guns***, but they want to tell women what to do with* **their bodies***!"*

> *(June 14, 2011) Tom and J note airlines' recent price increases, joke around that the companies could save money by charging "those wide-ass flight attendants." Sybil says calmly and forcefully throughout their ribaldry: "No. No. No." Then she summarizes with cold disdain: "Tom and J, I'm not playing your little reindeer games."*

*(June 25, 2008) Tom and J enjoy themselves disparaging aging women's appearance. Sybil calls them on it, and they demur, with the classic comics' excuse that everyone is fair game for humor. Sybil: "Oh come on, now come on—just stay **off** the ladies!"*

*(March 6, 2012) Sybil reports that Rush Limbaugh has apologized for calling a law student [reproductive rights activist Sandra Fluke] a slut and a prostitute. She articulates with great relish—this was early on in the multiple-sponsor stampede away from Limbaugh: "He has lost **seven** advertisers to date."*

Sybil could become very contentious on violence against women and girls:

(June 16, 2007) Crew discusses step-parenting. Issue of incest comes up.
Tom: You know, before Oprah, we didn't hear about that—a man touchin a stepchild . . .
*Sybil: I beg to differ. I think we **did** hear about it. She goes on to explain that the crimes pre-existed the feminist movement's organizing to make them public political issues.*

*(June 3, 2008) Crew comments on singer R. Kelly's court case. Tom labels the teenage girl witness who engaged in a ménage a trois with Kelly a "thief." Sybil erupts: "He had sex with a **child**. And she stole a **watch?! I'm sorry.**"*[39]

(June 16, 2008) Caller says that because of recently publicized rape cases, "Maybe now these young girls will put some clothes on and act right." Sybil quickly responds: "We mustn't say that what women wear has anything to do with how men react to them!"

*(December 5, 2011) "We've got word of a black woman, Kalisha Madden of Detroit, gone missing, but no one's talking about her. That's why **we're** here."*

(December 11, 2014) Crew discusses new rape accusations against Bill Cosby. Tom Joyner queries, Why did the women wait as long as forty years to come forward? Sybil gives an eloquent defense: "I believe them because of the history of sexual assault." She explains about victims' deep feelings of shame and fear, particularly when the man is powerful and could affect their careers.

*(October 10, 2017) Everyone is discussing the avalanche of rape and sexual harassment charges against the now-disgraced film mogul Harvey Weinstein. Sybil reports that the famous designer Donna Karan has tweeted that the women were "asking for it" because of their scanty dress. Sybil, with outrage: I ask **what century** she's living in to say those things!?*

(December 5, 2017) Crew discusses the burgeoning post Trump-election #MeToo movement. Sybil, Tom, and visiting comic Lavell Crawford seriously report new sexual harassment claims against various male celebrities. Then Tom says: "I get these texts every time, why don't the women bring it up earlier?" Sybil goes into full-throated defense of these women because of the fear—fear of hurting

*their careers, or just losing their jobs—they may have children to take care of. Lavell asks, what if it's "just looks." Sybil is again eloquent: "Yes, it's a gray area, and women can sound like children—'He **looked** at me!' But the men KNOW what they're doing. She then offers a summary of behavior that will bring about progressive change: "If you are doing it, STOP IT. If you are a man and see it done, Say SOMETHING. If you are another woman, say something!" She's very careful to acknowledge that men may be victimized . . .*

Later: Tom reports that dozens of texters are writing in, "Preach, Sybil!" "Tell'em, Sybil!"

And, quite clearly countering long-term stereotypes of feminists as prudish and humorless, Sybil always stood for women's rights to sexual pleasure as well as LBGTQ rights:

(June 22, 2009) Singer Eric Benet is guest in the Red Velvet Cake Studio. Benet is widely acknowledged to be seriously fine. Sybil is known to be straight and single.

Benet: Tom, Sybil is looking lovely. She is rocking an Issey Miyake gown (Sybil laughs delightedly) with glass slippers.

Sybil: Four-inch Jimmy Choos!

Benet: Tom, can I take Sybil home?

Sybil emits a series of excited dolphin-like squeals.

(March 21, 2009) Crew discusses report that women are having orgasms when working on gym bicycling equipment. Much ribaldry.

Sybil: Matter-of-fact, throwaway line: "Couple of D batteries and I'm good."

(May 10, 2013) Crew, as is their wont, is obsessively discussing Kerry Washington as Olivia Pope in the hit television series Scandal. *Tom and are J upset, or say they are upset, that Olivia has had so many sexual partners. Sybil pours withering scorn on them—why shouldn't she have multiple partners? Tom brings up the safe sex issue: "They're showin everything else, why don't they show a condom wrapper?" Sybil is dismissive: "They're **implicitly** there!"*

(January 27, 2005) Male caller: "I'm callin about Tavis (Smiley) sayin gay marriage isn't a government issue." Goes on about diseases ravaging Scandinavian countries, how black community already has high AIDS rates. . . . "So gay marriage is our issue. Tavis knows something about God . . ."

Sybil: Have you talked with your gay friends about this?

Caller: I don't have any gay friends!

*Sybil: You know, sir, you **do**. And that's why this is **not** your issue.*

(February 15, 2007) Former NBA player John Ameche has come out as gay and written a book.

Sybil: I wish you a lot of luck—it will be interesting to see what comes of this. And good luck with the book as well!

(October 14, 2008)

Tom: Our text message question of the day is, Do you believe gay people should be allowed to adopt?
*Sybil: I think **why not**? There are so many needy children!*
Sybil also defended her territory—her news announcement time—against crew members' efforts to hijack her reports for extensive joking:

(February 17, 2012) Sybil reports that interracial marriages are at an all-time high in the U.S.

J: That's great! Now you don't have to hear it! [implying that Sybil objects to his predilection for white women]
Sybil: HEAR WHAT???
Tom and J go on, lost in the bit, won't give up the mic.
*Sybil, openly disgusted: Go on wich your little **bits** of news!*

Sybil's radio voice, her tone—clear, intelligent, fact-filled, progressive, hectoring, often exasperated—is extraordinarily attractive to me, perhaps because I identify so profoundly with her political positions, and most particularly with her middle-aged, battle-hardened, anti-racist/feminist/social-democratic weariness. But I am only one of Sybil's millions of female and male fans, listeners who are grateful for the reliable information she purveys—recall the poignant working-class man's call so he could write down and follow up on "endometriosis" out of love for his suffering wife, and the Richmond, Virginia, clerical worker's appreciation of *the facts* that the *TJMS* furnished. And the *TJMS* audience often showed its appreciation for Sybil's trenchant defense of her politics, for her witty comebacks against "the boys" in the post-Myra J and Ms. Dupre years:

(August 29, 2013) Texter: Sybil you're a strong woman to work with those two nuts!

(May 22, 2014) Texter: Sybil, do you ever feel like an eighth-grade teacher to those two?

*(June 25, 2014) Texter: Sybil, I feel for you, workin with those two **fools**!*

*(March 1, 2017) Texter on Sybil's comments on Omorosa, Trump's "black friend" from The Apprentice: Sybil's **shade** is so **classy**. It's like church-mother shade. She just lays it down and quietly walks way.*
*Tom: I **love** it!*

*(February 16, 2018) Texter: Sybil for President! She's mean **and** sweet!*

Even the former President of the United States (probably coached by his staff) is a Sybil Wilkes fan.

> *(October 22, 2014) President Obama is on the phone. They ask him midterm elections voter suppression questions:*
> President Obama: *Well, listen, let me make a couple of points. First, Sybil, are those two guys behaving themselves?*
> Sybil: *No, sir.*
> President Obama: *Well, at least there's **one** adult on the show!*

And Sybil would stand her ground against Tom Joyner—despite his status as her boss—to lay out a more social-democratic, less beholden to the sponsors, vision of the world. They tangled on July 18, 2006, for example:

> *The crew discusses a new NAACP report on U.S. corporations. Target did not respond to NAACP queries. Tom Joyner comments that everyone could just shop at Wal-Mart. Sybil demurs, pointing out that Target has merchandise Wal-Mart doesn't carry. Tom Joyner notes sharply that Target also doesn't advertise on the TJMS.*
> Tom: *Always follow the money, Sybil!*
> Sybil: *(sardonic disgust) Yes, the **green trail**.*

And during a heated discussion about raising the minimum wage, on March 8, 2007, Sybil spoke strongly for it while Tom and J, as businessmen, complained that many employees weren't even worth the current minimum wage. After some back-and-forth, Sybil said wearily, "What's the answer?" "Stealin," was Tom's cynical response.

But later in the same broadcast, Tom brought the issue up again: "You cannot *live* on $5.15—and if you get three jobs, you got no life!" J contributed the immigrant angle: "And the only people who *will* (work three low-paid jobs) are the immigrants, and 'we' don't want them here!" They ended up conceding the debate to Sybil.

But even Sybil, like Homer, has been known to nod. Or to allow herself to cross the line from serious progressive into infotainment reporter. She did so when the late Maya Angelou visited the show, and Sybil asked her if she had ever dated younger men. Angelou, no stranger to queenly airs, got up on her high horse and read Sybil the riot act for her violation of propriety—"making Sybil come correct" as Professor D. Soyini Madison wrote me with great happiness—and Sybil repeatedly apologized. The crew never let Sybil forget her lapse, and J memorialized it in yet another brilliant murdered hit, which they replayed the day they announced Angelou's passing:

(May 30, 2014) Audio of former show:

Sybil: Dr. Angelou, off subject. We are talking today about older women and
*   younger men. Have you ever had that in your life?*

*Angelou: Well first of all, that's **not** the way to address anyone.*

Sybil: I'm sorry, I apologize.

Angelou: I mean not in public!

Sybil: I did not mean any disrespect.

*Angelou, hectoring: I **know** that, but this is the way you **learn**!*

Sybil: Yes, ma'am.

J swings in: Sybil, I have a message from Robin Thicke [he then sings new lyrics to
*   Thicke's "The Sweetest Love"*[40]

Ooh-oh, oh baby!

Why did Sybil ask Ms. Angelou if

She was down with dating younger men?

. . .

J then relishes Angelou's put-down—"She chewed out her butt so good!—and ends
*   with great falsetto satisfaction: "She got all up in Sybil's butt!"*

Tom Joyner and J Anthony Brown: Feminist Man Dance

But even if we magically eliminated all women crew and guests from the *TJMS*, the male crew members, from the earliest years on—despite their irredentist demands to be allowed their coarse, silly sex jokes and to make fun of everyone's appearance, political correctness notwithstanding—actually have consistently feminist and gay-positive records. One transcendently silly example of their overall tone was the sometime-in-the-2010s creation of the Friday-morning "Man Dance:" Tom Joyner would intone, in sermonic introduction, "This is the day that is given unto men to dance—with other men." Then a particularly lively funk number would play, overlaid with Tom's and J's shouts, grunts, and cries of joy as they mimicked (they were probably most often not even in the same production studio) dancing together. The entire ridiculous shtick was clearly designed, beyond simply being wonderful fun, to mock any potential homophobic audience response. It reminded me often, inescapably, of the 1970s and beyond term and practice of "political lesbianism:" We heterosexual feminists would deliberately allow ourselves to be identified as lesbian in public—as in the classroom—so as to share the social burden with our sisters and to proselytize for gay rights.

TJMS demonstrated the obvious progressive political intent of the Man Dance when President Obama announced his support for gay marriage on May 9, 2012.

On May 10, the entire show was engulfed with audience responses and crew and guest discussions. But comic Chris Paul, in his Morning Minute, had the last broadly humorous word:

> Chris Paul announces and endorses President Obama's support of gay marriage. "But I want to make it absolutely clear that I do **not** support Friday-morning man-dancing on the TJMS!"

Let's look at the male *TJMS* crew members' treatment of women's and girls' intelligence, women's rights/single mothers, violence against women, sexual rights, male responsibilities for children:

> (July 28, 2005) Tom says that Boy Scouts waited for President Bush three hours in the hot sun, and that many fell out [fainted]—even adults. "I hate to admit this, Sybil, but women are smarter. You would not find **Girl Scouts** waiting for President Bush in the hot sun. **No**, uh huh.
> Sybil: **Hol**-la!
> (April 23, 2009) Crew reports singer Jennifer Hudson is pregnant.
>
> Tom Joyner: Congratulations!
> Sybil: Here's the other side. A text just came in saying we shouldn't be celebrating having a baby out of wedlock.
> Tom: **Sit down!** We just got over Easter! These Christians!
> Sybil: Well, we're **all** Christians . . .
> Tom: Well, how about this . . . If you're perfect, stand up! [long radio silence] Yeah, I **thought** so. We shouldn't criticize others unless we're perfect ourselves. [Tom is of course alluding to Jesus's command, in New Testament John 8:7, "He who is without sin, cast the first stone."]
>
> (March 19, 2007) A divorced woman with a teenage son and daughter calls in. Her ex supplies the son with condoms, but tells the daughter that she can't have sex. Entire crew is incensed: "This is sexist!" Later, a nurse calls in, says parents must supply birth control to their teenage children, specifically condoms "because of STDs, and not ruin their lives otherwise."

And male or female, the *TJMS* crew is clear on a woman's rights to contraception:

> (July 1, 2014) Sybil reports on the Supreme Court's 'Hobby Lobby" ruling.[41] She explains that a deeply divided Court ruled that for-profit corporations do not have to provide a full range of contraception in their health plans. She says, "This has set off a whole storm of controversy about women's rights and their future."
> Tom asks why "religious people" can't just refrain from using contraception? Sybil explains the details . . .
> Tom: I don't get it!

Sybil: [presciently] This is something that's going to go on for a long time.
Later in the show, Chris Paul wraps it up with male feminist wit: He notes the irony
that companies like Hobby Lobby don't want to pay for contraception, but have
no objection to providing Viagra and Cialis, "because the Bible says 'Do not
spare the rod!'" [crew snickers]

Over the decades, the *TJMS* gave a large number of medical guests air time on
"Get Well Wednesdays." But in 2015, they hit the trifecta in choosing Dr. Drai, a
gay male feminist ob-gyn and media personality.[42] Extraordinarily good-humored
and profoundly campy, Dr. Drai simultaneously offered excellent advice and high
entertainment:

(May 29, 2015) Dr. Drai fulminates against the use of vaginal douches: "The
*vagina's a **self-cleaning oven**, honey! Don't put anything in there! [crew lost*
in hysterics]

(February 17, 2017) Crew discusses the widespread newer pattern of women
removing their pubic hair. Dr. Drai warns that it is a dangerous practice: "Oh
my God! Pubes have a purpose, ladies!" [shouts of laughter]

And the male crew also speak strongly about fathers' responsibilities for children:

*(February 18, 2008) A woman caller says her ex is stalking her: "I have had **hor-***
***rific** experiences!" He has confronted her in public places, yelling, "You should*
be home with the kids!"
*J, instantly: He aint with the kids **neither**!*

While Sybil always led the pack in protesting misogyny in the media, the male
crew would mix in with anger, and in the following case, both contempt and a
healthy dose of *Schadenfreude*:

(March 14, 2012) Tom announces that 140 companies have now cancelled their
advertising on Rush Limbaugh's show.
*J: Does he feel it **now**?*
Tom: And he's still abusin women! Still talkin noise!
*J: that's all he **can** do, is talk noise!*

And the iconic Chris Brown/Rhianna domestic battery case, in which she went
public with a shocking photo of her bruised and battered face, stung the crew, male
and female, to fury:

(February 11, 2009) Tom: Under no circumstances should a man raise his hand to
a woman! And a woman should leave an abusive relationship.

Sybil: . . . I always tell young people to walk away from the heat of battle.
Tom: The First Lady went down to the social services office yesterday and talked to
some young girls. Good job, Michelle!

Even Huggy Lowdown, known habitué of strip clubs, always wittily drew the
line on male sexual sanity. When Congressman Anthony Weiner was first caught
sexting, the crew was astounded[43]:

(June 7, 2011)
Tom: **Why** *do these dudes keep takin pictures of their manhood and mailin them*
to women?
Huggy: Tom, he was a respected Congressman, with a powerful position. Now he's
*just another freak-ass with a cellphone!—***Don't tweet ya meat!***
All, in unison, with great gusto: Don't tweet your meat!
(And this line, quite rightly, became a celebrated, often-repeated nostrum on
the show.)

Sometimes the *TJMS* audience had no need of the crew to set them straight on
women's status issues—they just wanted to share with the community of the air
women's ability to appreciate *TJMS* humor in even the most extreme circumstances.
On February 9, 2016, for example, a husband texted in that he was driving his wife
to the hospital to have their baby:

If yall don't stop, she's gonna laugh herself into deliverin in the car!

And sometimes the crew would simply use others' words to express their respect for women, especially single mothers. They did so on May 9, 2014, when
they replayed the NBA Most Valuable Player Kevin Durant's entire televised acceptance speech, a tearful paean to his own single mother—"We weren't supposed
to be here . . . you sacrificed for us . . . you didn't eat so we could . . . you're the *real*
MVP!"—with the sentimental Boyz 2 Men hit ballad, "A Song for Mama," playing
in the background.[44]

On LBGTQ rights, here are Tom, J and Melvin, back in the Dark Ages of 2004,
dealing with a caller on Melvin's Love Line:

(February 25)
Woman caller: I'm anonymous from Milwaukee.
Guys: Hi Anonymous!
Caller: And I got a long-term problem. My girlfriend goes off and won't tell me
where she's goin.
Tom: Same sex, same problem! We always say that, and it never changes!
Melvin: That's it!
J: And people say they don't like gays, but it's all the same.

And here are Tom and J, responding to a Roland Martin interview with a be-nighted black pastor in DC who opposed legalizing gay marriage in the District. The pastor's argument was that there was no civil rights parallel, because while black people's status is obvious, you can't "look at someone" and know they are gay.

(April 27, 2009)
J: Snickers. "Huh! You can't look at someone and tell they're gay!"
*Tom: Except at the Mall in Atlanta! Minister, have you looked at your **choir**?*
Tom and J, snickering more: Oh, Rev, Rev!
Tom: Why can't you just leave gay people alone?
J: Just like we always say . . .
Together: Same sex, same problems!

When the film *Brokeback Mountain* was first released in theaters, J was ready with his pro-gay statement:

(January 31, 2006) It's an excellent movie, a straight-up love story. . . . It's become the test for women to see how secure you are in your manhood!

But the crew always reserved their right to poke fun at every population. Here they play on a major Southern city's reputation as the capital of black gaydom:

(August 18, 2005)
Tom: Ms. Dupre, Your Psychic Friend, knows there's two things they can't keep on the shelves in Atlanta . . .
Ms. Dupre: "Donna Summers CDs and cognac!"

And also in 2005, the crew used a nonblack celebrity announcing he was gay to extoll the presumed greater toughness of black LBGTQ Americans:

(November 7) Sybil reports that George Takei [Star Trek] just announced he is gay.
*Myra J: He **been** gay. He aint **just** gay.*
*Tom: Sheryl Swoopes just called. She said, Aw, come **on**, man! That the best you **got**?*[45]

When comedian Wanda Sykes announced that she was a lesbian and had gotten married, Tom J were agog, but completely game. Comic Sheryl Underwood, visiting the show that day, gave a wild, deliberately working-class homegirl, tour de force performance:

*(November 14, 2008) Sybil! Wanda Sykes **gay**!? Hush yo mouth, girl! . . . She still my friend, though . . . I thought she be rockin a natchul cause she a certain age . . . do yo thing, snack on, girl!*

Tom then asked Sybil if he should get them a George Forman grill as a wedding present (yes), "Not a pair of curling irons?"

Sybil, instantly: No, cause she's rockin that fro!

And here is a very relaxed Tom Joyner, having announced Home Depot's "Girls' Night Out" promotion, responding happily to a campy cross-dressing texter:

(October 21, 2011)
Texter: Tom, are we invited too? You know, the boys in heels?
Tom: Yeah, come on by!

With reference to transgender issues, the *TJMS* again very early on simply normalized the transgender community, made them family. Back in 2012, guest comic Dominique, deliberately using "low-status" black speech and the then-current joking term for vagina, laid it out:

(April 10, 2012) Crew discusses news that the Miss Universe pageant will now
*   accept transgender contestants.*
Dominique: If she have a va-jay-jay, she a woman!

Transgender actor and activist Laverne Cox was a much-hyped "friend of the show" since the hit Netflix series *Orange Is the New Black* debuted in 2013. She appeared on the *TJMS* August 17, 2015, to publicize her role as "Deathy" in the just-released Lily Tomlin film *Grandma*:

Tom: I first met Laverne Cox at the BET awards, and then I found out she's my
*   homie, from Mobile, Alabama!*
Crew asks Cox about her pre-Orange life—she worked in a drag-queen restaurant,
*   "although I'm not a drag queen, I'm a transwoman!"—I took acting classes, and*
*   took every opportunity to pursue my career.*
Sybil: Coming from Mobile, Alabama, it could not have been easy . . . ?
Laverne Cox: Explains that it was difficult, she was "very feminine" and was
*   bullied, but she had a very supportive church environment.*
*   . . .*
Sybil: I know you've done a lot of work in the transgender community. . . . [she
*   wants to know if there will be an autobiographical film] . . . I have to say I have*
*   a lot more interest in you than in the most famous transgender person we have*
*   in the news [obviously Caitlin Jenner].*
Cox says it's far too early to imagine such a film, acknowledges her luck and suc-
*   cess, but pivots to the political: "We are in a state of emergency. Last week four*
*   transwomen of color were murdered. . . . This year sixteen transwomen have*

been murdered . . . *I've been very inspired by Black Lives Matter. These women matter! We need to* **say their names.**"
Crew offer supportive murmurs. Sybil again thanks Cox "for all your work."

On September 9, 2016, Sybil solemnly announced the death, at age fifty-nine, of The Lady Chablis, a transwoman from Savannah, Georgia, and well-known performer from *Midnight in the Garden of Good and Evil*.

Crew, sincerely: Awwwwwww!

J Anthony Brown, despite his clownish behavior, bitter divorcé status, and [white] womanizing reputation, repeatedly took up the cudgels for single mothers, and for women's and gay rights in general. And he went out of his way to protest violence against women. On May 8, 2015, to mark Mothers' Day, J murdered neosoul singer Calvin Richardson's "Hearsay," which has the refrain, "It's not about me, it's about you." He honored single mothers' burdens, strong discipline, pride, and hopes and fears for their children's futures. "You talk to kids to wipe their booties," J sang, "Let's keep it real!" He praised single mothers for breaking their necks paying bills, playing both "mom and daddy," and despite it all, enjoying their lives: "You wear high shoes!" The song wraps up with every mother's desire: "Keep hopin that yo kids gon be straight!"[46]
And here's J on fathers' innate responsibilities:

> *(January 4, 2006) Woman caller says she has two baby daddies. Her youngest is three months old, "and my baby daddy acts funny with her . . . he said he don't want it."*
> J: *"Well, he don't have to want it to take care of it!"*

J's commentaries on the general pains and indignities of middle age could be remarkably insightful, and compassionate about women's—particularly working-class women's—circumstances. Note, in this wildly funny, pissy sendup Pharrell's light-hearted, youth-oriented viral 2013 pop ditty, "Happy," how J moves nimbly across gender/sexual identities[47]:

> *(February 21, 2014)*
> *I eat like crazy, so I'm gainin weight [gender neutral]*
> *New Year is here, still I'm outta shape [ditto]*
> . . .
> *Laugh along if you live with a man who's growin boobs [female-oriented unless gay male speaker]*
> . . .
> *You left your man, now you want 'em back [likely female]*

His new girl is white, she got a lotta back [booty] [definitely female]
. . .

While everyone on the *TJMS* becomes incensed over violence against women and children cases, J's artistically composed reactions were particularly rhetorically effective. As the National Football League scandals heated up in the fall of 2014, for example, with the *TMZ* release of the videotape of then-Baltimore Ravens running back Ray Rice beating his fiancée unconscious in an elevator, J repurposed the famous old jazz/pop anthem about the enticements of life on the street into an indictment of male violence against women and a sexist, greedy, exploitative sports organization:

> *(Sept 19, 2014) "League Life" [to the instrumental track of "Street Life," 1979 hit*
> *by Randy Crawford and The Crusaders]*[48]
> *Recitative:*[49] *Rest in peace Joe Sample [Crusaders founder, keyboardist, died the*
> *previous week], We gon miss ya, Not tryin ta diss ya!*
> *NFL league life, kids leave college and turn pro*
> *League life, they get rich and go lo-co*
> *League life, the NFL don't do a thang*
> *League life, until the sponsors pull away*

J then moves to solutions—"Let the players smoke some weed . . . . It just might calm them down." He then gives stern prescriptions: "Hitting women, it's a crime . . . beat opponents, not your wife."

J then finishes the tour de force sendup with a finger-wagging kindergarten-teacher recitative:

> *Now remembuh, if they aint in uniform, and they aint on the field, and they don't*
> *have a helmet on*
> **Don't hit no-body!**
> *Play ball. Now play nice!*

Indeed, J sometimes was the most hard-line crew member on violence against women issues. For example, the *TJMS* followed the long unfolding of the Bill Cosby drugging and rape allegations, reporting as each new woman accuser came forward, as each Cosby defender recanted, as each former sponsor dropped his name, and then as Cosby's very self-damning some-years-old sworn deposition was leaked to the press. Cosby then hired a new, highly competent black woman attorney, Monique Pressley, and she appeared on the *TJMS* on July 27, 2015.

The crew was clearly impressed with her forceful clarity. Sybil labeled her a "tough sistah," but J shot right back: "She's just a good lawyer representin a *rapist*!"

Finally, back in 2005, many years before we as a nation shifted to majority support for gay rights, J, with an assist from Sybil, asserted celebrity Ellen De Generes's butch sexual prowess so fondly—as if she were a much-admired male buddy—that I was left dumbfounded and madly scribbling:

> *(May 30, 2005) Crew is discussing gay celebrities, then veers off onto Ellen giving her new girlfriend an emerald ring.*
> *J: Ellen can serve it up! No question about that. Don't let the funny dancin fool you . . .*
> *Sybil: Ellen's got it down!*
> *J: No question who's wearin the boots there!*

In 2012, J one-upped himself in characterizing Ellen's sexual prowess (echoing the old sexual bromide, Once you go black, you can't go back) in a conversation again begun by an evangelical Christian texting in:

> *(April 12)*
> *Texter: You're not born gay! God does not make mistakes!*
> *J: (disgusted) Oh, there we go with the Christians!*
> *Tom: What about Anne Heche? She was with Ellen and then she went straight . . .*
> *J: Well, there's your answer right there! That's Ellen! After her, you got **nowhere to go** but a man!*
> *All laugh.*

In 2009, three years before President Obama's famous "evolution" on gay rights, J, with help from Sybil and Tom, engaged a stridently conservative evangelical Christian caller with logic, a profound sense of universal human rights, and high humor:

> *(April 21) Woman caller repeats common televangelists' lines—"God created Eve from Adam's rib. It was Adam and Eve, not Adam and Steve!"*
> *Sybil: Where is Steve in the Bible? Where does the Steve part come from?*
> *Caller: Well, he's not in the Bible, but Adam is!*
> *J: Well, Steve's **here**, what are you gonna do with him?*
> *Caller: He needs to get a woman.*
> *J: He doesn't want a woman!*
> *Tom: What scripture are you reading from?*
> *Caller: You need to read the Bible.*
> *J: That's an old Christian trick. They don't know the Bible, so they throw it back on you.*
> *Caller: It's Leviticus 13: A man should not lie with another man.*

J: *Yall gonna have to figure out what to do with Steve, cause Steve's here. Whatta*
we gonna do with Steve?
Further back-and-forth with caller: J manages to make her laugh repeatedly, even
though she claims that Steve's "spirit comes from the Devil."

J further distinguished himself in 2012 in a wonderful progressive gender/sexuality two-fer. Jacque Reid was interviewing a guest, a married lesbian activist. Tom said, "We always say, same sex, same problems (guest laughs) but you're sayin, same sex, different problems?" She started to answer, but J interjected, "Because ladies make less money than men." Interviewee happily agreed. A little later in the conversation, he became more explicit: "They make less even when they're doing the same job."

Sybil: J, I am so proud of you!

The *TJMS* crew were as mesmerized in 2015 by the Bruce/Caitlin Jenner story as were other media outlets. J responded early on with approval and compassion:

(February 5, 2015) More power to him! He must've been suffering!

That did not stop J, however, from later murdering Percy Sledge's iconic 1966 soul hit, "When a Man Loves a Woman,"[50] to comment acerbically, offensively, and hilariously on the media circus surrounding Caitlin Jenner, her age, and her genital status. "When a man becomes a woman," J sang on June 5, 2015, "we can't talk of nuthin else." He characterized Jenner as "way beyond his damn prime," and thus "a cougar, is what she will be." He finished with a flourish, imagining that "he's gotta be in pain" wearing a thong, since Jenner "still has his manly meat!"

The *TJMS* audience in general was wildly appreciative of J's comic gifts and sharp political wit. But one morning a fond and highly skilled caller simply stopped the show.

(June 18, 2009) Clearly Southern working-class woman calls in, says "I have a
Father's Day song for J." She proceeds to sing a beautiful, slow, melismatic alto
gospel, with line-ends "Yes He did, Yes He did." Sybil interjects proper black-
church vocalizations in correct time. When the woman finishes, crew praises
her lavishly, asks for the tape. For the next few minutes, Tom, J and Sybil keep
breaking delightedly into pieces of the song.

Respectability Politics and the *TJMS*

For some decades now, African American scholars and political commentators have offered critiques of "the politics of respectability." The term was historian Evelyn

Brooks Higginbotham's 1993 coinage to describe the "lifting as we climb" gentility and charitable efforts of the *fin-de-siècle* black women's church movement. Higginbotham stressed the inherent political contradictions of this bourgeois activism:

> On the one hand the politics of respectability rallied poor working-class blacks to the cause of racial self-help, by inspiring them to save, sacrifice, and pool their scant resources for the support of black-owned institutions. Whether through white-imposed segregation or black-preferred separatism, the black community's support of its middle class surely accounted for the development and growth of black-owned institutions, including those of the Baptist church. On the other hand, the effort to forge a community that would command whites' respect revealed class tensions among blacks themselves. The zealous efforts of black women's church organizations to transform certain behavioral patterns of their people disavowed and opposed the culture of the "folk"—the expressive culture of many poor, uneducated and "unassimilated" black men and women dispersed throughout the rural South or newly huddled in urban centers.[51]

Higginbotham was especially concerned with gender, with the ways in which these African American women "asserted agency in the construction and representation of themselves as new subjectivities . . . contested racist discourses and rejected white America's depiction of black women as immoral, childlike, and unworthy of respect or protection.[52] She noted that the Baptist women condemned "immorality" among both whites and blacks, among both "high society" and the poor.[53] And she pointed out that their notions of proper behavior, of the necessity of disciplining the poor away from "the street" and dance halls, were shared by white Progressive Era reformers like Jane Addams.[54] But Higginbotham also noted that "[r]espectability's emphasis on individual behavior served inevitably to blame blacks for their victimization and, worse yet, to place an inordinate amount of blame on black women."[55]

In the years since Higginbotham's pioneering work, considerations of "respectability politics" have expanded to include a range of contemporary critical stances vis-à-vis language and physical comportment, gender relations, sexuality, and family and household forms. And it is now applied to many populations beyond black Americans.[56]

Clearly, there are many overlaps between family values ideology and respectability politics: false nostalgias for a past that never was, the browbeating stance that there is a narrow range of proper behaviors, the claim that Others must reform themselves to fit within that range. And they both purvey the notion that mass adherence to "proper" behaviors would bring about beneficial social change—whether to reclaim a "Godly Republic" or to magically bring about mass social mobility. Or both.

We can now see that for decades—in fact the entirety of the period encompassing this new scholarship and commentary—without, to my knowledge, ever using the term, the *TJMS* proudly, insistently, and complexly dissented from respectability politics with regard to its family values dimension.[57] It normalized single mother-hood and celebrated the struggles and triumphs of women raising children without male partners. "Hats off to single mothers!" as J Anthony Brown yelled out one morning. It stood up for women's rights, broadly. It protested violence, and sexual violence, against women and children. It simply normalized gay expression—"It's all the same"—decades before most of the rest of the country caught up. And yet again, journalists and scholars, of all races, have nearly entirely neglected the very influential politics of this majority black counterpublic. But the *TJMS*'s interven-tion into black respectability politics actually engaged with far more than gender and sexuality.

4

Partyin with a Purpose

TJMS *Race, Class, and Age Politics and Aesthetics*

Also unless it's neo-soul, rare groove, or old school-you won't hear it
here. Want radio hip-hop? Go to that white kids' club in the suburbs . . .
—Urban Dictionary, "Grown&Sexy"[1]

A *TJMS* jingle in 2015 addressed their sleep-deprived, overworked adult audience: "When you wake up in the morning but your butt don't seem to move" . . . "You
need sumpin sumpin pumpin that'll get you good to go." And of course the solution
was "as simple as turnin on your radio! Come on yall, it's the *Tom Joyner Morning
Show!*" Parliament Funkadelic intoned in 1975, in their "P. Funk wants to Get
Funked Up:" "Do not attempt to adjust your radio . . . we have taken control . . . we
will return it to you as soon as you are grooving."[2] That is exactly what the *TJMS* did
for decades—it "took control" of the black radio waves to get its audience grooving,
entertained, informed, and active. Or, as they began to announce in 2015: "*TJMS*—
Entertain. Empower. Inform." Thus the show's aesthetics and its politics were profoundly intermingled. Its dissent from the politics of respectability, we have seen,
involved the assertion of all black women's dignity, worth, and rights, and the open
promotion of LBGTQ rights—even back in the Dark Ages of the Don't Ask/Don't
Tell 1990s. But respectability politics is also fundamentally about *class, race,* and
apprehensions of economic mobility.

Respectably Black

Political scientist and African American Studies scholar Fredrick Harris, in the
journal *Dissent,* summed up the historical evolution of the politics of respectability
and its capitulation to rightist interpretations of ongoing black poverty in the post-
Jim Crow era:

> What started as a philosophy promulgated by black elites to "uplift the race"
> by correcting the "bad" traits of the black poor has now evolved into one of

the hallmarks of black politics in the age of Obama, a governing philosophy that centers on managing the behavior of black people left behind in a society touted as being full of opportunity. In an era marked by rising inequality and declining economic mobility for most Americans—but particularly for black Americans—the twenty-first century version of the politics of respectability works to accommodate neoliberalism. The virtues of self-care and self-correction are framed as strategies to lift the black poor out of their condition by preparing them for the market economy.[3]

Thus respectability politics shares a "blame the victim" pedigree with 1990s underclass ideology and its 1950s–60s forbear, the culture of poverty.[4] And indeed, as the late Americanist historian Michael Katz documented in *In the Shadow of the Poorhouse*, elite Americans have been blaming the impoverished for their own condition since the colonial era. Katz notes three obfuscations that allow and encourage this misapprehension: the denial that normal capitalist economic functioning invariably produces impoverished groups despite individuals' best efforts; the artificial distinction between "deserving" and "undeserving" poor, with only the former worthy of charitable efforts; and the failure to admit inherent governmental involvement—and thus its causal role—in all aspects of economic life.[5]

Many scholars from a variety of disciplines, and a range of political movements, have opposed this profoundly self-serving denial of the causes of poverty, and of economic inequality more generally, across American history. Let's focus here in particular on contemporary black respectability politics and its opponents.

There has been no dearth of social actors—from black ministers to the Urban League to a variety of politicians and commentators—espousing respectability politics in the century-plus since Higginbotham's *fin-de-siècle* black Baptist women were active. Perhaps the most publicized recent expressions, though, have been those of comedian and cultural icon Bill Cosby—many years prior to his exposure as an alleged, now convicted, serial rapist. Cosby's notorious 2004 "pound cake" speech, an address at a gala for the NAACP Legal Fund and Howard University, cemented his reputation as the elite scold of poor black Americans for "not holding up their end of the deal." Specifically, Cosby excoriated black criminality, illiteracy, female-headed households, and hyper-consumerism. He threw in disgust with "black" given names for good measure: "Names like Shaniqua, Taliqua, and Muhammed and all that crap." And he poured scorn on black Americans shot by the police, and rationalized police violence against poor people of color—words that are now far more chilling in the wake of recent highly publicized deaths, including those of Trayvon Martin, Michael Brown, Walter Scott, Samuel Dubose, Eric Garner, Freddie Gray, Laquan McDonald, Tamir Rice, Terence Crutcher, Jordan Edwards, and so many others. Cosby characterized these young African Americans as people who "get shot in the back of the head over a piece of pound cake! And then we all run out and we're outraged, 'Ah, the cops shouldn'ta shot him!' What the hell was he doing with the pound cake in his hand?"[6]

Black feminists have weighed in on respectability politics as well, focusing on the long American histories of white degradation of black womanhood and disrespect of black women's bodies—as E. Frances White put it, riposting on Sigmund Freud's coinage, "the dark continent of our bodies."[7] Many African American feminist historians have documented black women's historical "culture of dissemblance," as Darlene Clark Hine coined it, in response to omnipresent white (and black) male danger.[8] Historian of science Evelynn Hammonds, in a wide-ranging essay on black female sexuality, put her finger on the key question: "How can black feminists dislodge the negative stereotyping of their sexuality and its attendant denials of citizenship and protection?"[9]

One key popular-cultural phenomenon—the extraordinary success and thus public sphere dominance of Tyler Perry's many stage, screen, and television vehicles—has captured significant black feminist attention for its capitulation to respectability politics.[10] Many commentators have noted these dramas' stereotyping of black American women as either helpless and victimized, or as man-eating viragos, both in need of religious uplift and the "right" black man—or as the wonderfully comic, over-the-top persona of Madea, played by the cross-dressing Tyler Perry himself.

African Americanist literary critic Robert J. Patterson notes the numbers of ways in which Perry's productions define black American women as a priori troubled and in need of masculine aid: "Perry presents marriage as requisite for black women's happiness and consequently, no man will want to marry them when they are angry, overbearing, emasculating, emotionally unstable, or otherwise unfit for patriarchal coupling."[11]

In an insightful essay, black feminist professor Brittney Cooper acknowledges the profound attractiveness of Tyler Perry's productions: their verbal wit, use of down-home Southern cultural material, and familiar Christian messages: "The women in Perry's films reminded me of women I knew. And, as an evangelical Christian and regular church attendee, I found the sermons and faith themes in his movies poignant and instructive."[12]

But Cooper also describes her evolution toward a stance highly critical of Perry's productions: "Perry's exploitation amounts to what I refer to as a kind of *narrative colonization*. Narrative colonization occurs when black men use cultural, political, or theological mandates that sanction male supremacy to reframe black women's stories and black women's lives in terms of dominant male-centered narratives that that are sympathetic to patriarchy."[13] Cooper ends in adjuring black women to "create dynamic, dialogically based interpretive communities that make room for black women as cultural producers, critics, and audience."[14]

One particularly trenchant critique of black respectability politics is political scientist Adolph Reed's 1996 essay, "Romancing Jim Crow."[15] Reed was specifically interested in contemporary black visions of a less-troubled segregated past. In arguing that "current nostalgia for the organic community black Americans supposedly lost with the success of the civil rights movement is . . . frighteningly shortsighted and dangerous," Reed pointed to the plethora of cultural commentary—journalism, books, films, essays, "the talk show circuit"—to that effect. He roundly declared that "[t]his sort of nostalgic theory is dangerous on two counts: it falsifies the black past; and it serves reactionary and frankly racist interests in the present."[16]

Reed pointed out that, just as most people who imagine they had past lives are always sure they were aristocrats, not peasants, in those lives, so the black boomer vision of the idyllic segregated past is always from the perspective of the black elite:

> Class ideology, in fact, permeates and drives the current nostalgia . . . Nostalgia for the Jim Crow black world . . . keys its imagery of the Fall to the putative loss of petit bourgeois authority in the Bantustan—for example in William Julius Wilson's prattle about the middle class as a force for moral order and propriety among the poor. . . . Memoirists who pine for the lost community of Jim Crow tend to have middle-class parents, who typically strove to insulate their offspring from the regime's demeaning and dangerous realities, especially from contact with whites.[17]

But neither Cosby-like hectoring about modes of dress and behavior nor Perry-esque visions of female souls lost to drink, drugs, and promiscuity finding redemption through church, family, and appropriate heterosexual male guidance, nor elite boomer nostalgia for the Jim Crow past, are actually hegemonic among the bulk of contemporary black Americans. On the contrary. Fredrick Harris, for example, introduces his *Dissent* piece with a contemporary instance of black respectability politics "accommodating neoliberalism": In 2013, a black charter school in Tulsa, Oklahoma sent a little girl home because her hair was in an "unusual hairstyle"—dreadlocks. Harris is rightly outraged about this and the other rules "devised by black elites, with the backing of the state and the support of ordinary blacks who believe in their efficacy. . . ."[18] But I happened to be listening when the *TJMS* covered this story, on September 10, 2013, and their take on it was profoundly different. "Ordinary blacks"—at least on this show and among their millions of listeners—do *not* support these "rules devised by elites."

Early in the show that day, the *TJMS* crew didn't realize the school was black-run, so their outraged response was that the administration was racist. When they got the details straight later in the morning, Tom Joyner announced them, and then said angrily and incredulously: "Snooty! Snooty in *Tulsa*?! And I've *been* to Tulsa." The rest of the crew piled on about black Oklahomans putting on airs and hurting little children.

Both the *TJMS* response to this story, and Harris's lack of familiarity with that response, heard by millions of black and other Americans, illustrate yet again the show's "invisible" counterpublic status. But more importantly, they also illustrate the *TJMS*'s larger dissent from the politics of respectability, a dissent that interestingly melds working-class and racial pride, "movin on up" mobility hopes, a particular "old-school" black aesthetic, and a form of working-class black baby boomer nostalgia worlds removed from the bourgeois form that critic Reed excoriates.

First, the *TJMS* moved far beyond Myra J's focus on financially strapped "single moms." The crew as a whole assumed that their entire audience, women and men, is largely black working-class, and they invoked and celebrated that status. Tom Joyner and J Anthony Brown even "took on" working-classness—laid claim to it through their own childhood and adolescent experiences, although they are both now well off. As we have seen, they often teased Sybil Wilkes—whose grandfather was a doctor, whose parents were better off than theirs, and who attended a private non-HBCU university—in this vein.

One rich example of this class teasing occurred on March 3, 2008, when then-Senator Barack Obama appeared on the show after his very successful Super Tuesday electoral results. In a relaxed mood, Obama played along with Tom and J's threat to take Sybil's "black card" because she had never had her phone cut off. Obama smoothly and wittily negotiated his own complex class status for the radio audience: "I have never actually had my phone cut off, but I *have* gotten that red notice!"

Sybil's middle-class background—and thus failure to understand the economic strains felt by working-class people—came up again in a discussion of car foreclosures:

(July 23, 2014)
Tom: Ok. This is the time of the month when we see the tow trucks out, repossessin cars.
J: It's so sad, man . . . [He asks Sybil if she ever had her car towed.]
Sybil: Well, almost . . .
J: Whaddya mean, almost?
Sybil: Well, they said I was parking in a no-parking zone . . .
J: No! No! For non-payment!
Sybil: Oh! No, never. She asks [sincerely] if they repossess cars after one missed payment?
J: Well, a couple of months . . .

Sybil has difficulty understanding how people fail to make car payments. J narrates the long-ago tragic loss of his "brown on black" Pinto: "It hurts! It's the worst feeling in the world. And sittin on the bus, rollin past the finance company with my face pressed up against the window, lookin at my car parked there."
Tom: [mixed deep sympathy and milking the joke] Oh, it's so sad!
J: [ditto] So sad!

But more important here is the show's daily normalizing of and identification with working-class status. Imagine a television network news anchor reporting (if they would even bother) a bus strike. (Subway strikes are different, because so many urban professionals around the country use the Metro, the MTA, the T, the El, BART, etc.) Management and labor might be quoted. But the *TJMS* reported the Milwaukee bus strike on July 1, 2015, *from the perspective of regular bus passengers.* They discussed the difficulty of getting rides to and from work during a strike, and waxed poetically witty on the sad spectacle of "bus people" trying to catch rides with their car-owning friends:

> Tom: *People with cars treat bus people bad.*
> J: *(overlapping) Yeah, people with cars treat bus people **bad**!*
> Tom: *They make you go everywhere they wanta go before they take you where you need to go!*
> J: *That's car people, man. **Low down**.*

"Car people" are obviously hardly uniformly middle class. This is by and large a working-class majority, car-necessary, rapid-transit-poor country, after all. And one of Tom Joyner's long-running grievances/obsessions is the ups and downs of the price of gas—what price spikes mean for his listeners and their ability to get around. What the *TJMS* crew seem to be doing here instead, specifically, is taking a stand against people setting themselves above others, against making micro-class distinctions in daily life:

> *(October 10, 2005) Express Yourself [older call-in feature]: Who is the person who thinks they're the boss of you but they're not?*

Notice, in rapid-fire back-and-forth with the crew here, how the female crew members automatically know what (largely female) healthcare job acronyms mean. Also note Sybil's witty and somewhat cruelly expressed point about the politics of naming:

> Myesha: *Verna. We both are LPNs.*
> Tom: *What is a . . .*
> Sybil and Myra J duet: *She's a licensed practical nurse!*
> Myesha: *She just sit there when people come in and I have to do it all.*

> Unica: *Miss Viola, we work in the school cafeteria. She's about 46, I'm 31.*
> Sybil: *Don't you think it's the fact that you call her **Miss Viola**?*

> *(March 21, 2006) Express Yourself: "Who's the uppity, snooty family member?"*
> Caller: *She's workin with too many white folks, and now everything's "ghetto."*
> Caller, Angelique: *Complains about her sister changing her name from Thedra to Renee, and won't eat certain [implied: soul] foods anymore.*
> Caller: *My cousin Debra who turned into DebORah.*
> Caller: *My cousin's wife—she's a Mary Kay rep. She wants to lighten the whole family up—we're dark-skinned.*

While part of the critique here involves reproof of those who criticize black-ness or "act white," this stance is worlds removed from some scholars' claim that poor African American children often stigmatize successful peers as acting white.[19] The *TJMS* crew, in fact, relentlessly push educational and occupational mobility. No, the desire here is to maintain identification with those who are struggling, to encourage them to come forward, and to help them, to constitute, genuinely, a community of the air—often bringing tears to the eyes of this sen-timental listener:

(October 5, 2005) It's the Christmas Wish—in earlier years, the TJMS gave "Christmas gifts" to the needy once a week, all year round. The request letter is from Taquita, a nursing student in Flint, Michigan whose home furnace just died. Tom announces that they will replace her furnace.
Tom: I'm comin, Taquita! We got you!
Sybil: And some heating oil!

(November 2, 2005) Woman caller: I'm in Columbia, South Carolina, and I want to know where I can find enough money to pay for my son to finish at Hampton [an HBCU in Virginia].
Tom explains to her how to apply to the Tom Joyner Foundation, which is specifi-cally set up to aid students going to HBCUs.

(March 31, 2009) Cash call [guess the numbers and win $1000]
Florence calls in, screams the numbers.
Tom: You just won ONE THOUSAND DOLLARS!
Florence: Still screaming: You don't know! I NEED this! I'm about to be evicted! Oh Lord! Thank you, Jesus!

(May 14, 2014) Thursday Morning Mom letter from a ten-year-old girl in Orlando, Florida: "My mama has been battling diabetes, and in March she had to be in the hospital for a week and lost her job. She's been trying to find a new job, but so far no luck. She is two courses shy of her AA [junior college] degree but needs a laptop to complete her work. (Girl says that her mother doesn't like her daughter to "see her like that"—beaten down) On top of all that, I'm being bullied in school. (J and Sybil respond angrily, in disbelief. Threaten to go find that boy and "whup his ass.")

Not only did the *TJMS* aid this woman and her daughter financially, but audi-ence texters were deeply moved and quite helpful: Several wrote in offering extra money—Tom told them where to send it, that 100% of it would go to the mother and daughter. One offered to help Sybil and J whup the bully's ass. Finally, a woman wrote in: "I'm in Orlando and I'm an HR recruiter. Can you connect me with this Thursday Morning Mom so I can help her get a job."

Later in the show, Tom announced:

Text Tom Club: The texters are steppin up to help our Thursday Morning Mom.
I love you! I love you!

Another example of the crew framing a question that assumes members of the audience struggle with straitened circumstances:

(October 5, 2005) The question of the day is, What have you sold or given away
and wish you hadn't?
Lavelle: I sold my DVD/CD duplicator.
All: Why?
Lavelle: I don't know, I thought I needed the money.
Sybil: Don't you know that could make more money with it?
Lavelle: [sighing] I know, I know.
J: So we can call you a fool?
Sybil: Let's duplicate that!

And even Sybil has sufficient familiarity with working-class life to participate compassionately:

(March 15, 2013)
Texter: Tom, this new app is the bomb! I'm at the laundrymat, and now I can listen
to you instead of the old crazy man talkin loud!
Sybil laughs, and adds: In those hard plastic chairs!

Sicko and Socialized Medicine

Identifying with working-class and poor black Americans also implies thinking through their difficult life circumstances and debating how to improve them. And a key arena always needing improvement in American life is healthcare. Long before President Obama's first term, and the difficult and heavily contested passage of the ACA (Obamacare, or the Affordable Care Act), the *TJMS* was on the case on the issue, taking the most radical tack:

(March 21, 2006) Tom comments on a recently released statistic: Black women die
of breast cancer at a rate 20% higher than white women.... He responds: "We
*need health care in this country—you **hear** that, Bush?!"*
(July 11, 2007) The following year Michael Moore was a guest—his film Sicko
had just been released. First, they play a clip of Moore yelling at Wolf Blitzer on
CNN about the scandal of the American medical system.

Tom: *And anything that affects Americans . . . disproportionately affects black Americans. . . . Break it down, Michael! . . . in simple terms like you were talking to your grandmother . . .*

Moore: *Here's the truth. We have a health care system based on profit . . . no other country does this. Everywhere else, if a doctor wants to take care of you, he just does it!*

Sybil interjects with details from the film, guiding the discussion . . . *"I also think that we should not put another vote in a ballot box until every member of Congress has seen this film—especially a certain woman!"* [then-Senator Hillary Clinton, running for President]

Moore: *Yes! Too many Democrats want to play this game with private insurance . . .*

(February 27, 2008) A woman caller explains that her son has very crooked teeth and is ashamed of his appearance, but she can't afford to pay for braces for him. Tom fulminates anathemas against our medical system. "We need universal healthcare!"

Sybil: *I'm just playing devil's advocate, but what would Tom say when people say universal healthcare would be socialized medicine?*

Tom: *Then let it **be** socialized medicine, because what we've got now is no good!*

African Americans are also heavily represented in the health professions—particularly nursing. And through *TJMS* I discovered yet another aspect of American white racism of which I had been unaware:

(February 19, 2013) Jacque Reid interviews a black nurse from Michigan and her attorney: A white father covered in swastika tattoos demanded that no black nurse touch his baby in the NICU. The hospital, shamefully, acceded to his racist demand. The TJMS is then hit by an avalanche of texts from black nurses from all over the country, saying this is nothing new. They had all had experiences of white hospital and nursing home patients refusing care from black health professionals.

(These narratives reminded me inescapably of my bedside experience of my father's August 1984 death at O'Connor Hospital in San Jose, California. As he took his last stuttering breaths, I melted down. A Jamaican nurse came into the room, and, with profound compassion, nodded meaningfully to me, then leaned over, caressed my father's face and closed his eyes. In my agony, I couldn't then thank her, but I was deeply grateful.)

Black Work, Black Pride

Callers and texters, as we have seen, regularly announce their job titles. *We're administrative assistants, thank you very much!* And we can survey the working-class/

middle-class range of the *TJMS* audience over the years through those titles. We also can see, in the way that the crew interacts with their audience, how they work together to normalize working-classness, and to bring a particularly black-identified aesthetic *joie de vivre* into often-denigrated, stressful workplaces and their workers:

> *(November 4, 2005) Woman cash call winner: "I work for Kansas City Power and Light. I've been there twenty-six years. I listen every day!*
>
> *(November 7, 2005) Tammy wins the cash call. She says she's in Radiology, in Billing, and she gives Tom the names of three friends to call next. We can hear Allison's phone ringing through Tammy's because they're all in the same office. Allison gets the numbers right too, and wins $1000. That's $2000 going out at once.*
> Sybil: **Zapped** by the radiology department!
>
> *(May 15, 2006) Anthony wins the cash call. They ask him what he does. "I'm a trash man."*
>
> *(April 18, 2006) Michelle wins the cash call. "I'm workin for Coca-Cola. I'm a forklift operator."*
>
> *(March 27, 2006) Syreta wins the cash call. What does she do? "I'm a nurse."*
> Myra J: Girl, throw a bedpan in the air!
> Sybil, instantly: Like you just don't care![20]

Like you just don't care.

And listeners will use their work expertise, often hilariously, to school the crew. On April 8, 2009, for example, J and Tom were being typical cranky middle-aged males, bemoaning the horrific process of cleaning out one's digestive tract in preparation for a colonoscopy, arguing that it wasn't necessary:

Tom: It's a dirty job, doc, but you signed up for it!
J: He should see it the way it **always** is!

Sybil expostulated against them, unsuccessfully. Then a gastrointestinal nurse texted in her expertise with a down-home country twist, leaving me, and I'm sure millions of other listeners, laughing helplessly:

> "The chitlin hasta be **clean**!"

Sometimes texters or callers let the crew know, with high wit, that they hadn't thought through their audience's economic circumstances:

> *(October 15, 2012) TJMS has a guest attorney on, stressing the necessity of writing a will.*
> Texter: Who's gonna write a will for three pair of shoes and a raggedy SUV?

Or at times audience and crew collaborate in blackly humorous "class" takes on tragic realities:

(March 9, 2006) After the perpetrators of black church burnings have been caught:
Male caller: You're talkin about those young men who burned the churches, they [police] got a break from the tire tracks ... if they were black, they never would've found them!
Crew get the point immediately, laugh happily, assert that they buy all their tires used.

Crew members, as well, regularly portrayed a black world that is resolutely working class.

Ms. Dupre's Lucky Numbers often incorporated that surround, and note here her radical critique of finance companies preying on the poor:

(May 25, 2005) Count the number of businesses in your neighborhood have signs on them sayin "Open 24 Hours a Day" but they aint never open ...

(November 9, 2005) Count the number of broken chimneys in your neighborhood.

(November 30, 2005) Count the number of ads for paycheck loan companies ... I mean, it's like a whole drama bein played out, and it's just draggin people down, loanin them money they can't pay back!

And we've seen Myra J's Single Mom World, in which mothers are financially strapped, cleverly overcoming obstacles, and, with wit and style, creating a Good Life for all:

(August 22, 2005) Myra J offers a list of necessary end-of-summer preparations:

> 1. *Make sure everyone in the house reads at least two books—matchbooks don't count!*
> 2. *Get yourself a Brazilian wax. Just make sure a fine Brazilian gives it to you!*
> 3. *Buy yourself a fur coat. Put it on layaway.*
> 4. *Buy a heater for the back room.*

Or, to return to the bus issue:

(July 18, 2013) Crew asks, assuming deep audience expertise: How do you tell a safe bus driver?
Texter: You know a safe bus driver when he wears a short-sleeved shirt with the sleeves rolled up! [crew lost in laughter and approbation]
Texter: A safe bus driver always has a gut—man or woman!

Frequently, listeners called or texted in where they were and what they were doing (usually laughing uncontrollably, singing along, or dancing, as I was) in response to a particularly funny comic bit or musical jam—and in the process revealed their range of working- to middle-class jobs, and often their disparate locations:

(October 27, 2005) Male caller, in response to a joke: Oh no! You know I'm drivin a truck, and I can't get you where I'm at, but I listen to you [in the truck] every day!

(May 25, 2012) You mofos are off the chain! I work at a cleaners, and almost pressed my hand!

(Same day) Can you play some music nobody wants to hear? These people want me to work!

(Later) I was jammin so hard this mornin, I danced all the way from Raleigh to Greensboro!

(May 30, 2012) Sybil, make them stop! Tom and J are gonna make me lose my good city job!

(November 9, 2012) It's not easy to wobble in a cubicle, but we got it on! All three of us, thick sistahs! ["The wobble" is a popular black line dance—after it came out, TJMS played the song every Friday. Tom would yell: "It's Friday! Act like it!"][21]

(January 25, 2013) Drivin my FedEx vehicle but didn't stop me from pullin over and doin the wobble!
(Same day) Tom, I'm transporting a prisoner, but it didn't stop me from doin the wobble on the side of the road!

(February 22, 2013)

Texter: To the officer who let me wobble out of a ticket—thank you, boo!
J: She must be fine.
Tom: She must be.
Sybil: **He might be.** *[laughs dirtily]*

(April 18, 2013) Every Friday my co-workers look at me crazy because at eight I'm still sittin in my car in the parking lot, doin the wobble!

(April 26, 2013) I'm in the office jamming by my damn self! I'm a teacher, and the best way to prepare for a bunch of fourth-graders is to dance!

(February 6, 2014) I'm an electrical lineman, dancing in my bucket thirty feet in the air!

(May 9, 2014) I'm in the ER and everyone is doin the wobble and the dougie![22]

(June 6, 2014) Wobbling my ass off on the way to the Brown's Ferry [Alabama] nuclear plant!
(Same day) Our crossing guard in Augusta [Georgia] is doin the wobble!

(June 12, 2014) Tom, I drive public transportation in Cincinnati, and you playin "Hooks" is killin me! [*The O'Jays' 1973 "I Guess You've Got Your Hooks in Me," one of the all-time great old-school love songs*]23 I'm doin my best not to sing out loud!

(July 24, 2014) I'm cleanin my keyboard! Tom and J had me laughin so hard coffee is everywhere! A co-worker is waving a church fan over me!

(July 25, 2014) Blastin my horn, drivin an eighteen-wheeler, doin the wobble!
(Same day, different texter) I think I backed it up too much! [*"backing that thang up" is part of the wobble dance*] My butt caught fire on the kitchen stove!

(June 5, 2014) A range of texters respond to wobble song:
—Doin the wobble with my students on last day of Catholic school!
—Doin the wobble while feeding the homeless
—Doin the wobble on my way to work at Blue Cross

(September 25, 2015) Working in Philadelphia and I stopped writing citations to do the wobble!

(October 22, 2015)
Wobblin while deliverin newspapers
Wobblin at Johns Hopkins Hospital
Wobblin at Wal-Mart with my cart of food and TJMS blastin from my phone

(February 19, 2016)
Wobblin with three white co-workers, they HAVE to wobble because it's MY car!
Wobblin in the produce section in the supermarket in Columbia, South Carolina!
Wobblin on Amtrak on my way to New York
I was wobbling so hard, I knocked my wife's dentures off the table and broke them!
    But I don't care, she needs to lose some weight anyway.
Sybil: Wow! Wobblin AND ignorant!

(February 17, 2017) Doin the wobble in the bathroom with my wife in Omaha!

*(November 19, 2017)*Wobblin in my car on the way to work Gonzales, Louisiana
Wobblin on my tractor trailer in Ashville, North Carolina!
Doin the wobble celebrating my Sigma Gamma Ro upcoming Founder Day!
Wobblin on Moreland Ave in Atlanta, on my way to work at Emory!
Doin the wobble with my knee brace!
Seventeen degrees in Flint, Michigan, laying concrete, doin the wobble!
At the gym, doin the wobble in Miramar, Florida!

(December 8, 2017)
Doin the wobble with crew 509 garbage detail in Lexington, Kentucky!
I'm at work in the parking lot doin the wobble in Cincinnati!
Wobblin at my desk in Nashville, Tennessee!

(December 15, 2017)
On my way to school in Dallas, doin the wobble!
On I-70 in St. Louis, doin the wobble in my car!
Doin the wobble on the way to primary care in Baton Rouge!
Doin the wobble in Memphis in front of Graceland!
Doin the wobble in NGS [a large health corporation] in Harrisburg! With co-workers!
I'm in my truck on the way from Dayton, Ohio!
Doin the wobble in Toledo!
Doing the wobble on the orange line in the DMV!
Doin the dougie/wobble in the red state of Alabama!
Doin the wobble deliverin newspapers in Mansville, Ohio!
Doin the wobble with my ten-month old grandson in Little Rock!

(January 19, 2018) Wobblin in the Chi, gettin ready for work!

(March 23, 2018) Doing the wobble at Blue Cross/Blue Shield in Columbia, South Carolina!

(March 30, 2018) Doin the wobble in Norman, Oklahoma before the big teachers strike!

(April 20, 2018)
I'm doin the wobble in NOLA on my way to St. Augustine high school!
Doin the wobble in my FedEx truck in Shreveport
Doin the wobble while celebrating 4/20—"Jamaica style!"
Doin the wobble at my desk at HUD!
Doing the wobble in Atlantic City!

(August 10, 2018)
Goin to John Deere in Davenport, Iowa, doin the wobble!
Doin the wobble at my job in North Haven, Connecticut!

(September 21, 2018) Doin the wobble in my car on I-70 in Ohio, scarin all the colonizers [post-Trump phrase meaning racist whites]!

Or listeners may just text in their appreciation of *TJMS* humor:

(August 5, 2014) I'm sittin here in the guard shack laughin my head off [at a J Anthony Brown bit]

Office workers, truck and bus drivers, teachers, students, health workers, charity volunteers, construction workers, electricians, dry cleaning workers, prison and security guards, sanitation workers, traffic officers, delivery workers. From Connecticut, New York, New Jersey, the District of Columbia, Pennsylvania, Ohio,

Michigan, Illinois, Iowa, Maryland, North and South Carolina, Florida, Georgia, Alabama, Kentucky, Tennessee, Arkansas, Oklahoma, Louisiana, Texas, Nebraska, and other sites far and wide. This is the black working-class community of the air, sharing amusement and camaraderie, and setting the groove to get through another long, stressful, underpaid workday.

Often, the *TJMS*'s very construction of a question for its audience assumed working-class status, and callers could be magnificently witty and deep in response.

> *(May 16, 2005)*
> Tom Joyner: *"Today's Express Yourself is, tell us about repo [repossession] . . . Tell us about when your stuff was repo'ed!"*
> Male caller: *I **am** the Repo Man. I've seen it all . . .*
> *[Crew starts teasing about women offering sexual favors to keep their cars. Caller demurs.]*
> J Anthony Brown: *But tell me this, what if she's **Halle Berry** fine?*
> Caller: *I can't put all that fineness on the electric bill.*

Another Express Yourself question assuming working-class status:

> *(November 7, 2005) How do you stretch a dollar?*
> Woman caller. *My daughter has this boyfriend and his mother has five kids. She buys a huge bag of potatoes and gives each child a potato. She says, choose how you want it.*
> Male caller: *Whenever I go through a drive-through restaurant, I save the cup and then I get a refill and don't have to buy another drink.*
> J: *He's savin money, but that's **nasty**.*

And a very revealing and lengthy third example. Notice how these listeners' job-training efforts versus their present job statuses often reflect well-known American class and color barriers to achievement:

> *(November 29, 2005) Express Yourself: I went to school for blank and instead I'm working as a blank:*
> Woman: *I went to school for fashion merchandising and now I'm a corrections officer.*
> Woman: *I went to school to be a nurse and now I'm a truck driver.*
> Andrea: *I went to school to be a CNA [Certified Nursing Assistant], and now I'm a school bus driver.*
> Man: *I went to school to be a photographer and now I'm an apple candy seller.*
> Portia: *I went to school to be a computer engineer and now I'm a high school math teacher.*

Tom: *Why . . . you could be makin plenty of money and not be scared all the time!* **Bless** *your heart!*

Renee: *I went to school to be a piano teacher and now I'm a Certified Nursing Assistant.*

Tom: *And you play piano at the nursing home?*

Renee: *(with a sense of irony) Yes I do!*

Ricky D: *I went to school to be an elementary schoolteacher and now I'm a tree surgeon.*

Ray: *I went to school to be a law enforcement officer, which I did for six years. And now I'm an engineer on the railroad.*

Kat in Buffalo: *I studied to be an accountant, but I became a UPS driver.*

Avis: *I studied to be a nurse, but I'm a high school teacher—special ed.*

Mohamed: *I studied music, wanted to be a singer. But I'm a delivery guy for Direct TV.*

Shonda: *I took classes to be a psychologist, but now I'm a baker—gourmet cakes.*

Woman: *I studied Business Administration, but now I'm a letter carrier.*

J: *So you went from BA to BS!*

Caller, deep Southern accent: *J, it pays the be-ulls, it pays the be-ulls!*

Sometimes callers "bring out" inherent debates among the crew, as did the feisty Unique:

Unique: *I studied to be a nurse, but now I'm a stripper.*

J Anthony Brown: **Hell**, *yes!*

Sybil: *You been waiting all morning for this!*

Unique: *I couldn't afford nursing school, so I became a stripper. On a bad day I make $1000. It's no low-class about it, it's definitely upscale. But guess what?—My uniform is a nurse's uniform!*

All: *Wild laughter.*

It's no low-class about it. A small percentage of exotic dancers like Unique, for a very short period in their lives, may make decent money. But the sad reality for most exotic dancers in the era of neoliberal corporatization is that they must pay a "stage fee" just to be allowed to perform, and are expected to share tips with DJs, bartenders, and other staff. Stripping is a precarious working-class job, with no benefits, no retirement plan, and an automatic expiration date.[24]

Callers may also yank the crew away from their understandable desire to milk the joke, back down to the grim realities of many jobs:

(August 14, 2006) *Cash call winner. He says he works for the sanitation department. "I'm a garbageman."*

Myra J: *You're a* sanitation engineer.

Caller: *Man, and I need the money.*
Tom: *What's the best stuff you ever found out there?*
Caller: *Oh man, I drive a front-end loader, we find bodies, people sleeping overnight—It's **dangerous** out there!*

Or a listener may reach out to correct the crew's ignorance of their working conditions:

(February 26, 2013) *Crew had been bemoaning winter storms, snowy roads.*
Texter: *Tom, I'm a snowplow driver. You asked how snowplow drivers get to work—we go to work **before** the snow starts and stay til the roads are clear!*

A working-class listener may simply tug the heartstrings:

(March 14, 2014) Response to "What are you doin this weekend?"
Texter: *This is Mack from the DMV. I'm going to ask my boo to get married and re-tire from the Single Moms' Club! [title of Tyler Perry film that had just opened]*
Crew: *Awwwww, that's nice!*

Or the show may comment, with high amusement, on the not entirely legal ways in which working-class people pay their bills:

(April 20, 2005) Crew discusses upcoming Monday Night Football game. J: "The bootleg man is gonna be busy this week, baby!" All laugh.

Of course, the show does have its share of professional-class listeners:

*(October 18, 2005) Question of the day is, Who on TV can you **not** stand?*
Woman caller: *It's Nancy Grace! I'm an attorney, and she's an awful, awful advo-cate. She deliberately ignored all the cases of missing black girls.*
Tom: *All that cryin!*
Caller: *It's fake!*

(March 28, 2007) The crew is discussing Alzheimer's disease. A woman calls in to urge that people always go to the doctor, because "it could be other conditions which are treatable."
Tom and Sybil: *Did you go to the doctor yourself for this reason?*
Caller: *I **am** a physician!*

(January 14, 2013) Texter: I'm a surgeon and I'm fixing to do a hysterectomy and I can't get J's song [a murdered hit] out of my mind!
(October 18, 2013) Texter in response to "What are you doin this weekend" question: This weekend I'm going to be inaugurated as President of Dillard

University [an HBCU in New Orleans, thus the texter must have been Walter M. Kimbrough, or his assistant texting for him].

At times, the crew can't resist teasing their audience:

(December 9, 2008) Cash call. Middle-school teacher calls in, wins. Crew asks her is she in school right then? Yes, she is.
Sybil, utterly being herself: Where are the children? Their participles are dangling as we speak!
Tom: That's alright, with the salary she gets, she needs the money!

Frequently the *TJMS* crew, as we saw in the bus strike example, identified with and talked about news events from "the other side," the working-class laborers' perspective mainstream media rarely even imagine:

(April 25, 2005) The question of the day is, "What did you do to mess up that good-a [ass] job?"
Woman: I went to the TJMS [a sky show] and told them I had a doctor appointment!
All: Laughter, shouts of Oh no!
Sybil: Why didn't you go to the doctor afterwards?
Caller: I did! But I didn't get a letter!

Later caller, demonstrating that some listeners are middle class:
Woman: I lost a good-a job in college trying to pledge [to a sorority]!
Myra J: Girl, you tried to do all that?
Caller: Yes I did.
Myra J: And what did you pledge?
Caller: Delta Sigma Theta. [The largest black women's sorority, founded at Howard University in 1913.][25]

Later the same morning, we are back in working-class territory:

Male caller from Tallahassee: I was shift supervisor at a recycling plant, and one of the guys dropped the n-word on me. I picked him up and put him through a table.
*J: One question—were you **acting** like the n-word?*
All: laughter

Another example of the *TJMS* automatically thinking through the working-class workers' point of view:

(August 9, 2006) Sybil reports that because of the "shoe bomber," American airports have instituted new stringent controls on the items, liquids in particular, that passengers may bring on board.

Tom: If you know someone who works security at the airlines . . .
Melvin: You might get some great gifts!
Crew goes on about the possibilities—liquor, perfumes . . .

Sometimes the crew joked at their working-class audience's expense about bad food habits and poor consumer choices:

(April 27, 2005) Ms. Dupre's Lucky Numbers.
Count the number of salads you ate this week.
   [long hilarious crew discussion of how the number is probably zero for most of their listeners]
*J: I **know** you aint never had a salad!*
Ms. Dupre continues: Count the number of people you know with no car but they
   got a wide screen television.
All: Laughter and snide remarks.
J: They takin the bus!

And crew members may themselves assert their own low status through humor. Ms. Dupre, for example, consistently *played* working class:

(April 29, 2005) Ms. Dupre plays a clip from the Oprah Winfrey show. She claims
   that Oprah "stole my stuff" and that she is suing her for billions.
Sybil, highly amused, asks Ms. Dupre what she's given away [a la Oprah's various
   extravaganzas]—any cars?
*Ms. Dupre: I've given away **bus passes**!*

Or the job may be accomplished—class asserted—through a simple shout-out, as Tom Joyner did on May 15, 2014: "This one's for everybody on the *third shift!*"

The crew may identify profoundly with its hardest-pressed listeners:

(May 9, 2013)
Texter: Yall make getting up and goin to work at a job I know I'm losin in two
   weeks possible!
Crew: Awwwwwwww!
Tom: Bless your heart! Bless your heart!

(November 1, 2013) Sybil announces cuts to SNAP [food stamps]. "Fifteen per-
   cent of the U.S. population get food stamps!"
Tom: [disgusted, sardonic] Just in time for the holidays!

The *TJMS* also defined the class and race identity of their audience through invoking *black space*—neighborhoods, cities—and government's characteristic racist neglect and/or oppression:

> (*August 22, 2012*) *Crew discussion of West Nile cases in Houston. Tom asks the audience: Are they spraying [insecticide] in the hood? They instantly received dozens of texts, most simply saying no. But others were inspired to mordant, cynical humor—*
> *Tom: But this is the best one: "Yeah, they sprayed in my area. With a twelve-ounce can of OFF!" [crew loses it]*
> *Later texters: "Yeah, they dropped off fly swatters.' "Yeah, they sprayed—bullets!"*

J Anthony Brown's many "jacked up Christmas" songs also reflected a vision of black working-class/impoverished space, with simultaneous baleful realism and nostalgic sentimentality. On December 10, 2010, J sang a brilliant takeoff of the carol, "Do You Hear What I Hear?" He ran through sound, sight, and smell:—"Ghetto sounds blend into the night."—"Crackheads looking for a rock."—"Doin hair and making barbecue." He then wished everyone a Merry Christmas, and adjured them to "stay safe in the hood!"[26]

Wobblin in Uniform

Despite the *TJMS*'s radical protests against the racist criminal justice system, quite a few black police call or text in to the show. Here is a poignant conversation a month after the Katrina disaster in New Orleans:

> (*October 5, 2005*) *I'm a disgruntled police officer from New Orleans. Those of you who were here from Day One, we had to scrounge, just like everybody else, to provide for our families . . . We were not paid . . . My wife had to take the kids to another state. We're being paid now, but no overtime.*
> *Tom: Well, God bless you, man . . . We know it's a struggle for you trying to care for your family and the city at the same time!*

Some police simultaneously protested and enjoyed being sent up stereotypically:

> (*May 16, 2012*) *J and Tom do a "doughnut alert" bit, mimicking a police dispatcher announcing a fresh batch.*
> *Texter: Tom, that is **not right**! I'm a Chicago police officer, but I'm laughin my ass off!*
> *And some police were just happy with the snarky progressive comedy:*

(August 13, 2012) Texter: I'm pulling over before I wreck my police car [in response to wonderfully nasty skit about Pat Robertson]. Keep'em comin, I need it!

Even White House Secret Security agents have been known to communicate to the *TJMS*:

(April 15, 2009) Tom and J do a well-timed bit on Bo, the Obamas' recently acquired White House dog.

Tom: Oh, the dog is so cute! But you wait, playa, it is only-a-matter-of-time

J: Only-a-matter-of-time before he steps in

Tom: [instantly] A steamin pile!

*Later, Tom says: When we did that bit, I got a text from I think a Secret Service agent, because I know Secret Service agents listen all the time. And he wrote, I signed up to take a bullet, but not for **that**!*

Serving and former military members were also fans:

(April 20, 2005) Call for Your Psychic Friend Ms Dupre:
Male caller: I've been in the military, and this woman's been waiting for me. I want to know what the future holds.

(February 11, 2009) A male army nurse calls in, just back on a leave from Afghanistan, says he slept only two hours last night. Tom asks him why he went into the military instead of working stateside? "Well, Uncle Sam paid for my training." Sybil asks him how long he has to stay in Afghanistan. "Well, it's indefinite". . . . "I just want to let yall know that we listen to you over there."

(March 15, 2013) Crew had been discussing wives' revenge on unfaithful husbands:
Texter: My wife ironed my military uniform with [particularly black-identified] red velvet cake!
Sybil and Dominique [guest comic] laugh uproariously.
Tom, equally amused: Any other cake would be alright, but not red velvet!

(May 22, 2014) Poignant texter: I'm an OIF [Iraq war] veteran . . . and when I was in country, your show kept me alive.

(May 28, 2014)
We're ten deep in the gym shower in Fort Belvoir [army training center in Virginia] doin the wobble!
J: [playing on the gay interpretation] Now that is just wrong. Five deep, OK. But ten?!

(June 12, 2014) Texter: Tom, I'm away from my office doing barracks-room inspections, and the app allows me to keep up. Thanks!

(October 31, 2014) I'm wobbling in my military uniform even though I know it's against policy!

(September 9, 2016)
Doin the wobble on a C130 on the way to Afghanistan!
J: God bless you! Make it home, make it home!

(December 8, 2017) Doin the wobble in Osan air base in Korea!

TJMS financial advice is also curated with their working-class audience in mind. Sometime in the 2000s, financier Mellody Hobson, who is also married to film-maker George Lucas, began doing a "Money Mondays" spot.[27] Despite her great wealth, Hobson tailored her presentations to an audience likely to be in straitened circumstances and vulnerable to predatory financial institutions:

(December 7, 2015) Hobson reports on the 7% of the American population that
is unbanked, and that twenty-six million Americans do not have enough credit
history to get a credit score—how difficult it is for people, and that President
Obama has a new plan to help them.
Tom asks, "What about debit cards?" Hobson explains that you have to have a
bank account to get a debit card.
Crew teases Hobson for not mentioning that she just attended the Kennedy Center
honors event the night before because George Lucas received an award.

But the *TJMS* audience can be quite sharp, and will correct reporting that is inaccurate or insufficiently accounts for working-class and poor people's lives and needs:

(January 29, 2018) Hobson had given a too-optimistic interpretation of the
Trump-era Republicans' giant tax cut bill, which was designed to provide
nearly all its benefits to the already wealthy[28]:
Texter: In response to Mellody Hobson, the overwhelming majority of companies
aren't giving away anything! And the increased deficit will have to be paid by
ordinary people. Look for cuts to Social Security and Medicare!

Playing with Language, Class, Race

As we have seen, the *TJMS* crew, guests, and audience *play* with language. They code-switch across so-called proper English usage and a wide variety of regional black dialects. They began the show with a ban on "cussin" (which loosened somewhat over the decades, as it loosened in American culture generally), and crew members, as we have seen, created gloriously witty euphemisms—shiggity for shit, diggity for having sex—that audience members have taken up and circulated. They also picked up and circulated newish black slang, often derived from hip-hop culture, such as "sidepiece," "took me a minute," "ratched," "trap queen," "ride or die"[29]—and, of course, "woke." Ken Smukler, the white election analyst who provided extraordinarily angry, linguistically creative reports each presidential election season, adopted show euphemisms and added his own: Smukler played with his own name, using it to mean "fuck." As in: "Tell them to get the **smuk** out of here!"

As well, crew, guests, and audience members deliberately used words and phrases widely circulated in mass media to stigmatize racial minorities *to the opposite effect*. That is, as we will see, they call criminal *white people*, no matter how wealthy or elite, "gangsta," dope "slingers," "Crips and Bloods doin drivebys," etc. Thus they de-Otherized racially charged language that functions to define black Americans as innately criminal—deliberately undercutting what George Lipsitz has labeled the "possessive investment in whiteness" that is central to discrimination against people of color.[30]

One of the key elements of Huggy Lowdown's performance is his linguistic creativity—including intonational contour (lots of falsetto and extended vowels), word choice, rhyming, alliteration—and particularly in the way he greeted each crew member as he began each morning's performance. The greetings frequently sent up black "colorism"—that is, tension among African Americans over skin tone—as Tom is quite light, Sybil, J, and Huggy dark:

> (*February 21, 2010*) *What's up, my Milano cookie-colored kinfolk?*
> *Sybil: I* **love** *that!*
> (*August 17, 2012*) *Addressing Tom Joyner: To the brutha whose cul-uh Crayola has yet to discov-ah!*
> (*October 12, 2012*) *And to J, the darky full of malarkey!* [*influenced by the recent Joe Biden Vice Presidential debate*]
> (*October 7, 2016*) *Tom Joyner, AKA "Fifty Shades of Beige!"*

The crew also sent up stereotypical "white" English and slang, as when Sybil Wilkes impersonated a young white male Obama supporter speaking to a black coworker during the 2012 presidential election:

> (*November 6, 2012*) *Duuude, are we gonna win this thing or* **not**?

But perhaps the most astounding and effective linguistic play I've ever heard on the show was an example of "comic blackening" during the run-up to our tragically misguided invasion of Iraq in 2003. The *TJMS* crew was discussing then-Secretary of State Colin Powell's address to the United Nations, in which he claimed that Iraq had weapons of mass destruction. They "working-classified" the very dignified African American general and diplomat. They assumed he was dutifully lying for the Bush Administration, and imagined for him an epiphany, a moment of truth, in which he "went colored," stopped in the middle of the speech, and announced to United Nations Secretary-General Kofi Annan:

(February 6, 2003) *"Brother Kofi, I aint got nuthin, I can't front yall"*—kicking over his chair as he stalked out.

After comics Keegan-Michael Key and Jordan Peele, many years later, created the brilliant character "Luther," President Obama's "anger translator," I revisited this compelling *TJMS* moment, and realized that the show had paved the way for them.

We Are the World on *TJMS*

The crew's and audience's civil rights vision always also encompassed all other Americans of color, and all black people everywhere. They embraced the Caribbean in particular. After the devastating Haiti earthquake of January 2010, the *TJMS* tried to travel there to provide an internet café for survivors, so they could reach family and friends on the island and in the diaspora. They continued for years to report on ongoing devastation, epidemics, and the failures of outside agencies to provide real lasting infrastructural, medical, and other aid. Jeff Johnson, their key outside news expert in that period, traveled to Haiti with BET directly after the earthquake, and angrily asked listeners to call the Christian Broadcasting Network (CBN) to complain about Pat Robertson's characteristically outrageous reaction:

(January 14, 2010)
*Tom: That **fool**! Tell people what he said!*
Jeff Johnson: Explains that Robertson claimed that Haiti was cursed because they had fought Napoleon for their freedom.
*Tom: Well, what about Limbaugh? He said the President responded **too quickly**!*
Jeff: Well, Limbaugh is using the George Bush response manual—how long it took Bush to respond to Katrina!

D L Hughley also weighed in on Robertson and the Haiti tragedy:

*Tom, you know I'm always able to find humor in anything, but this Haiti situation has me befuddled . . . Well, three things characterize Haiti: 1. Bein black, 2. Bein poor, and 3. Having **no** natural resources people can rape and oppress them for! . . . God bless Haiti!*

And the *TJMS* crew was always aware of the multiple-country diasporas that have flowed together to make and remake "black America:"

(February 18, 2014) Sybil reports on a major earthquake in Barbados: "If you have folks there, you may want to check on them."

Al Sharpton came on the show on April 24, 2013, to comment angrily about the Republican-controlled Senate, having failed to pass any gun control legislation, turning to immigration restrictions:

> *Some are trying to use the fact that the [Boston marathon] bombers are Chechen [to rationalize restrictions]. The face of immigration was Mexican, now they're trying to make it Chechen! [He notes that many newer immigrants are Caribbean blacks.]*
> Tom: *Tell it, Rev!*
> Texter: *Yeah, tell it, Rev! I'm from the Bahamas, naturalized.*

D L Hughley, Los Angeles-based, has been particularly concerned over Mexican Americans' legal and political status in the United States. On May 7, 2009, D L laid out his vision of American imperial appropriation:

> *Happy Cinco de Mayo! You know it's funny where we take people's land, and then we give them a **day**! [crew lost in approbation]*

The following year, D L repeated and hilariously elaborated his anti-racist history lesson:

> *(April 29, 2010) Now, I'm against illegal immigration, and I'm concerned about people crossing our borders and taking our jobs. And that's why I'm supporting building a wall on the **Canadian** border! [Hughley enumerates long list of Canadian entertainers active in the U.S.] . . . California, New Mexico, and Arizona, up until the 1800s–1900s, were all **Mexico**![31] They're just comin home!—maybe they forgot sumthin?*

Hughley returned to the attack after Arizona passed the notoriously racist SB1070, the "papers please" bill, and the Phoenix Suns announced they would wear jerseys emblazoned with "Los Suns" in protest:

> *(May 6, 2010) I want to commend the Phoenix Suns—I've never seen the **owner** of a team take a political stand. I don't understand people sayin they're takin our jobs. We're all the same! Maffack, Mexicans are just blacks with good hair! [crew loves it]*

And *TJMS* programming encouraged cross-racial solidarity in the workplace— On May 4, 2012, the show did their annual *Cinco de Mayo* programming, and a listener texted in:

> *Tom, that Cinco de Mayo tribute had me cryin, I was laughin so hard. I played it for my Mexican co-workers—they loved it!*

During the summer 2014 media firestorm over Central American children fleeing from deadly violence in their own countries, asking for asylum in the United States, the crew was extremely sympathetic:

> *(August 1, 2014) Crew discusses Congress's failure to pass an immigration bill because of Republican obstructionism. Tom explodes: "Waitaminute! What about the children on the border? They're **real people**!"*

And the *TJMS* followed the "Linsanity" over Chinese-American NBA player Jeremy Lin, then leading a turnaround for the New York Knicks, and deplored, *as if he were black,* the incessant "funny" racist attacks on him, by both fans and sportscasters. On February 17, 2012, for example, the crew was outraged over journalists hounding his family in Taiwan (although Lin is American-born), and called for them to "leave them alone!"

The crew attended as well to the horrific massacre of Sikh Americans at their *gurdwara* (temple) in Oak Creek, Wisconsin, on August 5, 2012. The following day, Sybil reported sympathetically on the facts of the attack—the shooter, Wade Page, was an Army veteran who was a white supremacist. And the crew followed up on August 7.

Similarly, during the U.S. Ebola crisis, when affected nurses were being quarantined and treated at Texas Health Presbyterian Hospital in Dallas, Tom asked Sybil on October 17, 2014:

> *OK, now how are our Ebola patients?*

The patients at the time were two nurses, one black, and one Vietnamese American. It didn't matter. They were *ours.*

And Arsenio Hall, on the show on May 10, 2018, remarked of the Koren Americans whom North Korea had just released:

> *By the way, our citizens are free now!*

Ours.

The 2018 caravan of terrified Central American families attempting to reach the United States to seek asylum, and the spectacle of the Trump Administration forcefully separating the children, even babies, from their parents, and housing them in cages, spurred the *TJMS* to repeated compassionate protest:

> *(June 19, 2018) Gwen Ifill of the NAACP Legal Defense Fund begs the audience to call Congress to pressure them to reunite these children with their parents.*

> *(June 20, 2018) Sybil says she is so upset about the children that she can barely function. Al Sharpton calls in, furious: "This must end! It should remind us*

*of when they separated **us** from our parents. So you cannot sit by and say it's Mexicans, not us . . . Donald Trump has gone a bridge too far in many areas. This is one he has crossed . . ."*

Tom asks how Sharpton got in to see the children . . . He explains they've been using clergy to get in . . . Sybil says its common to let clergy visit gangsters, mobsters. Why not these children?

Then Chris Paul comes on, asserting that the UN Human Rights Commission should have thrown the U.S. out because of this atrocity.

And the *TJMS*'s "we are one" vision includes the globe's Muslims. Long before 9/11, African Americans, in part because of the history of American Black Muslims and the heroic status of the martyred Malcolm X, tended to be much more comfortable with Islam than most white Americans.[32] Jokes about the superiority of the Fruit of Islam as bodyguards were common coinage on the show. (They repeatedly, facetiously suggested that President Obama hire The Fruit, known for their discipline and probity, for protection, instead of the scandal-plagued Secret Service.)

After the horrific ISIS-connected Paris attacks of Friday, November 13, 2015, the show took time for a serious discussion on the following Monday, November 16.[33] Both crew and audience were outraged that Republicans were blaming President Obama for the attacks, and were clear that the blame lay with George W. Bush's failed post-9/11 wars and the chaos, impoverishment, and refugee crises they created.[34] Sybil went out of her way to make anti-racist and anti-Islamophobic points: that the global press paid nowhere near the same attention to Muslim extremist attacks on ordinary people in *Africa*; and to note acerbically that the vast mass of the globe's two-plus billion Muslims had no connection to, and were firmly in disagreement with ISIS and other terrorist sects.

TJMS could even imagine the lifeworlds of Somalian pirates—at least with a humorous edge[35]:

(April 9, 2009) Comedian Rudy Rush is on: "I know a bunch of Somalians—they come here and drive cabs for a few years. Then they go back to piratin, jackin everybody over there.

Tom: This is the Martin Luther King Drive of the seas, they jack everybody up!

Rudy: That's the first time that crew said: "Hey, you know we got a black president!" [does extremely bad Somalian accent] "I dunt ca-a-a-re!"

J then got into the act, pretending to be a Somalian pirate, with a significantly better accent:

*Good morning Tom Joyner, I cannot speak for long, I am eating up my anytime minutes right now. We did not plan this well at all! The first thing we would like is a bigger boat—oh, did I tell you, it is **ripe** in here? We need a boatload of Febreze!*

Aside from joking about the poor living conditions on pirate boats, the crew debated whether to focus on tanker ship defense, or on the appalling state of the Somalian economy, and the role of poverty in encouraging certain kinds of crime:

(April 13, 2009)
J: I got nuthin, you pass my house with a truckload of watermelons every day, see what happens! Now they're called pirates. Back in the day, they were **settlers**!
Tom: Just arm the ships, alright? It's either that or pay millions in ransom.
Sybil: I think we have to think about these people and how they're living in their native countries.
J: The haves are always goin to have a problem with the have-nots takin what they got!

(April 20, 2009) The single captured Somalian pirate is in the U.S.
Sybil: What I don't like is the press asked him to smile!
J: Watermelons, slavery . . .
Sybil: And he's **done** already! It's over for him. They'll be saying he feels no remorse. And he's sixteen!

Finally, the TJMS crew often note instances of interracial solidarity and empathy in daily life. After the terrible June 17, 2015, white supremacist massacre of black congregants and their pastor at the Charleston, South Carolina, Emmanuel AME church, for example, President Obama gave the heartfelt eulogy, and sang "Amazing Grace," at the funeral of Reverend Clementa C. Pinckney.[36] Sybil reported on June 29, 2015, that she happened to be at an Asian-run nail salon at the time the eulogy was broadcast live on television: "The whole place stopped **dead**." Then, at the end, "everyone stood up and applauded!"

Country Black

The TJMS crew also enjoyed and played with the Southern-based black linguistic creativity some audience members exhibit. One example is so astonishingly brilliant that I had to puzzle over whether or not it might have been rehearsed, and not just be pure joyous improvisation:

(March 3, 2006) Melvin's Love Line
(Obviously middle-aged, working-class, country Southern man) This is Le Roy [Sybil starts laughing uproariously]. [He continues with total sincerity]: And I want to know what do I do to keep my sugar-wooger Mabel?
Entire crew lost in wild laughter and chants of sugar-wooger
J: This is OLD SCHOOL. This is an old school problem. Sybil, you don't know nuthin about it . . .

*Melvin: [simultaneously sincere and over-the-top]: Sugar-wooger **loves** you. You*
    don't have to do nuthin.
Le Roy: But it's hard out there.

Tom, J, and Melvin instantly sing, in unison, to the tune from the recent film Hustle
    & Flow:
"Cause it's hard out there for a sugar-wooger."
All fall out.

Sometimes Southern callers displayed such wonderfully antiquated language
and unique imaginations that the crew could only marvel:

(April 26, 2005) Question: What would you do if it was your last twenty-four hours?
Woman caller: First I'd sit down with my loved ones and pray for a few hours. . . .
    Then I'd commence to robbin banks and side-swipin cars.
Sybil: Side-swipin cars!
J: You committin crimes they don't do anymore!
Sybil: What is this, Ma Barker?

In 2018, Tom demanded that Sybil repeat an anecdote from her own Chicago
history. While this narrative is hilarious in and of itself, it also comments on the
"Delta country" speech of many working-class black Chicagoans who arrived from
the South in the Great Migrations:

(February 20, 2018) Tom begs Sybil, "Tell it again!"
Sybil: Well, this was the year Soul Food *came out [1997], and I went to see it.*
    There was this elderly couple seated directly in front of me. [In the film, an adul-
    terous couple is having sex, only to be confronted by the man's wife. The elderly
    man turns to his wife and complains] "He aint even wraynched off!" [crew lost
    in laughter and repetitions of "wraynched"]

But at other times, the *TJMS*, in classic black comic tradition, hit back hard when
callers displayed poor grammar. The crew, like many other black radio DJs, were
never behindhand in correcting callers' English, sometimes with the witty cruelty
of the hook at Amateur Night at the Apollo:

(September 30, 2005) Melvin's Love Line
Myron from Shreveport: I'm twenty-nine, I'm going to voc-tech . . .
Melvin: Let me guess! Heating and cooling? [yes] Yes, you sound like a man full
    of freons!
Myron: I just can't find the right woman.
Melvin: Sybil, meet Myron. Myron, meet Sybil.
Sybil: Myron, I need some references.

J: And she don't do trade school, cause I've already tried.
Melvin: Tell me this, do you have a gold grill?
Myron: I have one gold teeth.

Loud dial tone.
Crew, yelling: That was it, one gold teeth. He said the bad word, and Sybil hung up on him!
Sybil: [defensively] It was just reflex!
(August 4, 2008)
Woman caller talking about education: I didn't went to Auburn, I didn't went to Princeton, but I got an education at UNC Wilmington! [crew cuts her off, makes fun of her grammar]
Tom asserts: "I'm going to pull UNC's accreditation!"
(July 13, 2009) Ongoing discussion of male infidelity. John from Milwaukee calls in, admits to being unfaithful to his wife. Tom asks him why he is outing himself on the air?

John: Sometimes your opinion just gotta be spoke!

*Tom, instantly, with wonder and deep happiness: Sometimes your opinion **just gotta be spoke!?***
J: I don't have to say nuthin!
Sybil: Repeats John's statement, and collapses in wild laughter.

Tom, quoting Tyler Perry's Madea: Who learned you how to speak?
  Later in the show, they revisit John's statement:

Sybil: Peals of laughter. "Truer words were never spoke!" Lost again in laughter.
Tom: I'm so embarrassed—to be an African American male.
J: Sometimes you just want to be a woman, huh?

And in fact, the crew was so taken with John's malapropism that they excerpted it, and played it during commercial breaks, on and off, for months afterward.

After J Anthony Brown left the show at the end of 2016, Joyner replaced him with an array of performers, each present on a different day of the week. One of them, Arsenio Hall, well-known for his creative but short-lived (1989–94) television show, invented a bit, Dear Black People—obviously a reversal of the comedy series *Dear White People*—which the crew and many audience members took up enthusiastically. "DBP" is intended as an in-house check on foolish, narrow-minded, or inappropriate behavior, as in:

(October 9, 2017) Sybil: Dear black people: If you can afford nice clothes and a car, you can afford to get your raggedy-a mouth fixed!
(Same day) Tom: Dear black people, don't talk about the man keepin you down, if your resumé is a half-page. The only people with half-page resumes should be junior high students and Donald Trump Jr! [crew loves it]

(Same day) Texter: Dear black people: There are a lot of tasty varieties of fish other than catfish!

(Same day) Another texter: Dear black people: No socks with thong slippers!

(July 30, 2018) Sybil: Dear black people: when your ringtone is the dirty version of Tank's "When We," turn it off before you go into church! [37]

But most often, "DBP" functions as linguistic correction, with audience members chiming in with a vengeance:

Arsenio: Dear black people, the word is prostate, NOT prostrate! By the way, we're glad you're getting yours checked!

(November 27, 2017) Texter: Dear black people: It's Santa Claus, not Santy Claus!
(Same day) Another texter: The seasoning is called paprika, not pepper-ika!
(Ditto) The word is business, not bidness!
*(Ditto) If you can't pronounce it, leave the word alone! Like interesting—it's **not** inneresting!*

And crew members will also correct "hip-hop English," as in the very common, and quite charming, use of "conversate" instead of "converse"—which shows up, for example, in Mary J Blige's lyrics, among others. Comic Damon Williams did an early-morning feature, Seriously Ignorant News, and on October 21, 2014, he exclaimed:

It's seriously ignorant! As serious as people thinkin "conversate" is a word! It aint a word, people!

But crew members and audience often split the grammatical difference when music is involved. On March 2, 2011, for example, Tom played Jennifer Hudson's latest hit, "Where You At.[38] He came back on the air, praised the song, and proclaimed that "even the English teachers don't mind her bad grammar." But later in the show, he reported:

*Oh, the texters didn't agree with me! [The show was flooded with texts from English teachers who said, yes, they **did** mind her bad grammar. One wrote: "It makes my ears bleed!"]*
*J, setting up the joke: Sybil, what **should** she say?*
Sybil: Where are you!
*J: But **that** aint a hit! [all laugh]*

Sybil herself cleverly split the difference in a "DBP" bit:

*(October 9, 2017) Dear black people: It is "sup-posed to!" **Not** "posed to." And by the way, you're **posed** to know that!*

Finally, the crew took a heterodox line on perhaps the most important "black language" issue: the use of the n-word. On July 10, 2007, comic D L Hughley read a careful statement *against* the NAACP's new stand that the n-word should be banned. He called it merely symbolic, "when black Americans continue to be poorer and unhealthier than white Americans." He exclaimed: "There've never been funerals for "kike" or "Wop," because they're too busy running their own businesses!" He summarized: "The only power the n-word has is the power we give it."

The crew received his argument very favorably:

Sybil: *You know what, you're preaching the same words that J has been for a long time!*

J: *You saved us, man!*

Tom: *And he weighed every word—you really don't want to mess this up!*

Thus the *TJMS* straddled a difficult linguistic/political contradiction, one encapsulated in their "Entertain. Empower. Inform" catchphrase. On the one hand, they know that the inability to speak standard, mainstream, middle-class English can harm black Americans' employment and mobility prospects. And so they frequently engaged in cruel banter, the message of which is that their working-class audience, for their own social and economic sakes, should be able to code-switch. On the other hand, for both aesthetic and black pride reasons, they cherish class- and regionally based African American linguistic variety and creativity and exhibit it themselves. They attempt to use language to entertain, but also to empower and inform.

Grown and Sexy: *TJMS* Parties with a Purpose

The many *TJMS* celebratory institutions—the earlier Sky Shows, the annual Fantastic Voyage, and the Labor Day Family Reunion—parallel *TJMS* language ideology. They were designed simultaneously to raise charitable funds, to draw in younger listeners while providing them with college scholarships, and to sediment a "Grown and Sexy" political aesthetic through which adult to middle-aged working-/middle-class black Americans defined themselves as physically attractive, fun-loving, intelligent, and progressive. (Originally, you had to show a voter registration card for entry to a Sky Show. If you weren't registered to vote, tables were set up and ready to register you right there.) Thus "getting in the groove" asserts black adult aesthetic engagement, personal self-confidence, and social responsibility.

Ironically, the "grown and sexy" (G&S) phrase actually derives from rap—specifically, from a line in Jay-Z's 2003 song, "Excuse Me Miss," in which he intones: "This is for the grown and sexy, only for the grown and sexy."[39] Two years later, singer/songwriter Babyface produced an album simply named *Grown and Sexy*.[40] Use of the phrase quickly became ubiquitous among black Americans, specifically for generational boundary-drawing purposes. G&S indicates the assertion of adult status, clothing, music, comportment—and often for the quiet, rather than flamboyant, assertion of financial well-being. The online "Urban Dictionary" beautifully sums up the grown and sexy gestalt:

Ebonics for: "Don't even think of showing up at my function in
in baggy jeans, Air Jordans, platinum chains, bandanas, and 3x white t-shirt. If you're not custom tailored, Armani or Versace—stay your ass home! . . . Also unless it's neo-soul, rare groove, or old school-you won't hear it here. Want radio hip-hop? Go to that white kids' club in the suburbs . . . And approach a Sista' with a little finesse. Leaning up against your homies' Escalade does not constitute "having game" . . . feel me?"
RADIO ANNOUNCER: "FUNK JAZZ WEDNESDAYS at the ICE HOUSE LOUNGE in downtown. Doors open at 10PM.This party is for the GROWN AND SEXY."
#mature #sophisticated #upscale #tight #hip vibe[41]

Thus a rap phrase became common currency among adult black Americans, and came, bizarrely, to signify the exclusion of rap and hip-hop as "white kids'" music, the glorification of black adult/middle aged music—"neo-soul, rare groove, or old school"—and the assertion of the superiority of responsible age over careless youth, of finesse over flamboyance.

The *TJMS* special events, cruises, and family reunions exemplified this adult musical/social responsibility aesthetic. The free 2012 "Take a Loved One to the Doctor Health Festival" in Philadelphia flaunted guest experts like U.S. Surgeon General Dr. Regina M. Benjamin, White House chef Sam Kass, and a range of black physicians, as well as middle-aged comics Dominique and Damon Williams, "old school" singers like Johnny Gill and Monie Love (who is a hip-hop artist but graduated to old school through the aging process), and gospel singer Tamela Mann.

The 2013 Family Reunion in Orlando, Florida (regularly sponsored by Allstate), featured a free family expo with guest gospel, R&B, and hip-hop artists, and a range of politicians and pastors. There was a "Represent Night," in which families were encouraged to wear their own family reunion t-shirts, and a "White Night," where everyone wore all-white clothing. Most moving was the "We Are One Family Town Hall Forum"—a year after Trayvon Martin's death—which featured Trayvon Martin's parents, Sybrina Fulton and Tracy Martin, and their attorney Benjamin Crump, as well as a Florida state senator, and U.S. Congresswoman Corinne Brown. Also featured were neosoul artists Lyfe Jennings and Raheem DeVaughn.

The 2014 Family Reunion included a full complement of neosoul stars—Tank, Kem, Joe, Babyface—the O'Jays founder Eddie Levert, as well as gospel artists Smokie Norful, Yolanda Adams, Tasha Cobb, and James Fortune. Al Sharpton and progressive radio host Michael Baisden were on hand to provide political heft.

The 2016 "Tom Joyner Foundation Fantastic Voyage" (sponsored by Ford) was an extraordinary entertainment blowout. It celebrated the twenty-fifth anniversary of the film *Five Heartbeats*, with all the original cast members, and included three cast members from the classic black television comedy *Good Times*. The musical lineup ranged across old and new school: Diana Ross, Patti LaBelle, Charlie Wilson (from the Gap Band, in his second career); neosoul singers Jazmine Sullivan, Angie Stone, and Vivian Green; "Golden Era of Hip-Hop" stars, including Rakim, Big Daddy Kane, and Rob Base; West Coast hip-hop stars Bone Thugs-N-Harmony and DJ Quick; and a Gospel Explosion with a rich array of star singers—Pastor Shirley Caesar, Hezekiah Walker, LeAndria Johnson, Tamela Mann.

Every year, the crew hyped these events for months, while simultaneously recognizing that they were often beyond the financial reach of many in their audience. They offered payment plans, and frequently suggested room-sharing to cut costs. Thus the inherent contradiction within the "grown and sexy" frame—you can be a responsible, fully employed adult, with excellent politics and musical taste—and still be broke.

Finally, being grown and sexy also means you can and should use your biting wit against anyone—including your radio show crew—and that they should take, with good humor, what they dish out:

(*January 25, 2005*) *Crew discusses Oscar nominations. J asks, "Anything for*
    Drumline? [*He was in the film*] *Best fat man in a purple shirt?* [*crew laughs*]
Sybil: Oh, there is a nomination: Quickest to video! [*all laugh*]
. . .
J: Is there a nomination for best bootleg?
Sybil, wrapping up the shade: That would be Drumline.
(*July 6, 2102*) *Tom reads woman's text at end of show: Dang, Tom Joyner! You*
    jamming like you got **hair** *this mornin!*

Even a solemn discussion can degenerate into a cutting session on the *TJMS*:

(*April 10, 2013*) *The documentary on the exoneration of the Central Park 5*
    has just come out. Huggy mentions it, and then a texter opens the door to the
    onslaught:
"Tom, did you see Reverend Al in the documentary?" [*crew goes wild, describing*
    Sharpton's former appearance—fat, gold medallions, the long permed hair]
J: I got to see it **just for that**!

"Church Mess": Threading the Needle on Religion

The *TJMS*, as we have seen, departed from the black-church piety of Tyler Perry's many film and television projects, and of a variety of other black popular cultural vehicles. At the same time, they threaded the needle across the observant Christian/ agnostic/atheist range through crew declarations and *en passant* references. Through them, over the years, it became clear that Sybil is churchgoing, Tom a backslider, and J an atheist—"I'm good without God!"

But J always also made it abundantly clear that he grew up in the black church, is more than familiar with biblical teachings and black sermonic conventions, and is profoundly critical of the crazier fringes of Christian evangelicalism—and of Christian hypocrisy. When a woman Sunday school teacher called in to report, on May 3, 2005, that she was telling her children that the Second Coming was close, J responded flatly:

How close? I heard that fifty-three years ago, is it any closer now?

And J also repeatedly claimed that evangelical Christians were particularly likely to break Biblical sexual commandments:

*(October 21, 2005) Sky Show in Tallahassee. J to particularly wild audience dancer: What in the **hell** is that!? . . . What church you go to, with your **nasty self**? Cause I always say: the bigger the Christian, the bigger the freak!*

And thus also J's hilarious but short-lived character, "The Reverend Richard Adenoids III," who intoned wildly offensive announcements in a comic black ministerial voice to the backdrop of black church organ music[42]

(May 2, 2005) We have free tickets for the hit play, "Dark-skinned Women Who Act Siddity." Anyway! [crew catcalls] Free tickets for "The Blacker the Berry, the Bigger the Butt." [laughter and protest] Old men with earlobes the size of hams will meet in room . . . Anyway!

(June 27, 2005) Lost line in the Last Supper: One of the disciples said, I may be out of line, but I sure would love a deviled egg!"

(October 24, 2005) Today's church announcements are brought to you by Pauline's Pigfeet Pizza . . . People who can draw flies will be meeting in room 4.
Sybil: J, you are going straight to hell!
J: We have a bible verse . . .
Crew: From?
J: The Last Supper . . . When one of the disciples said to the waiter: Are yall hirin, cause this thing aint payin!
Sybil: Oh my gosh, Mr. Brown, your rocket is waiting!

The crew, circa 2015, inaugurated a wonderful comic bit—"Church Mess"[43]—J or Tom would chant, barker-like, what may have been intended to be the *Batman* introduction—"DA DA DA DA DA DA—*Church mess!*" and then savor an account of the latest scandal or outrage from televangelists, like Creflo Dollar begging for donations to fund his own personal jet, or the missteps of little-known local pastors and their families, reported with relish by alert listeners nationwide:

> *(December 7, 2015)*
> *Texter: Our church mess is from the pews. Our pastor's wife sings extremely loud and tries to out-sing the choir. Everyone complains about it but no one will talk to her. What should I do?*
> *Tom: Everyone should sing louder and wrong-er than she does!*

Nevertheless, the *TJMS* frequently played contemporary gospel, and hosted guest pastors like the highly successful T. D. Jakes. Tom and Sybil often jousted over whether talking with pastors and playing gospel on-air "counts as church" for the backsliding host.[44]

Hard Times Black

The 2008 recession, as we would expect, ramped up the *TJMS* and audience commentary—again, primarily from the perspective of working- and middle-class people. Early on, Tom did announce that "our revenue is down probably 60%" (January 28, 2009). And the crew was aware of and commented on the ongoing, and accelerating, decline of hard-copy newspapers and magazines:

> *(April 3, 2009)*
> *Tom: And have you seen* The Chicago Tribune *lately?*
> *Sybil: It's **thin**!*
> *Tom: It's like a pamphlet!*

But overall the show focused on ordinary people falling on hard times, and both crew and audience worked to eke black [in both senses] survivors' humor from the disaster.

> *(Same day)*
> *Tom Joyner: Oh man, all these layoffs! Ten thousand at Corning Glass yesterday? . . . So what's doin well?*
> *J: Liquor stores are doin well—lines around the block!*
> *Tom: Breastaurants, like Hooters . . . McDonalds . . . soup . . . lipstick! How much is a tube of lipstick?*

Sybil: Oh gosh, it varies.

Tom: Anybody can afford a tube of lipstick and feel better.

Sybil: Just ask J!

Tom: I have a friend in the business [strip clubs] and he says men are coming in just to eat from the buffet!

(January 29, 2009) Tom: Oh man, the economy is really bad out there . . . if you have a good job, don't leave. Not even to go potty! Cause somebody might be in your chair when you get back!

(January 30, 2009) Crew asks, "In this recession, what's been laid off?"
Caller: Fruit got laid off from Fruit of the Loom!

J: [laughs] And you know the grape got laid off first! They laid off the brother first!

Texter: [banal but predictable] My wife laid off the sex in our marriage.

Texter: [brilliant, mordant humor] The KKK had to lay off a K. They couldn't afford the sheets!

Tom: This just in! Speakin of layoffs, if you go to a Superbowl party, you just get the chips. You have to bring your own cheese!

Then they play Jazmine Sullivan's fabulous 2008 neosoul hit, "Bust Your Windows"—"I bust the windows out your car, And no, it didn't mend my broken heart."[45]

Tom comes back on: This just in! Due to the cutbacks, women are usin the same brick to bust out cars. Then they have to pass it on!

Sybil and J laugh and catcall.

And the *TJMS* presciently reported on the necessity of re-regulation of the financial industry, years before the 2010 passage of Dodd-Frank, and then the 2011 founding of the Consumer Financial Protection bureau:

(March 28, 2008) Jacque Reid has Lynette Khalfani—"ask the Money Coach"— on to discuss the ripple effect in the economy of the subprime mortgage crisis.

She asks her: "Well, if President Obama fired Bernanke and appointed you, what would you do?

Khalfani: I think [what's necessary is] government regulation of the mortgage and banking industry. [she goes on to describe the general issue of predatory lending] It's going to take a multi-pronged approach.

The *TJMS* audience provided a running commentary on the "when Americans catch cold, blacks get pneumonia" riff:

*(October 8, 2008) Let me tell you how black people know the economy's goin bad—it's **cold** all over the house!*

And even when Clear Channel, possibly for political reasons, yanked *TJMS* off the air in Chicago, a few months after the 2008 election, listener reaction underlined the working-class nature of the base audience:

(March 29, 2009)
Tom: Just got a text from Chicago postal workers—they're upset!
J: Oh dang, that's a group you do NOT want to upset!

Four years later, Sybil announced that the U.S. government was considering abolishing Saturday mail delivery as a cost-cutting measure (February 6, 2013). While MSNBC's Ed Schultz covered the story better at the time, focusing on the fact that the USPS is self-funding and only in financial trouble because Congress forces it to over-fund its own pensions, the *TJMS* crew did respond in terms of both stressed workers and customers. First Tom worried about reduced delivery cutting into postal workers' checks. Then, the next day, the whole crew spent time fussing over the possible consequences of no Saturday deliveries for Social Security, disability, and other fixed-income recipients—"What if the first of the month falls on a Saturday, And Monday is a holiday?"

And even comic Sheryl Underwood, a lifelong Republican, would swing into action on union rights:

(December 4, 2010) Sheryl criticizes the Senate for holding up the appointment of
*   a TSA chief "because the very qualified candidate is a **Negro**, and for collective*
*   bargaining—which is our right as Americans! Tom, am I right, don't police and*
*   firefighters and pilots all have those rights?"*

As well, the *TJMS* covered Detroit's long bankruptcy agony from the perspective of working-class black Detroiters being denied their pensions and city services.

(February 24, 2014)
Tom: I feel so sorry for the retired people in Detroit whose pensions are bein cut!
Sybil: You work hard all your life and—the one thing you think you can count on!

Even when celebrating African Americans' heft as consumers, the *TJMS* always circled back to the majority who are struggling:

(March 27, 2009)
Sybil gives a detailed report: In four years, black Americans will be spending a tril-
*   lion dollars a year. Thirty percent of black consumers are under eighteen, and*
*   70% of sales are online. "Black Americans are strong consumers."*
Tom: Just think what it would be if we were all employed!

Crew segues to a discussion of black unemployment, which has been consistently twice that of whites since the 1940s.[46]

The morning of November 8, 2008, the horrible economic realities too many African Americans face came home to the show: a man called in from Holland, Illinois, and said that he was suicidal. Tom exclaimed, pained: "Don't play, man!" But the man was not playing. He had been out of work for a very long time and his wife had abandoned him. The crew asked him had he tried a church, while they scurried around off-air and found him a life coach. He and the life coach returned to the air on November 20, and he reported on his recovery process and the daily prayers he was saying. They played the segment over a background of slow gospel numbers.

Working-Class Boomer Nostalgia

We have seen Adolph Reed's disgust with the narcissistic bourgeois nostalgia of some black baby boomer writers and filmmakers—their representations of past worlds in which their relatives were leaders, local aristocracy, with no analysis of or compassion for the majority of poor and working-class African Americans inhabiting those same past worlds. But the *TJMS*'s uses of boomer nostalgia were utterly distinct. They were staged entirely from the unheralded bottom rungs of the black American past. Theirs is the nostalgia of anti-respectability politics, a nostalgia for their youth in past working-class worlds.

One recurrent, hilarious example of this "Alternate Boomer Nostalgia" was the crew's creation of a category, Country Fun, meaning what did you—the largely middle-aged to elderly listener—and other kids around you do to amuse yourselves in your impoverished rural Southern childhood?

> *(April 10, 2012) Crew does riffs on Country Fun: watching bugs fly into the bug-zapper on the front porch. This then stimulates a mass of texters:*
> —*Using an old mattress for a trampoline*
> —*Wearing your long johns and putting a towel around your neck and calling yourself Super N-Word*
> —*Hiding grandma's teeth, then going outside and listening outside the window while she cusses!*
> —*Rolling down the hillside inside a tire—and I'm a girl!*
> —*Using a broomstick as a horse*
> —*Hitting a hornets' nest and seeing who can get home without getting stung*
> —*Hearing on the school intercom that the hogs got out and we've gotta go home and catch'em*

(June 21, 2012) Returning to the topic:
—Skatin on watermelon rinds
—After butcherin a hog, blowin up the bladder for a ball

(June 27, 2012) And more:
—Takin turns pullin each other across the yard on an old piece of vinyl!

Country Fun reflects the realities of the ongoing American "black belt" population in the Southern and Southeastern states, as well as the Southern origins of the
waves of black Great Migration[s] to northern cities.[47] And it reflects the fact that
those regions—the black belt and the industrial North and Midwest—were the base
of the *TJMS* audience. The crew—in this case, respectively, Alabama- and South
Carolina-born Tom and J, the very northern, urban, and middle-class Sybil con-
spicuously left out—imagined black Americans their age, with their working-class
Southern-roots backgrounds, unashamedly remembering less than elite childhood
activities. Activities marked not only by class and often rurality but by the clever use
of the scant materials at hand to fashion amusement. As American Studies scholar
Farah Jasmine Griffin has written: "The South . . . continues to be a place that suffers
from a racist legacy. Nonetheless, it is also a haven of African-American history and
community, a site of the ancestor, and for some African-Americans, it is still home."[48]

Being "country," then, carries a range of meanings on the *TJMS*—some, as we
have seen, very positive, others less so—one of dozens of characteristics ripe to be
comically sent up:

(January 4, 2006) Ms Dupre: If your slogan for the New Year is "More grits in
*2006," then you **country**.*

In the earlier *TJMS* years, a frequent visitor, the elderly "Mrs. Leonard,"
represented both "country," with her quavering Southern accent, and the crew's
amusing but often ditsy parental generation. Mizz Leonard, as Sybil, always her sole
interlocutor, pronounced her name, was in fact actor Kevin Woodson, the "man of
a thousand voices," who also played Melvin. She was delightful, as was Sybil's elaborately polite respect for her elder:

(October 23, 2005)
Mizz Leonard: There wasn't so much history when I was a young girl!
Sybil: Yes, ma'am.
And they got that TNN or whatever, on all day and night.
*Sybil: That's **CNN**, Mizz Leonard.*

But Alternate Boomer Nostalgia doesn't necessarily have to invoke "country." It
could just be "back in the day," as in the crew's query to their audience on October
31, 2016, about "back in the day" Halloween costumes:

Texter: We had to dress up as Bible characters!

*Texter: We were so poor, I would have to put on my big brother's clothes, and go as **him**.*

Or it could be "old-school," as we have seen, and in this delicious vignette:

(April 20, 2005) Tom, to caller, What's your name?

Woman caller: Willie Autry! [squeals with happiness]

J: That's old-school!

*Tom: It **is**! Is your name Willie Mae?*

*Caller: It **is**!*

All: Delighted with themselves and their superior state of old-schoolness.

But the crew would also simply lament, with their unique snark, the inevitable processes of aging and death:

(July 26, 2005)

Tom: Another one of the Four Tops died . . .

J: Not good on the marquee: "One Top"

*Tom: Man, they're falling right and left! Man, there's only six singers **left**! . . . Call the O'Jays, see if they OK in this heat.*

J: [laughing] Bring them some water!

. . .

Discussion on being "old-school":

Tom, pretending to be a questioner: So were you on the bus with Rosa Parks?

J: Yes, Sybil, we get damned tired of that!

Sybil [milking the joke, wonderfully enjoying her relative youth to the utmost]: What was it like? That first experiment with the peanut?

"These Children!" Pissed-Off Black Boomers

Age and class came together in the prototypical ways in which the *TJMS* and their audience construed the generation gap. We have seen the "grown and sexy" framing, and Myra J's repeated assertion of mothers' authority over children, of the necessity of discipline and rules. The crew as a whole certainly framed "kids today" in the classically cranky—generation after generation is the same—American adults' complaints about present-day youth ease and privileges: how they should better appreciate parents' efforts for them. But they and their audience added a particularly working-class African American flourish, a bite, to that well-trodden comic pathway. These are hard-pressed, witty, pissed-off black boomers.

(August 2, 2005) Today's question is, "What is on your back to school list that your child must have?"

Woman caller, obviously enraged: This child wants a brand new damn car! She's sixteen, just startin to drive. And she wants not just any old car. She wants a 2003 or better!

J: My mama did not have these problems! We didn't even dare show her the pictures in the Sears catalogue!

Male caller: J, I feel your pain! In the early 70s, I asked my Daddy for a pair of Converse and he told me I was a fool! And now my son wants a pair of shoes called Air Force that cost $130!

Woman caller, exasperated: They are eleven and fourteen. The eleven-year-old needs a Palm Pilot and the fourteen-year-old needs a laptop. Mama doesn't have a Palm Pilot!

Sybil: How many names does a Palm Pilot hold?

Caller: About 1500.

Sybil: And how many friends does she have?

Caller: About three!

Sybil: Mama, run the numbers for her!

The crew could wax downright vindictive in their commentary on ill-behaved or criminal children and teenagers.

(October 6, 2010) Crew discusses forty-five-year-old Memphis man who was annoyed with teens wearing sagging pants, and shot at them.

Tom: And I know the question—did they pull up their pants?

*J: **Hell** yeah!*

(May 23, 2005) The crew discusses a video repeatedly shown on television news of an old male bus driver physically retaliating against the child passengers who had been hitting him:

Tom Joyner: They keep showin it over and over and we just love it! That bus driver!

J: Oh man, there's two kinds of people, the old and the scared. They will snap!

Tom: This old man, he gets it straight, baby!

*J: Sometimes you just have to **choke** a child!*

(January 3, 2006)

Tom: Washington, DC . . .

Sybil: Not good news.

Tom: Former Mayor Marion Barry was robbed at gunpoint . . . after giving some youts

J instantly interrupts: Youts!?

Tom: Like My Cousin Vinny—a few dollars for helping him carry his groceries.

J: His kente wallet!
Tom: He's a man of the community, and the community robbed him.

(March 31, 2009) Tom reports on a school secretary who got into trouble for
    beating a third-grader with a belt.
Long radio silence.
*Sybil: Well, **somebody** had to!*
Crew goes on to talk about the smack that kids talk today, etc.

And the *TJMS*'s sympathy for baby boomers victimized by youth was broad-based, transracial—not just for black Americans. The crew commented pointedly and sympathetically, on June 22, 2012, on the viral video of a *white* school bus monitor, Karen Klein, being remorselessly hectored by foul-mouthed students.[49] And their sympathy for all teachers was very broad-based. On January 11, 2018, Sybil went on an extensive rant about the poor *white* Vermilion Parish, Louisiana, schoolteacher who was arrested and handcuffed for asking a question at a school board town hall[50]:

> *She wasn't even a black woman! She was protesting the supervisor getting a raise,*
>   *and teachers hadn't gotten raises in forever. It was unbelievable! Even the gov-*
>   *ernor said that nothing in her behavior warranted that.*

And working-class black boomer nostalgia can also simply involve musing on the extraordinary technological, economic, environmental, and cultural shifts of the last several generations, and thus young people's ignorance of children's ordinary life experiences in earlier decades:

(February 8, 2018) Question to listeners: What will your kids never experience?
Texter: The one thing my child will never experience is eating the big hot pickle with
    the candy inside!
My kids will never experience a woman with real eyelashes!
My kids will never see the candy lady's house . . . [crew beside themselves with
    memories of various cities' "candy ladies"]
Jumpin double dutch and singin the songs
Runnin to the Good Humor truck or Mr. Softee ice cream
Makin money by collectin bottles for the deposit
Stayin out til the streetlights come on
Rotary dial phones!
My kids will never get that Sears or JC Penny catalog
Kym, Sherri, Sybil, in unison: And Spiegels!
Puttin lightning bugs on our ears for earrings!

And audience members were not behindhand in commenting on the difference age makes:

> (April 17, 2013) I appreciate you so much more now that I'm in my thirties. It allows me to learn, laugh, and live better!"

Alternate Boomer Nostalgia, of course, also encompasses musical memories, the soundtracks of the lives of black (and some soul-music obsessed other) Americans of a specific class and age range:

> (December 5, 2012) A texter responds to the TJMS playing the late Charles Brown's 1947 black classic, "Merry Christmas Baby":[51] "I remembered how my Aunt Bea used to call my Daddy and sing that song to him, tipsy. Good memories!

> (October 21, 2014) The crew is broadcasting from Macon, Georgia. They discuss a James Brown exhibit, and recount admiring tales of Otis Redding's performances.
> J says: "He invented skinny jeans, man! And they were shiny!" [they then play a medley of Redding's hits]
> Texter, specifying his deep nostalgia: I just had a Crown Royal moment!

And Alternate Boomer Nostalgics can also be insufferably smug about their superior Grown&Sexy musical taste:

> (October 30, 2014) The crew report that a new Nielsen survey of "conscious consumer" black American musical preferences indicates that they choose R&B first, at 34%. Next in popularity is gospel, then hip-hop, with rap in final place. The crew loudly gloat, then joke that rap and hip-hop are "really R&B" because they steal [sample] from it so much.
> Texters then weigh in, complaining, "What about jazz?" Tom pretends to be a cool jazz DJ, then segues to the very un-jazzy soul-pop El DeBarge's "After the Dance."[52]

The crew would also eat its own for comic relief on the "generation and music" issue. In August 2005, when Little Milton died, Tom and J discovered that the decade-younger Sybil didn't know who he was, and teased her mercilessly. Again, on October 16, 2013, it came out that she had never heard of The Meters [the original New Orleans Neville Brothers band], and she was, quite rightly, subjected to withering disdain.[53] January 14, 2014, they posed the question: If there were a cruise [as in their annual charity event] with entertainers "who have passed on," who would you invite?

Tom: Oh, that's easy! James Brown, Luther, Marvin [Gaye], Gerald [Levert], Michael [Jackson], Johnnie Taylor and Tyrone Davis!

Sybil then admitted, astoundingly, that she'd never heard of Johnnie Taylor or Tyrone Davis, and she got it in the neck again.[54] (I'm not even going to mention all of the late *female* greats Tom might have listed.)

Alternate Boomer Nostalgia also encompasses Black Boomer Cussedness in protesting the substitution of white music in "black space":

(February 3, 2006) The crew is discussing the Superbowl.
Tom Joyner: How crazy is that, you gone come to Detroit and you don't have **Motown**? *You have The Rolling Stones!?*

And they would claim classic, untouchable status for certain black cultural productions, often not the most transcendent:

(August 2, 2017) They report that a country and western singer has covered Sir Mix-a-Lot's "Baby's Got Back." They play a segment.
Tom: That's sacrilege!
Comic Bill Bellamy, imitating Lionel Ritchie from the Commodores: "That song has no va-yuh!"

But the crew will happily contradict themselves on blue-eyed soul issues. On March 5, 2010, they threw themselves enthusiastically into a fake announcement, in the style of late-night television infomercials for oldies music, and then just kept sucking dry the self-mocking joke:

Tom: Bad Boy Records [a rap label founded by Sean "Diddy" Combs][55] presents the first compilation of White Songs Black People Absolutely Love! . . . Hall & Oates, The Rolling Stones, Elton John . . . .
But there's more! Act now and we'll throw in a CD of white songs black people listen to with the windows rolled up! [They cited the Beach Boys' "California Girls." I identified with this one, as a literal California girl, with deep embarrassment, although I'm much fonder of "Good Vibrations" and "Sail on Sailor."]

And Black Boomer Cussedness, as we have seen in the *TJMS* characterization of Eminem vs. The O'Jays, includes the castigation of "these kids'" failures to understand soul music and its history, and their assertion that old-school musicians were more skilled and hard working. Eminem came in for more harassment, and assertions of black superiority, when comic Dominique commented brilliantly on his claim that he forgot his lines in a concert because of taking the sleeping medication Ambien:

*(October 19, 2011) Rock'n roll, sex and drugs, that's what it **called**. How you gon say it's Ambien? . . . DMX done **crank**, an **he** remember **his** lines!*

(January 3, 2006) Discussing the late singer Phyllis Hyman.
Tom: I would say, in her day, Phyllis Hyman was the Beyoncé of her time.
Sybil: Beyoncé's gonna kick your butt! Next time she sees you . . .

(January 18, 2006) Crew plays a magnificent funk song.
Tom Joyner: That song has got to be thirty, thirty-five years old. [It was then actually twenty-six years old, but who's counting?] And it still holds up! "Take Your Time" by the SOS Band.[56]
*Sybil, world-weary: But do they **listen**?*

(March 8, 2006) They play Alicia Keys's 2003 title track song, "Diary/Secrets."[57] *At the end, she intones, with falling melismatic intonation contour, "Bring it down," the volume falls, and the song ends in a piano solo. But the crew mistakenly heard her say "Break it down" (I did as well, and only discovered the actual line through searching the song's lyrics):*
Tom: That's not a breakdown! Someone's got to tell Alicia what a breakdown is!
Crew rings changes on breakdowns—"A real breakdown is, 'Let me talk to you a little bit.' If Gladys [Knight] was here, she'd say . . ."
Tom, theatrically: These children! These children!

At times, though, the *TJMS* simply notes its audience's adult/middle-aged status, and invites listeners to share with them their rueful awareness of the coming of old age:

(January 23, 2006) Express Yourself: What's the "old people" thing you find yourself doin?
Steve: I find myself drivin slow—in the fast lane—and I'm only thirty-three!
Georgia from Birmingham: When my knees catch up with my body when I get up in the morning!
Teresa from Detroit: Gargling with Listerine!
This is Miriam from Indian Head [probably Maryland]: When I walk in a room and I don't know why I'm there!
Patricia from New Orleans: I'm pullin hairs outta my chin!

Two moving *TJMS* vignettes illustrate its "community of the air" fusion of black celebrity culture, middle-aged working-classness, and beautifully unashamed male African American sentimentality: After Whitney Houston died in 2012, the *TJMS* dedicated the entire show to her, and played her posthumous duet with R Kelly, "I Look to You":[58]

(February 13, 2012) Two separate male truck drivers text in that they had to park on the side of the road because hearing the duet made them burst into tears. Then a listener texted in that a [black] policeman started crying, while writing her a ticket, listening to the duet on her car radio.

On the fiftieth anniversary of Martin Luther King Jr.'s assassination, April 4, 2018, the *TJMS*, as they did for every anniversary, put together a beautiful mashup of appropriate music, news accounts, and MLK speeches. A texter wrote in that

I'm a U.S. Marine, and that tribute had me cryin like a three-year-old!

Another offering showcases listeners' sophisticated, witty responses to "fine" black celebrities, simultaneously sending up "old-school" behavior:

(February 9, 2012) Woman texter: When Denzel [Washington] was on, I was tryin to throw my panties through the radio!

Finally, in a rational attempt to draw in "these children" as an audience, despite their annoyance with them, in 2012 the *TJMS* created a regular DJ mashup they called "Old School/New School," in which soul or funk classics were mixed with recent hits. This mix was extremely popular with the *TJMS* audience, precisely because it allowed parents to enjoy music with their children:

(May 8, 2012) Old School/New School: DJ Steve Silk Hurley mixes Chaka Khan with Drake.
Texter: I really love the mix you just played . . . I'm singin the Chaka part, the only part I know—and my son's singin Drake!

Sometimes the *TJMS*'s best efforts to expand their youth audience didn't work, though. Trina, a clerical in her twenties, like many younger black Americans, told me in 2016 that she used to listen to the *TJMS*, but didn't any longer: "It was always inspirational, helping the youth and all that. But I don't listen anymore. Because I'm younger. I only did it cause my *Mom* was in the car and she made me!"

TJMS Celebrity Politics with a Twist

As we have seen, the *TJMS* paid a great deal of attention to black celebrities and to celebrities in general. But it did so in a particularly progressive black way. The crew solemnly noted the birthdays, deaths, and the death anniversaries of both

American and South African civil rights leaders—W. E. B. Du Bois, Rosa Parks, Martin Luther King, Jr., Malcolm X, Coretta Scott King, Mildred Loving (of *Loving v. Virginia*), Supreme Court Justice Thurgood Marshall, Julian Bond, Andrew Young, Congressmen John Lewis and Elijah Cummings, Nelson Mandela, Bishop Desmond Tutu, etc.—and of a variety of black artists and intellectuals—poet Gwendolyn Brooks, historian John Hope Franklin, writer Maya Angelou, singers and musicians like Millie Jackson, Fats Domino, Curtis Mayfield, Bob Marley, Nancy Wilson, Charlie Parker, Marvin Gaye, James Brown, Luther Vandross, Michael Jackson, Gerald Levert, Bobby Blue Bland, B. B. King, Sarah Vaughn, Dinah Washington, Eartha Kitt, Lou Rawls, Prince, Chuck Brown, Donna Summer, Natalie Cole, Whitney Houston, Tyrone Davis, Little Milton, Bobby Womack, Maurice White (of Earth, Wind & Fire), Chairman of the Board, Aaliyah, Dennis Edwards (of the Temptations), Marvin Junior (lead singer for The Dells), Clyde Stubblefield; gospel great Edwin Hawkins, actor Sidney Poitier, singer and actor Della Reese; comics like Richard Pryor, Bernie Mac, Charlie Murphy, Nipsy Russell, and Dick Gregory; iconic radio DJs like DC's Petey Greene; *Soul Train* founder Don Cornelius; and playwright August Wilson. Thus they created a uniquely "black calendar": We were led to memorialize black political sacrifice and achievement, and African American artistic creativity, all the year round, and to punctuate our days, weeks, and months through that remembrance.

That memorialization could also take comic forms, as did Tavis Smiley's very witty takeoff on Michael Jackson's child endangerment trial. A month after attorney Johnny Cochrane's death, Tavis claimed to have found a memo in his effects, which he proceeded to perform[59]:

(April 28, 2005)
Just because he has kids but not a wife
Doesn't mean you should send MJ up for life!
You know yall should let MJ moon-walk out of here today
I should know, I've seen worse, I had to represent OJ!

Michael Jackson's death, on June 25, 2009, was a news earthquake, a globally recognized phenomenon. But the *TJMS*, while they treated Jackson's passing solemnly, and dedicated a show to mixes of his music, also commented on the widespread mourning in their own inimitable, utterly hilarious way, folding in an acknowledgement of multiple black American worlds and the *TJMS*'s presence in all of them. This may be the wittiest piece of improvised comedy I have ever heard:

(June 29, 2009) Discussion of Michael Jackson's death
*Tom: Man, even the **thugs**! I was at a Chucky Cheese with the baby [a grand-*
*   child], and this thug was there with a thug baby . . .*
J: Thug baby!

Tom: He had a thuggish diaper ..

*J, overlapping: Oh yeah—went **real low***

Tom: And he came over and said [mimics thug] "Tom, Tom, I feel your pain, man!" Man, it says something about Michael Jackson's crossover when even the thugs—

J, inspired, instantly caps the story with a Prince reference: "When thugs cry!" [crew lost in hysterics]

The *TJMS* celebrity humor could also simply pull back the curtain on distinguished African American individuals, revealing their true down-home selves:

(February 16, 2015) Tyler Perry dishes on Oprah Winfrey's weekend party for her new television channel, OWN. He tells the crew that the very best moment was the sight of [the much feted, very dignified, elderly] actor Cicely Tyson dancing barefoot on a chair while holding a plate of greens. [crew beside themselves]

But the *TJMS* was also a comedy show with progressive politics. Thus it gave no quarter when discussing misbehaving or criminal celebrities, as we have seen with its treatment of Bill Cosby—and it was frequently cynical concerning reports of noble celebrity actions. The crew was merciless, as well, in going after rightist black politicians and celebrities.

Back during the George W. Bush Administration, for example, well-known black conservative Condoleezza Rice, who served first as Bush's National Security Advisor and later Secretary of State, came in for her fair share of well-deserved calumny. On September 10, 2001, I emailed a friend about a fabulous *TJMS* bit that combined withering disdain for Rice's anti-civil rights politics, especially given her upbringing in a Southern hotbed of segregationist resistance, and commentary on her unusual "black" name:

I just called you . . . wanted to tell you that the Joyner crowd was commenting on Condoleezza Rice coming out against reparations, with wonderful shit like "and she grew up in Birmingham! And her name is Condoleezza! She needs reparations just for that!" Then they went off on how her parents would have to go to church after the whole world saw her on "Meet the Press," and what their brethren would say to them.

They were still at it in 2005:

(January 25, 2005) The crew report with glee on Senator Barbara Boxer's (D-California) vigorous questioning of Condoleezza Rice on Bush Administration incompetence leading to 9/11—"the surgery continues!"[60]

J: It's one thing to go up in there, but Barbara Boxer's got that miner's cap on . . .

Sybil: [milking the gag] With the light . . .
J: [finishing it with a flourish] That's just not right!

Later that morning, J returned to the agony of Senator Boxer's dressing down of Rice. He simultaneously twisted the knife and yet showed some empathy, through blackening and working-classifying the notoriously rigid and withdrawn conservative diplomat. J "became" Rice, arriving home after the congressional hearings: Slamming the light on, throwing her keys on the couch, kicking her shoes across the floor . . . opening a can of wieners and eating them right from the can. Then she makes "the call," [to a presumed secret boyfriend] and says, "Come on over here right now. I've had a bad day."

Back during President Obama's first term and Michael Steele's short-lived leadership of the Republican National Committee, the crew were merciless:

> *(March 4, 2009) They assert that Rush Limbaugh is the actual head of the Republican Party, as Michael Steele was just forced to apologize to him.*
> *J: We need to send Michael Steele cases of juice. Cause he **got** none! [loud laughter]*
> *Tom: Michael Steele! He's the head of the Republican Party!*
> *J, instantly: No he's not!*
> *Tom: Michael Barbecue Steele!*
> *J: Cause they're havin him for dinner!*
> *Sybil: HMIC! He's the Head Meat in Charge! [playing on the old acronym HNIC, Head Negro in Charge]*

Supreme Court Justice Clarence Thomas was always a favorite *TJMS* target. The crew remained aghast at his passivity, his hyper-conservative politics, and his deadly effect on the Court:

> *(June 24, 2009) The Reverend Al Sharpton is on. Clarence Thomas had just voted against the Voting Rights Act.*
> *Sharpton: I just wanted to see what an Uncle Tom really looks like!*
> *Tom: Eight to one!!! The only vote against voting rights! How can a black man rise to Supreme Court justice and vote against everything that got him there?!*
> *Sharpton: It's a vote against everything that you are. That is not conservatism, that's insanity . . . J, you can't even think of a joke, can you?*
> *J, lugubriously: Not on this one.*

And for many years, during R Kelly's indictment and trial (2002–08)[61] for having sex with underage girls, Tom Joyner refused to play his music at all. Some years after the not guilty verdict, he resumed doing so. But R Kelly was always on notice with the *TJMS*:

> *(January 21, 2016) Sybil reports that R Kelly has given an open interview with GQ Magazine. He said he suffered sexual abuse as a child, and he is aligning himself with Bill Cosby.*
>
> Tom: *Do you **really** want R Kelly on your side if you're Bill Cosby?*
>
> Sherri Shepherd [guest comic]: *I just started listening to "Step in the Name of Love!" You're gonna make me **boycott** you **again**?!*
>
> [And indeed they did, on April 24, 2018, in response to a challenge from visiting #MeToo founder Tarana Burke]

On the same day, the crew both demonstrated its cynicism and skewered a right-wing black celebrity:

> 1. *Crew discusses reports of actor/singer Jamie Foxx saving a man from a burning car wreck on the street outside his house. J speculates that Foxx "set it up": "It **is** Hollywood! Maybe he had a stuntman. I've seen Jamie's house, and from the gate to his house is a loooong way!"*
>
> 2. *Crew discusses actor and Fox News commentator Stacy Dash's latest outrageous statements:*
>
> Sherri Shepherd reports that Stacy Dash said we should get rid of BET and TVONE.
>
> Tom: *For**get** Stacy Dash!*
>
> Sherri: *She better hope she stay **cute**!*
>
> J: *She gonna stay **stupid**, that's for sure!*

During the 2016 election season, Republican nominee Donald Trump fielded a tiny group of black supporters, including reality television star Omarosa Manigault (who had been on *The Apprentice*). On September 23, 2016, Sybil reported that Omarosa had asserted the day before that "they will have to bow down to President Trump."

The crew simply branded her a hopeless sycophant, with the nastiest possible language, given their ban on "cussin":

> Tom, with great disgust: *How brown is her nose right now?*
>
> J: *You can't even see it! Her head's all up in there!*
>
> Later, texter: *Omarosa's nose is plugged up! She can't breathe!*

After Trump was elected, gave Omarosa a White House job, and then ignominiously fired her, the *TJMS* had a field day.

(December 14, 2017) First Huggy Lowdown got his licks in:
Everybody and their sidechicks are talkin about Omarosa, you hear that, Tom? . . . Did you know at the barbershop, Tom, they had that "how long will Omarosa last" pool? [crew loves it]

Then they hosted journalist April Ryan, who had broken the story[62]:

Crew asks Ryan about pushback against her story?
Ryan: The Secret Service says, the Secret Service was not involved in the termination process for Ms. Manigault, nor for her escorting off the complex. The only thing they did was deactivate her pass. I stand by my story. I've been doing this for twenty years, but I've never had anyone say I'm running a vendetta against anyone . . . I was getting information from inside and outside the White House.
Crew asks, What about Omarosa's reported altercation with General Kelly? Ryan reports that her access had been cut off, she confronted Kelly and there was an altercation. She was animated, cursing, and vulgar.
Sherri Shepherd asks Ryan about the possibility of Omarosa being welcomed back into the black community. Ryan says, "I don't know. There is a disdain for her in the black community, a large-scale disdain."

And the pissed-off *TJMS* audience did not disappoint. Texters that day wittily expressed their exquisite "large-scale disdain":

Texter: With Omarosa walkin into the private residence, thinkin she's Olivia Pope!
Texter: Don't forget what happened to Chrisette Michele! [The singer who performed for a Trump inaugural ball, and was then shunned by black Americans]
*Tom, relishing the cliché: Chrisette Michele can't even draw a crowd with a **crayon**!*
Texter: Omarosa was never part of the black community! Sayin people would have to bow down to Trump was just the last straw!

Then Huggy Lowdown returned to continue the takedown. It was a Friday, the day in which he names the Bamma of the Week:

Huggy: Let's count down these contenders ten days from Christmas and the fourth day of Hanukkah!
Contender #2, I don't want to say her name, but it rhymes with I'm supposedta!

He details a significant number of Trump's words and actions with reference to race that the *New York Times* has deemed untruthful and racially insensitive—his birtherism with reference to president Obama, calling for the Central Park Five to be

Figure 4.1 Comics and newer crew members Huggy Lowdown and Chris Paul. Photo reprinted with permission from Huggy Lowdown and Chris Paul.

executed, and never apologizing when they were exonerated after spending years in jail, labeling Mexican migrants criminals and rapists, praising white supremacists—all with no response from Omarosa.[63]

Sybil joins the bit, and interjects, in her church voice: Come **on** *now!*

Then, at the beginning of her regular newscast that day, Sybil played audio of black news anchor Robin Roberts, with great relish, using Ice Cube's dismissive kiss-off phrase from the black 1995 film *Friday*: "Bye, Felicia!" Sybil characterized Roberts's summation as "the sound heard across the world."

Finally, Chris Paul contributed in true holiday mode: He murdered Jose Feliciano's wildly popular "*Feliz Navidad*," changing the phrase to "Felicia Goodbye!" The song worked wonderfully to diss Omarosa. The last lines were: "They dragged her black ass out the White House, and deactivated her key card!"[64]

Comedian and television and radio host Steve Harvey also capitulated to a meeting in 2017 in Trump Tower, and was mercilessly dogged for it. On February 21, 2017, Keegan Michael Key of the very successful comedy show "Key & Peele" was on-air plugging his new horror film *Get Out*. Comic Lavell Crawford asked him,

Is it like the Trump elevator? When black people go up and then come down it, they're all hypnotized like Steve Harvey! [crew goes wild]

When Kanye West, who has demonstrated an infinite capacity for crazy, announced his support for Donald Trump on social media in April 2018, late-night hosts quite properly roasted him. But Huggy Lowdown really nailed him, using local knowledge, on April 24, 2018:

> *Kanye West, you are the Bamma! . . . [he is now so embarrassing that] we've got* **Chicago** *people sayin they're from* **Schaumberg***! [a northwest suburb with only a 4% black population]*

But they weren't finished with Kanye. On April 26, the *TJMS* went after him again with a black flourish. Chris Paul named and shamed him:

> *Kanye's lost his mind messin round with Kardashians!*
> *No man should have all that crazy!*
> *Kanye thinks we should all forget slavery!*

When Trump appointed neurosurgeon Ben Carson Director of Housing and Urban Development, the *TJMS* crew and audience had a field day with his conservative statements that we are "beyond race" while he was busy destroying what regulations HUD had in place to ensure enforcement of fair housing laws.

> *(March 7, 2018) Ben Carson referred to black slaves as "immigrants" in his first speech to HUD employees. The TJMS is utterly disgusted with him, and the texters weigh in with witty cruelty:*
> *Tom: My favorite text this morning came from someone who said, "Yes, and the Tuskegee Experiment was the first free clinic!*
> *Next texter: Ben Carson said that hangman's nooses were just safety harnesses!*
> *Last texter: Huggy got me this morning with "HUD spelled backwards is DUH!" Perfect for Ben Carson!*

The crew also reserved particular animus for Conrad Murray, the disbarred doctor who was convicted of responsibility for Michael Jackson's death. Murray appeared on the show to publicize a book on Michael Jackson he had just published:

> *(August 5, 2016) Crew harasses Murray for his exploitation of Michael Jackson's memory. He denies it, but Sybil has read his book, and declares that "there's nothing in it that you couldn't get from the tabloids!"*
> *Audience member texts later: Dr. Murray is gonna need a surgeon to remove that foot that Sybil shoved up his butt!*

The *TJMS* would also attack black celebrities they deemed embarrassing:

(May 2, 2012) Sybil announces that Deion Sanders and Bobby Brown are on Matt
    Lauer [obviously, before his disgrace] and Good Morning America today.
J: What's this, ig'nt black men day? On morning news shows?

But as we saw in the first chapter, the *TJMS* also paid attention to white celebrities, in a variety of ways. They very much like CNN news anchor Anderson Cooper, for example, particularly after his serious, on-site, activist coverage of the Katrina disaster in 2005. But when gossip sources reported that Cooper's boyfriend had been unfaithful to him, the crew used the news both to repeat their gay rights stand—as they did, repeatedly, for Ellen De Generes—and for comic relief:

(August 13, 2012)
Crew: What'd we say? Same sex, same problems!
J, sardonically, naming the notoriously homophobic restaurant chain: Let's have
    some Chick- Fil-A and make up!
Sybil pretends to be Cooper's boyfriend: You're never here! I only see you on
    television!
*Tom, milking the joke, takes on Cooper's persona: You **knew** what I did when we*
    got together!

Former Vice President Joe Biden was always a favorite. On midterm election day 2010 (November 2), Blackamericaweb.com ran a story the point of which was that "Joe Biden *is* hip-hop." They called him an "extra cool customer," and praised his swagger, excellent clothing taste, penchant for swearing, connections to ordinary Americans, and the fact that he worked himself up the ladder from the working class.[65]

And the crew were cynical, biting, and brilliant in response to Barbara Walters's memoir, in which she revealed she had had an affair with Edward Brooke, the late black Republican Senator (1967–79) from Massachusetts[66]:

(May 28, 2008)
Tom: So Sybil, how's Barbara Walters' book doin?
Sybil: It's at the top of the best-seller list!
Tom: So when it starts droppin, she's gonna have to reveal some more dirt!....Maybe
    she had an affair with a player in the Negro League!
Sybil: Laughs wildly, then effortlessly mimics Walters' lisp to nail the joke: I
    wemembah Satchel Paige!

The *TJMS* and its audience would also note white celebrities' failures to racially integrate their projects:

> (April 25, 2012)
> Texter: *Isn't it strange that Jim Carrey never had any of his* In Living Color *people on any of his movies?*
> Sybil: *I hadn't thought of that!*
> J: *He's had **penguins** on those films, but no black people!*

The crew and guests would also confer "honorary black" status on certain white artists, by virtue of their style and substance. The comic Sinbad, for example, was visiting the show on June 28, 2007, and the subject of the now-deceased (2010) R&B singer Teena Marie[67] came up:

> I don't call Teena Marie white, man. She aint crossin, she aint passin, she's us . . .
> Joss Stone aint even close. She try too hard. Teena aint even tryin.

Another "blue-eyed soul" example: Robin Gibb, of the white Australian band the Bee Gees, well-known for their mega-hit *Saturday Night Fever* soundtrack, died May 20, 2012. On May 30, Sybil announced his memorial services. Then she muttered resentfully and under her breath,

> And they **were** a black group!

Finally, the crew and guests would occasionally protest against infotainment altogether, argue against our national obsession with celebrities and celebrity news:

> (May 5, 2005)
> Tom: *They talkin bout who Paula Abdul screwed, Pat O'Brian's dirty phone calls, and **where's Osama bin Laden?!***
> J: *Yeah!*
> Sybil: *Don't we have **deeper** issues? People are losing their jobs . . .*

> (June 3, 2007) *Jacque Reid points out that the media are all over Paris Hilton, but are not covering the story "of the black college woman, Stephanie Harris, who has been missing since Memorial Day!"*

> (February 19, 2009) *D L Hughley comments on the brouhaha surrounding the New York Post's offensive "Obama monkey" cartoon. "People need to take Obama's example, and say 'I've got things **to do**!' Why do we get upset about a cartoon . . . when major corporations knowingly let contaminated peanuts be sold? How come we don't get **just** as mad about things like that? . . . When people's lives are at stake? When corporations put profits above safety?*

(October 28, 2010) D L Hughley again: Well, Thomas Joyner, we are five days away from what looks like a transformative election in which it's likely that the Democrats will lose the House [they did] ... and all anyone wants to talk about is LeBron James and Charlie Sheen!

(November 2, 2011) Al Sharpton is lamenting American's distraction by infotainment: We need to maintain focus on the economic crisis and not be distracted by ... the fact that Kim Kardashian is getting a divorce after seventy-two hours or seventy-two days or what-evah it is [J snickers]. ... With fifteen million unemployed in this country, we have to keep our eyes on the prize and hold on!

TJMS Whiteness Studies

The *TJMS* crew thus frequently enjoyed themselves both praising and criticizing white as well as black celebrities. And in general, the show welcomed white listeners, while reserving the right to characterize white Americans humorously—part of a long black comic tradition. Elements of this tradition are the claims that whites are awkward—they (we) talk funny—as we have seen—lack rhythm and style, can't dance. They have unconscious white privilege: they tend not to be aware of external dangers, because they are so much less likely to be exposed to them than are black Americans. For that reason, they are far more likely to court danger, to engage in reckless and foolhardy activities—swimming in shark-filled waters, sky-diving.

This notion of white foolhardiness fueled endless seasonal jokes about white people's idiocy in swimming in shark-infested water:

(June 27, 2005)
Tom: So the big news today is a shark attack off the coast of Florida ...
Sybil: Yes, they say a surfer found her ... there are some thirty attacks a year ...
Tom: How many black people?
J: One or none. Black people don't do that! If your ankles get wet ...
Myra J: I'm screamin!
Tom: Black people just wade in the water, they don't go in!

(June 29, 2005)
Tom: In case you haven't heard, white people, the beach is open!
J: [megaphone voice] Back in the water, white people first!
Tom, milking the joke: And the beach is back open?
J, ending with a sadistic twist: Eat'em while they're hot!

And then there is the ridiculous "African safari trophy hunt" phenomenon, largely the province of wealthy Western white males (like Donald Trump's sons). The *TJMS* noted, on March 7, 2013, that there had been a spate of lion-killings of safari visitors. They snarkily labeled the victims, in mimicry of the National Pork Board's advertising campaign, "the other white meat."

Whites are also noteworthy for jogging in dangerous weather:

> *(November 16, 2015) Texter talks about white people out jogging while there's a weather alert.*
> *Sybil: Nothing stops white people from jogging! They're like the Post Office—neither rain nor snow nor sleet . . .*

Or the audience would just comment on white failure to dress properly for extreme weather:

> *(May 20, 2014) Texters had been calling out whites for wearing flip flops during the recent hailstorms in Chicago.*
> *Tom: Here's a white texter: "Black people wear those knit hats in August!" [crew loves it] That's fair! That's fair!*

Comic D L Hughley also played with the "foolhardy whites" stereotype to make a serious point about common dangers for black Americans and the stubbornly consistent economic discrimination they face:

> *(July 22, 2011) Commenting on people being swept off a ledge into Yosemite falls: You know how you always know it's white people? Black people get killed by drive-bys and the police, as **nature intended**! If black people want excitement, we'll apply for a home loan! [crew loses it]*

The comic Earthquake rang the same changes in commenting on his abrupt departure from the U.S. military—he quit at the point of the first Gulf War:

> *(February 15, 2007) I don't mind practicin for war, but they playin for real! I coulda stayed in DC to get shot at!*

As we would expect, the *TJMS* also lauded black parental strictness as opposed to stereotypical white laxity producing spoiled children. On March 5, 2014, for example, Tom brought up the case of the New Jersey teenager who was suing her parents for financial support after she had moved out of the house.[68] The crew was aghast:

> *J: "Uh—**white people** mess!"*
> *Crew talks about how this situation "just wouldn't happen to black people . . . Nobody could do that to a black mama!"*

The crew also used black athletic achievement and bodily strength as comic fodder, mining the white U.S. conundrum that American Studies scholar Nicole

R. Fleetwood has anatomized in her discussion of Serena Williams and LeBron James: "[O]ne of their shared characteristics is their unabashed ambition and ability to dominate their respective sports without mitigating the threat of their blackness, intelligence, and physical prowess to appease white patronage or hierarchies."[69]

> *(April 20, 2005) Black Yankees outfielder Gary Sheffield was hit in the face by a white Red Sox fan while attempting to retrieve a ball. He swiped back, then stopped himself and returned to the game.[70]*
> *Tom: You need to do this as a public service. [tell white people not to go after blacks] They get drunk, they don't know what they're doing.*
> *J: How many white people have to get knocked out before they learn?*
> *All: Uh huh!*
> *J, grandly: This has been a **public service announcement**, white people!*

But you don't have to be black for the *TJMS* to celebrate you getting your licks in against racist whites. After American boxer Rod Salka wore "America First" shorts to his April 2018 fight with Mexican boxer Francisco Vargas, Vargas beat him to a pulp.[71] The event was widely covered, but Tom's vindictive gloating at the come-uppance was of a different order. Comedian Don DC Curry was visiting the show that morning, April 16, 2018, and masterfully tied up the crew's take: White people need to be aware of the "oppression strength" that people of color can draw on when the offense is just too great.

And of course, the crew and guests played with the "black don't crack" presumption that whites age more rapidly than blacks:

> *(September 2, 2009)*
> *Comic Sheryl Underwood, discussing the relatively new technology of high definition television: "High definition is the dose of truth you **don't** want to pay!*
> *Tom: You right! [crew laughs loudly]*
> *Sheryl: And it's hardest on **white people**!*

Another common "white people" theme is their (our) stereotypical willingness to lay out cash for overpriced, overhyped commodities. Starbucks comes in for its fair share of calumny here:

> *(January 10, 2006) The crew discuss a bomb found in a Starbucks.*
> *J: And white people are still there! What does it take to make them stop goin to Starbucks?*
> *Tom: And there's a **bomb,** and they still don't drop the price of a cup of coffee!*
> *Crew goes on about being embarrassed because they claim they can't pronounce the Italian names of Starbucks drinks.*

In 2018, the crew followed the racist event in a center city Philadelphia Starbucks, in which a white female barista called the police to come and arrest two black men who had arrived early for a business meeting. A white woman videoed the incident, which went viral instantly. By the time the two men were released without charges, at midnight, they were already famous, Starbucks had fired the barista, its CEO requested a personal meeting with the men, and was scrambling to make things right to avoid a boycott/losing market share.[72]

The crew and audience had plenty of angry snark to offer:

(April 16, 2018) Tom shares a text from a woman complaining that she couldn't convince a white co-worker that the incident was racial profiling. He editorializes both sadly and jokily, "It's so hard to keep white friends nowadays!"

Sybil: "It's very simple—[say] You're **wrong**!" But she goes on to point out the white woman who videoed the event and all of the whites "who have supported black people in these situations."

Al Sharpton then reported on the National Action Network meeting in New York City that day. Yes, Starbucks had contacted them, but "Tom, you know when I was a baby, I learned the difference between pacifiers and milk . . . What we must do is go for real change! . . . When we see people being arrested for nothing in Philly, training is just a pacifier. Don't be a baby and go for the pacifier! Be part of real substantive change! . . . How you gonna teach people to deal with blacks in half a day? That's a nice first step . . . but what are you gon do institutionally with reforming the police?"

(April 20, 2018) Huggy comes on, names the now-fired barista "venti racist cappuccino."

Then they play "The Wobble," because it's Friday. One texter humorously and pointedly linked her participation to her response to the racist incident:

Doin the wobble, passin a Starbucks on my way to Dunkin Donuts!

White inability to dance, of course, is always a ripe topic for comic treatment. One listener wrote in on February 7, 2013:

Tom, I taught all my Caucasian co-workers to do the wobble. The whole white race thanks you!

But a listener texted in, on October 13, 2017, that he would be DJ-ing a high school reunion that weekend:

It's a mixed class. Tom, I have to **close my eyes** when I play the white people's music, because when I open my eyes, they're dancing **off beat**!

The *TJMS* will also joke about white ignorance of African American history and contemporary realities. When Beyoncé headlined the Coachella festival and brought down the house, the crew exclaimed over the racial explicitness of her choices—bringing in a HBCU college marching band, singing what is known as the "black national anthem"[73]:

(April 16, 2018)
Huggy: [exclaims over the excellence of her performance] Sybil, do you know how
*many white people have Shazamed that **new** song "Lift Up Every Voice and Sing"?!*
Then Don DC Curry raised the game: "She took'em to college. I heard that
Beyoncé's performance was such a black college experience that people left with
student loan debt!" [crew loves it]

But the crew, as we've seen, is meticulously honest, and sometimes the comedy turns on black audience appreciation of "white" music:

(August 18, 2014)
Texter, reporting on weekend activities: "I went to a Jimmy Buffett concert."
[Tom reads the text, and then gives a loud "Hmmmm"]
*Sybil: Oh, so **you** were the one!*
J: Somebody's datin white!

Of course, the logic can run in the opposite direction:

(October 14, 2014)
Texter: I saw a white woman bobbin her head to the [TJMS] mix in her car!
J: She's datin black!

And there is also the not uncommon phenomenon of black American ignorance of the racial status of "blue-eyed soul" performers. On October 16, 2014, for example, the breakout English soul singer Sam Smith ("Stay with Me")[74] appeared on the show, to the immense befuddlement of audience texters. They had not realized that he was A. white, B. not American, but English, and C. openly gay. No one was judgmental about any of those statuses, just sorely puzzled.

And the *TJMS* also highlighted the ongoing double standard for black versus white American behavior. The 2008 presidential race, when vice presidential nominee Sarah Palin's daughter Bristol was revealed to be pregnant and unmarried, provided a rich example:

(August 4, 2008)
D L Hughley [visiting the show]: When a white girl gets pregnant, they get a movie
and awards [likely a reference to the 2007 film Juno *and Ellen Page's Academy*

Award].[75] *When a black girl gets pregnant, they get a visit from a social worker and a pack of condoms!*

The double standard, of course, also applies both to criminal wrongdoing and academic achievement. In this vignette, the *TJMS* melds those racial facts:

(February 20, 2006) The crew discuss the discovery that the CEO of Radio Shack had falsified his resume, claiming two BAs he never received.
Tom, in high dudgeon: And there's a black man listenin to this, with a PhD. and drivin a taxi!

Black Americans are also painfully aware that to many white people, "we all look alike." The crew sedulously noted examples in public life:

(March 30, 2006)
Tom: Whippin some butt news: Let's go to Cynthia McKinney.
Sybil explains that [black] Congresswoman McKinney hit a Capitol police officer who refused to recognize her.
J: Was he white? [He was.] (World-weary): Yeah, happens all the time.
Tom and J go off on a riff about Sam's Club guards not recognizing fellow black workers.
*J: Oh, black people, **don't** assume white people remember you! . . . See, they don't have to! . . . Unless you servin food! If you've got a tray! [crew laughs and catcalls]*

The crew also sent up pervasive white fear of black people. Here they sardonically imagine a Martin Luther King, Jr., Day parade, hitting the "fear" mark straight-on:

(January 16, 2005) Mock MLK parade.
Tom: And here comes a float full of frightened white people!

But the crew weren't yet finished. They instantly moved on to the widespread assumption that black men will sleep with *any* white woman, because of the status inherent in whiteness:
*Tom: Oh look! There's the association of black men married to **fine** white women!*
Sybil: [relishing her humor] Small group!
Tom: They're in a Mini-Cooper!

Finally, the crew became violently angry—along with the rest of progressive America—at the racist calumnies against President Obama and his family, which began before he took office in 2009, and sedimented into a constant background noise from a hard-right constituency. In the following brilliantly improvised performance, Tom, Sybil, and J collaborate to wrest black—in all senses—humor from that phenomenon. They accomplished it through an extraordinary mashup—with yet another swipe at Starbucks—of commentary on the notorious American sentimentality over cute animals, and on the lower social value of blackness in humans:

> *(September 24, 2012)*
> *Tom: Oh—playa, did you see the sad news, sad news . . . uh, the baby panda died.*
> *Sybil: In—the Washington Zoo*
> *Overlaps J: This is white people news—*
> *Tom & Sybil: Yeah—J: Yeah, this is white people news.*
> *Tom: Yeah, the baby panda died.*
> *J: Yeah, they're gonna be sad today.*
> *Tom: There's gon be some* **sad** *white folks at Starbucks*
> *Simultaneously,*
> *Sybil: Ohhh my God . . .*
> *J: Yeah!*
> *Tom: I'm tellin you that right now.*
> *J: Now the* **killings** *in Chicago and around the country . . .*
> *Tom: Don't care nuthin bout that, but that baby panda die*
> *J: Man, that baby panda died?*
> *Tom and Sybil: Um-hum, sad.*
> *Sybil: That is baad.*
> *Tom: It's really really bad. [laughs sardonically]*
> *J: An he's half-black and they STILL sad*
> *[all laugh]*
> *Tom: Half-black!*
> *[All laugh again]*
> *J: An they're weird, they care more about a half-black [elongating the words] bear . . .*
> *Sybil: Than they do about a half-black man!*
> *J: A half-black president!*
> *Sybil: [laughs]—That's right!*
> *J: [falsetto laugh] Can't figure out white people, man!*
> *Tom: Can't figure'em out!*
> *Sybil: And just when you think you HAVE figured it out . . .*
> *J: Now they just LOVE the half-white panda . . . But a . . .*
> *Sybil and Tom overlap: Half-white president? Mm-mm!*
> *J: [laughing] Ain't happenin, man!*

In the tense run-up to the 2012 presidential election, elderly actor Betty White announced that she was supporting President Obama for re-election. Guest comic Dominique rang the changes on the news, both praising White and using the endorsement to comment on white racism, employing a common black religious phrase:

(May 14, 2012) Well kudos to her!—Cause 90-year-old white people, they bout **invented** racism! Guess she don't know when she gonna go, want **to get right with God!**

The issue of racist whites and their actions against Americans of color became much more serious in the age of Trump, with renewed permission from above for appalling racist behavior. On September 11, 2018, Tom asked the crew had they lost white friends because of Trump? Kym Whitely and Sherri Shepherd exclaimed that indeed, they had had to cut off a number of "clear people." A texter wrote in that "it's so hard to keep white friends nowadays!" Another wrote with passion:

I just had a colonizer [racist white person] tell me that Obama was taking credit for the economy, and that **he** was the most divisive president ever! So I **gave** it to him! But then Sybil intervened, pointing out all of the progressive whites organizing and demonstrating for antiracist causes: "There's white people who are **blacker** than **we** are!

The crew would indeed sedulously and positively attend to the lives, actions, and deaths of progressive whites. When lifelong news anchor Walter Cronkite died, in 2009, they devoted a long segment (put together by DJ Mike Stark) to Cronkite's civil rights and anti-war reporting, as well as his heartbroken announcement of President Kennedy's 1963 assassination. The audio clips, as was common in tributes to black celebrities, were backgrounded by key cuts from relevant soul hits: The Temptations underneath civil rights news, Marvin Gaye with the announcement of Kennedy's death, Edwin Starr's "War! What Is It Good For?" with anti-war reporting, "Has Anybody Seen My Old Friend Martin"—from the memorial song "Abraham, Martin, and John,"[76] with Cronkite's announcement of Martin Luther King, Jr.'s assassination.

Similarly, when actor James Garner died on July 19, 2014, Tom Joyner noted both that he was part-Cherokee, and that he had been active in the Civil Rights Movement. (He helped to fund and was a participant in the 1963 March of Washington.)[77] Joyner editorialized:

You see all this information about James Garner on TV, newspapers, and the internet, but you only see his connection to the Civil Rights Movement on blackamericaweb.com!

And back in the beginning years of the show, Joyner initiated a "bit," in honor of his highly paranoid brother—"hidden racism." That is, crew or audience members would claim to have found a new example of American racism that was so wide-spread that it was hidden in the details of daily life. They introduced the bit with an audio clip of a man intoning the phrase, heavily electronically altered, "wa-waed," to sound syncopated and ghostly. The bit allowed the *TJMS* and its huge audience to poke fun at themselves, to send up the twitchy, knee-jerk response that every single element of mainstream white life is deliberately racist:

> (July 14, 2005) Caller: Hidden racism! I want to know why all the **wheat** bread is at the back of the truck!
> (July 21, 2005)
> LeRoy calls in: "They're gonna rename the BWI airport for Thurgood Marshall, but it's 'B W Marshall.' When they renamed National Airport for Reagan, it became 'Ronald Reagan National.'"
> Tom: I see it. If it's a black man, the name comes second.
> Sybil: Oh!
> Tom: Sybil, you see it now?
> Wa-wa Machine: Hidden racism!
>
> (October 20, 2005)
> Tom: Sybil, I saw the promo for Prison Break." **No** black people! In prison??
> Sybil: Go on, now, it's . . .
> Machine: Hidden Racism!

But as we have seen, the *TJMS* had a significant white audience, and over the years I have heard a number of touching tributes:

> (January 25, 2012, the day after President Obama's State of the Union address) Tom reads: Texter, from the 832 [Houston area]: I'm a forty-two-year-old white man and I say, "That's **my** President!"
>
> (March 6, 2012) I'm a thirty-five-year-old white country boy. Country music is my favorite, but I listen to your show every morning!
> Sybil: We appreciate you!
> Tom, deeply moved: How about **that**?
> (September 21, 2016) With reference to the police killing of unarmed South Carolinian Walter Scott: I'm white, and Sheryl Underwood had me in tears this morning! I **hate** to see black people bein killed!

And white listeners will even correct the crew on racial stereotypes:

> (July 31, 2017) Crew has been discussing their assertion that it's fine that Game of Thrones and Power are broadcast against one another, because "only white people watch Game of Thrones, and only black people watch Power!"

*Texter: This white woman **loves** Power!*

And sometimes black *TJMS* listeners will report on positive encounters with whites:

*(May 30, 2014) Texter: Was drivin home in Jackson, Mississippi, was next to an elderly white lady bobbin her head. I rolled down my window and it was **you**! She said "YES! TJMS!"*

(October 7, 2016) Texter: Birth of a Nation *was excellent! The white man next to me turned around with tears in his eyes and said, "I'm sorry!" And then he left!*

Four days later, more *TJMS* listeners had white *Birth of a Nation* audience narratives:

Texter: Went to Birth of a Nation, *and white folks were breakin their necks runnin out afterwards.*

Texter: Took my white co-workers to Birth of a Nation *yesterday, and water cooler conversation was **so different** today!*

Or audience members may simply note "aberrant" white behavior and their responses to it:

(October 31, 2016) Texter: I went to see Madea [Tyler Perry's latest film] on Friday, and there were so many white people I felt like a minority!

But sometimes all the interracial goodwill just doesn't work:

(June 18, 2013) Woman texter: I broke up with a guy who said he didn't like your show because you make white folks uncomfortable! [crew exclaims in amusement, appreciates her loyalty]

I personally experienced this simultaneous "acceptance/shade" African American take on white people one afternoon some years ago. I had won free tickets through V103 to see neosoul singer Lalah Hathaway, Donny Hathaway's daughter, perform in Bronzeville, an historically black Chicago neighborhood. A former graduate student (white, in a mixed-race family) and I drove to the Southside venue and stood outside on line with hundreds of other people, all black, snaking around the building. I chatted with the women behind us in line about the glories of Luther's first hit, "Never Too Much," singing the lyrics and embarrassing my student to death. Just then, a thirty-something black woman leaned far out of the passenger window of a car driving past us on the busy street, waved her arms wildly, and shouted in high good humor, "All hail to our **Caucasian** sisters!" We were a hilarious sight, sticking out like two little marshmallows in a large cup of coffee, and she was letting us know.

"Goin Black"

And then there are "whiteness studies" versions of the multifarious ways in which the *TJMS* crew, like other African American comedians, practiced comic "blackening." First, they blackened high-status whites to highlight the lack of difference between their behavior and behavior that is stigmatized when associated with African Americans. Second, *TJMS* crew and guests would assert that white people caught in scandal often should or will "go black" to escape their situations.

A brilliant example of blackening high-status whites: After the death of Pope John Paul, and with the installation of Pope Benedict, the crew took a page from Virginia Woolf's Depression-era era critique, in *Three Guineas*,[78] of high-status male ritual peacocking, underlining the parallels between Catholic and black rap star (and *TJMS*) ritual:

> *(April 25, 2005)*
> *Tom: Playa, did you see the new Pope's installation? What a Sky Show!*
> *J: He came wid it!*
> *Tom: He blinged up.*
> *Sybil: [describes the details of the Pope's installation in the tone of the*
>   *New York Times]*
> *J: He was blingin, man.*

Or blackening President George W. Bush to highlight his lying incompetence:

> *(January 10, 2007)*
> *Tom: So President Bush will come on TV tonight and admit he made a mistake in*
>   *Iraq, but still ask for more troops?!*
> *Sybil: So, you're saying President Bush is like a **trifling brother**?*
> *J: You know it! . . . Bush is like a guy who owes you money, and comes to you sayin,*
>   *Look, I know I owe you money, but I need another twenty!*
> *[crew laughter and agreement]*

Then there was the revelation that celebrity bike racer Lance Armstrong, long lionized as both an athletic star and a cancer survivor, had taken and had perhaps even sold illegal performance-enhancing drugs.[79] The *TJMS* comically but meaningfully turned him into a ghetto drug addict/dealer:

> *(October 11, 2012) Tom: According to them, Lance Armstrong wasn't just dopin,*
>   *he was slingin!*

There are multiple examples of brilliant *TJMS* improvisations noting that well-known whites in trouble are "goin black:"

Tom Joyner announced sardonically on June 29, 2005:

Black folks had another victory in court yesterday! A big one!

Sybil: A lot of people don't realize—they see this white man in action . . .

Tom: HealthSouth. The government went in there and charged that he'd stolen some money. This white man [Richard Scrushy] went and joined a black church [Guiding Light, in Birmingham] and got him some black lawyers. . . . And when this came down on him . . .

*J: He went **black!***

Tom: Now when Tyco and Enron go up, they'd better know what's good for them!

*J: Go **black!**[80]*

And in July that year, as the Valerie Plame [CIA officer whose identity the Bush Administration purposefully leaked, thus destroying her career, in vengeance against her husband, Joseph Wilson, a career diplomat] scandal heated up, with both George W. Bush and his "brain," Karl Rove, implicated, President Bush announced that they would be attending the Indianapolis Black Expo.[81] The crew swung into action:

(July 14, 2005)

Tom: They are deep in it, playa! Over this Karl Rove stuff. So what do you do when it gets deep? You go black!

*Sybil, performing incredulity: What?! You can't go to the NAACP convention, but you can go to the Black Expo! Talkin about your economic program, which is not doing **anything** for black people!*

*J: Sybil? Have you ever **had** the black love incense? [referring to rumors that Rice was Bush's mistress, and the crew's earlier, and hilarious, claim that she had demanded he bring that and a bootleg of the latest Lil Kim CD back to her]*

When it became clear that President Obama's first appointment for Health and Human Services Secretary, former South Dakota Senator Tom Daschle, owed significant back taxes, he withdrew his candidacy. The *TJMS* imagined them both as working-class black, talking in the Oval Office:

(February 4, 2009)

*Tom: You **know** how it went! [He and J play the characters]*

Obama: So you're good, man?

Daschle: I'm straight!

Obama: No problems?

Daschle: Naaaaah.

Crew loses it, claims that whenever anyone says "Naaaah," you know there's a
  problem.
They ask: And what do you say to the press after you've embarrassed the President
  by not paying your taxes?
*J: You aint gon be-**lieve** this!*
Tom, with relish: The more white people [screw up], the blacker they get!

Similarly, during the period of the Obama auto bailout in order to save the industry during the Great Recession, the *TJMS* blackened and working-classified the auto executives coming to DC, hats in hand, begging for federal funds to save their companies:

(February 18, 2009)
Tom: They're comin back, askin for more money. It goes like this:
Obama (Tom): Hello?
Auto executive (J): Barack, what's up? Got the money. But we'll need another—I
  gonna throw five atcha. We really need seven, but I'll go with five.

Roland Martin would also get in the blackening game, as when he excoriated the Republicans during Obama's first term:

(March 3, 2009) Stop behavin like the Crips and the Bloods doin drive-bys!

Finally, white comedian Gary Owen, who married black, and who openly admits that his career took off first on BET's "Comic View," and then when Kevin Hart cast him in a number of his films, was, as we have seen, a friend of the show.[82] Part of Owen's schtick is the disjunction between people's expectations about his and his wife's families versus the actual realities: "I'm from a trailer park in Ohio!" And he plays with other black/white stereotypes—such as the notion that all African Americans, unlike whites, know how to have a good time. Owen commented on November 18, 2015:

I went to tailgates for the Bengal Lancers game. The black tailgate had an actual
  DJ, and none of the songs were about the game. And man, they were dancing,
  *they were grindin. The white tailgates were **about** the game!*

The *TJMS* insistently indicted white racism while remaining open to progressive whites, celebrated hard-working adult black Americans, and engaged in philanthropic partying. It set a race/class/gender/sexuality political groove for the nation. But how exactly did the *TJMS* actually engage in *politics*, rather than just political discourse and self-help? Let's consider the show's involvement in political struggles, in tragedies affecting black Americans, and in American electoral politics.

5

Activism, Disasters, Elections

Black Radio at Its Best

Don't forget radio or internet. McCain didn't do any radio.
—Chuck Todd, *How Barack Obama Won*[1]

... [L]istening is a dynamic historical and cultural practice, an
embodied critical sense shaping how and what we think, *and* an ethical
act shaped by our thoughts, beliefs, experiences, and ideologies, one
both subject to discipline and offering agency.
—Jennifer Lynn Stoever, 2016[2]

Broadcasting alone has a clear shaping effect on the American, or any, public sphere—and thus on what is sayable or not, believable or not, what is news or not. But various forms of media circulation are not the same as actual political activism, not coterminous with the tedious and labor-intensive actions of door-knocking, phone-calling, marching, demonstrating, meeting-going, organization-funding, voting, policy-writing, legislating, and judicial decision-making that constitute actually changing how a government functions, how people's lives can or cannot be lived.

The *TJMS* though, unlike many media platforms, constituted itself from the start as simultaneously opinion-shaping and activist. (Although they were nowhere near as seriously political in the early years—a *TJMS* ad in the *New Haven Advocate* back in 1995, when the show was one year old, touted its offerings only as "music, humor and sports.") But we have seen Tom Joyner's pre-*TJMS* interference with Texas Highway Patrol speed traps for his black constituency, and the early Joyner/Smiley battles, joined by audience members, against a variety of corporations on behalf of their African American customers.

I have labeled the *TJMS*'s politics "progressive," in the contemporary sense: broadly anti-racist, feminist/pro-LBGTQ, economically left-populist, anti-imperialist, environmentalist. And we have seen abundant examples of crew members, guests, and listeners articulating those political perspectives. But what political projects have they engaged, and have they actually *accomplished*? What exactly has *TJMS* political activism looked like? Rapper L L Cool J announced in 1985, meaning something a bit different, "I *know* I can't live without my radio."[3] How has the *TJMS* helped black Americans use radio to engage in political action?

Saving HBCUs

The *TJMS*'s most prominent form of activism is their intensive and consistent commitment to the welfare of HBCUs and their students. Since founding their HBCU fund in 1998, they have raised and distributed $65 million to 20,000 students. A twenty-something African American woman, a Howard University graduate, when informed of my project, asked me pointedly: "Are you covering how much Tom Joyner has done for HBCUs?" And Tony, the paint store manager whom we have met before, immediately pointed to *TJMS* HBCU scholarships when I asked him about the show, volunteering: "I'm an HBCU grad!" While it may seem, on the surface, that keeping black colleges solvent and awarding their students scholarships are not exactly elements of revolutionary activism, HBCUs do indeed provide a key opportunity to working-/middle-class African American students who might otherwise be discouraged from pursuing their chosen fields in mainstream public and private colleges—and thus from experiencing economic and social mobility. Xavier University in New Orleans, for example, deliberately constituted itself several decades ago as a premiere science/pre-med institution, and is responsible for a significant percentage of the younger black American doctors, pharmacists, mathematicians, engineers, and bench scientists practicing today.[4]

And thus Tom Joyner can be quite bloody-minded about payment for the cruises and family reunions. When audience members write him, pleading for discounts, he responds flatly: "Kids gotta go to college!"

As is the case into the present, the *TJMS* has always reported civil rights news, and their own political engagements, both straight, and with a humorous twist. On August 8, 2005, for example, they commented on their own participation in a march honoring the fortieth anniversary of the Voting Rights Act. The crew teased J Anthony Brown about his unsuitable "gators"—wearing alligator skin shoes rather than running shoes to the march. But Tom came to his defense:

> Tom: *I'll tell you one thing—Martin Luther King, Junior didn't march in Nikes! I've been to the museum and I've seen his suits and shoes. He marched in Stacy Adams!*
> J: *And those marchers today, they are **bigger** than the old marchers.*
> Tom: *Well, the old marchers were marchin every day, protestin something.*

The show will always treat a tragedy, however, whether at home or abroad, "straight." But their appropriately solemn reportage has an extra bite—an anti-racist, social democratic, and often anti-imperial consciousness—most often missing from mainstream media coverage.

9/11, *TJMS*, Invisible Black Victims

The national emergency and extraordinary tragedy of the terrorist attacks of 9/11 left the *TJMS* crew, like the rest of the world, horror-struck. But they quickly organized themselves to accomplish what others were not managing: focusing on racial minority victims—who were a significant percentage of those killed and were barely noticed by mainstream media—and articulating an anti-Islamophobic, anti-war perspective on the crisis.

I was not then yet actually transcribing from the show, but I did write to and talk with friends contemporaneously about the crisis—as we all did, in our shock and agony—and lauded *TJMS* programming. I was particularly struck by their efforts to get beyond know-nothing, xenophobic vengeance, and to dig into actual American Middle East foreign policy history and its role in the making of al-Qaida.

> (September 18, 2001) Black radio here has actually been great, using Marvin Gaye to forward a non-bellicose response, lots of love for one another, and bringing in ministers to criticize Bush's "dead or alive" bullshit.

> (September 20, 2001) Joyner is great this morning . . . everybody's finally on the same page re us creating Saddam, bin Laden, etc., and why "everybody hates us." If only white radio were as good!

> (Same day, different friend) TJMS discussing the special on the Taliban/bin Laden on TV last night, good focus on the blowback point, which their callers emphasize has been clear all along, just not in our media.

I have been able to piece together more *TJMS* 9/11 coverage and responses through the show's observations of each subsequent anniversary of the tragedy. Audience members, having watched television specials, would call in, as did Keeta on September 11, 2006, asking: "I just want to know, where are all the black faces of 9/11?"

> *Tom: I understand, and that's why we're here . . . when it happened, we noticed too and found and helped [9/11 victims of color]. And Reverend Al Sharpton made the point, 9/11 happened early in the morning, when all the workers had already arrived, but most of the executives and administrators hadn't. More than a third of the victims were black or minority.*

The *TJMS* crew deliberately searched out black 9/11 victims' families and aided them. On the 2006 anniversary, they honored New York City firefighter Vernon Richard, whose daughter's college tuition they had covered.[5] She came on the show to thank them, laud her father's courage, and announce that she was just starting graduate school.

The show was also consistently clear about the lack of any reason for George W. Bush's 2003 invasion of Iraq, the falsehoods flowing from the White House about weapons of mass destruction (WMDs), etc. And again I wrote to friends with deep appreciation:

(March 24, 2003) Joyner is delightfully consistently anti-war. I'm getting news from them I don't even get from the left listserves.

(March 25, 2003) Are you following Joyner? Nonstop antiwar. I keep crying whenever they talk about the poor black woman POW [Shoshana Johnson. She appeared on the show after she was released.][6]

On the 2008 anniversary, Sybil reported bitterly on the vast gulf between the number of those who were killed on 9/11 (2996) versus the number of Americans—4755—killed in combat by that date in our unnecessary wars in Iraq and Afghanistan.

On the 2012 9/11 anniversary, DJ Mike Stark created an extraordinary five-minute audio segment that combined actual panicked police and firefighter 9/11 radio transmissions, early news anchor efforts to report the tragedy, a black woman speaking about turning to the Book of Revelations (sampled from the great Curtis Mayfield's "If There's a Hell Below"),[7] backgrounded by Bebe and Cece Winans' gospel standard "Don't Cry," Marvin Gaye's haunting "Mercy, Mercy,"[8] and Tom Joyner's solemn, stumbling 2001 commentary:

We're gonna try to do the best we can to report and try to sort out the confusion from the facts, as well as our own hearts and minds, with this tragedy.

Then Tavis Smiley articulated the conundrum of fighting against a non-territorial religious terrorist organization:

How do you win against folk who think that giving their life is the way to make it to Heaven?

But Reverend Al Sharpton then warned, speaking both of the 9/11 victims and our targets in Iraq and Afghanistan, that

We've got to remember that there's human life here, innocent life, none of whom did anything, in any way, that remotely deserves what they receive.

Tom Joyner summed up their scrambled but compassionate and truth-seeking broadcasting:

> *This is black radio at its best!*
> *Sybil, intensely: Yes it is!*
> *Tom: Nothing special. It's just what we do.*

On the 2014 anniversary, Tom recalled that in 2001, first

> *We observed a moment of silence . . . then we went to work! That's when we started the blackamericaweb fund. And unlike the other charities, we went directly to the victims. . . . The cops, the firefighters . . . we personally went to about forty families.*
> *J: And everybody [in the early days] had hope [that their loved ones were still alive]—because they didn't* ***know.*** *They said they were leaving things as they were, so when they came back, it was the same.*

A woman then texted in:

> *[On 9/11] I was listening to you-all on my job—we didn't have a television then. I thank you for being there!*

Like other progressive news outlets, the *TJMS* was also bitterly amused by President George W. Bush's easy evolution from bellicose saber-rattling about catching Osama bin Laden "dead or alive," to casually remarking, after the U.S. intelligence services and military failed to do so year after year, that he didn't know and was "truly not that concerned" about where bin Laden was.[9]

On the 2006 anniversary, Tom Joyner threw out the challenge:

> *Can I get someone just to yell, "Where's Osama bin Laden?" at the president? I'll pay you $1000!*
> *J picks up the challenge, but the rest of the crew warn him about "how much trouble" he could get into for, as Myra J put it: YWB! Yelling While Black!*

Black Katrina

But the key national political importance of the *TJMS*, and its simultaneous mainstream media invisibility, became even more apparent in the aftermath of the disaster of Hurricane Katrina in 2005. On August 29, the U.S. airwaves were filled with warnings of Hurricane Katrina's onslaught. But few media outlets connected the hurricane's potential damage to the American wars in Iraq and Afghanistan and their costs, much less to the corrupt practices of the Bush White House. On the *TJMS*, though, the commentary was pointed and prescient:

> Tom: *Thirty billion estimated in claims for Hurricane Katrina. I just want to know, Sybil, how much is the war in Iraq costing?*
> Sybil: *Oh my goodness, I don't know.*
> Tom: *I'm just askin, why can't all that money go towards saving people's lives in the path of the hurricane?*

Later in the show, Tom and Sybil commented favorably on Gold Star Mother Cindy Sheehan's summer-long demonstration against the Iraq war, and her efforts to force President Bush to meet with her.

> Tom: *Martin Sheen—the president on the* West Wing*—he went to visit the lady on the lawn?*
> Sybil: *Not only him, but Al Sharpton . . .he told her, at least you've got the **acting** president of the U.S.*
> Tom: *Go 'head, girl. You stay **on** it.*
> J: *Here's to you, white lady!*

On the same morning's broadcast, the Joyner crew addressed the global political economy of oil and hemispheric relations, snidely linking in (using rapper Kool Moe D's phrase) the recent scandal of a notorious American fundamentalist's call for the assassination of a democratically elected Latin American president.

> Tom: *So Jesse Jackson is in Venezuela, talkin with President Chávez—and this man has just said he wants to help poor Americans with their heating oil—and they say this winter is going to be the worst . . .*
> Sybil: *How you like me **now**, Pat Robertson?*

On successive days, though, as Katrina decimated New Orleans and brought the entire Gulf Coast region to a halt, the Joyner crew abandoned all other news to focus on the outrage of the federal government's failure to protect New Orleans and to evacuate the overwhelmingly black and poor population left behind. But they also began organizing their own relief efforts, as well as articulating a critique of mass media coverage of the disaster:

> (September 6, 2005)
> Tom: *Turn the TV **off**, will you?*
> Sybil: *Stop watching it! It's like crack!*
> Tom: *I know, and I'm getting depressed watching it. And they don't have but five pictures. . . . Here's what we've come up with. The families who've taken in*

*families can't get any form of relief. So we're gonna help the people who're trying
to help the people who have no hope.*

Joyner went on to explain that they had made a decision to give out prepaid
credit cards to individuals who registered through any church (they did not have to
be church members) because of tax law restrictions. The crew pledged $80,000 of
their own money and solicited donations from their working-/middle-class black
audience. Only three days later, they had amassed $580,000, and less than two
weeks after that, they had raised $1.5 million, had already sent out 500 credit cards,
and had another 300 ready to go in the mail.

Meanwhile, after the first shock of the disaster faded, Americans began to realize
the multiple institutions destroyed by the hurricane and federal relief failures, and
American colleges moved to enroll evacuee students and to give displaced professors
temporary positions. The first wave of relief, however, went out only to Tulane,
a largely white school. But there are three predominantly black colleges in New
Orleans—Xavier, Dillard, and Southern—and, unlike white-majority America, the
Joyner crew were aware of them, and had already moved by September 9 to ante up
$1 million of their own money to give out $1000 scholarships to 1000 displaced
students from those three schools. By October 4, they had disbursed $1.3 million,
and by October 17, $2.4 million.

Thus the crew literally put their money where their mouths were—they kept
funding Katrina survivors for a full year—and their anti-Bush coverage and jokes
gained in heft and bite. They returned to their well-worn outrage over white
Americans' valuing nonhuman animals over black Americans' lives:

*(September 15, 2005) Tom: It's happening, just like we said—it's happening. Our
people are still homeless . . . and we're getting stories about people missing pets—
like these **dolphins**.*

As Alan Watty's haunting "Hurricane Song" laid it out: "Then it hit me, ain't nobody comin to get me. . . . Once again, the color of my skin reminds me things ain't
changed."[10]

And members of their audience displayed the economic sophistication of union
organizers in evaluating how the White House dealt with reconstruction funding:

*(Same day) Woman caller: What's on my mind is President Bush says he cares
about the people hurt by Katrina, but he's awarding contracts to his cronies like
Halliburton and says he won't make them pay the prevailing wage!*

Despite the *TJMS*'s extraordinary level of private philanthropy, the crew
never stopped hammering on the federal government's responsibility for hurricane relief, and their abject failure to do so in the case of Katrina. Crew members

played wonderfully with black slang to display their utter contempt over Bush Administration failures to provide timely disaster relief:

> *(September 23, 2005) Ms. Dupre, whose New Orleans home had been destroyed, to a live Las Vegas, Nevada Sky Show audience:*
> *Ms. Dupre: You know the new thing—we no longer say CP [colored people's] time—it's officially FEMA time!*
> *Tom: It's not CP time, it's . . .*
> *Vast, laughing, noisy crowd: FEMA TIME!*

It is an old cliché that disasters bring to light underlying social processes, expose inequalities about which the general public has become complacent. And certainly we saw, in the wake of Hurricane Katrina, a short-lived wave of press coverage of black poverty and social vulnerability in New Orleans, and in the U.S. in general.[11] Myself familiar with black New Orleans, I was startled, for example, to find the social characteristics of the lower Ninth Ward, the most devastated New Orleans neighborhood, thrust into national consciousness. (But the journalists all missed the now doubly ironic street kids' rhyme, "I'm from the Nine, and I don't mind dyin.")

Desperately seeking heart-warming stories amid the horror and gloom, the American press also reported extensively on local and national disaster relief efforts, from bake sales to benefit concerts to Red Cross organizing. But missing from this vast wave of coverage was, beyond a few references on the black-run afternoon National Public Radio show, any acknowledgment of the impressive relief launched by the Joyner crew, much less their magnificently unbridled daily reportage on and critiques of the Bush White House.[12]

> *(September 12, 2005) Tavis Smiley, Tom Joyner, and J Anthony Brown get into the mix:*
> *Tavis: If we gon clean up public housing, let's start with the White House!*
> *Tom: How many black Christians think that God did this to New Orleans because there's so much sin there?*
> *Tavis: Hey Tom, Bourbon Street is only so long, how about Pennsylvania Avenue?*
> *J, mimicking President Bush's very late New Orleans photo-op: I've got my sleeves rolled up, lookin like I'm workin, wavin at nobody . . .*
> *Tom: And black people, do me a favor, DON'T let him take his picture with you . . . and I won't be mad at [black New Orleans mayor] Ray Nagin if he just elbows him in the **throat**.*
> *J: Come on, Nagin! You the closest one!*

Not only did the national press miss the mordant wit of these well-known commentators (imagine the flurry of attention had Jon Stewart done a white version of this diatribe on *The Daily Show*), they entirely failed to register the fact that this wildly popular show was, in the weeks following the disaster, broadcasting daily the voices of evacuees and of those who were aiding them. The imagined community of the air, the black counterpublic, was operating at full force, just beneath mainstream American radar:

> (September 14, 2005) Enraged woman caller: Ms. Dupre, can you tell me what the difference is between them shoving us in the Superdome and them shoving us in the boat back in Africa?

Audience members called in to complain about widespread corporate profit-gouging, taking advantage of people's desperation, and to explain their individual efforts to ameliorate that evil:

> (Same day) Houston caller: She complains that U-Haul's rates are too high, that they are exploiting evacuees, so as a U-Haul employee she is discounting their rentals: "I'd lose my job behind it, but I just can't do it."
> Sybil: I commend your efforts, ma'am. Good luck to you.

And individual listeners called to testify about their personal horror, and about the benefits of TJMS efforts:

> (October 4, 2005) Woman caller: I was calling to thank you for what you've done for Katrina victims. Our father was the one who was trapped in his attic for eighteen days, and the day he was found, we received a check from you for the other evacuees, and we were able to use a portion of it to reunite him with us. . . . It is just a blessing.

Because of the entre nous character of the show, listeners felt free to call in to complain, with biting wit, about the inevitable misery ensuing after taking in evacuee friends and relatives:

> (October 5, 2005) Male caller: This is Vaughn, I got two hurricane victims stayin with me 'bout a month, they holdin out on me, how do I get them politely not to eat my food?
> J: What's the one thing that they ate that really set you off?
> Caller: Bacon! It's history!
> Sybil: You know, you are gonna have to have your bacon at work.
> Ms. Dupre: [fake hysteria] Hide the bacon! Hide the bacon!
> J: Put it in a book. You know they aint readin!
> Tom, same day: All right, FEMA claims they'll have people out of shelters and into temporary shelter by October 15th.
> J: Yeah, right.

Sybil: [sardonic] Well, they are not known for their timeliness.
All: Wild laughter

The *TJMS* is so universally well-known among black Americans that it even served as a local town hall during the crisis. On September 13, after an evacuee woman in Shreveport called in, claiming destitution and lack of local support, another Shreveport woman phoned in to rebuke her, having recognized her voice and circumstances: *"I guess she don't think holy people listen to you in the morning."* This woman's church had given the first caller extensive help already, and she was outraged at her dissemblance: *"You know what? God don't like ugly."*

And six months into the crisis, the *TJMS* and its listeners continued the radical Katrina conversation:

(February 21, 2006) Express Yourself: I'm a good religious person, but if I weren't:
Myra J: I'd run down to Florida and get all those FEMA trailers, and I'd drive them to the Gulf Coast, and I'd say, Here ya'll, [falsetto] Free! Free!
*New Orleans woman, relocated to Athens, Georgia: First I'd whup Bush's ass, then I'd take him back to New Orleans to my parents' neighborhood where a **barge** is sitting where my parents' house was!*

Spike Lee's highly effective Katrina documentary, *When the Levees Broke*, came out in August 2006, and the *TJMS* invited him on the show.[13] A wonderfully unbridled conversation ensued:

(August 17, 2006) J suggests, before Spike Lee comes on, that he should have ended the documentary as he did his first film, School Daze: with the protagonist facing the camera, screaming "WAKE UP!!!!"
Spike Lee mentions that he was in Italy when Katrina hit, and noticed that Italian media, unlike their U.S. counterparts, showed actual footage of dead bodies in New Orleans...
Tom: So you're saying that the government controls the networks?
Spike Lee, sardonically: Oh, you know that?

Tom then said that he was "mad enough" about the government's failed response to Katrina that he was thinking of throwing copies of *When the Levees Broke* over the White House fence. J and Sybil warned him of the dangers of such an act.

The next day, the *TJMS* had a Sky Show in Washington, DC. Tom harangued the huge crowd about *When the Levees Broke*, repeating his desire to throw a copy of the film over the White House fence. He told the audience, "Show it to your kids!"

Myra J shouted, "Show it to your teenagers!—cause this is **our people**!" She went on to point out that today's youth will need to fight "as we fought" for civil rights.

Male audience member: Throw the tape, Tom!
Another male audience member: We got your back!

The following week, the crew was still on the Katrina case. On August 21, 2006, multiple audience members phoned in to catcall the Bush Administration. Representative Maxine Waters [California] came on the show and used crew and audience fury as a springboard to articulate a progressive Democratic perspective, and to call for maximum voting participation in the upcoming midterm elections.

The crew then returned to the ongoing outrage: Where was the funding Bush had promised? Sybil pointed out that there was no aid for ongoing social services in New Orleans: "They're operating on just 25% of pre-Katrina revenue in that city."

> *Tom: And what about the levees? It's hurricane season and they still haven't repaired the levees! [He takes seriously the conspiracy theory, widely believed in New Orleans, that authorities deliberately "blew" the levees to flood black areas and spare the wealthy parts of the city.]*

Two days later, the crew read a Wednesday Christmas Wish letter from a Katrina victim living in a FEMA trailer and attempting to repair her home. Her insurance company had refused to pay to replace her appliances. The crew educated their audience: insurance companies would not pay for Katrina damage to belongings.

> *Tom: Because of Spike's documentary, we **do** understand now. We will cover for you what the insurance company didn't! [Long disquisition on how Ms. Dupre had not yet received a penny from her insurance company, nearly a year after the disaster.]*

The *TJMS* kept up their outraged coverage of the sequelae of governmental failures for years after Katrina. The following vignette could serve as an antineoliberal classroom lesson in Why We Need Government and What It Should Do for Us:

> *(August 29, 2007) Al Sharpton is on to observe the Katrina two-year anniversary. Crew takes a call from a New Orleans firefighter who describes the impossibility of doing his job, given that there is still insufficient water pressure for the hoses to function.*
> *Tom: That's basic! You have a tragedy, and the infrastructure has to be rebuilt!*
> *Ms. Dupre: Things we pay taxes for, things we **purchase**!*
> *The crew goes on to discuss ongoing Katrina-related health problems in New Orleans:*

*Ms. Dupre: I'm telling you, one week we had one hundred funerals, and I am **not** telling you a lie!*

Al Sharpton: And they keep tellin us we can't leave Baghdad, but after two years they aren't in New Orleans!

"Go Shawty!" *TJMS* and the Environment

Environmentalism—concern with and activism against pollution, climate change, and the carbon emissions causing it—is the final plank in the twenty-first-century syncretic American, and global, progressive vision. Without its success, of course, human life on earth is ultimately doomed. And here the *TJMS* has historically been weakest, at least in terms of radio broadcasting—we can see, from their Katrina coverage, that they provided little focus at the time on the hurricane's (and the Army Corps of Engineers') damage to the fragile Louisiana coastline and wetlands. But the crew's online and in-person presence is far more obviously green. One possible reason for this relative overall neglect is widespread racial minority awareness of the long history of affluent whites paying far more attention to the welfare of "appealing" nonhuman animals—songbirds, dolphins, whales, gorillas, chimps, pandas, penguins, polar bears—than to the lives of people of color in the United States and around the world.

But over its broadcasting history, the *TJMS* audience has been hearing increasingly about a range of environmental disasters, whether Acts of God or human-caused—like Hurricane Katrina in 2005, as we have seen—the BP Gulf oil spill in 2010, the Fukushima nuclear plant meltdown following the tsunami of 2011, the multiple and devastating hurricanes, fires, and earthquakes of 2016, 2017, and 2018. This coverage is often married to stinging indictments of careless governments and profiteering corporations—and increasingly, of environmental threats. And the crew and their audience have never exhibited any climate change skepticism. They have always accepted the realities of global warming as settled science, and are very aware of environmental racism:

(March 5, 2012)
Tom: Man, this weather! Tornadoes, and it's not tornado season. Volcanos!
J: Over in Hawaii. And glaciers melting.
*Tom, dripping sarcasm: But there's **no global warming**! It's all good!*

(July 16, 2014) Dr. Mark Mitchell, the co-chair of the National Medical Association's Environmental Task Force, is their guest on Feel Good Wednesday.
*Tom: According to this study, **none** of us are doing well! Climate change is significantly affecting communities of color—come on, Doc!*

Dr. Mitchell: 89% of physicians are seeing injuries related to severe weather.

Sybil: So we're messed up wherever we live!

*Tom: So what do we **do**?*

Dr. Mitchell: Avoid being outdoors between eleven and seven during ozone emergencies.

Tom and Sybil: But besides that?

Dr. Mitchell: Call your governor—say you want to reduce emissions from power plants!

Sybil regularly announced both Earth Day and Arbor Day since at least 2008, and frequently boasts about the high mileage of her Prius, a gift from their sponsor Toyota. Huggy Lowdown celebrated Earth Day in 2010 by repurposing the spirited black birthday chant:

Go shawty, it's your Earth Day!

There was a "One Nation Working Together" March on Washington on October 2, 2010, with Bill McKibben and many other prominent environmentalists, and heavy union and minority involvement, co-sponsored by the African American Environmental Association. Tom Joyner moderated a segment of the program.[14] And, despite their generally wildly pro-Obama stance, the crew would counter the former president on environmental (as well as anti-war) issues:

(April 5, 2010) Tom comments on the California and Mexico "Easter earthquake" of April 4:

That earthquake is a sign from God . . . and the sign says "Stop That Offshore Drilling!"

Sybil: It's a sign from God?

*Tom: It **is**.*

*J: Isn't the President **for** offshore drilling?*

*Tom: **Yes he is**.*

The *TJMS* covered the April 2010 Deepwater Horizon explosion and oil spill in the Gulf of Mexico with facts, intense impatience and a sense of helplessness, unmitigated anger at corporate malfeasance, and a soupcon of conspiracy theory. On April 29, Sybil reported that the spill was far worse than had been believed—5000 barrels a day from the new leak. On May 6, the crew discussed the ongoing disaster and admitted their need for an expert to interpret the information coming out. On May 12, the crew reported on and responded to the British Petroleum executives being questioned by Congress:

Sybil gives a cogent account of congressional questions and BP answers. She recounts Senator Mary Landrieu asking about compensation for lost tourism dollars, and the executive saying, "Uh, that's a question mark."
Tom: *And they had **attitude**!*
Sybil, *wittily defiant: Question mark **this**, mister! There's four million gallons of oil on the floor of the bottom half of our country!*

Al Sharpton came on the show on May 26 to accuse BP of major crimes. (His analysis was exactly the same as that of journalist Howard Fineman's on Keith Olbermann's show on MSNBC the night before. The only difference was that Sharpton's statement *rhymed*.)

On June 1, Tom was back on the issue in high dudgeon, and moving into conspiracy theory territory:

Sybil, this oil spill!
Sybil: *It's got to you! Ok, Josh Bauer [of the television show 24], what do we do?*
Tom: *They're letting it go on to embarrass the President!*
J: *Nah—but is it helpin BP?*

On June 4, Sybil reported with great satisfaction that President Obama had slapped a $69 million fine on BP to cover the cost of cleanup and was heading back to the Gulf that day to view ongoing efforts. The next day, the *TJMS* expressed their own sympathy for oil-fouled wildlife by comically blackening them:

Tom: *And those poor pelicans! Did you see them? They got this look on their face, like this is some bullsh—here! This is jacked up! And then you see another pelican, and they say, "They got you too, man?"*

On June 11, Sybil played James Carville's statement accusing BP of obviously lying—the spill was at least twice as large as the corporation was admitting.

On June 15, Sybil played audio of President Obama's tough statement on charges and fines against BP. Then she intoned with intense pride: "**That** guy? That guy is **President of the United States**!" Later in the show, Tom reported on the plight of black fishermen in the Gulf and criticized media neglect of their existence: "Sybil, you would think there's *no* black fishermen on the Gulf!" Then on June 18, Tom Joyner brilliantly and sarcastically ventriloquized hard-right-wing Congressman Joe Barton of Texas, an oil company apologist[15]:

Ah am just so a-shamed as a white man to see that those up in the White House have done to you, BP, jackin you up! Ah haven't been so a-shamed since they made me go to school with a black girl!

On July 12, Sybil reported on an NAACP report that people of color were doing a disproportionate share of the dangerous cleanup jobs in the Gulf. Finally, on July 16, the *TJMS* was able to report that BP had capped the leak:

> Tom: *I called this eighty-six days ago. Anytime they wanted to, they could've capped this leak! They just wanted to make the president look bad!*
> Sybil: *I think you're onto something!*

On July 26, Sybil reported that BP's CEO Tony Hayward had finally been fired, but was given a $17 million golden parachute:

> J, scathingly: *I don't see firin and seventeen million in the same sentence!*
> Tom: *Meanwhile, poor people back in the Gulf . . . .*

On March 3, 2014, Sybil reported Bill McKibben's group 350.org's March 2 demonstration against the Keystone XL Pipeline at the White House, and the hundreds of arrests, while mainstream news sources gave it very little coverage.

Disasters concentrate the media mind and illuminate variations and disjunctions in a nation's political consciousness. But reportage of and responses to day-to-day politics also reveal how publics and counterpublics differently articulate what the key issues are and how to respond to them.

Tavis Smiley: Shutting Down Capitol Hill

In the pre-Obama 2000s, Tavis Smiley was Joyner's key political partner and the *TJMS*'s primary "inside the Beltway" political analyst. He continued their effort to protest lack of black representation in American mainstream media:

> (*August 2, 2005*) *Tavis reports on a new Urban League study that calls it "Sunday Morning Apartheid"—the whiteness of Sunday morning political talk shows. "More than 60% of shows have no black guests! . . . More than 70% of all black guests are three people . . . and you can guess who: Colin Powell, Condi Rice, and Juan Williams . . . Maybe they think that because we're in church we can't go on TV! Maybe they don't know we have three services!*

Tavis also fought to keep various black television shows—such as *Living Single* and *New York Undercover*—on air, and harassed ad agencies to hire African Americans and run ads in black venues.[16] And he would partner with political guests to urge the huge audience into massive collective action, although it often failed to turn the tide. Here are two examples.

During the Democratic Senate filibuster against the (ultimately successful) confirmation to the Supreme Court of the extremely conservative judge Samuel Alito, for example, Senator Ted Kennedy appeared on the show:

*(January 31, 2006) Ted Kennedy: I can tell you . . . this nominee has his fingers on
   the scales of justice . . . he's against people of cullah.*
Tom: *We've heard that Samuel Alito is no friend to the African American commu-
   nity. We want to know how we can help with this filibuster?*
Kennedy points out that Alito had ruled that all-white juries were "fine."
Sybil: *A jury of his peers, huh? [barks a laugh]*
*Kennedy: We need your listening audience to call in . . . ask their senators to stand
   with Kennedy and Kerry!*

Later in the show, after Sybil had announced the death of Coretta Scott King,
Martin Luther King, Jr.'s widow, Tavis Smiley came back on:

Tavis: *Less than twenty-four hours after Coretta Scott King passes, the Senate will
   vote on a Supreme Court nominee who promises to reverse King's legacy! [He
   announces the general phone number of the U.S. Senate so listeners can call their
   own Senators to protest.]*

In 2007, President George W. Bush nominated Leslie Southwick to the Fifth
Circuit Court of Appeals. Southwick was known for upholding the reinstatement
of a fired Mississippi social worker who had referred to a black co-worker as a "good
ole n————." He had also, in dozens of cases, upheld prosecutors' rights to strike
black Americans from juries, but denied the rights of defense attorneys to strike
whites from juries.

Tavis Smiley, following the NAACP's aggressive organizing against the Southwick
appointment, asked listeners to bombard Senate offices with phone calls expressing
their displeasure. On June 21, 2007, Tavis came on to report that "apparently we
have scared the bejesus out of the U.S. Senate!" On October 30, he complained that
the Democratic Senate was allowing the Southwick appointment to go forward. He
asked listeners to call Senators Harry Reid and Dianne Feinstein to complain. Two
hours later, a woman caller reported in that Senator Reid's staffers were saying that
their office had been bombarded by calls, and to please tell the *TJMS* that Senator
Reid had not voted for Southwick. Sybil clarified the point: Reid had *allowed* the
Southwick nomination to go forward.

Woman caller: *Oh! Then I will call them back!*

Unfortunately, in the end, Southwick was confirmed.[17]
The *TJMS* also engaged directly in civic activism, encouraging their enormous
audience to participate as American citizens. A key example is their wildly enthusiastic Obama-era campaigning for black involvement in the 2010 United States
Census. They went so far as to charter a bus plastered with 2010 Census advertising, and drove it around the country. Younger comic Chris Paul also crafted a brilliant "Poli Sci 101" song on April 9, 2010, encouraging black census participation

and explaining its functions, hilariously set to the tune of Biz Markie's furiously disappointed-suitor song "Just a Friend"[18]: I have never seen a popular-cultural vehicle that better explains the absolute necessity of "big government" to the proper functioning of a country—and Chris Paul even displayed feminist care in specifying "congresspeople." He began by asking "have you ever wondered how they allocate money from the government for the cities and states," then went on to demonstrate that that is one of the functions of the Census. He adjured African Americans to participate fully, because "if they don't know how many people are there, then they'll just have to spend all of that money elsewhere!" Paul then specified that the federal government funds schools, bridges and tunnels, senior citizens, children in need, etc., and proclaimed, "if you don't help the community, then you're just a **fool**!

Paul went on to lay out the necessity of being counted so as to get the proper number of congresspeople for your district, and to debunk conspiracy theories about the federal government's use of census material to harm people—"You won't be deported, evicted, or arrested!"—theories that, sadly, now hold more than a grain of truth in the punitive, hyper-militarized Trump era, with the proposed citizenship question addition to the Census. He ended with a deliberately youthful, slangy call to participate: "Yo! This is real business! Get involved, and get counted! Represent! The US Census 2010!"

A Tale of Four Elections

But the *TJMS*'s most dramatic set of political engagements, of course, has been with U.S. presidential elections. They were always aware of gerrymandering and voter suppression, and celebrated the civic virtue of voting. In 2018, a texter dramatically demonstrated their real-world effectiveness:

> *(October 30) My parents never voted, and I didn't either—until I listened to the TJMS and learned about [the news]. Now we all vote in every election! Thank you, Tom Joyner!*

The show was relatively uncritical of President Bill Clinton during his two terms (1992–2000)—and for that reason I was not then as enthusiastic an audience member. (With other American progressives, I was furious over his draconian crime bill (1994), the slaughter of welfare (1996), "Don't Ask, Don't Tell," and the repeal of the Glass-Steagall Act (1999), which, with other financial deregulations, paved the way for the 2008 recession. And over NAFTA, which so impoverished rural Mexico, by allowing U.S. corporations to flood the country with cheap foodstuffs, that it triggered a huge increase in out-migration, "Mexicanizing" for the first time the American South and Eastern Seaboard.)[19]

But the go-go economy of the 1990s, the low unemployment rate, and Bill Clinton's notorious charm and comfort level with African Americans help to explain why the *TJMS*, and the country at large, gave him high approval ratings. In the 1990s, it was only in the minority precincts of radical scholarship and activism that we saw strong critiques of these Clinton White House policies.[20] In the post-2008 recession/Black Lives Matter present, it can be difficult to remember just how normalized, how commonsensical in the 1990s were notions of an innately criminal and feckless black and brown American underclass deserving only punitive treatment, of the clearly inferior character of female-headed households, and of the necessity of unleashing businesses from the "unfair" trammels of financial and other regulations.[21] Or perhaps it is not so difficult anymore, given the horrifying return of all of these false political claims with Trump's 2016 election.

Ironically, the Monica Lewinsky scandal also helped Bill Clinton. Ordinary Americans, and black Americans in particular, saw Republicans' attempts to impeach Clinton over what they considered to be a private affair to be prudish grandstanding. Novelist Toni Morrison's labeling Bill Clinton the "first black President" in 1998 fit with a larger African American vision of Clinton as both a "player" and punished for it.[22] J's excellent and much-repeated takeoffs of Bill Clinton during those years drew from these common apprehensions.

I was listening to the *TJMS* during the 2000 election cycle, and noted their vociferous support for Gore/Lieberman, but it was only during the 2004 presidential race that I really began to pay close attention and to transcribe their programming.

The entire show was mobilized for months, first in voter registration drives, and then in pull-out-the-stops get-out-the-vote efforts in the Southern black belt and in northern and western cities. John Kerry and John Edwards appeared on the show multiple times, and the crew replayed segments of both presidential and vice presidential debates, mixed extraordinarily cleverly with 1960s and 1970s anti-war soul music.

The morning after the first Kerry/Bush debate, they made a tape loop of Bush's bumbling ums and uhs, and let it run, interspersed with clips of Kerry in eloquent anti-war attack mode, over Edwin Starr's 1970 hit, "War! What is it good for? Absolutely nothing." After the vice presidential debate, *TJMS's* show-ending mix first staged Cheney making domestic economic claims and then Edwards riposting with facts, ending with his punchline, "I don't think the country can handle four more years," with the Bee Gees' "Jive Talking" playing in the background. They finished with Stevie Wonder's version of Dylan's "Blowing in the Wind," with a voice-over of Cheney's claims to experience and Edwards flashing back that "there's a bright light now flickering and the president and vice president don't see it. John Kerry and I believe we can do better." After the second presidential debate, the crew played segments from Kerry's assertions about the importance of civil rights and Bush's failures in that domain, with the Chi-Lites' "For God's Sake, Give More Power to the People" running behind him. They segued into Bush's set of claims about his civil rights record over Cameo's clear indictment of lying, "You talkin out the side of your neck, you gonna get what's comin to you yet." They ended with Kerry's peroration on his civil rights plans, laid over Curtis Mayfield's beautiful falsetto in "Keep On Pushin.'"[23]

During the period when a number of states allowed early voting, the crew expanded and fanned out, broadcasting simultaneously from multiple polling sites, each with long lines of black voters. Their biting commentary, with its references to the state atrocities of the 1950s–60s Civil Rights era and their parallels to the new universe of gerrymandering and dirty tricks, was deeply moving:

> (October 22, 2005) Comedian Tricky, in Houston, expounds on Republican dirty tricks to slow down the black vote, sending men spraying pesticide and using leaf blowers around the line: "That's all you got? We had dogs and hoses!"
>
> Ms. Dupre, in Las Vegas with a giant crowd waiting to vote, reports that a white guy showed up with a baseball bat: [with great, dignified sarcasm] "He thought something was amiss."
>
> J, in Nashville: We been dogged one time, we aint gonna be dogged no more!

On October 29, the crew ran a Sky Show in which they marched—with Michael Moore!—from the Jackie Gleason Theater in Miami to a polling place—and were yet again ignored by mainstream and all progressive media.[24] On election day, the *TJMS* crew continued to document Republican dirty tricks. Voters from Lansing, Michigan reported that they were getting phone calls claiming that Kerry would legalize gay marriage (this *was* 2005, after all). The actress Kerry Washington—yes, *that* Kerry Washington, she has been a Democratic Party activist going back that far—from Florida, reported on calls to black voters there stating that "today is Republican voting, tomorrow Democratic voting," or that "you can vote from your home." The crew distilled tension and outrage into high humor:

> J: It is not true that people with weaves can't vote! It's not true that men over three hundred pounds can't vote. Weave your fat behind to the polls! . . . They tryin, man. You gotta give'em credit. They got every kind of tricks.
>
> Tom: But we've got so many people.
>
> J: We got more people than they got tricks!

Well, J was wrong on that one. After Kerry conceded the election, most U.S. news sources turned on a dime, becoming instantly self-flagellating—Have we been too liberal?—and pandering—Oh, the intriguing virtues of "moral values" voters! But the *TJMS* was irredentist, solid, a breath of fresh progressive air after the craven witterings of the mainstream media:

> (November 3, 2004) Tom: We all of us are sittin here lookin like John Kerry. We all got long faces. I'm playing Negro spirituals.

Woman caller from Alabama: (outraged and disbelieving) What happened?

Crew: Everything always happens in Alabama. We did our thing, they did theirs. We outnumbered.

Woman caller: How come they claim 98% of the vote is counted when some people couldn't vote til 3:56 a.m.?

J: Listen, we looking for something, but you aint got nothin.

Tom: The forecast in the next four years for black people is pretty grim. Social services, gone. Medical care, gone. We've got to step up and do for ourselves.... Meanwhile, how does the rest of the world look at us? All I've seen is Tony Blair...But the rest of the world: they hate us. All you have to do is go out of the country—that's some scary stuff.

J: There's a letter for each year: H-E-L-L.

Caller: I just wonder if George W. Bush really won, or if some trickery can be suspected?

J, elaborately sardonic: Hmmm, let's see, is the government involved in trickery?

Caller, with a comment that resonates even more painfully after the 2016 presidential election: You know, you need to really get on Virginia. You know they supported Bush big-time! All these people in trailer parks with no teeth ... they don't care that Bush hurt them as long as he don't help us!

Usually, when J Anthony Brown "murdered another hit," his humor turned on the wars between the sexes or popular cultural absurdities, but not on the day after the 2004 election. Then he slyly pulled off a trickster lament with commentary on Republican dirty tricks and a post-Patriot Act "police state" sting in its tail. He prefaced the song with a statement: "This is so tough ... First of all, I did not know who was going to win the election. So I was all set to sing 'Hit the Road, Bush'" (as in Ray Charles' hit, 'Hit the Road, Jack')[25] ... So J rewrote his song to account for the new reality. "Hit the road, Bush" became "I take the jokes back!" But he referenced Republican dirty tricks—"Oh you won the election with your voting machine"—and pretended to be terrified of being charged for violating the Patriot Act: "And you got the I-R-S, don't wanna start no mess! ... Zip my lip up when I'm onstage!"

Let me give the last prescient post-election word to a *TJMS* listener, one that again raises goosebumps in the current American political climate:

(November 4, 2004) Woman caller: We might as well have the KKK, with Bush in office.

Sybil: Ma'am, we haven't seen the KKK in the last four years, what makes you think we'll get them now?

*Caller: I'm sayin, **we might as well**.*

*Tom: If you work with this lady in the office, **don't** get into it!*

And, in fact, the *TJMS* acted as that "lady in the office" with regard to George W. Bush's remaining time in the White House. They never let up on their absolute disdain for him, and maintained their radical critique of the dominant U.S. public sphere:

> *(February 10, 2006) Tom: So the top story this morning is that President Bush, while trying to get people behind the Patriot Act, announced that he stopped a terrorist attack in 2002?!*
>
> *J: White people need a word that's equivalent to NP! [Negro, please!] vast crew laughter*
>
> *Melvin: And they really need that! No one calls him on anything!*
>
> *Sybil: And here's one thing: the polls are going up in support of secret wiretapping! . . .*
>
> *Tom: And they're controlling the media! I didn't hear one artist say anything at all at the Grammys . . .*
>
> *Sybil: And everyone needs to see George Clooney's* Good Night and Good Luck! *It stinks of the McCarthy period, which is what we're experiencing again.*

> *(March 24, 2008) Sybil, repurposing the old anti-Vietnam War chant: "Hey hey George W. Bush, how many lives have you crushed? . . . We are now marking four thousand U.S. deaths in Iraq.*

> *(May 15, 2008) D L Hughley is visiting the show. He comments on San Francisco Giants' Barry Bonds' indictment concerning his alleged steroid use: "Isn't it amazing that you can get indicted fourteen times for lying about baseball, but you can't get indicted **once** for lying about a war?"*

The Road to 2008: The Obama Effect

There is no dearth of scholarly and journalistic analyses of Barack Obama's historic 2008 presidential election victory. In fact, we could say that the narrative of that particular campaign—its personnel, politics, key turns in the road, public relations—has been done to death.[26] But while Obama's racial identity was and is a central focus of mainstream press and public attention, there has been very little concern with the actual public deliberations among the working-class minority Americans whose heightened activism and voter participation played a major role in putting Obama in the White House, and in keeping him there.

Instead, commentators have heaped well-deserved praise on Obama's campaign team, on the tightness of its organization and secure command of the ground game. Much has been made of the youth vote for Obama—ironically, though, reporters Chuck Todd and Sheldon Gawiser, running the numbers afterward, concluded that "it's important not to overstate the youth vote in Obama's victory," as "the youth share of the vote was 18% of the electorate [in 2008], just one percentage point more than in 2004." They rammed home the statistical reality—"[I]f no one under the age of 30 had voted, Obama would have won every state he carried with the exception of two: Indiana and North Carolina."[27]

Todd and Gawiser, The Pew Research Center, the Joint Center for Political and Economic Studies, and others have also come to other heterodox conclusions about the relative importance of various sectors of the American electorate to Obama's 2008 win. Despite much journalistic ink spilled on a vision of white male racist animus against Obama, he nevertheless received 46% of all white male votes, even though "not since Carter has any Democratic nominee earned more than 38% of the white male vote."[28] As David Bositis of the Joint Center points out, "[in] all states outside of the South, Obama received significantly more of the white vote—more than any Democratic nominee since Lyndon Johnson."[29] As well, many commentators noted the increasing importance of the Latinx vote, but most focused on Latinos' roles in the Southwestern and Western states. Post-NAFTA migration patterns, however, have spread Latinx populations across the U.S.: "If no Latinos had voted, McCain would have carried Indiana."[30]

As well, despite overwhelming press and scholarly attention to Obama's racial identity—and, during the campaign, on whether black Americans would judge him to be "not black enough" or "too black"—very little attention has been paid to actual black American apprehensions of the campaign and election. In fact, there was almost no mainstream media coverage of black American media or organizing efforts. Ironically, in reviewing both journalistic and scholarly analyses of the 2008 vote, I found a serious quantitative study of the role white racism may have played in denying Obama the landslide he might otherwise have gotten, given President Bush's overwhelming unpopularity and the Autumn 2008 financial crash—but not a single explicit consideration of the actual electoral college effects of the *increased black vote*.[31]

The Pew Research Center reported that two million more black Americans voted in the 2008 than in the 2004 election—nearly matching, for the first time in history, the turnout rate of white Americans—and 95% of them supported Obama. Black women had the highest turnout rate of *any* population of voters, and black youth turnout was higher than that of "young eligible voters of any other racial or ethnic group in 2008"—another historic first.[32] Even though, as seems likely, black voting alone did not secure Obama's victory, it is surprising—or perhaps not—that scholars paid so little attention to exactly what role it did play.

The *TJMS* crew were profoundly engaged in covering Barack Obama's 2008 campaign and election. The show's anchors also had extraordinary access—not only multiple on-air interviews with Barack and Michelle Obama, Joe Biden, and other Democratic Party heavies but physical access to the Obama headquarters on Election Day. They gained this access because the show was partly Chicago-oriented and represented one of Obama's key national electoral bases. But it was also, and more importantly, the result of the show's enormous audience and extraordinary engagement with the Obama presidential campaign, and before it, with many other Democratic Party candidates and office holders, back to President Clinton's two terms.

The Obama Campaign: Early Coverage

As we have seen, the *TJMS* crew and commentators have tended, from the show's inception, to support the Democratic Party in general, and specifically, black Democratic politicians.[33] But that stance by no means translated into automatic support of Obama's candidacy, despite Tom Joyner's own fervent early support.

On February 23, 2007, Cathy Hughes, president and CEO of the black media company Radio One, (and creator of Quiet Storm programming) was on the show, complaining that Obama was too inexperienced and did not necessarily have a pro-black agenda. J and Tom demurred. Tom came out explicitly: "I want a black president!!" On February 28, Tom commented that "a lot of black people with money are supporting Hillary Clinton because, let's face it, after eight years of Clinton in the White House, a lot of black people made money!" He went on to state that nevertheless he was giving money to the Obama campaign instead.

The *TJMS*, like most political commentators and the public at large, assumed at the beginning of Obama's campaign that he had little chance of garnering sufficient white support to mount a credible primary challenge to Hillary Clinton:

(April 4, 2007)
Woman caller: The world is comin to an end! I just drove by a white guy with an
    Obama sticker on his car! In Jacksonville, Mississippi!
Crew: wild laughter, sardonic remarks
Sybil: Does he know!?
[crew assumes she means Obama, again sardonic remarks]
Sybil: I mean the white guy!
Crew: Various fantasies about people putting Obama stickers on white people's
    cars to drive them crazy.

Meanwhile, the show also served as an early warning system for racist calumnies against Obama:

(April 5, 2007)
Woman caller: My supervisor had the audacity to call Obama Osama bin Laden!
Crew tells her not to lose her job behind her reaction. Tom: "Just give him—The
    Eye. And go on."

But the show's sensitivity to racial slurs against the candidate did not translate into full-on support for some time. On July 3, 2007, for example, in an exchange mirroring divisions among black Americans, given long-term support for the Clintons, Tom asserted that black Americans had the best chance ever to put a black man in the White House. Sybil demurred for feminist reasons, making the point of Hillary Clinton's generally progressive political stances but also slyly referencing the widespread false rumors of her lesbianism: "I don't know, Tom. Hillary comes pretty close to being a black man!"

On January 22, 2008, show regular Tavis Smiley took Obama to task for his positive statements about Ronald Reagan in his interview with the editorial board of the Reno, Nevada *Journal-Gazette*. Hillary Clinton's campaign and many other politicians and bloggers had already criticized Obama,[34] but Smiley's point was specifically with reference to Reagan and civil rights history: "What *wasn't* said? That Reagan started his presidential campaign in Philadelphia, Mississippi!" Smiley reminded listeners that Philadelphia, Mississippi, was notorious as the site of the 1964 lynching of civil rights workers James Chaney, Andrew Goodman, and Michael Schwerner, and that Reagan had deliberately used that historical resonance, in "dog-whistle" style, to woo white racist Southerners.[35]

Apprehensions of Clinton's candidacy were also quite mixed, up until the Bosnian "sniper fire" incident. On February 4, 2008, a Chicago woman caller articulated a version of the "Hillary means Bill" line quite common then in mainstream media, but with a new black interpretation: "Black people don't realize that if we put Hillary in the White House, she'll bring Clinton back and he didn't do nothing for black people!" J instantly capitalized on this statement, improvising to the tune of Justin Timberlake's then-current "I'm Bringin Sexy Back" ("Them other boys don't know how to act!"[36]: *"She's bringin Clinton back, Yeah! He get all naked, don't know how to act!" [crew lost in hysterics]*

And yet only one day later, Super Tuesday, Hillary Clinton was on the show, commending the *TJMS*'s partnership with the NAACP's hotline for voting problems.

The Super Tuesday elections and caucuses—through which Obama won thirteen of twenty-three contests and gained 847 delegates to Clinton's 834—ended Clinton's definitive Democratic lead. Like mainstream media in general, the *TJMS* significantly shifted its coverage of the Democratic race after this major win. But while mainstream outlets covered Obama's new lead as a "story," the *TJMS* covered its specific meanings for black Americans. J, for example, revisited his murdered hit two days after Super Tuesday, re-orienting the spoof in commentary on the elections, with an anti-war twist, while interpolating a joke bearing on his own notorious predilection for white women: "I think I'm voting black, Yeah!, I like white women . . . but he will get us out of Iraq!"

A week later (February 18), D. L. Hughley was on-air, commenting on the effervescent air among black Americans, given Obama's multiple Super Tuesday triumphs: "I remember when everyone was sayin they wanted a President they could have a beer with—who knew it'd be a **forty ounce**!?" But three days later (February 21), Hughley narrated his college-age son's recent horrific experience: he had sent him to a neighborhood jewelry store to pick up a check the store had waiting for him. The store's security guard immediately assumed that he was a robber and pulled a gun on him. The boy came home shaken. Hughley said flatly and presciently:

> As much as things have changed, our black children are still goin through some of the things we had to . . . While I believe that Barack Obama will be president next year, we will **still** be black in America.

Obama himself displayed a relaxed and playful side in his post-Super Tuesday March 3 call to the show, riffing on the Clinton's camp's post-election complaints: "Clinton's people tend to complain a lot . . . I played a lot of basketball—and you can't complain to the refs!" Even comic Sheryl Underwood, now entirely converted from Republicanism—at least for this election—got in the mix, celebrating Obama's vote-getting abilities with ironic commentary on the "saints or sinners" syndrome: "*And* he got white women sweatin and fallin out, and he aint even sing or play basketball!"

Black Sniper Fire

It was, however, Hillary Clinton's "misspeaking" on the campaign trail about having come under sniper fire in Bosnia in 1995 that was the turning point for the *TJMS*, as it was for many other media outlets.[37] But again, the *TJMS* crew and their guests articulated a particularly black-sensitive perspective on the imbroglio. Major American media mentioned in passing that the black comedian Sinbad (as well as white singer Sheryl Crow) had been on that particular flight with Hillary Clinton and had denied the sniper fire story. But the *TJMS* rode the story for *eight days*, both drawing out its racial subtext and using it to bury Clinton, symbolically, as a credible presidential candidate.

> (*March 25, 2008*) *D L Hughley is on: And when the lie wad'n workin, what did she do? She went to Jeremiah Wright! . . . Sinbad! He was there! And you know that big light-skinned brother knows what bullets sound like! [And what did Clinton say?] Well, he's a comedian! That's what people say when they mean that lyin jigga!*

(Later) Tom: You can't mis-speak about dodging sniper fire! She didn't mis-speak, she just straight-up lied!

(March 27) J, still on topic: I can forget my keys, I can forget my glasses, but I'd remember bein shot at!—and I have!
Tom: No, no playa—only white people can say they forgot . . . Even white people are sayin—uh hunh! [explicitly black articulation] [all laugh]

(March 28) Huggy Lowdown, the Celebrity Snitch, announces the "Bamma of the Week" every Friday.
Huggy: Hillary Clinton, you are the Bamma of the Week, Week, Week! Hillary said that bull-shiggity about bein under sniper fire! Tom, she lyin like a brother in jail talkin about how much money he had on the outside!

Later. Sybil played an audiotape of the actual pilot's calm description of landing in Bosnia in 1995:

*Not only weren't there any bullets flying around, there wasn't a **bumblebee** flying!*
(Later) D L Hughley is on again: Yeah, well, white people always lie about getting shot at!

(March 31) The comic Sinbad himself is on the show:
*Hillary Clinton got stronger and stronger and more adamant about it . . . And then these blogs started doggin **me**.*
Tom: When did you hear [about the controversy]?
*Sinbad: I heard the same time as everybody else . . . [describes his internal reactions] Man, where did that come from? Lemme think about this. Were there gunshots? **No** . . . But think about it—there was a press corps on that plane. There was all that footage. What did the press do? Did they just buy it? . . . I had no idea it was gonna hit the fan. Wham! [Sinbad is pointing out that it made no sense to criticize him for denying the sniper fire story when abundantly available video footage would disprove Clinton in any event] . . . No, I don't regret it. You don't regret the truth.*

Later in the conversation. Sinbad rhetorically addressed Clinton:

I'm on the plane with you! When did I lose credibility? "He's just a come-dian!" . . . I lost a lot of respect [for her] . . . know what you're seeing now?—A sense of entitlement. "How dare Barack Obama?" . . . When he won Iowa the whole campaign freaked out! . . . [half-jokingly] If I disappear, ya'll know what happened! Look for me, people, look for me.

Of the Reverend Jeremiah Wright & Others

As the sniper fire issue faded in the media, the Jeremiah Wright controversy reignited. To reprise the history: The Obama campaign had begun to distance itself from Wright—in whose Chicago Trinity United Church of Christ Barack and Michelle Obama had been married, and their two daughters had been baptized—as early as Obama's announcement of candidacy on February 10, 2007. Wright had been slated to give an official benediction at the event and was disinvited when the campaign staff evaluated his record and shied away from his more controversial statements. The first upsurge of press attention and direct attacks on the Obama campaign vis-à-vis Wright's past sermons took place over March 2008, leading to Obama's specifically crafted March 18 speech on race and Wright, "A More Perfect Union." (It was in this phase that, as we saw, D L Hughley, like many other commentators, accused Hillary Clinton's campaign of attacking Wright and his association with Obama in order to deflect attention from her false statements about having been under sniper fire in Bosnia.) After a spate of evaluations of the speech—largely positive in mainstream media—popular attention to the issue faded, until Reverend Wright began, in late April 2008, a series of very flamboyant public appearances. A media free-for-all ensued—led by rightist outlets—leading to a second, harsher Obama statement in an April 29 press conference.

It was at this point that the *TJMS* intensified its commentary on the issue.

On April 29, Tom Joyner noted with a sneer that Wright was on the front page of the *New York Post*. Later that morning, Tavis Smiley came on the show for a lengthy commentary: "Jeremiah Wright was minding his own business, heading toward retirement, when he inadvertently became a political football." Smiley went on to note the unbalanced media coverage of Reverend Wright's so-called anti-white, anti-American views versus New Rightist, former Nixon speechwriter, former presidential candidate, and then-current MSNBC commentator Patrick Buchanan's March 21 blogpost, entitled "A Brief for Whitey." Buchanan wrote the essay in response to Barack Obama's March 18 speech, but it is merely a rehash of the specifically anti-black racist statements for which he became notorious decades ago.[38] Buchanan actually had the nerve to write, in this 2008 publication, that "America has been the best country on earth for black folks . . . [they were] introduced to Christian salvation, and reached the greatest levels of freedom and prosperity blacks have ever known . . . no people anywhere on earth has done more to lift up blacks than white Americans . . . [g]overnments, businesses and colleges have engaged in discrimination against white folks."[39]

Smiley began, "I've been waiting for over thirty days to see what they [media] would say about the Buchanan story! How is it that a former presidential speechwriter and a former presidential candidate can get away with this? . . . How come Buchanan's racist rant never got media lift-off?" He went on to query why "MSNBC hasn't checked Buchanan . . . How long before Buchanan steps over the line? He's got chalk all over his shoes!" (And in fact, MSNBC did not fire him until 2012.)[40] And Smiley definitely had a point: the key Frank Rich *New York Times* and E. J. Dionne *Washington Post* columns making these parallels between *Republican* presidential candidates and their close ties to scarily racist, right-wing ministers did not appear until May 4 and May 2, respectively.

The following morning, April 30, Smiley again warned that "we've got to be careful that we are not pushed into some fratricide . . . Wright has been subjected to one of the most ruthless scrutinies. . . ." He pointed out how little had been made of Mitt Romney's [and John McCain's] embrace of right-wing televangelist John Hagee, who was violently anti-Catholic (labeling the Church "the Great Whore") and claimed that Hurricane Katrina was God's wrath on New Orleans for gay rights activism. Smiley went on to assert that "They came after Reverend Wright . . . to try to derail Barack Obama's candidacy . . . the white media is having a field day! . . . No one asked Rudy Giuliani when he was running how he could be a member of the Catholic Church and not support their tenets. . . ."

The next morning, May Day 2008, Smiley asked listeners to tell mainstream media to pay attention to Pat Buchanan's racist screed: "When they say Wright, you say Pat!" He continued in call and response tradition:

Tavis: Wright!
Tom and Sybil: Pat!
Tavis: Wright!
Tom and Sybil: Pat!
Tavis: Wright!
Tom and Sybil: Pat!!

Smiley continued: "I can't begin to tell you of the overwhelming email I've received from folk who had never heard of this Buchanan piece! . . . Who knows? Senator Obama may be the first black who gets a pass from white people, but we have to remember the distinction between anger and righteous indignation." He went on to expatiate on widespread white terror of angry black men: "We will resist the effort to portray us like we're stuck on stupid . . . HIV is *not* caused by whites in conspiracy to infect blacks, but *we do know* about the Tuskegee experiments! . . . Remember this, when Reverend Wright lied, no one died. When Bush lied, more than 4000 died!"

The following morning, May 2, D L Hughley commented on Obama's distancing himself from Wright. Hughley pointed out that Wright had had a consistent politics for twenty years, and that Obama was being disingenuous to deny knowledge of it: "He [Wright] said something *we* say in private, in public."

Later that day, J tied up the threads of black opinion on Obama and Wright in a tour de force murder of the old 1972 Luther Ingram hit, "If loving you is wrong, I don't want to be right"[41]: J intoned hilariously in his chorus, "Now pastor you aint wrong for clearin your name and such, But Obama's damn near president, and it's time for you to hush!"

At the same time, the *TJMS* crew became even more pressing in their suggestions to Hillary Clinton that she drop out of the presidential race. On May 8, Tom Joyner began a picket-line-type chant, which he repeated multiple times with great gusto:

Move Hillary, get out the way!

And Sybil responded, articulating her own political quandary by repurposing the song, "And I Am Telling You, I'm Not Going," from the musical *Dreamgirls*, made a hit in the 2006 film version by Chicago native Jennifer Hudson.[42] Sybil sang instantly, in response to Tom, *as Hillary Clinton*: "And I am telling you, I am not going! This is the best job I want to have!"

Moving Toward November 4

From May 2008 until Election Day, the *TJMS* was increasingly dedicated not simply to Obama's candidacy but to the efforts to register and safeguard the ballot for black Americans. The show teamed up with the NAACP—with the Teamsters Union providing financing—establishing hotlines to enable registration and report voting irregularities. (During this period, Tavis Smiley, who had remained critical of Obama for not articulating a "black agenda," was subjected to withering audience criticism, and quit the show. But I suspect that an earlier event, in which the magnificent Aretha Franklin teasingly addressed Tavis as "booger puddin"—to the rest of the crew's and the audience's wild delight—might also have been a contributing factor.)

The director of the NAACP's hotline, Ken Smukler, appeared frequently on the *TJMS*, particularly around state primary election dates, and increasingly as November 4 loomed, commenting with high wit on both deliberate voter fraud and state-level bureaucratic incompetence.[43] Smukler's performances—his flash-bang references to celebrities and current events, his vocal glissandos and machine-gun delivery, and his neologisms, including playing with his own surname—reminded me inevitably of the hip white radio DJs who "played black" in the years before stations hired black DJs. Note the way in which Smukler wraps rather policy-wonky voting information in ripped-from-the-headlines political and celebrity humor.

> *(May 6) Well, it's the fine line between trickery and shiggity! [Smuckler explains multiple voting problems in North Carolina and Indiana primaries] Yesterday it would've been easier to find a Cinco de Mayo party in Laredo, Texas with Pat Buchanan doing the Mexican hat dance than it was to find your poll location in North Carolina!*
> *[wild laughter from crew]*

(September 19) Tom, it is easier to find an R Kelly song on the Tom Joyner playlist this week [TJMS banned Kelly's songs because of his alleged abuse of young girls]—it is easier to find Wesley Snipes's signature on an IRS form [Snipes did prison time for tax evasion]—than it is to find your polling place . . .

(October 2) It is easier to find a Wall Street broker celebrating the third-quarter earnings with Cristal and a lap dance than it is to find your poll location!

(October 14) It is easier to find [American Idol *winner and closeted gay*] Clay Aiken judging a wet t-shirt contest in a Girls Gone Wild *video than it is to find your poll location in America.*

(October 21) The shiggity hit the fan in Jacksonville, Florida yesterday. At some point, all eight early voting centers shut down yesterday . . . And you know what the Secretary of State said? "This is democracy working!"—Yeah, maybe in a Third World country!

(Later that morning) Get this, Sybil—they say machines should be working and referred me to a second number. What do you think they said at the second number? Call the first number! [He tells people in Duval County, Florida listening to TJMS to call in if they have problems with early voting.] It's like what I say, J, all the time: Shut your pie hole and do your smukin job! [crew laughter]

(October 22) [Smukler reports that the first day of early voting, the NAACP responded to 11,000 calls from frustrated voters.] It is easier to find Michael Vick signing autographs at the Westminster dog show [Vick did prison time for animal abuse] than it is to find your poll location in America!

(October 27) Smukler reports that the NAACP has now received a total of 96,000 calls reporting voting problems.

October 28) Smukler sings to the tune of Stevie Wonder and Paul McCartney's 1982 hit, "Ebony and Ivory[44]:" Trickery and shiggity live together in perfect harmony. . . . It is easier to find Roland Martin acting as a personal shopper for Sarah Palin at Neiman Marcus than it is to find your poll location in America! . . . In Georgia, it's déjà vu all over again. They have learned nothing in Gilmer County. We have reports of people waiting six hours in line! . . . In Palo Pinto County, Texas, the machines kept switching votes from straight Democratic to Republican . . . In Florida, Hialeah voters had an unusual visitor this week, a guy named Juan who offered to help people fill out their ballots and take them in!

(October 31) Re Halloween party costumes: I'm going as a voting machine. When you push McCain, it lights up Obama! [reports of voting machine glitches] Let me tell you, Tom, a glitch is when you're romancing your sweetheart, the Viagra kicks in, and your Barry White CD starts skipping! That's a glitch! When your voting machine messes up, that's not a glitch! [Crew beside themselves with laughter]

On November 3, Ken Smukler interviewed Teamsters Union President James Hoffa. Tom noted that Roland Martin had reported the Teamsters were going door to door "straightening out" their members who were thinking of voting for McCain. Smukler noted that the Teamsters provided money and supplies to the Civil Rights movement in the 1960s. Hoffa emotionally—choking up—described a photo in his office of his father and Martin Luther King, Jr. together at the memorial service for slain civil rights worker Viola Liuzzo, who was the wife of a Teamsters member. Hoffa: "This is a time in history we can all be proud of—getting the country away from the big corporations that have been ripping us off, and back to working people." Tom warmly thanked Hoffa for funding the NAACP Voter Hotline.

The Election and Its Afterlife

(November 4, 2008, presidential election day) The TJMS broadcasting from Obama headquarters in Chicago:

Roland Martin, then-CNN newscaster, greets longtime Democratic insider Donna Brazile, who had worked for Hillary Clinton's campaign.

Donna Brazile: My boo!... I voted for Obama in DC... I credit Senator Obama with this because he understood the political process and used it ... as of this moment more than seventy million people will have received a door-knock or a phone call.

Sybil: That's community organizing at its finest! [sardonically referring to Sarah Palin's repeated attacks on Obama's community organizing background]

(Later, same morning)

Al Gore: This is a day the Lord has made! [quoting from Psalm 118]

Tom Joyner: [slyly] You know a little something about being robbed of an election!

Al Gore: Well, it's time to turn the page ... we've been breaking records with early voting. I'm on pins and needles, Tom. It's not already done, it's still to do!

(Later)

Barack Obama: Referring to TJMS presence in his campaign headquarters—I want to make sure, now, that everybody's behaving around Tom Joyner!... We're seeing long lines around the country, in some cases rain, and the key thing is who wants it **more** ... I wish that my grandmother had been here to see this, and I wish that my mother ... But having my daughters with me..

Sybil: [departs gushingly from her rather reserved, tart persona] But how cool was it that your grandmother was able to vote for her grandson Barry?

Obama: She was able to vote absentee, and she told me that she was very proud.

(November 5, 2008, morning following the presidential election)

Tom, beside himself: Think of all the votes they stole, and he won Florida anyway!... So when you go to work today ...

Roland Martin: Oh, people not **goin** to work today!

[crew lost in laughter]

Tom: *This just in, this just in!* **Fox** *still won't call it! [loses it]*

(Later that morning)

Michael Cottman, Blackamericaweb.com staff writer:

Tom: *What's up, man? Ooooh yesterday, we were in the Obama campaign headquarters . . .*

Cottman: *First of all, I have never heard so many "Halleluiah, Praise the Lord," so many times in my life! When they saw our press passes, their faces lit up!*

Tom: *We were right next to photographers from all over the world! And we knew the world was watching! [reference to Vietnam-era demonstration chant, The whole world is watching]. . . . And Al Jazeera, they were really enjoyin sayin [terrible Arabic accent] Blackamericaweb! Blackamericaweb!*

(January 16, 2009, four days before presidential inauguration) George Clinton, the funk musician, is on the show, reporting that he will be performing at the Inauguration.

Tom: *George Clinton! You're a prophet!*

George Clinton, naming titles of his own songs from the 1970s and 1990s: Chocolate City! Paint the White House Black![45]

We can see in these excerpts the nearly hysterical bated-breath conversations on the eve of the election, shared with former Vice President Al Gore and Obama himself; and finally, triumphal anti-rightist (references to Fox News and Republican voter suppression dirty tricks) and globally oriented (Al Jazeera) celebration, with both the self-aggrandizing reminder of the *TJMS*'s key access to the Obama campaign and an historical eye cocked to the recent past in which the notion of a black president had been only a funk musician's clever dreamsong.

The *TJMS* and the NAACP hotline project received more than 300,000 phone calls in 2008, registered nearly 100,000 voters, and protected black voter access in primaries and on November 4, in dozens of states, providing enormous benefit to Obama's and other Democrats' candidacies, efforts that were rewarded by multiple Barack and Michelle Obama and other Democratic politicians' appearances on the show. And yet American mainstream media never covered the story. Not even Keith Olbermann's then-newish or Rachel Maddow's brand-new MSNBC evening news programs mentioned the project or the *TJMS*'s electoral importance, despite their shows' progressive, pro-Obama slants.

But the *TJMS* audience knew what time it was. A woman caller on January 16, 2009, summed up the role of their community of the air:

*I just want to thank you. . . . It was because of Tom Joyner that the rest of the black media came around . . . [Obama] was the longest of long shots . . . and you came out for him **so early**! . . . When Tom Joyner came out for Barack, there were three believers: Barack, Michelle, and Tom!*

TJMS and Obama's First Term

As we have seen, the *TJMS* crew covered the run-up to the election and its af-termath with near-hysterical effervescence. And a certain amount of political vengeance. The morning after George W. Bush's January 15, 2009, farewell address, DJ Mike Stark put together an artfully nasty mix of excerpts from the speech, followed by newsclips disproving Bush's claims and satirically connected musical interludes. A small selection: Bush's "Tonight I'm filled with gratitude to Vice President Cheney" was embedded in Junior Walker's 1965 Grammy-winning song, "Shotgun." And his infamous Katrina crisis exclama-tion, "Brownie, you're doing a heckofa job," was followed by Allen Watty's "Hurricane Song:" "Get me off this rooftop, Can somebody rescue me?" The mix finished up with 1990s girl-group En Vogue's angry anthem, "Lies, lies, using lies as alibis."[46] Joyner summed up: "Aren't you glad you missed the speech last night? We did it *right* for you!"

While murdered hits and mixes tend to make use of old soul and funk music and other dusties, I also remember the period of Obama's election for the particu-larly relevant songs on constant rotation across all black radio in those months: the Detroit gospel group The Clark Sisters' magnificent 1981 reggae-infused hit, "You Brought the Sunshine." will. i. am's two 2008 Obama campaign songs—"Yes We Can" and "A New Day." And gospel group Mary Mary's jubilant 2008 hit "Get Up." They were the soundtrack of adult black America's triumph.[47]

And the Inauguration, of course, had its own awe-inspiring soundtrack. Millions either attended the star-studded, talent-stocked inaugural events, or watched them on television, and remember Aretha Franklin spectacularly singing "My Country Tis of Thee" at the ceremony. Jamie Foxx expertly mimicking the new president to his face, and the elderly Pete Seeger's duet with Bruce Springsteen of Woodie Guthrie's "This Land Is Your Land" at the Lincoln Memorial concert. Beyoncé singing Etta James's "At Last" for the new presidential couple at one of the inaugural balls.

But the *TJMS* didn't just watch this historical Inauguration on TV. They *went* to the Inauguration and broadcast it. Before the ceremony, they played a mix of Martin Luther King, Jr.'s 1963 March on Washington speech underlain by Marvin Gaye's "What's Goin On":

*Tom: Oh man! I know he's feeling the pressure. Barack Obama has to follow **that!***
J: He gon come widdit!

Obama himself made a courtesy call to thank the crew for their unstinting support, during which Sybil begged to be introduced to Reggie Love, his [very attractive, twenty-eight-year-old] body man. Obama responded with acerbic wit:

> *"Oh, come on now, he's a little **boy**!" He also recounted his daughter Malia's warning about his inaugural speech: "First African American president? Better be good!" And I was like, **dang**!*

And the crew disclosed their own awkward technical difficulties during the Inauguration show:

> *Tom: We had to be here at four to broadcast at six—and the security is so tight— and we had to walk&walk&walk. . . . Let's figure this thing out . . . we've got two college grads (him and Sybil) out in the cold! And we've got a dude from Denmark Tech (J) in the warm! . . . And people kept stopping, sayin "Tom! They messed up this city!" And I said, "**You** did that! You voted!"*
> *J: [heartfelt] And it's needed!*

Huggy was beside himself:

> *Today is the day Barack Obama is finally in the building—and it's a historic day, kinfolk! Today I woke up cryin—Mr. 44 is in the door! Dress warm, bammas! Cause it's gonna be cold as shiggity!*

The following day, they were still het up and celebrating. They were beside themselves over the sheer numbers of the inaugural crowd—circa 1.8 million:

> *Tom: And all those millions of people who attended the Inauguration—and not* ***one*** *arrest!*
> *Sybil: Not **one** person actin the fool!*

Sheryl Underwood was in excellent witty form:

> *Aretha was sharp! That was a sharp, Sunday-go to-meetin, I'm-about-to-sing-and- tear-it-up hat! And was Joseph Lowery not off the chain?*
> *The other persuasion—the vanilla people—they did **not** bring their A game! They was standin on top of statues and porta-potties!*

Huggy Lowdown had a series of wildly happy comments on contemporary race mores to add:

> *I haven't seen that many white people cryin for a black man since Jimi Hendrix at Woodstock in 1969! . . . and when the Queen started singin "My Country Tis*

of Thee," I saw Lincoln snappin his fingers! . . . Do you realize we now have the **first president** *to appear on* **club flyers***!?*

Al Sharpton was on hand to warn repeatedly against misconstruing Obama's role and powers:

Tom: People in the media are comparing Obama to Dr. King.

Sharpton: Dr. King was the leader of a movement challenging the government. Barack Obama is a politician who **is** *the government now. He works by consensus . . . it's a real trap for us to make Obama Dr. King. There must be a role for those who take the unpopular stands!*

The show's happy triumphalist bubble was soon punctured by the ongoing recession, Obama's difficulties with Republican members of Congress, and the very clearly connected resurgent racism associated with Tea Party protests against the Democratic healthcare initiative. The *TJMS* articulated their own and their audience's incredulous, defensive outrage against early racist attacks on the White House.

(August 11, 2009) Sybil reports on the phenomenon . . .

Tom: You know what, playa?

J: McCain people!

Tom: Those are the same people . . . I haven't seen people mad like this since McCain was running against Barack Obama!

J: And what are they mad about?

Tom: Have you seen **who's** *in the White House?*

(August 12, 2009) Sybil reports on town hall disruptions again.

Tom: Mentions poster of Obama with a Hitler mustache.

J: Did you see the one where they made him The Joker?

Sybil: Come on, people!

The crew and audience continued, weaving together a witty put-down of Tea Partiers as foolish, spoiled children whose racist unfamiliarity with black Americans would terrify them into silence if confronted with them:

(August 12, 2009)

Male caller: "What's up with these hearings?! It's white folks gone wild! It's like McCain rallies on steroids!"—Caller goes on to say that it's "old folks behaving like spoiled kids! They need graham crackers, chocolate milk, and a nap."

Sybil suggests Benadryl.

(Later)

Tom: We came up with a solution to the town hall meetings—you need to bus in a busload of black folks! That'd cut all that clownin down!

J, with sardonic emphasis: Waaay, WAY down!

The crew also enjoyed the spectacle of a dignified, informed, intellectual *black* President, after centuries of black Americans being treated with disdain and condescension by whites, testily putting down a bumptiously rude white journalist, Ed Henry, then of CNN.[48] Note how they comically impute to Obama a range of middle-aged black working-class gestures of contempt:

> *(March 25, 2009) Beginning of show:*
> Tom: *Did you see it, did you **see** it?!!*
> J: *Did I **see** it!*
> Tom: *It's better than Idol!*
> Tom: *So we're talkin about the press conference when President Obama shot that reporter down!*
> J: *Did you see him rollin his eyes? If he had false teeth he woulda been rollin them around in his mouth! [crew enjoyment]*
> Sybil: *And that reporter has an ice pack on his butt!*
> Tom: *Don't worry, sir, the swelling **will** go down!*
> J: *He didn't say it, but you know he was thinkin it, "You mother—!"*
> *[crew lost in shouts of laughter]*
> *(Later in the show)*
> Tom: *Did he roll his eyes?*
> Sybil: *I think he even clicked his tongue.*
> J: *And then he went "Uh hunh, uh hunh." He went up in there, man!*
> . . . .
> Sybil: *The tweeters went crazy last night!—"Obama slams CNN doofus," "Henry, you got spanked, deal with it!"*
> . . . .
> Tom: *And the only thing that was missin was, "Here's my response, right **here**.*
> J: *It's like the whole room went D-A-A-Y-M!*
> *(End of show) Woman caller channels and blackens Ed Henry: "What the **hell** was I thinkin, me and my dumb behind!" [crew loves it, repeats with variations]*

The *TJMS* also followed in detail the road to the 2010 passage of the Affordable Care Act, Obama's signature piece of legislation, with much anxiety and calls to activism:

> *(December 16, 2009) Al Sharpton attended the second Obama White House Christmas party the day before. He expounds on the hypocrisy of Republican Senators talking about Christmas while holding up a real healthcare bill—urges people to call their senators. "It's not a game, this is real. This is life or death!" Sybil asks is the current bill worth it?*
>
> Sharpton: *If this bill goes down, I think we are looking at no health care for the rest of our lives! [exactly what Senator Ron Wyden said on Keith Olbermann's show the night before]*
> Tom: *Call your senator! That's right!*

The show was also caught up—as were all U.S. news media—with relief at President Obama's successful May 1, 2011, order of the Navy Seals attack against Osama bin Laden in Pakistan. Their response, however, read the event uniquely through a black pride lens, and was also noteworthy as commentary on Obama's besting of a silly, untruthful, self-claimed billionaire whom none of us then took seriously:

(May 2, 2011, 5 a.m.)
Tom Joyner: Oh! Mission accomplished for real!
Sybil: God bless America!
J: Whatchuknow! Tom Joyner, he's dead! He left the building . . . And Sybil, Wasn't that gangsta? Just when The Apprentice *was gettin good! . . . What a great day! He took out bin Laden and Donald Trump! . . . And Trump had to be hospitalized!*
Tom: ???????
J: He had to have Obama's foot removed from up his ass!
  (Later) J describes after the speech: And the only thing that was missin was cowboy boots and swingin doors! . . .
(Later) The crew on U.S. public reaction:
Tom: And they celebrated!
Sybil: From sea to shining sea.
*Tom Joyner. Good. Good! It's a good day. [deeply emotional] Big Chief! [referring not only to Commander in Chief but to black New Orleans Mardi Gras Indians' "Big Chief"] That's **my** Chief.*
(End of show)
Tom: Oh, it's a good Monday morning!
J: It's good if you're black!
Audience member texts: "He shoulda walked off and pumped his fist!"
They play a segment of Obama's White House Correspondents' Dinner speech [in which he jokes about birther—and Donald Trump's in particular—fantasies about his non-American origins], interspersed with Justin Timberlake's 2007 hit "What Goes Around Comes Around."
*The crew adjures their audience: Now don't give white people shiggity today at work—just **roll** your eyes. [all laugh]*

While here the *TJMS* crew are too celebratory and Old-West macho for my own taste, they are nowhere near as violently so in the wake of the killing as were large public crowds of young white Americans—or as was, for example, *The Daily Show's* Jon Stewart, who in his reportage that evening actually pointed to a cartoon depiction of a U.S. map in which Florida-as-penis suddenly became erect and grew large hanging testicles.[49] And the *TJMS* crew at least linked American triumph over a terrorist enemy to a critique of the false warmongering claims of the previous President—"Oh! Mission accomplished for real!"—and the nation's first black President's verbal jujitsu in besting an absurd yet simultaneously powerful (we didn't yet know how powerful he would become) celebrity enemy.

Nevertheless, the *TJMS* crew and contributors repeatedly expressed chagrin that, now that their candidate inhabited the White House, they no longer had as much access to him and his staff. Most amusingly, President Obama had appeared on the show January 19, 2009, and asked what he could do for Tom Joyner, given the show's monumental efforts for the campaign. Joyner asked to be invited with his granddaughter to the White House Easter Egg Roll. President Obama: "Alright, you got the hookup." But after the event, Joyner relayed his great disappointment (April 14, 2009). He hadn't even gotten to talk to the First Family, and "I registered 100,000 people and he gave me *one egg!*"

Sybil: "Could've been worse! You coulda supported McCain and gotten short-armed!" Listeners and crew then descended into clowning, deriding Joyner for having received only "uh egg."

But this self-amusement also periodically morphed into more serious criticism—into the claim that the president was not responding adequately to his black American base. For example:

> (November 4, 2009) Tom: *All I'm sayin is the president needs to talk to his black*
> *base!—We are here for you, but you can't take us for granted!*
> J, *in the quavering voice of an old black man: You aint called since you left!*

Despite its incessant edgy humor, the *TJMS* is also capable of subtlety and restraint in making its political points. In its regular feature, "Real Fathers, Real Men," listeners nominate a man—who is not necessarily a biological father—whose behavior exhibits self-sacrifice for others, usually children. On September 15, 2009, ten weeks after the conservative-dominated Supreme Court had ruled for white firefighters, against the New Haven, Connecticut, Fire Department's affirmative action plan,[50] Salvatore Consiglio (whose Italian American status is fairly obvious) called in to nominate his New Haven Fire Department co-worker, Kenneth Oliver, Junior (obviously black), as that day's Real Father, Real Man. Consiglio, a firefighter, testified that Oliver, a paramedic, had saved his life and the lives of many others: "With all the problems in the New Haven Fire Department, race has never been an issue with us." His statement was an obvious counter to the Supreme Court's ruling, and the crew limited itself to heartfelt exclamations—"Yeah!"—after Consiglio's testimony, letting it speak for itself.

Finally, the *TJMS* periodically expressed disappointment with and opposition to some White House policies—most particularly military policy. The show has a long anti-war record, and Tom Joyner and Sybil Wilkes are particularly outspoken in this regard:

(December 2, 2009) Tom and Sybil summarize President Obama's December 1 speech and war plans.

Joyner: So, I don't like that decision—but what can I do? Here's what I'm gonna do. Every month I'm givin a scholarship to a veteran [of Iraq or Afghanistan] to go to an HBCU.

(July 22, 2010) Tom comments on secretary of State Hillary Clinton's recent meeting with Pakistani leaders: Alright, Secretary of State Hillary Clinton went to Pakistan and said to Pakistani officials, "You know where Osama bin Laden is and he's in Pakistan," right? So why are we in Afghanistan?

Sybil tries to explain that there are now al-Qaida operatives in Afghanistan, the rationale for going after "his people."

Tom: Ok—it's just me.

Sybil: No, no you're not alone! And that's why the president is losing a lot of his supporters.

They discuss the 5500 American lives to date lost in Afghanistan.

Tom: And how many died in 9/11?

Sybil: [heartfelt, and always grammatical] A lot fewer!

(January 27, 2010) Tom goes on an anti-war rant: War isn't workin! So how about this? Let's take our butts home . . . there's got to be a better way!

And Sybil was quite tart about Obama's disappointing selection of his Chicago friend, the neoliberal Arne Duncan, as Secretary of Education, signaling his continuation of George W. Bush's failed education policies of teaching to test, encouraging privatization through charter schools, and increasingly punitive classrooms:

(January 14, 2009)

Tom to Sybil: What about your homeboy from Chicago for Secretary of Education?

Sybil: He's not my homeboy, but what's your point?

Tom: Well, they've got some of the worst public schools in the country there!

Sybil, with withering sarcasm: But he plays a heckuva basketball game!

(Of course, the later spectacle of Betsy De Vos's rightist administration in the Department of Education under Trump makes Duncan look like Bernie Sanders.)[51]

While Tom and Sybil disagreed with a number of President Obama's policies, their overall support was never in doubt. Not so some other African American journalists, politicians, and intellectuals. Tavis Smiley, allying with Cornel West, spent a great deal of time in the Obama years writing and speaking against him.[52] An early, hilarious contretemps with Al Sharpton on the *TJMS* gives us some of the flavor of those disagreements:

(February 23, 2010) Tavis Smiley is on for the first time in years. He condemns Obama and other black leaders and announces a "Black Agenda" meeting to take place in Chicago on March 5.

Then Al Sharpton calls in, furious. Smiley had characterized him as telling President Obama that he didn't need a black agenda. Sharpton explained that he had met with the president about the jobs bill, "because a 'black bill' would never pass!" Sharpton attacks Smiley for "runnin around the country buck-dancing for Bill Clinton!"

Tom: Man—[laughs]—Reverend Al! You know what, Sybil, it's too bad he was on a cell phone cause he couldn't slam the phone down when he was done!

[crew laughs, makes more jokes] They finish the segment by playing War's famous 1975 song, "Why Can't We Be Friends."[53]

Later in the show, they host the distinguished Harvard Law professor Charles Ogletree, who says he had also received a letter from Smiley, but "I will be in China the whole month." Ogletree calls for an honest discussion "about what Obama can and cannot do." He reports that he regularly presses the president on a variety of issues.

Radio Silence in Chicago

A few months after Obama's victory and Inauguration, Clear Channel Corporation suddenly threw the *TJMS* off the air in Chicago, replacing it with Steve Harvey's far less political, and much less popular, morning show.[54] It was a major shock to the city, and to the crew. Joyner exclaimed, "We lost the mothership, yall!" Friends were emailing me in horror. After some months, Joyner was able to buy a black radio station in Gary, Indiana, 106.3 FM, to continue broadcasting in the region, but the signal was never strong enough, and, after awkwardly streaming the show for some time on my computer, I ended up buying an iPhone so I could listen to the show on the *TJMS* app. But many Chicago listeners just gave up. As Ray, a Home Depot worker, said to me,

I miss the TJMS. *But I'm listening to Steve Harvey, because 106.3 is just too staticky!*

Five years later, Ervin, a skilled manual worker, told me:

Ervin: I listen to Steve Harvey now, but I can't stand the giggles and all that. So I like Tom Joyner. They're better!

Me: And they've got politics!

*Ervin: Oh yeah! They **bring** it! Tom Joyner brings it!*

And a forty-ish man walking to Methodist Church services in 2017 was greatly interested in my project, and explained that while he no longer listened to any black morning shows, his wife listened through the *TJMS* app:

We love Tom Joyner! He's better than them all!

Isiah, a pharmacy technician in his twenties, told me that while he doesn't try to listen to the *TJMS* now, he has fond memories of listening to it while biking to school when he was a young child in the South. Tony, the paint store manager whom we have met, discoursed with solemnity about the importance of the "Chicago radio icons"—Tom Joyner, Herb Kent, and Doug Banks—and how Joyner was thrown off the air, while Kent and Banks had recently died.

But also in 2017, an accidental conversation with a local elderly blues musician— "I'm 83, darling!"—underlined for me the fact that most people living their busy daily lives do not necessarily notice what exactly they are hearing. I mentioned the show, which set the nattily dressed gent off on a tear: "They just play bubblegum! And they do nothing to advance the race—dragging us down, with all those n——— jokes!" He repeated that phrase several times. I realized that he was probably confusing the *TJMS* with Steve Harvey's show, which, since the Clear Channel putsch in 2009, is the only adult black morning radio show, aside from gospel, easily available on the dial in the Chicago area.

Fighting for 2012

The *TJMS*'s muted criticism of the White House, its defensive circle-the-wagons posture—including ambivalent coverage of Occupy Wall Street protests (Sybil was positive, Tom doubtful), and even of Obama's declaration for gay marriage, for fear of harm to his re-election prospects—continued into the run-up to the 2012 elections. This tendency was enhanced by the ongoing racist attacks on the First Family and the under-reported Republican state legislatures' swathe of voter-suppression legislation. (Until Spring 2012, only progressive outlets like *The Nation* and MSNBC seemed aware of this ALEC-organized conspiracy to strip the franchise from minorities, youth, and the elderly, all heavily Democratic constituencies.)[55] *TJMS*, hyper-aware of this phenomenon, consistently reported on it. Al Sharpton, for example, spent his regular Wednesday spot on April 17, 2011, explaining ALEC's secretive and effective blanketing of state legislatures with voter suppression laws.

And the *TJMS* reanimated, with the NAACP, the 1-866-MYVOTE-1 hotline, with promos from a range of black celebrities—NAACP Chair Ben Jealous, Wendy Williams, Samuel L. Jackson, Mary J. Blige, Eric Benet, Angela Bassett, Bill Bellamy, Monie Love, Robin Thicke (white, but at that time married to a black woman, the actor Paula Patton). At the same time, they focused on Department of Justice remedies available at least to former Jim Crow Southern states, and twitted Tavis Smiley and Cornel West's self-involved early criticisms of the President[56]:

> (*November 8, 2011*) *Ken Smukler reviews voter-suppression laws state by state—but he points out that "the last defense against voting-restrictive acts in Voting Rights Act states is Eric Holder and Barack Obama. Do you hear that, Cornel West?" [repeats query pointedly and angrily] Smukler explains that multiple states are asking the Justice Department to allow them to waive Section 5 of the VRA*[57]

The second key track of *TJMS* 2012 election coverage was of course the Republican primaries. Here the crew and audience shared with the broader American media and public a fascinated astonishment with the array of bizarre characters and statements. But from a specifically black progressive perspective—and unlike some other black media outlets—they were outraged by Herman Cain, and beyond mirthful at his comedown over sexual harassment charges. Recent addition younger comic Chris Paul, on November 8, 2011, brilliantly "murdered a hit" to Prince's "Purple Rain"[58] to mark the occasion. He began with audio of one of Cain's victims testifying. Then he spoke, instead of the "Purple Rain" recitative: "A GOP candidate is in trouble, A GOP candidate is in shame . . . because "all these women claim they were harassed by Herman Cain!" Paul's chorus, instead of "purple rain, purple rain," was "Herman Cain, Herman Cain!" And he rose to such heights of wit as "But first you said racism wasn't true, I guess unless it involves you!" "You . . . can't stop chasin white behinds . . . Your wife is gonna whup you, and she might knife you, and cut off Herman's Cain!"[59] (For those who know "Purple Rain" well, just reading the replacement lyrics without even hearing Chris Paul sing them can incite gleeful hysteria. I emailed my transcript of the song around to interested parties at the time of the broadcast. A black university administrator wrote back that he was shouting with laughter so long and hard while reading it, that his staff burst into his office, fearing he was having a heart attack.)

And the *TJMS* wasted no time in articulating biting criticisms of Mitt Romney. On May 1, 2012, Sybil played an audio clip of Romney saying bin Laden's death shouldn't be politicized. She then summed up:

> *That's flip-flopper Mitt Romney who said he wouldn't go after bin Laden, then said he would've, now saying the killing of bin Laden shouldn't be a campaign issue. [crew laughs and catcalls]*

On June 22, D L Hughley was on, wittily sending up Romney's upper-class racist condescension:

> *So Romney went to speak to some Latinos. **He** thought he was going to a housekeeping convention! And he's goin to see the NAACP. He thinks he's goin to see The Help! [crew loses it]*

Michelle Obama phoned in to the *TJMS* on August 10 to report on the stakes of the election: "It's a choice about how we want our democracy run—whether we'll actually **tackle** global warming!" [among other issues] Tom then announced that for this election they were partnering with The Urban League, the National Action Network, and the NAACP in order to fight voter suppression and get out the vote.

The crew reported extensively on voter suppression efforts in a variety of states. On August 14, Roland Martin gave details of Ohio Republican politicians' voter suppression policies: "The problem is, the *TJMS* registered all these black voters across Ohio, and now the Republicans." He implored the *TJMS* audience to call the Ohio Secretary of State to protest. Tom Joyner, bitterly: "When did Ohio turn into **Mississippi**?"

By August 16, Roland Martin was able to announce: "So, the pressure definitely worked there!" The Ohio Secretary of State had announced expanded early voting. But a Pennsylvania judge had upheld that state's voter ID law. Pennsylvania State Senator Vincent Hughes phoned in to exclaim angrily: "It's a gangsta move!" Tom energetically agreed: "No other way to put it! Straight-up gangsta!"

Tom Joyner articulated the distinction between the original Obama campaign and his re-election on August 23: "In 2008, we were proud—in 2012 we're scared!"

The crew covered the details of the Republican National Convention, but Huggy Lowdown's contemporaneous spirited put-downs were priceless:

> (*August 29*) *Yesterday the message at the Republican National Convention was "We built it!" But it should've been, "We bullshiggity!" [crew very happy] ... Y'all hear Uncle Buck's [Chris Christie's] keynote? It was all about* **him**! *... And there was enough in that suit to make uniforms for all the Newark schoolkids for a* **year**! *... And stop playin! ... We* **still** *don't know who the Tin Man is! [his regular characterization of the wooden Romney—crew lost in laughter]*

D L Hughley summed up the Republican National Committee's rightist politics and War on Women in a pithy feminist put-down:

> (*August 30*) *I think the Republicans want to shrink the government so much that it actually fits into a woman's vagina! [crew shouts of laughter]*

The *TJMS* appreciated the 2012 Democratic National Convention both for its politics and its aesthetics. Huggy Lowdown commented on it as spectacle:

> (*September 5*) *I haven't seen a lineup like that since Berry Gordy started* **Motown**! *... In the DNC we don't believe in talkin to chairs [reference to Clint Eastwood's infamous RNC performance], we talk to real live people! ... One night! That one night has already eclipsed the entire Republican Convention! ...*

(September 6) Bill Clinton was so good that Clint Eastwood's chair gave him a standing ovation!

(September 7) The TJMS *plays President Obama's entire DNC speech with Curtis Mayfield's deeply moving 1964 classic "Keep On Pushin" in the background. Tom warns listeners in advance: Now get your Kleenex out. If you drivin, park on the side of the road!*

Huggy Lowdown *responds to Obama's nomination speech: Pastor Pres delivered an elegant Sunday sermon . . . all he needed was the Chicago Mass Choir! (crew very happy) Tom, J, and Sybil, after seein the President, I don't know how anyone would want to go for the Tin Man and the Scarecrow!*

(Later, same day) D L Hughley comes on to sum up the Republicans: Clint Eastwood is a prototypical Republican: he's old, white, rich, out of touch, and talks to people who aren't even there!

The *TJMS* crew, like the rest of the country, were beside themselves over the release of Romney's notorious taped "47%" statement in September 2012. A jubilant David Corn, Washington bureau chief of *Mother Jones*, the journal that broke the story, came on the show on September 19:

*David Corn: What Romney is saying is that **everyone** who voted for Obama is a **moocher** . . . telling that to all the rich folks in the room, the "strivers."*

Al Sharpton followed Corn, and drove home the message:

*When you feel that **seniors** are freeloaders, you are not fit to lead the country!*

Although the sheer number of hours they spent discussing the upcoming elections was fewer than in 2008, the *TJMS* crew were wired to a fever pitch in the last weeks before the November 6 election, and continued to report the news with particular attention to (not only African American) race, class, and gender angles. On September 27, they noted sardonically that Romney appeared before *Telemundo* [actually, it was *Univision*] "with a spray-tan so dark it looked like he was pretending to be Latino!" Michelle Obama came on-air October 3 to rally the troops in advance of the first debate, and the crew announced a "debate party" to be held on Facebook. 3000 people joined Facebook simply to participate in it. On election night, more than 150,000 people participated.

White comic Gary Owen, on October 5, 2012, told a hysterically funny "shifting race relations" story about watching the first Obama-Romney debate with his black wife: "And she's mad at **me**! I told her, I'm not Romney, I'm **Biden!**"

Like progressive media in general, the *TJMS* crew were shocked by Obama's poor first-debate performance, but quickly rallied. On October 5, D L asserted that "I'm firmly convinced he was suckering him in . . . it was rope-a-dope!" President Obama gave them a precious interview—the sole public event in which he discussed the first debate—on October 10. Tom baldly asked him what had happened. Obama responded: "I think it's fair to say I was just too polite, because, you know, it's hard to sometimes just keep on saying that what you're saying isn't true. It gets repetitive. But, you know, the good news is, is that's just the first one. Governor Romney put forward a whole bunch of stuff that either involved him running away from positions that he had taken, or doubling down on things like Medicare vouchers that are going to hurt him long term."

Given consistent, years-long mainstream and even progressive media neglect of the *TJMS*, I was startled to find that that very afternoon Obama's quote "I Was Just Too Polite" was a *Huffington Post* headline, and then was used that evening, with attribution to the show, on NBC, CBS, CNN, NPR, and on every MSNBC evening news show.[60]

The *TJMS*, as we have seen, reserved a real fondness for Joe Biden, as an authentic, often wildly funny, compassionate Democratic politician. To my knowledge, people had either forgotten or never noted Biden's role—as a key member of the Senate Judiciary Committee—in ensuring the confirmation to the Supreme Court of Clarence Thomas, and in preventing Anita Hill's and other women's testimony about his sexual harassment from being taken seriously. The day after his vice presidential debate with Representative Paul Ryan in 2012, they played a nearly seven-minute long set of extracts from the debate—highlighting Biden's signature high amusement at the untruths his colleague was retailing, such as his opposition to Obama's stimulus bill when he'd been caught applying for money for his district from that legislation—"With all due respect, that's a bunch of **malarkey!**"— introduced and underlain by B B King's version of "Joe Cool."[61]

The first vice presidential debate, on October 11—in which Joe Biden definitely schooled the much younger and poorly informed Ryan, sent Huggy Lowdown into a series of joyous Ryan take-downs:

> *Oh man, the Democrats' Shawshank Redemption! Young Ryan was lookin at Joe Biden the way a deer looks at an SUV! . . . Lyin Ryan was sweatin and drinking water. . . . He did say that Romney was uniquely qualified.* **Uniquely qualified!** *Paul Ryan, you are* **uniquely qualified** *to be the Bamma of the Week, Week, Week!*

The *TJMS* also continued its pedagogical role through this period. On October 15, the crew and guests reported on the sinister rightist billionaire industrialists, the Koch brothers, and their vast and secretive infusions of cash into a variety of hyper-conservative causes.[62] A texter wrote in, confusing them with the Coca-Cola Company, swearing to boycott Coke. The crew clarified with high humor, then began joking about druggies being confused by their reporting too, imagining it was about cocaine. Tom Joyner gleefully and hilariously summed up: "My apologies to the Coca-Cola Company—and to the drug dealers!"

And the show actually broke real news the same day: They hosted an anonymous white woman employee of Florida's Westgate Properties, whose CEO had ordered all its employees to vote for Romney. Tom repeatedly exclaimed "bless your heart!," praising her for coming forward to report this illegal activity. She responded, sweetly: "Thank you for having me, I feel the same way you guys do."

After the second presidential debate on October 16, in which President Obama wiped the floor with Romney, the crew was beside themselves. 200,000 people had participated in their Facebook debate party. Huggy exclaimed, "That debate was great! President Obama went all Tony the Tiger on Mitt Romney's ass!" One texter in an all-white office wrote, with consummate *Schadenfreude*,

> *Work is pretty quiet today. Office doors are closed. [crew laughs long and hard]*

Mike Starks then played an extraordinarily clever debate mix which wonderfully used the O'Jays' 1975 "You've Got to Give the People What They Want," interlaid with Obama and Romney statements. Roland Martin came on directly afterward, in fine form: "If there was a theme song last night, the President would've been singin 'Whoop That Trick!'" (from the 2005 film *Hustle & Flow*).[63] The crew immediately latched onto the vision of Roland saying precisely that on CNN, and being summarily fired:

> *J giggles maniacally.*
> *Sybil responds, "Squealin like a pig! That's all he needed! J and Tom gave him permission to do it, and he's gonna go on and say it, and the next thing, he's gonna be on suspension!" [Martin was in fact fired by CNN the following year, along with half-a-dozen colleagues, as part of new-ownership housecleaning.]*

The *TJMS* audience, alert and witty, had all the comebacks. After the third presidential debate, on October 22, they responded to Sybil's comment that the president won the debate "like the champ that he is!"

> *(October 24) Texters:*
> *This morning the Romney camp woke up VOMITING!*
> *Tom, the white people at work haven't come in yet!*
> *Sybil, NOW will you stop watching* The Apprentice? *[because Donald Trump, even then, was still making false announcements that he was about to reveal President Obama's "secrets"].*

A November 1 texter, showing both how closely she was following election dirty tricks and also how well she'd digested *TJMS* slang, wrote in: "Ken, they're *smucking* in Pennsylvania!" And indeed, Smukler kept up his torrent of poll-location and dirty tricks information to the very last minute. On November 5, he reported that authorities were illegally telling people they could not vote, and that voting machines were down all over the country. While he was speaking, texters alerted him that 177 people had failed to receive absentee ballots on Miami, and that no voting machines were then working in Cuyahoga County.

As in 2008, the 1-866-MYVOTE-1 hotline played a key role in Obama's triumph. Ken Smukler reported that they were "at DEFCON 4" by 9 a.m. on November 6. They received an average of 3600 calls every hour, and found poll locations for 50,000 people, not to mention dispatching attorneys to hundreds of sites around the country where callers reported voter suppression. (And these numbers do not reflect the extraordinary work the hotline people did during the weeks and months before the election.) As President Obama joked on the show on October 17, "Here's what I know: when Tom Joyner is workin it, good stuff happens!" But American mainstream and progressive media remained oblivious to that good stuff, and to the vibrant black working-class counterpublic, hidden in plain sight.

This counterpublic was further instantiated both during early voting and on election day, as Republican state governments, attempting to suppress the Democratic vote, restricted voting hours and the availability of booths and ballots in minority neighborhoods, particularly in Ohio, Pennsylvania, and Florida. Extraordinarily long (and under-reported) lines ensued, with individuals waiting up to eight hours simply to cast their ballots, and the *TJMS* echoed Michelle Obama's plea: "Stay on line. Don't let them discourage you." The show created an instant "line culture" in repeated days' commands—"Everybody do the wobble in line!" or "Do a *Five Heartbeats* lines duel!" They kept asserting: "Black people know *how* to stand on line!" And they asked their listeners: "What can you do to make money on line?" Texters flooded Tom Joyner's phone with suggestions: Babysitting. Hair braiding. Powering up devices. Selling "Jamaican cigarettes."

Further elaborating the politics of this working-class black counterpublic, with its hyper-awareness of ongoing popular white racism but openness to the existence of progressive whites, the crew asked its audience: How can you tell that your white co-workers or friends voted for Obama? Texts flooded in: "They fist-bump you." "They ask you how to do the wobble." "They come in with big Obama stickers on their foreheads!"

In the immediate aftermath of Obama's re-election, the *TJMS* crew and correspondents like CNN's Roland Martin, MSNBC's Al Sharpton, even comics like Dominique expressed relief, joy, and profound exhaustion—the entire crew stayed up all night, and were broadcasting at 5 a.m. on November 7. Tom Joyner spent a certain amount of time complaining about the lousy music at the Chicago McCormick Place celebration, pointing out what would have been more appropriate soul classics: "They should have played Shalimar's 'Second Time Around!'

'Cool Mo Dee: 'How you like me now!' They didn't play 'Oh Happy Day,' they didn't play none a that!"

Guest comic Dominique then performed a gorgeous rant, in her trademark raw, uncut vocal style. What struck me at the time was not only the hallucinatory story she created of a determined pregnant woman conversing with her as-yet unborn baby, but also how many key political issues she managed to incorporate—economic polarization (and Dominique is a former DC postal worker, and performs working-class), racist discrimination, women's reproductive rights, black voters' fierce determination to exercise their franchise, and the embarrassing spectacle, on election night, of Karl Rove refusing to believe his own Fox newsroom's announcement that Obama had won. She even managed to insert a surprising homage to election statistician Nate Silver and his first book in order to enhance her put-down of Karl Rove:

> Tom baby! Tom, Sybil and J, what's goin **on** this morning, it went DOWN for us last night! . . . I feel so good, I been up allll night, I mean evah-body just partyin, it's a beautiful thing, Tom!
> Tom: Yeah if you missed the speech, cause it came on really really late last night, I'm gonna play it next . . .
> Dominique: Whooh, congratulations, Mr. President, oh my God! To the American people, they got it right! . . . to all the senators that won! Tom, I feel so good, I can buy a car now, Tom! [crew loses it] I aint got to worry bout ridin to work, and keep lookin at the thermostat to make sure I won't have to pull over and walk the rest of the way!
> Look J, I had to hold out. Cause I said if this thing don't go right, Mitt Romney gon take me back to **Spartacus**! I won't need no car! . . . I said . . . if this don't go right, I might, you know, get my bike game up . . . and you was goin to see me on the highway **bikin**! . . . A Huffy I was lookin at [crew in hysterics, shouting Huffy!]. . . . But good riddance! Ooh he tried, but thank God, I don't have to look at him no more! [crew exclaims in agreement] Bless his heart but good riddance! When he walked out there to do that speech, I said, Come on! Lyin-ass self, takin all long to get out here, come on out heah, so we can get this party started!
> Tom: Did you see how your people in DC voted? 91%!! Whole crew laughs and repeats the number.
> Dominique: Oh, it's understood in DC how it's goin down! . . . Every time I see the numbers in DC, I crack up laughin . . . ..
> Oh the way the people voted, and they stood in line . . . it just was **awesome**, Tom! I'm talkin bout one of my friend's grandmother had a stroke, and she said, "Take me out of rehab! I can kick this ball later! I can lift my leg later! But yall need to get me to the polls, That's where it goin **down**!"
> Tom: Did you see where this lady was pregnant, black lady, in Chicago—and on the way to the hospital, her water broke! On the way to the hospital, she said pull over—

Crew, in unison: I got to vote first!

. . . .

*Dominique: She did the right thing! . . . She said, the man I love put this baby in me, but I don't want to have the **next nineteen**, if I don't want to! She said, she told the baby, this what's goin down, can you hold off? The baby said, "Let's go, Mom!" . . . She stood right in that line! She was off the chain!*

Tom: If Mitt Romney got elected . . .

Sybil: Yes—she would have no control over her body!

*Dominique: No control over her body! Nah, when the contractions started hittin her, she started smartenin up, she said, I'm gon to have to have the baby at the **poll**, but I'm gon cast my vote!*

T, with J overlapping: Water broke!

Dominique: Yeah, the way Mitt Romney was doin things . . . he was taking us back to Little House on the Prairie! . . . [crew shouts]

Tom: Her contractions were five minutes apart!

Dominique and J overlap: That's determination!

Dominique: And it worked out, and guess what, Tom, we sittin high on the hog today! Good riddance to Milleford or what-evah his name is!

Sybil: It's Willard Mitt Romney.

*Whatever! . . . I'm glad he gon home . . . And Karl Rove—little Teddy Ruxpin[64]— [Sybil shouts the name, lost in laughter] Yeah, he need a hug—out there tryin to crunch numbers like Nate Silver! [Sybil loses it] You aint. . . . Go on, it's over! You don't know the signal and the noise! You a **dummy**, you wasted your money, you thought it was bought&paid. No it wuddnt!*

The *TJMS* celebrated the win that they had done so much to ensure. But they also pivoted instantly to the next political tasks. While mainstream media focused on "Obama's next crisis, the fiscal cliff," the *TJMS* and other black media began haranguing their audience on the necessity of staying mobilized and taking back Congress for the Democrats in the 2014 midterm elections.

Crew and audience also maintained their vigilance vis-à-vis the appallingly racist right-wing attacks that only intensified after Obama had won re-election. Tom went off on November 13:

Thehatethehatethehatethehate! The hate continues! He cites people claiming they will secede from the country because of the Obama re-election.

An angry and historically insightful audience member later summed up their (our) understanding of the no-win situation the president found himself inhabiting:

(June 20, 2013) Texter: Is the president the modern-day Jackie Robinson—doin a great job while people try to bring him down? [wild crew exclamations]

There was no show Thanksgiving Day 2012, but they played Obama's victory speech over a fabulous mix of cleverly relevant soul songs: five simply old-school triumphal—"Movin On Up," "Ain't No Stoppin Us Now," "Second Time Around," "Celebrate Good Times," and "Signed, Sealed, Delivered." The sixth was a clear reference to LBGTQ rights, Diana Ross's "I'm Coming Out."[65]

Ironically, the radio music I remember most clearly from the 2012 campaign period was not politically oriented or gospel-joyous. It was, rather, first the highly talented, James Brown-esque, black/Mexican Los Angeles-based singer Miguel's hypnotic breakout love song, "Adorn." I became obsessed with this new neosoul entry, which played for months, on heavy rotation, on every adult black station in the U.S. A Jamaican graduate student and I confessed to one another that we would simply play it for ourselves on constant repeat, day after day, never tiring of it. The second song was the reclusive but openly gay New Orleans composer/singer Frank Ocean's idiosyncratic "Thinkin Bout You," which draws the listener in through its low-key yet hallucinatory lyrics and style. In a universe characterized by widening inequalities and such high levels of hatred and violence, new and more expansive love songs can leaven the atmosphere and provide comfort.[66]

In 2012, black voter turnout exceeded that of whites for the first time in American history—another under-reported phenomenon. In fact, William Frey of Brookings calculated that overall minority turnout determined the 2012 Obama win[67] And much of the credit for black turnout goes not only to the much-ballyhooed "Obama ground game" but also to the *Tom Joyner Morning Show*, its eight-million-strong audience, and other black media. The Democrats "did radio," and black radio paid off.

6

Not "Radio Nowhere"

Racist Criminal Justice and TJMS Activism

> I do want to rescue from the critical guillotine the idea of a collective
> black critique, a collective sensibility, however contested it may be.
> —Guthrie Ramsay, Jr., *Race Music*, 2003[1]

> Power concedes nothing without a demand. It never did and it
> never will.
> —Frederick Douglass, 1857[2]

Black Lives Matter: *TJMS* and the Criminal Justice System

Decades after the heyday of the Civil Rights Movement and the widespread coverage of brutal beatings, dogs, fire hoses, bombings, and lynchings, mainstream American media temporarily yet again "discovered" ongoing police violence against unarmed minority Americans. This discovery was in reaction to the release and widespread airing of the videotaped 1991 Los Angeles Police Department's post-car chase violent beating of motorist Rodney King, and then with the subsequent trials and acquittals of all of the officers involved, leading to major riots in Los Angeles.[3] (I was working in my Northwestern University office on April 29, 1992, with V103 on the radio, when the not guilty verdict came in. They interrupted the music to report it, and the woman DJ kept repeating in shocked expostulation, "I just don't *believe* it!" I didn't either.)

But mainstream media soon once again largely lost interest in ongoing police violence against minority citizens, until George Zimmerman shot and killed the innocent, unarmed teenager Trayvon Martin in Florida in 2012. Not so the *TJMS* and other black media sources, which never stopped reporting on police abuses. As we have seen, Joyner himself began his DJ career in Dallas warning black motorists where the local highway patrol had set up speed traps, attempting to save his audience from both the expense of speeding tickets and the danger inherent in police traffic stops of black motorists. And the *TJMS* has for more than two decades consistently covered race and criminal justice.

That coverage was quite extensive—including the broad swathe of American crime and punishment across class, race, and gender, articulated from a progressive perspective, without fear or favor. In 2007, Bruce Springsteen, perhaps reflecting on driving cross-country, lamented the "radio nowhere" all across the dial, how he was "searchin for a world with some soul . . . is anybody alive out there?"[4] But the *TJMS* was not just alive, kicking, and soulful on the dial and the internet: they were furious, fact-filled, and activist. Sybil Wilkes, for example, regularly announced instances of noteworthy crimes committed by African Americans. She would frequently detail some heinous, or simply bone-headed, criminal case or abuse of power, and then say, with a mixture of sorrow and exasperation: "And yes. He (or she) *was.*" It was assumed that the audience will share her distress, embarrassment, and stern determination not to flinch from hard realities. On October 19, 2016, for example, Sybil reported that

> *A 911 operator is charged with hanging up on callers . . . she apparently hung up on*
> *more than eight hundred! Crashanda Williams . . .*
> Tom Joyner: **Crashanda?!** *[authentically upset]* No! No!
> Sybil: **Yes**. *She could often be heard saying, "Ain't got no time for this!"*
> *J makes fun, tries to turn it into a comic bit . . .*
> Tom Joyner: **No!** *I'm so embarrassed!*

On January 9, 2017, Sybil reported that a man shot a police officer in Orlando.

> *"And yes, he **was.**"*
> Tom Joyner, distressed: Oooooh!

These frequent vignettes reminded me inescapably of my 1970s experiences with the Italian Americans with whom I was working for my dissertation research. One older *paesan* said to me, reflecting his intense self-consciousness about Italian American involvement in organized crime: "Oh, when I read about a criminal, I just pray that his name doesn't end in an e, o, i, or a!" But that defensive stance is now a mere echo of the long-ago past for us older WOPs. It never ended for African Americans, and not because, as the poorly informed imagine, blacks (and Latinos, per Donald Trump's baseless claims) are unusually criminally minded.

No, the *TJMS* and its audience are also painfully aware of the *facts* about race and crime in the U.S.—as opposed to the myths widely accepted by many white (and other) Americans and mainstream media as a whole. Contra screaming newspaper and online headlines, and "if it bleeds, it leads" television news coverage, most crime in the United States is committed by white individuals, and whites commit hate crimes against people of color with high frequency, almost always with impunity.

The criminal justice system is rigged against black and brown Americans—the long-term differential (and thus racist) penalties against crack versus powder cocaine, widespread prosecutorial over-charging of black and brown Americans, long-term profiling and "stop and frisk" police actions in minority neighborhoods, and the "school to prison pipeline" are only the tip of the empirical iceberg proven by carefully executed and widely ignored criminal justice research.[5] And, of course, police of every race tend to harass, falsely arrest, and often murder unarmed people of color at high rates.[6] As Ramsey Guthrie notes in my epigraph, there is a collective black critique, however contested it may be. And as Frederick Douglass declared, alas, more than a century and a half ago, it is only through repeated, insistent political demands that we can force those in power to cease this incessant drumbeat of daily racist incidents through teaching by example and appropriate punishment of wrongdoers.

Former *TJMS* commentator Stephanie Robinson, for example, a lecturer at Harvard Law School, frequently ranted about disparities in the criminal justice system. On December 11, 2008, she asked:

> *Sybil, did you know that most crimes are committed by white people? No! Because in the media all you see is Ray-Ray in a do-rag and handcuffs, rather than a white man in a suit and tie who is defrauding us all of millions! Rod Blagojevich! [former Governor of Illinois, impeached in 2009 and convicted in 2011 of multiple felonies]*[7]

The Reverend Al Sharpton will always agitate about police abuse, and comment with appropriate outrage on the extraordinary unfairness of the criminal justice system:

> *(October 22, 2008) Former [Chicago police] Commander John Burge, who tortured many, many black prisoners, **finally** was arrested! But he was arrested for lying to a grand jury! **Not** torture!*[8]

For Sybil Wilkes, this outraged reportage was simply her daily responsibility:

> *(September 18, 2015) Sybil reports that a fourteen-year-old kid was wrestled to the ground and beaten by police **for jaywalking**. The incident was caught on video, but the police department is not apologizing.*
> *Tom: And I don't want to hear any more about how it's just a few—get rid of the bad ones! Your union is protecting them! Get rid of them!*

Comedian and actor D L Hughley (see Figure 6.1) made key, telling comparisons of the differential treatment of black Americans versus others accused of similar

Figure 6.1 American actor and stand-up comedian D L Hughley. Photo courtesy of Carl Clifford; cropped from original image. CC BY license.

crimes. He was particularly vitriolic—and hilarious—about the sexual abuse of children by Catholic priests, and the Church's long-term, and clearly criminal, efforts to prevent these priests from being exposed and punished:

> *(April 17, 2008) We will let people do **anything** in the name of religion! If Michael Jackson was a priest with a collar, he would never have been put on trial, they'd just assign him to another record label! . . . The Catholic Church has paid out more than TWO BILLION in child sexual abuse cases since 1950!*

D L has also been eloquent about white supremacist militia violence against people of color, and how little attention it garners from mainstream media. He said presciently, six years before Donald Trump was elected president, with the concurrent uptick in white racist hate crimes[9]:

> *(January 13, 2011) I'm not even scared of terrorists anymore—I'm scared of **crazy white guys!** [He goes on to explain that they believe the world is laid out for them, and when they don't get whatever they want, they explode.] Black people, they don't have those expectations. When they lose everything, they just go home to Mama and them! [crew appreciation]*

Hughley, along with the rest of the *TJMS* crew, tirelessly argues for gun control, and specifies who is to blame for our nation's backward, out-of-step gun policies—we are alone, in our lack of gun regulations, among the entire rest of the industrialized world.[10] Like many other progressives, he notes the criminal hypocrisy of rightist anti-abortion yet pro-gun stances, and manages to wring high comedy from the tragic realities:

> *(January 25, 2013) D L dogs National Rifle Association head Wayne La Pierre for his appalling demand that there be no background checks for gun ownership. "We need to talk about gun murders as **really really** late-term abortions! **Then** the right wing would be for gun control!"*

The *TJMS* audience, as well, chimed in frequently on this issue, often with biting wit:

> *(January 23, 2013) Texter: If marijuana is a gateway drug, what is an assault rifle a gateway to?*

With reference to black-on-black violence, the crew was consistently upset, but equally consistently pointed to the widespread availability of military style weapons, and the pure hypocrisy of profiteering gun manufacturers and their lobbying group, the National Rifle Association (NRA). Like all U.S. urban mayors, the former Obama administration, medical professionals, and the public at large, the *TJMS* and its audience desperately long for sensible gun control laws, and call out those responsible for the failure to pass them.[11] Many years before the February 2018 Parkland, Florida, mass shooting of students and teachers, and the surviving high school students' fearless demand for gun control and de-fanging the NRA, the *TJMS* crew and audience were calling for a boycott of that grotesquely powerful institution:

> *(March 4, 2009) Eleanor Holmes Norton, Congressional Representative for the District of Columbia, is on, urging listeners to call Congress and the Senate and tell them to strip "gun rights" out of the Washington DC voting rights bill.*
> *Tom: Elaborately, theatrically surprised: "What do guns have to do with DC voting rights?"*
> *Holmes Norton: **Now** you get it!*

> *(March 5, 2014) Texter, presciently: Let's boycott people who support the NRA!*
> *(Same day) Texter: We should call Florida the Gunshine State!*

> *(July 17, 2015) They have a full crew discussion of the Chattanooga attack.[12] They aren't interested in the terrorism aspect. All focus is on the easy availability of guns, the total illegality of gun shows. J shouts: "Shut it down!" Tom and Sybil*

explain that it's not so simple—we have the Second Amendment, and the active lobbying of the NRA to maintain false interpretations of that amendment. They keep repeating that "the NRA owns Congress." Tom expostulates, "Follow the money!" He says repeatedly that the NRA claims it represents gun owners, but it doesn't—it only exists for gun manufacturers' profits.
(November 4, 2015)

Tom: That situation in Chicago with the nine-year-old and twenty-year-old bein shot . . .
*Sybil: But here's the thing Tom—it's **every day** in Chicago!*
*Tom: GUNSGUNSGUNSGUNSGUNS! I'm **so tired** of people sayin guns don't kill people!*
Crew discusses "safe guns," which have to be unlocked by a single owner . . .
Tom: I could live with that!
J: Let's just get rid of these guns! The gun shows, you could close that, and high taxes . . .and why do you need a bazooka?
Sybil: Or AKs!

*(February 16, 2017) Huggy Lowdown is on a rant against Republicans in Congress who have just made it legal once again for the mentally ill to buy guns, because President Obama is no longer around to veto their crackpot legislation. "But the one we really wish had **pulled out** is Trump's dad! [crew reacts wildly] Who the hell thinks it's a great idea to give crazy people guns? Republicans are like old strippers dancing on the pole—with the NRA stuffin dollar bills in their bras!"*

As we have seen, the *TJMS* was always angrily aware of the differential criminal justice treatment of black versus white celebrities. Tom Joyner in particular can lurch into conspiracy theory territory on this issue:

(June 7, 2007) Sybil announces that Paris Hilton has been released from jail after only three days [for driving while intoxicated, with a suspended license]. Crew chimes in with amazement, jokes about her being white.
Sybil, dripping sarcasm: You hear that, Lil Kim? [the rapper who was jailed for a year for lying to a grand jury about the actions of members of her entourage during a shooting incident][13]
Tom Joyner: This is some 24 stuff! [He notes that George W. Bush scheduled a congressional vote late last night on racist judge Leslie Southwick.] It's a conspiracy to distract our attention from that! Are you with me on this, Sybil?
Sybil: After six–seven years of the Bush White House, I am!

The show was also hyper-aware of, and saddened, by badly behaving black politicians—they were originally friendly with Ray Nagin, Jesse Jackson Jr., and

Kwame Kilpatrick—and then not so much, after they fell afoul of the law. But the crew also sedulously noted how much more likely African Americans are to be prosecuted:

> (March 27, 2014) Crew announces that the mayor of Charlotte, North Carolina has resigned over bribery charges, and the mayor of Homer, Louisiana has been arrested for fraud.
> Texter: Does the FBI go after white politicians like they do black?
> Tom: You know [laughs]—We make it so much easier!
> Sybil: We are low-hanging fruit!
>
> (March 28, 2014) Sybil reports on the latest New Jersey Governor Chris Christie scandal.
> Tom: [sardonically] And meanwhile, the mayor of Charlotte . . .
>
> Crew riffs angrily on white politicians getting away with crimes for which black politicians go to jail.

Black-on-black crime came home for the crew in 2009, when the news broke that the black-owned and -patronized Chicago-area Burr Oak Cemetery had "lost" large numbers of bodies. It was a horrible tale of greed gone mad, with workers digging up bodies and discarding them elsewhere in order to re-sell the plots.[14] Sybil discovered that no one seemed to know where her father's body was. The crew treated the scandal and Sybil's pain both seriously, and with shovels of caustic black humor:

> (July 13, 2009)
> Tom: Sybil went to Chicago—to find her daddy.
> J: Her **dead** daddy.
> Sybil: That's right.
> Tom: J's gonna make a t shirt that reads Help Find Sybil's Daddy!
> J: And on the other side—We Know He's Dead.

The Cook County Sheriff Tom Dart got involved in the crime, and tried to help grieving families locate their loved ones. The story came to an end for Sybil, but not without yet more teasing:

> (August 19, 2009) The crew reminds the audience that Sybil's father's body, along with hundreds of others, is missing from Burr Oak Cemetery. They explain that J leaves a ticket from him at every concert he does, "hoping he'll show up." And he also leaves one for Johnny Mathis.
> J: Because Sybil's father loved Johnny Mathis!
> Tom, slyly: Not that there's anything wrong with him. [playing on Mathis's gayness]

After a commercial break, Sybil reports she has finally located her father's head-stone online, where Tom Dart has had investigators' photos posted.

And of course, the *TJMS* doggedly covered the constantly expanding number of cases of exonerated black prisoners over the years. (Since DNA evidence was first accepted in 1989, more than 2100 innocent people have been exonerated and released from prison.)[15] On April 3, 2015, for example, they celebrated death row inmate Anthony Ray Hinton, proven innocent and freed after thirty years in prison.[16] On January 16, 2018, they had Anthony Graves on the show: an innocent man who had just been released after eighteen years behind bars.[17]

The "criminal justice" story came home for the *TJMS* again when it turned out that Tom Joyner's own great-uncles, Thomas and Meeks Griffin, had been falsely convicted of murder—by an all-white South Carolina jury—and executed in 1915. Henry Louis Gates, Jr. actually discovered the connection and proof of their innocence—he had had the genealogical research done in preparation for having Joyner on his show, *African American Lives 2*. They shared the information with law enforcement, and Joyner traveled to South Carolina on October 13, 2009, to watch state officials sign the pardon documents.[18]

The *TJMS* was also very involved with the Jena 6 case—in which six black Louisiana teenagers were convicted for the beating of one white teenager. (The backdrop was escalating racist tensions in the town, including white students hanging a number of nooses in a symbolic tree.)[19] When one of the teenagers was released, they erupted in joy:

(*September 17, 2007*) *Tom Joyner plays a phone message from Michael Bales's attorney announcing that his conviction has been reversed. Melissa Bales, Michael's mother, also calls in to "let people know that injustice will not be tolerated." The discussion among the crew and guests is interspersed with the intense, shouting chorus from Aretha Franklin's famous 1968 feminist anthem, "Think": "Freedom! Freedom! Freedom! Freedom!"*[20]

Sean Bell, New York City

With reference to police violence against innocent black citizens, the *TJMS* family was particularly incensed and insightful over the Sean Bell case. The twenty-three-year-old unarmed New Yorker had left his strip-club Brooklyn bachelor party on November 25, 2006, with a group of friends, and was driving away, when they were chased by armed plainclothes police. He attempted to flee in his car and all the police opened fire, killing Bell and severely injuring two of his friends. Some of the officers were finally indicted and stood trial but were found not guilty[21]:

(April 25, 2008)

Tom: In New York, they have found the detectives who killed Sean Bell not guilty on all charges.

Sybil adds relevant details, then repeats with fury, "On all charges!"

Tom: Not guilty on all counts! I'm trying to get in touch with Reverend Al—I know he's there on the scene. He was so worried—

Sybil points out that the feds may now enter the scene and bring their own charges against the officers.

Tom: No gun. Getting married the next day. And FIFTY BULLETS!

*J: This—uh—in your gut, it **just hurts**.*

Sybil: People . . . white people will just not understand . . . you cannot argue and tell me justice has been served!

J: [sarcastic white voice]: But you don't know how tough it is to be a cop!

*Sybil: We have cops in our **families**!*

*J: White people are NEVER treated the way **we** are—in LA, I've seen grown-ass men sittin on the ground, cuffed, over bent over the hood of a car . . .*

Four days later, the *TJMS* hosted Sean Bell's fiancée, Nicole Paultre Bell, who had taken his surname and had been very involved in the movement protesting his murder. They asked her sympathetic questions about the strain of keeping up the protest while holding down a full-time job and raising two children.

Trayvon Martin, Hoodies, the Political Economy of Racism

It is only in the past few years that we have begun to see non-minority journalistic venues (*The New York Times, The Washington Post, Salon.com, The Huffington Post, The Atlantic*) shift into reporting adequately on these horrifying race realities. Sybil Wilkes, for example, covered the 2012 Trayvon Martin case for nine full days before the *New York Times* took notice. And then, on March 25, they published a summary piece about the case's "long journey to national attention," once again failing to acknowledge the insistent drumbeat of a major news source for eight million Americans. Let's consider the details of that drumbeat.[22]

Sybil first reported, on March 9, 2012, that "a seventeen-year-old kid was shot and killed [on February 26th] by a neighborhood watch person in a gated community." On March 13, Roland Martin and Sybil discussed the case, as details had been coming out in local Florida newspapers. Martin reported that there was a Change. com petition demanding that George Zimmerman be arrested. On March 19, the whole crew engaged in an extended discussion, attempting to nail down the facts and expressing sorrow and outrage.

Tom: Why has this man not been arrested yet?

*J: Well, when you're white and you kill black, that's **gray**!*

Sybil, bitterly: The other way, not so much.

*Tom, disgusted: So **that's** it.*

Sybil reports facts about George Zimmerman: He was twenty-eight, had wanted to be a police officer but didn't make the cut, and had called the police fifty times in the past year as a "neighborhood watch person."

On March 20, Jacque Reid interviewed Trayvon Martin's family's attorney, Benjamin Crump, who revealed that Trayvon was on his cell phone talking to an out-of-town woman friend up until Zimmerman attacked him. Hardly the profile of someone intending to commit a crime.

The next day, Al Sharpton came on to announce a national rally in Sanford, Florida, where the murder took place:

*Since we've all gotten on it, the Department of Justice has announced an investigation, but the killer is still not arrested." He noted that it had now come out that Zimmerman was not even a bona fide neighborhood watch person—so how could the police NOT charge him? "And now we've gotten the [911] tapes released, and he was told not to follow, and he followed anyway . . . and for three days the child was lying there dead, and they say he didn't have ID. The father was calling the cellphone, and the police didn't answer! [agonized] How could they do that to the **family**?*

Sybil noted the same day that the police who dealt with Zimmerman "have bad records."

The following day, March 22, an agitated Tom harangued Sybil: "Why hasn't Zimmerman been arrested? Why don't they fire the police chief?" Sybil pointed out calmly that power flows from the top. Tom still expostulated, making an interesting historical parallel:

It's like after 9/11 we went to Iraq instead of finding Osama bin Laden! It doesn't make any sense to me!

Commentator Stephanie Robinson came on the show in a later hour, heartsick and furious with mainstream media coverage:

*Who could justify killing this young man under **any** circumstances? Matt Lauer pressed Trayvon's mother on whether he had a criminal background or was possibly "agitated!"—As if that would justify **shooting** him!*

The next day, D L Hughley articulated a parallel lament to President Obama's statement that same day, instantly deprecated by the right, that "if I had a son, he'd look like Trayvon"[23]:

> Trayvon Martin is every black parent of a male child's greatest fear—it's almost that you want your child to wear a shirt that says: "Don't shoot! I have a future!"

Then Professor Louis Henry Gates Jr. of Harvard—Skip Gates—phoned in to comment on the infamous Stand Your Ground legal doctrine:

> I wonder how many would stand their ground without a gun? Guns make **brave men** out of cowards!

On March 26, the Reverend Al Sharpton visited to comment caustically on the local police department's and mainstream media's collusion in smearing Trayvon:

> Like all of that has something to do with why he was killed!? ... The killer ... it is **his** background [arrested for domestic abuse] that would lead to him being violent!

D L returned that day to comment presciently, referencing the by then notorious hoodie that Trayvon had been wearing:

> It is ironic that a young black man has to dress **just so** in order **not** to get shot. ... If we let this go, I know that ... it will be open season on young brothers. ... What kind of world will our children live in?

On April 3, Sybil and guest host Skip Murphy discussed the ongoing case:

> Sybil, in sorrow and horror: You cannot dispute the 911 call that clearly shows Trayvon screaming for his life.
> Skip: Well, we're hoping that justice will be done.
> Sybil: We're hoping, we'll keep hoping, but it's taking a long time!

Sybil reported in disgust the following day that a Pew survey revealed that Republicans, and white Americans in general, a scant six weeks after his murder, "are tired of Trayvon."[24] Al Sharpton then noted black media's role in keeping the story alive:

> Don't forget—we broke the story! Roland and I talked to Sybil on TJMS! [National media] didn't want to cover the story in the first place!

On April 7, Tom Joyner reported that

Rush [Limbaugh] *is now saying that all the "fuss" about Trayvon Martin is about the re-election of President Obama!*
Sybil, with agonized sarcasm: So **that's** *why Trayvon got himself killed!*
Tom: And no one is sayin nuthin!

On April 9, Tom commented that

For all the people who participated in protest marches for Trayvon Martin, the grand jury meets tomorrow, and let's hope they bring an indictment! And oh! The hate continues!
Sybil: We've got to be vigilant! You can't let your guard down. . . . She goes on to detail the disrespect to President Obama.
J: They're **so** *mad! And It's not to help the country. They'd rather bring the country down.*

On April 10, a perceptive and sardonic texter asked the key question:

Tom, can someone please explain to me why you would **follow** *someone if you're in fear for your life?*

On April 12, family attorney Benjamin Crump commented in surprise on the eventual second-degree murder rather than manslaughter charge against George Zimmerman. The crew and Crump noted the defense's claim that they had no idea where Zimmerman was. Crump exclaimed: "Thank God for Attorney General Holder and President Obama, because we know he left Florida, but they cover the whole country!"

And as usual, the *TJMS* acted as the charity of last resort for black Americans experiencing tragedy:

Trayvon's parents, Sabrina Fulton and Tracy Martin, are on the show. Tom asks: You need some help? Some help with some bills?
Mr. Martin: Well, yes. . . . People are supporting us, but I've taken a leave of absence from my job.
(Later in the show) Texter: Tom you **are** *goin to Heaven!*

On April 17, Al Sharpton laid out the larger national political issues behind the Martin case. George Zimmerman was claiming innocence on the basis of Florida's Stand Your Ground law, despite the fact that he had stalked Trayvon Martin on public streets, and was obviously nowhere near his own home, defending it from an intruder, when he attacked him. Sharpton explained once more about ALEC, the shadowy right-wing American Legislation Exchange Council, which was responsible for the passage of Stand Your Ground laws in multiple states, as well as voter suppression, anti-union, and anti-regulatory legislation.[25] He discussed his National Action Network's protests against both legislative moves, and adjured the *TJMS* audience: "We'll have to keep watching them!"

During George Zimmerman's trial, the *TJMS* crew and guests were incensed over the defense's tactic of painting Trayvon as a criminal deserving his own assassination. No one was the least bit fooled by the double standard for black versus white adolescents. D L Hughley spoke for millions when he came on the show on June 14, 2013, and declared:

> *If a teenage boy could be given the death penalty for smoking weed and cutting class, wouldn't Justin Bieber be on death row right now?*

The crew and audience were very agitated over Rachel Jeantel's trial testimony [the young woman with whom Trayvon was speaking on his cellphone as Zimmerman began stalking him]: the painful spectacle of a working-class black teenager, completely unprepared for the national spotlight, being browbeaten by the defense attorney. As a *Washington Post* reporter put it, she "unwittingly became a proxy for pitched cultural debate, a stand-in for projections about race, class and especially all the things Americans—black and white—want, don't want and can't tolerate seeing in young black women."[26]

Sybil was upset over Jeantel's inarticulateness—"But Tom, it was difficult to understand her!" While Tom felt a paternal defensiveness for her: "I understood her just fine! . . . I feel so sorry for this little girl!" Joyner then began imagining what he could do to help her. Jeantel had said on the stand that she didn't watch the news, and was criticized for it. A compassionate texter identified with the young woman, and laid out her own take:

> *I don't watch the news—I get it all from yall! So if it aint around the water cooler or on TJMS, it aint news!*

On July 13, 2013, the Florida jury found George Zimmerman not guilty on all counts. On July 16, the *TJMS* had Rachel Jeantel on the show, and Tom Joyner told her he would pay for her education. And he did.[27] The crew reported outrages—that racist, right-wing retired rocker Ted Nugent blamed Trayvon for his own murder—while they were reduced to reacting:

> *Tom, horrified: And he got a round of applause!*
> *Sybil: Yes he did!*

Tom: That is just sick . . .
*Sybil, balefully: **That** is the America we live in.*

The next day, the show played a memorial tribute for Trayvon—with the Five Stairsteps' crooning ballad, "Oooh child, things are gonna get easier"[28] in the background—in mourning over the verdict, but picking up the pieces for yet more activism. Tom played extraordinary listener responses, such as this sadly insightful one from a black Southern working-class man:

> We **live** here—we **know** what race is here. The onliest thing we can do is change
> all these laws.

On July 18, Tom announced that there would be demonstrations on Saturday at federal buildings across the United States, "and I encourage you to go!"

Sybil: I'll be there!
J: [deadly serious] I'll be there too!

By July 19, the crew had a list of all of the planned federal building demonstrations on the Blackamericaweb.com website.

Eric Garner, Marissa Alexander, Michael Brown

The *TJMS*'s attention to police violence against people of color is far too granular and long-standing to allow a full accounting of their coverage of every case since 2004. But the Michael Brown/Ferguson events, preceded by Eric Garner's police chokehold killing in New York, and Sandra Bland's minor traffic arrest and then suicide in custody, were extraordinarily heart-wrenching, involved the first major Black Lives Matter demonstrations, and garnered enormous global publicity. How did the *TJMS* respond on a daily basis as those cases, and the new movement, unfolded?

Eric Garner, who was allegedly committing the minor offense of selling loose cigarettes, was attacked by Staten Island police officers, and brought down and killed by a chokehold on July 17, 2014, a Thursday. By the following Monday, July 21, the *TJMS* had Roland Martin and Don Lemon from CNN reporting extensively on the case. Everyone was outraged over the chokehold, which was illegal, the city's failure to arrest the officers involved, and reporting indicating that paramedics arrived, but then stood around, making no effort to help the dying man.

Al Sharpton reported in on July 23, the day of Garner's funeral, to protest yet again against the illegal chokehold, and to call once more for federal regulation of the police:

> *How do we stop police brutality? The same way we stop crime. When police know that they can go to jail . . . it will stop!*

Sharpton returned on July 28 to report that he was meeting with Garner's family about filing a federal lawsuit against the Staten Island police, who have a long-standing reputation for racism. "Seven of the top ten most sued police officers in New York City are from Staten Island, even though it's the smallest borough!"

Meanwhile, the crew was aghast at the ongoing governmental persecution of African American Marissa Alexander, an abused Florida wife who had fired a warning shot into the ceiling to deter her husband from attacking her. Contra Florida's Stand Your Ground law, Alexander, who had no criminal record whatsoever, was arrested, charged with aggravated assault with a lethal weapon, convicted, and sentenced to a mandatory minimum of twenty years. An appellate court ordered a new trial in late 2013, and released Alexander to house arrest. Angela Corey, the prosecutor, announced that she would re-prosecute Alexander, aiming for three consecutive life sentences.[29] The *TJMS* and many others were painfully aware of the contradiction: Alexander had actually been "standing her ground" within the letter of the law, and yet was charged, jailed, and convicted. Zimmerman's attack on Martin bore no relationship to the law, and was a cold-blooded murder, and yet Zimmerman—and Corey was in charge of that case as well—was judged not guilty. Tom went off on a rant on July 23, 2014:

> *What has she [Angela Corey] got against this woman? She was abused by this man! And he was coming after her! And she shot in the ceiling, a warning shot! And no one was hurt! And we went down to protest in Tallahassee!*

Michael Brown was killed in Ferguson, Missouri, on August 9, 2014, a Saturday. The *TJMS* was in full effect by Monday, August 11—providing all the information then available, with Roland Martin interviewing a local black television reporter for details. The crew was aghast and sorrowful, but also repeatedly called for nonviolent demonstrations. Comic Chris Paul, in his Morning Minute, laid out the furious black (and generally progressive) dissent from widespread, automatic mainstream media presumptions of the guilt of victims of police violence:

> *It's time to stop calling these people officers of the law and call them what they really are—HUNTERS! And our people are always in season!*

The following day, the *TJMS* hosted Benjamin Crump, now one of the attorneys for the Brown family, and Al Sharpton, who phoned in on his way to Ferguson. Sybil crisply laid out the opposing narratives of the Ferguson police and Michael Brown's friend, an eyewitness to the murder.

On August 13, Roland Martin interviewed a young black *Washington Post* reporter, Wesley Lowery (who later won a Pulitzer Prize, and is now a commentator for CNN). Lowery, with another reporter, was violently arrested directly after his phone conversation with the *TJMS*, on his first day in Ferguson, for simply sitting in a McDonald's restaurant.[30] Lowery's arrest was but one example of the phenomenon that alert journalists were chronicling: the extraordinarily unnecessary, horribly militarized, over-reaction by Ferguson police to street protests over yet another police shooting of an unarmed black male.

Al Sharpton then reported on the massive ongoing Ferguson protests in which he was participating, and commented on the police saying "that they don't want to release the officer's name because of threats, but many feel they don't want his name out there because he may have a record of violations." Sybil then smoothly entered the conversation with the Missouri State Attorney General's statistics on the state's history of racial profiling.[31]

On August 13, Tom went on an outraged rant over Lowery's arrest. Sybil and J, in order to introduce a lighter note, impersonated Yoda, joking that "the force is strong in that one." The following day, Chris Paul sardonically asked, assuming audience familiarity with civil rights history,

> *What **year** is this? It's like the police in Ferguson are using the documentary* Eyes on the Prize *as a **training video**!*

Sybil then reported that a St. Louis Alderman, Antonio French, had been arrested in Ferguson while documenting the protests and ongoing police violence, which led the crew into an angry exchange:

> *J: It's a war on young black men!*
> *Tom: It's like Iraq!*
> *Sybil: Except more information comes **out** of Iraq!*

On August 15, Sybil said grimly,

> *It is what it is—white man in uniform murdering a black child.*

Tom Joyner, beside himself, broke in:

> *That's murder! Arrest him! . . . Then have a trial.*

The crew then discussed how proud they were of President Obama's statement, and queried why Hillary Clinton had not yet said anything—although Sybil noted that she was "damned if she does, damned if she doesn't." They noted that Senator

Elizabeth Warren had flown to Missouri to work with Senator Claire McCaskill on the crisis. And Sybil reminded the crew and audience that there were now three ongoing cases of police murders with "no legal action. . . . Tom, this is the slowest I've ever seen! Nothing is coming out!

By August 19, the crew was beyond weary of waiting for law enforcement to move on the case, of watching police violence against nonviolent demonstrators, and of the violence and looting engaged in by a minority of the demonstrators:

> Tom: *The violence is being perpetrated by the police who have not arrested the officer who killed Michael Brown . . .*
> Sybil: *I'm not sure even that will stop it at this point.*
> Tom: *Maybe it's just gone too far. And now the President is sending in Eric Holder. [big sigh] So. Syb?*
> Sybil: *As you said, Tom, this could all be stopped.*
> Tom: *So put an end to it! Arrest the guy!*

On August 21, comedian and film and television actor John Witherspoon called in. Witherspoon had experienced the riots in Detroit after Martin Luther King Jr.'s 1968 assassination. He and Sybil energetically opposed music mogul Sean "Puff Daddy" Combs's claim that President Obama was not doing enough for Ferguson, explaining the limits on the Commander in Chief's powers. They then discussed black parents' horrifying but necessary task of teaching their children how to avoid being killed by the police—the notorious "talk" about which much has been written[32]:

> Tom: *I tell my children, and they tell their children—Do what the cops say!*
> Sybil and John Witherspoon point out that even if you do exactly what police demand, you may get beaten or even shot anyway. They make a strong case for ongoing activism and legal and policy changes.

On August 25, Tom and Sybil were broadcasting from St. Louis, as they had traveled to the area to attend Michael Brown's funeral. Roland Martin harangued the audience about the need for ongoing activism "after the TV cameras leave," the importance of "a moment becoming a movement."

> Tom: *And here's a story about Darren Wilson [the officer who killed Michael Brown]—He used to work in the police department in Jennings, Missouri. And the racial tension was so bad that they fired the entire police department! The corruption and racism was that bad![33]*
> Sybil: *Makes you wonder . . .*

Al Sharpton, who would be presiding over Brown's funeral, then reported that he had spent the day before with Brown's parents and their attorney Benjamin

Crump. The parents had attended a rally for peace in St. Louis, and asked that there be no protests that day out of respect for their son. The whole crew was aghast that $250,000 had been raised for Darren Wilson. They discussed the details of money extracted from Ferguson and other nearby black communities through abusive policing and a punitive justice system. (A few months later, legal scholar Richard Rothstein would publish the detailed and exhaustive "The Making of Ferguson," with the Economic Policy Institute. The piece lays out the historical political-economic evolution of a century of deliberate policies determining residential and school segregation in the region as a whole, and the concomitant rise of municipalities using their black populations as ATMs through targeting them for police stops, arrests, over-charging, high bail amounts, and excessive fees and fines—a reality that would be news to many white readers but already deeply understood by *TJMS* listeners.)[34]

Sybil reported that blackamericaweb.com would stream Michael Brown's funeral live, as well as a Michael Cottman interview with Attorney General Eric Holder. The following evening, they announced, there would be Radio One-sponsored town hall meeting at Harris-Stowe State University (an HBCU) in St. Louis. Tom remarked, "I hope all this energy goes to the *polls*, because that's how we make change happen!" Sybil pointed out that if you aren't registered to vote, you cannot be called to serve on a grand jury.

The *TJMS* finished out the show with a clever audio/musical mashup offering historical contextualization: actual audio footage from the 1965 Watts riots in Los Angeles, Presidents Lyndon Johnson's and Barack Obama's responses to each crisis, Ferguson march chants, testimonials from individual marchers, police megaphone commands, all underlain by the highly appropriate Steve Miller Band's 1976 crossover hit "Fly Like an Eagle" ("Time keeps slippin into the future"),[35] segueing into the gospel duo Mary Mary's triumphalist "It's the God in Me."[36]

While they were waiting for news from the Ferguson grand jury, and suffering through the disappointing 2014 midterm elections, the *TJMS* crew kept the heat on. J pulled off another brilliant, devastating political murdered hit on October 10, referencing both the Michael Brown and Eric Garner cases, repurposing Chris Brown's misogynist "These Hoes Aint Loyal"[37] into a manifesto against violent police:

[Recitative]
Cop: Sir, please put your hands up!
J: My hands are up!
Cop: Your hands are not up!
J: My hands are completely up!
Cop: He's reaching! BLAMBLAMBLAM! . . . Uh, I'm sorry. Was that a
    pocket comb?

J then sang, to a reggae beat, that "we are uptight" because "some of these cops ain't right." Interpolating features of Eric Garner's killing, J concluded that "as far as we done come, it's like 1939!" Referencing the huge progressive changes wrought by bystanders filming police violence, he concluded: "Hope and pray there's a camera on ya! . . . No, po-po aint loyal!"

Meanwhile, the *TJMS* kept their audience up to date on Michael Brown's case. On November 18, journalist Soledad O'Brien discussed her upcoming Ferguson/police violence special on CNN, "Black and Blue."[38] On November 21, Sybil reported that Michael Brown's shooter, Darren Wilson, would resign from the Ferguson police department. On November 25, the day after the evening announcement that the grand jury would bring no charges against Darren Wilson, an appalled and sorrowful crew reported the facts. Sybil said:

> Here we are on the day after the non-indictment came down, and we have seen protests, some peaceful, some not so. . . . She then read the full press announcement, and opened the TJMS phone lines: "This morning, TJMS is yours. We want to hear from you!

The *TJMS* interviewed attorney and St. Louis native Gloria McCollom about the case. McCollom was beyond exasperated by the incompetence and obvious racial bias displayed by St. Louis County prosecutor, Robert McCulloch: "They pretty much want to clear the guy!" Guest host Skip Murphy was aghast:

> How can this possibly be ok? How can you shoot someone who's not trying to shoot you? We've got to fix the system—but we always say that, don't we? What does that even **mean**?

On December 1, post-Thanksgiving, Sybil talked about holiday dinner discussions being dominated by Ferguson and the Bill Cosby case. Tom praised local NBA players for expressing their dissent:

> I was so proud of the St. Louis Rams when they came out with their hands up!
> Sybil: A lot of people were not pleased with that, and they're calling the NFL!
> Tom, sardonically: I don't think they're going to get into that, they've got their hands full!

On December 3, the nation learned that the Staten Island grand jury considering Eric Garner's strangulation by the police officer Daniel Pantaleo was bringing no indictment, and there were immediate protests around the country. Sybil reported that the show was receiving hundreds of texts from people engaged in demonstrations as far away as Paris. The *TJMS*'s Chris Paul responded to both cases in his prototypically sardonic manner:

> Dear Santa Claus, This year could you please bring black people in the U.S. what we need and want? Could you please bring us some **justice**??

The crew discussed both non-indictments, the protests, and shifting white American comprehension of racial justice issues. Sybil expostulated:

> I wasn't surprised about the non-indictment in Ferguson, but **this** one—what more do you **need**?!
> J: Nuthin's changed! Go back to Rodney King!
> Sybil and Tom: That's right! Nothing's changed!
> Sybil: I think what a lot of white people don't understand is that we are protesting the **treatment** of people of color.
> Tom: I think white people are beginning to understand—because you watch the protests in New York City, what do you see?
> Sybil and J: A lot of white people!
> Tom: And there's a new hashtag—white people talkin about how they were stopped by the police and **let go**.

The crew then switched to a broader historical perspective, commenting on the positive effects of the rise of social media:

> Tom: Back in the day, when we were protestin, you wouldn't find out who was protestin for at least a week! You had to wait til Jet Magazine came out!

For the rest of the year, the *TJMS* reported positively on the spate of Black Lives Matter and other protests around the country—from medical students staging a die-in to congressional staffers' hands-up walkout, to the major anti-police violence march in Washington, DC, in which many of the crew participated. Meanwhile, life went on, and Tom and Sybil were honored to attend the White House Christmas party, where President Obama reportedly told Sybil that she had "cute hair."

In these years, characterized by the disorienting drumbeat of repetitive acts of violence black Americans face in their quotidian lives, the *TJMS* has indeed been a site where, as Donna Summer reminded us, "love is found on the radio."[39] Not in this case the romantic love that soul balladeers have crooned about over the decades, but the communal love felt, instead, for one's oppressed fellow humans: the comfort, the political and social solidarity, the calls to activism—making Frederick Douglass's demands—the actual material help, the community of the air that the *TJMS* crew, guests, and audience offered one another as they built and rebuilt their progressive black counterpublic. As Sybil remarked, bitterly and accurately, many times over the years, "Hate doesn't take a holiday." And we need a respite from that overwhelming, ignorant hate, the respite that the *TJMS*, among other progressive media, provided. This is not "Radio Nowhere." It is *right there* on the radio dial, very much Somewhere, and that Somewhere is Progressive Soulsville.

We have seen that love, that aid, that solidarity in multiple instances of audience and crew empathy for and material aid to others—in the aftermath of 9/11, of Hurricane Katrina, of the Gulf Oil disaster, in the provision of HBCU scholarships, in concern for and publicizing the cases of missing black women and girls, in protests against police violence against unarmed African Americans, and in responses to multitudinous individual hard-luck narratives, including the extraordinary pain of grieving family members of unarmed individuals killed by police, who, as we have seen, often then appear on the show. As Sade sang, "I got the radio on . . . I can feel your sound."[40] But we also see this *communitas* in *TJMS* political discussion and commentary, in their presumption that audience members will identify with and act as citizens in accord with show's progressive politics.

7

The Trumpocalypse and Its Afterlife

> Donald Trump is operating the White House as a terror cell of racial
> grievance in America's broader culture wars . . .the exploitation of
> black bodies and the spilling of black blood are an indelible part of the
> American story, and how we deal with that says everything about *where*
> we are as a nation and *who* we are.
> —Charles Blow, "A Rebel, a Warrior, and a Race Fiend," 2017[1]

> Indeed, the greatest and most immediate danger of white culture,
> perhaps least sensed, is its fear of the Truth, its childish belief in the
> efficacy of lies as a method of human uplift.
> —W. E. B. Du Bois, 1940[2]

Moving Toward the 2016 election

During Obama's second term, the *TJMS* began inviting news anchor Joy Reid, whose role at MSNBC was growing, to visit the show and lay out civics details for its anxious and disappointed audience longing for faster progressive change.[3] On August 5, 2014, for example, Reid expostulated everyone:

> *If we want a better President, we need a better Congress! . . . So basically, Congress is the primary institution, and who's in Congress can **trump** the President anytime they want! They have such broad power that they can literally bring the government to a halt! And this Congress **has**. [She articulates FDR's and LBJ's relations with very different Congresses, then lays out the current Congressional math that prevents President Obama from achieving much of his signature legislation.] All of this is not to say that President Obama can't do anything . . . Black voters can make a **huge** difference!*

Tom Joyner and the crew enthusiastically thanked Reid, and a texter summed up audience reaction:

> *Joy Reid **brought** the government civics lesson this morning! Now I understand my government so much better! Thank you, Joy Reid!*

The *TJMS* changed as well during this period. Tom Joyner bought a New York City radio station, 103.9, WNBM (with Cumulus Media), and built within it another premier "Red Velvet Cake Studio" for visiting artists' performances. He bought a home in Harlem himself, probably—beyond personal reasons—in order to take part more easily in Eastern Seaboard black and other cultural events and to publicize the show more successfully through proximity to major national media sources.[4]

TJMS and the 2016 Campaign

As the 2016 presidential election approached, the *TJMS* kept up the pressure, following the race closely and urging their audience to pay attention, register, and vote. To my knowledge, they never referred back to their annoyance with Hillary Clinton for having "misspoken" during the 2008 race about experiencing sniper fire on a trip to Bosnia. (Nor did they reanimate Clinton's presumed complicity in the retrogressive Bill Clinton-era legislation—in part because they had not disapproved of President Clinton in the first place.) The crew instead was hyper-aware of the actual contemporary stakes of the race for most Americans' social welfare—and for both the rest of the world's human populations and the rapidly changing global climate— and consistently covered the issues.

And to my infinite glee, they managed—and manage—to be funnier and nastier about Donald Trump&Co than even the best American network and cable television political satirists—Samantha Bee, Bill Maher, Jon Oliver, Stephen Colbert, Chelsea Handler, Trevor Noah, Jimmy Kimmel, Seth Myers. In particular, both before and more importantly after the election, the various crew members vied with one another—and even with themselves—to coin the most scabrously disrespectful and simultaneously accurately descriptive epithets for Trump, easily beating out Bill Maher's often-repeated "whiny little bitch." Huggy Lowdown holds the current record, having coined, over just a few short, miserable years:

Trumplethinskin
The Orange Dude is All Kinds of Rude
A Grown-Ass Baby
The Pigpen of Politics
Baby Fat Hands
President Re-ject
Flatulent with a Comb-over
President Infomercial
Orange Roughy
The Pumpkin-Colored Race-Baiter

*Pumpkin Sniffle Latte—after the presidential debate in which he kept sniffling like
   a cokehead*
This Secondhand Prophylactic
The Billionaire Bigot Bozo
The Tangerine Fiend
40-Lie—as opposed to 45
Orange Lucious—as in the criminal Lucious Lyon in the television show Empire
Billionaire Butthole
MOTUS, or Moron of the U.S.
That Orange Stool Sample
Lego Fat Man
The Mar-a-Lago Duke of Hazzard
The Brainless Bigot
Putin's Pistachio Holder
*Commander Tissue-Shoes [after Trump was videoed walking up the Air Force One
   stairs trailing toilet paper from one shoe]*

And the *coup de grace*, the clever epithet that has incited the most hysterical
laughter among everyone with whom I have shared the list:

Toupee Fiasco[5]

And continuing the fake tan and authoritarian theme, Chris Paul hit it out of the
park with "Kim Jun Orange," "Orange Pinocchio," "The Orange Underwear Stain in
the White House," and "That Toupee-Wearin Traffic Cone!" "That Testicular Wart,"
and "That Toddler Without Testicles" also make the grade. Guest comic Arsenio
Hall contributed "Orange Satan," while news anchor Roland Martin came up with
"Orange Slob Square Hands."

TJMS listeners were equally wonderfully nasty in describing Trump. On May
11, 2018, after Chris Paul had delivered yet another Trump take-down, mentioning
what David Letterman used to repeatedly name "that **thing** on Donald Trump's
head," a texter with obvious country background wrote:

Trump's hair is like a chicken's ass in a high wind!

Trump's various allies received the same witty, nasty treatment, the apex perhaps
being when Chris Paul, at the point of hopelessly criminally compromised National
Security Adviser Michael Flynn's disgrace and ignominious White House departure, characterized him as "nuthin but a colostomy bag wearin shoes!"

During the primaries, the *TJMS* didn't at all ignore the surprisingly successful
Bernie Sanders campaign, but that campaign made it extremely difficult for them

to engage with him. On February 9, 2016, for example, Al Sharpton was on air, explaining that he was about to have breakfast with Sanders and to press him on civil rights policy. Tom interjected:

> Reverend Al, is this a closed meeting? [yes, it was] Well, we've been asking Sanders for weeks *to come on the show!* [with no response whatsoever]

Bernie Sanders did eventually appear on the *TJMS* on February 29, with a panel of questioners including Roland Martin, Al Sharpton, Don Lemon, Sybil Wilkes, and Jacque Reid. They queried him about his healthcare and education plans, and specifically pushed him on the welfare of HBCUs. Sanders stuck to his standard talking points—free higher education, and how he helped write the Affordable Care Act, but we have to improve it. He said that HBCUs had played "a phenomenal role in giving an education to people who might not have gotten one otherwise," but he had no response to the question of what he would do to aid them in this era of HBCU financial crisis.

Al Sharpton pushed Sanders on the broken criminal justice system, asking what sort of attorney general he would appoint. Sanders was forceful there: "An attorney general of mine would be extraordinarily aggressive in attacking the broken criminal justice system." Jacque Reid then pointed out that the *Detroit Free Press* and others were attacking the EPA for the Flint water crisis: "You've been paying close attention . . . you've even called for [Michigan] Governor Snyder's resignation." "Sanders: I met with people in Flint . . . I could not believe what I was hearing! . . . So we have to strengthen the EPA. We have to as a country prevent the companies from polluting our air, our water. If the state government is not interested in helping the people of Flint, then the federal government should move in aggressively."

Sybil Wilkes then queried Sanders on the race/gender intersection, pointing out that women only make seventy-eight cents to the male dollar, and black women even less. She asked whom he would name to his Cabinet. Sanders reached back to the 1990s Bill Clinton line that it would "look like America," and said that he believed in pay equity.

Afterwards, the crew found Sanders's performance underwhelming. Sybil sardonically noted: "I think he needs a little more time with us."

> Tom: *We've been tryin for six months to get Bernie Sanders to do this interview with us. And if he had done it before South Carolina, he would've done better, wouldn't he?*
> Sybil: *Yes!*
> Tom: *And you jammed him up about the **women**, Sybil! I love it!*

The witty and well-informed Ken Smukler returned to the show for the 2016 campaign, periodically reporting—with wildly relevant but often rather abstruse popular cultural references—on the shifting polls, Clinton campaign gaffes, and the alarming details of Trump's statements and actions, and those of his soon-to-be-proven-criminal campaign personnel:

> *(September 1, 2016) Good morning, Tom, Sybil, Kym, and Jay Antoine. The Donald's kvetching, Hillary's email vexing, and Anthony Weiner sexting! Sixty-seven days to go—and THIS is your Smuk report.*
>
> *When last we chatted, the conventions were in our rear-view mirror, the Donald was like an armadillo crossing Texas state highway 130, just north of San Antone—a few armadillo arms away from roadkill! His numbers went from dead even across the battleground states . . . to double digits after Hillary threw the Chaka Khan&Awe at him [as is Shock and Awe], day two of the Democratic Convention. The Donald decided that nothing seems more presidential than attacking the Gold Star mother of an American Muslim killed fighting for his country. Uh—that country, Donald, would be the U S of Smukin A! A move which led the Donald's poll numbers to plummet faster than Ryan Lochte's net worth after relieving himself of bodily fluids and any sense of dignity! [crew loses it] . . .*
>
> *I swear, Donald Trump kvetches, blaming all things that are attacking him on the media. It's like he's Chris Brown, channeling Charlie Sheen, blaming the LAPD for responding to a 911 call that came from **his** smuking house!*
>
> *The Donald attempted to reset by shaking up his campaign team! Look Tom, when Trump tagged Paul Manafort as his campaign manager, loyal followers of the Smuk report will remember, learned of this cat's ties to the Ukrainian thug in chief Viktor Yanukovych.[6] But the Donald threw Manafort under the Trump train when he's reportedly outed for taking cash payments from Dr. No . . .*
>
> *So Trump decides to reset his campaign with a dude named Steve Bannon. Who runs a rightwing website, whose theme song, if it had one, would be "Springtime for Hitler in Germany!" [crew hysterically appreciative] A website named Breitbart, which is as bright as a black hole and has the intellectual outlook of Bart Simpson. Seems Bannon doesn't only have a problem with Jews, he's got two domestic violence reports filed by his ex-wife. Which is PERFECT for Trumpville, a campaign that had just brought on Roger Ailes for debate prep. The chief of Fox News—the **former** chief of Fox news, the man who will be remembered for putting the **cock** in Fox![7]*

Smukler then rose to a pinnacle of male-feminist-ally satire, richly mining popular cultural references:

> *So Donald Trump completes the misogynistic cocktail: first a jigger of Corey Lewandowski, who roughed up a female reporter on the campaign trail. Add a splash of Roger Ailes, and garnish with a sprig of Steve Bannon. Really! Sybil,*

the campaign trail is the Isle of Misfit Boys, a campaign that should be recast as
*Fifty Shades of **Gross**!*

But Smukler didn't entirely let Hillary Clinton off the hook, judging her campaign
for sloppiness and poor optics:

> *But make no mistake, Tom: if Hillary becomes the forty-fifth president of the*
> *United States, it will only be because she ran a campaign against a man who*
> *every day runs a campaign that could best be described as "I'm fired!" Hillary's*
> *numbers soared after the convention, like the price of a two-pack Mylan epipen*
> *over the last decade! But then came an Associated Press story that claimed that*
> *the Clinton Foundation sold face time to the Secretary of State like a stripper*
> *selling access to the champagne corner! As we sit here today, here is the poll*
> *number that Hillary wakes up to every morning: 58% say Clinton isn't honest*
> *and trustworthy. That's according to the CNN poll, her worst number on rec-*
> *ord . . . which means her trustworthy number is south of the Donald's, a man*
> *who the Washington Post finds to lie or misstate the facts three times out of*
> *every time he opens his smuking mouth! (And in hindsight, we now know that*
> *this estimate was far lower than the reality: The Washington Post documented*
> *2140 Trump lies in only his first year in office. That averages out to nearly six*
> *lies each day.)*[8]

> *Think about this, Tom: Donald Trump, a man whose relationship with the truth is*
> *like me's relationship with Mrs Jones: they got a thing goin on, but it's only every*
> *day, at the same cafe at 6:30, and no one knows she'll be there! [Reference to*
> *well-known 1972 soul song "Me and Mrs. Jones"]*[9] *And this is the guy Hillary*
> *is losing to on trustworthiness, Sybil? WHY, Sybil, why?—because Hillary*
> *treated her Secretary of State emails like Anthony Weiner sexting emails of his*
> *ass to an avowed Trump supporter! . . .*

> *I mean what the **smuk** is going on here? . . . Memo to Hillary: as we've said before,*
> *an email problem is like the zika virus. Just when you think you've dealt with*
> *every email, another smuking mosquito flies into the neighborhood!*

> *[at the Republican National Convention] First, Rudy Giuliani comes on stage in*
> *Phoenix, wearing a Make America Great hat, looking just short of a senior*
> *passed out at the racetrack . . . really, this cat made as much sense as Kanye*
> *at the VMAs! Then Mike Pence comes onstage and opens up with his signa-*
> *ture "oil can, oil can"[as in, Pence is as stiff as the Tin Man in The Wizard of*
> *Oz] . . . . Then Trump starts out saying that he and the Mexican president spoke*
> *of the great contributions Mexicans made to this country. Now I'm pretty sure*
> *the Mexican president was thinking of Frida Kahlo, Diego Rivera, and Carlos*
> *Fuentes. And I'm equally sure that Trump was thinking of Eric Estrada, Freddy*
> *Prince, and Speedy Gonzales! Ándale! Ándale!*

*Tom, at the core of Trump's immigration policy is what he believes is our ability to choose immigrants who will thrive and love us. Trump calls it an ideological verification . . . it's a love test for Trump. I call it the Jose Feliciano test. Because Sybil, the **only** Mexican who will make it into the U.S. under the new Trump test is a Mexican that is blind and can sing a holiday tune! And that's the Smuk report! Sixty-six days to election day! . . . [lowers his voice and growls] Smuk on! Smuk **out**[10]*

Tom: Oh Sybil! It's so scary, it's nice to laugh at scary stuff!
Sybil: It's some scary times!

(September 8, 2016) Sybil reporting news of the day: Audio of Trump praising Russian president Vladimir Putin. Sybil, lost in outrage over Trump voters' blasé take on his admiration for Putin, shouts, "HE'S A DICTATOR!"

Throughout the campaign, for both self-interested and rationally strategic reasons, the *TJMS* was highly aware of one of the Clinton campaign's serious failures, the one rarely noted in mainstream media: unlike Obama's two presidential runs, and despite her genuine efforts to be inclusive—for example, her alliance with groups of mothers of unarmed black males slain by police—Hillary Clinton's campaign simply did not put real money and labor into get-out-vote organizing in black communities, and in advertising in minority media. And it was minority voters who had put President Obama over the top in both the 2008 and 2012 contests. On September 12, 2016, Roland Martin's interview with black pollster Cornell Belcher made those points abundantly clear. Revisiting this conversation with the election results in the rearview mirror, we can see that Martin's critique of the Democratic campaign strategy was painfully prescient. He understood the data far better, apparently, than did Clinton campaign operatives:

Roland: Let's get right to it. The polls are tightening and Hillary Clinton's lead is shrinking . . . [he gives details] But the real question is, what does this mean for black folks? What must Hillary Clinton do to ensure that she gets the turnout from the Obama coalition? We're joined by top pollster Cornell Belcher. Cornell, what's up? . . . So you released a recent poll where you talked about the ambivalence of young black voters? . . .
*Belcher: It isn't so much about the support for Hillary Clinton, but about the coalition, right? John Kerry did well among African Americans. African Americans disliked George Bush a great deal. But African Americans weren't the most likely voters in the electorate at that point. So you're talking about the expanding of the electorate. What we were able to do with the Obama campaign was **grow** the black vote. We got 43% of the white vote, the same as John Kerry did, but we won a **majority**. That was based off of increasing the percentage of African American votes, so that a state like Ohio, which was 12 or 13% under Kerry,*

became 15%, and we won that. . . . We got 140,000 more black votes out of Ohio than John Kerry did. And remember, Roland, we didn't win Ohio by a great deal, and John Kerry lost by 100,000 or so votes.

Roland: [agreeing with the analysis] In 2008, Obama leads **North Carolina** by 100,000 votes because of the **intensity** of black turnout.

Cornell Belcher: That's right! And the African American electorate is dispro-portionately younger voters now. We talk a lot about the millennials, but the millennials are key to this. . . . And then the Obama coalition sort of stepped back. And when they step back this time around—cause right now, in the ABC/ Post poll, she's not doing better with white voters than Obama did. She's what, 36–37%. We got 38% in 2012. I think its fool's gold to think that she's gonna do dramatically better among white voters than Barack Obama did.

. . .

Roland: Let's get to money, cause here's the reality. The Clinton campaign is bein aggressive in spending money, trying to flip Republican white women. Many of us say, look, you better ensure you are properly invested in black folks, because you're spending a lot of time and energy trying to flip conservative white women when you might be better served tryin to ensure massive black, Hispanic, young voter turnout.

Sybil, intensely: Do they **get** it yet?

Belcher: laughs—I can't answer that . . .

Roland: No, let me answer. He can't answer this, Sybil. [because Belcher was a nonpartisan pollster] I've talked to folks who have been talking to the Clinton campaign this weekend. NO! They don't get it!

. . .

Sybil: Roland, we're EIGHT WEEKS out! WHAT is the bottom line in terms of getting them to recognize this before the registration deadline is up, especially for these millennials?

Roland: Cornell?

Cornell Belcher: If you want the police to stop beatin you on the head and shootin people in your communities, you have to exercise your political power. You know, Barack Obama is President of the United States because of black power. Plain and simple. If you want to stop what's happening . . . exercise your power. . . . You cannot step back . . .

Tom: Roland, J was at a club, and he had an unofficial poll done at the club . . .

Sybil: They were asking, who's gonna vote for Donald Trump, and nobody applauded. They asked for Hillary Clinton, and he said it was **crickets**.

Roland: laughs

Tom: And then he asked who wished that you could have another term for Obama.

. . .

Tom Joyner: And the crowd went wild! I know there's nuthin scientific about that poll, but that says sumthin!

Belcher and Roland laugh.

Cornell Belcher: It does say something but again, we've gotta stop acting like it's all about Hillary Clinton! No, it's about us and our issues and our community! Even if you're not in love with Hillary Clinton, get out there and vote!

Roland: Here's a question though: Have you heard that ad on black radio, have you seen those ads on television? Because that's how you make the argument! So, for instance, I'm tryin to figure out why the Clinton campaign hasn't brought out the Central Park 5 to say, Hey, if Donald Trump had his way, we would've gotten the death penalty! And we were later exonerated! . . . Because the reason—Sybil just said: early voting is critical. We've seen North Carolina, where the federal court said, they had a laser-like focus on targeting black voters. Black folks turned out in the weeks of early voting and on Sundays . . . [and North Carolina has since slashed those opportunities] There's gonna have to be even MORE effort to make sure our folks are turning out!

Cornell Belcher: It starts with the campaign and also the Party and also outside groups . . . and so even if my Republican brothers [crew catcalls] are not for Hillary Clinton, they've gotta be for black power, and for being able to change what's going on in our communities!

. . .

Sybil: Cornell, you and your cute little suit have some work to do! [all laugh] Cause . . . her people are not getting the message!

Tom: Yeah!

*Roland: Well, guess what? I guarantee they're gonna hear this damn show! And I advise them to put some money behind a black effort because they need a **surge** of black voters. A 2.4% increase for Obama in Ohio in 2012. **That's how he won the state!***

. . .

Tom: Alright, good job Roland!

The *TJMS* displayed a distinctly feminist sensibility when Hillary Clinton fell in the street in Manhattan and was later diagnosed with pneumonia. The crew was sympathetic, and a woman texter summed up—and this was perhaps the only time I read or heard anything on national media admitting that, however we may agree or disagree with her specific policy positions over the years, what an extraordinarily hard worker Hillary Clinton always has been:

(September 13, 2016) Everyone knows that women push themselves more. We work sick all the time and don't say anything!

Clinton herself was back and on-air with the *TJMS* a few days later, and quite clear about her support for the full progressive 2016 Democratic Party platform. In a long interview—so painful to read post-election—with Roland Martin, Don

Lemon, and Sybil Wilkes, we see not only Clinton's articulateness, her clear policy proposals, her sensitivity to race-minority concerns and issues, and her prescient focus on Russian election-meddling and Trump's frighteningly cozy ties to a hostile foreign power but also CNN and *TJMS* correspondent Don Lemon's sometime tendency to focus away from real political and economic issues onto personalities. (Lemon left the show soon thereafter.)

> *Roland Martin: A recent* New York Times *story revealed that focus groups showed that African Americans are leery about your presidency. Beyond criminal justice, what are the three issues that impact African Americans that you can speak to get them paying attention to your campaign?*
>
> *Clinton: I'm well aware that I still have work to do, and I'm very committed to continuing to travel across the country to talk about and hear from young African Americans about the struggles that they face daily. Our campaign has hired a number of people, both at our headquarters and organizers on and off campus that are also having conversations about what's at stake in this election. And I also have a lot of sympathy, because think about what this millennial generation has faced. They entered the workforce during one the worst recessions in our nation's history.*
>
> *So what I'm focusing on is more good-paying jobs, I want to make college affordable, and that is a plan that I've been talking about and working toward since I got into this campaign. I also want to help everybody with student debt and that's a very high proportion of African American young people with a B.A., that come out with student debt. We're going to really help that get paid down and paid off so people can get on with their life.*

Clinton and her campaign had clearly done the policy-wonk work to come up with a package for struggling HBCUs:

> *I'm committed to helping historically black colleges and universities—in fact, I have a specific fund of twenty-five billion dollars that will really upgrade and support and provide financial assistance for young people, because I think the HBCUs are incredibly important in providing a pathway into the future. We're going to make sure that we deal with criminal justice reform, address gun violence and have a positive agenda to get wages up. Not only national minimum wage, but equal pay for women, helping small businesses, especially young people who want to be entrepreneurs. You know the fastest growing segment of small business in America are African American women. We're really putting out a very broad-based agenda, and the more young people hear about it, the more they know what I will do to help invest and fund employment, skills training and education, the more interested they become.*

Then Don Lemon tried to stir the pot:

Don Lemon: The former Secretary of State Colin Powell, in his hacked emails, has criticized you and your "minions" for trying to drag him into your email server problem. He concludes by saying "Everything HRC touches, she kind of screws up with hubris." How do you answer him and critics who say whether it's your emails, or disclosing your health issues, or even pointing out Trump's flypaper-like ability for attracting racially insensitive or "deplorables" as you call them, that somehow the message gets screwed up?

But Clinton stayed on point:

Clinton: I have a great deal of respect for Colin Powell. And I have a lot of sympathy for anyone whose emails become public. I'm not going to start discussing someone's private emails. I've already spent a lot of time talking about mine, as you know. What I think is really important about these emails is the chilling fact that the Russians are continuing to interfere with our elections. I have to say, I'm increasingly concerned about Donald Trump's alarming closeness with the Kremlin over the course of this campaign. It's deeply concerning and there's a lot that Trump should answer for. Because these attempts by Russia to interfere in the election go hand in hand with his closeness to the Kremlin and his flattery of Putin. It's not just me that is noticing this. Fellow Republicans, and foreign policy [leaders] and [those with] national security experience and NATO leaders. I'm going to keep raising the alarm about Russian influence and that raises questions about who Trump actually does business with.

Don Lemon: Can I just follow and say that by hubris [Powell] is saying that you're stepping on your message by hubris or arrogance or by not being transparent.

Clinton: Again, I'm not going to comment on anything that is said in a private email.

Lemon: Even to critics beyond the former Secretary?

I think I've worked very, very hard to be more transparent than not just my opponent but in comparison to anybody who's run. The medical information I put out, and we're going to put out more, meets and exceeds the standard that other presidential candidates, including President Obama and Mitt Romney, have met. I think the real questions need to be directed to Donald Trump and his failure to meet even the most minimalistic standards that we expect of someone being the nominee of our two major parties.

. . .

Sybil then yanked the interview back to the key issues of Trump's racism, xeno-phobia, and Islamophobia, and Clinton was ready to go:

Sybil Wilkes: I have a question about all the anger that's going on in our country in both race and religion. Colin Kaepernick is taking a knee in protest against what's going on with police and black citizens, and a Muslim woman in tra-ditional garb was set on fire in New York, and another group of women was attacked in Brooklyn. There is so much anger and so much ill will. Is there a way that you are going to try to bring people together to bring some understanding to all of this anger and hatred that we seem to be experiencing?

Clinton: Sybil, I am so concerned about all of this. I have said that Donald Trump has run a deplorable campaign. He's accepted support and been cheered on by people like David Duke, the former Grand Wizard of the Ku Klux Klan, and other white supremacists. . . . I do think we have to speak out against this hatred. Trump attacked a federal judge because of his Mexican heritage. He bullied a Gold Star family because of their Muslim faith. He promoted and he's still promoting the lie that our first black President is not a true American. He called women pigs and bimbos. I'm going to keep calling out the bigotry and hateful rhetoric that he's brought to this campaign because I don't think you can make our country great by tearing people down. I do really believe we are stronger to-gether. But I also accept the responsibility, making sure that we do everything we can to try to heal these divides to bring people together . . . .

In our campaign, we say "Love Trumps Hate" and we really mean it. I've talked a lot on the campaign trail about how we need more love and kindness. I gave a speech to the National Baptist Conference last week to talk about my faith, and the humility one should feel just to be a human being, never mind one seeking authority. We are not people of hate and we are not people who condone this violence, and I've cited a few of the examples that were just sickening. I want to be the president of everybody, not just people who agree with me or people who vote for me.

For people who have legitimate concerns about what's happening in the economy or what's been happening in their lives, we should get together and address those. We need to help people who've been left out and left behind, whether they're in the inner city or a community or Indian country or anywhere else in America. We will help you. But we will not tolerate racism and sexism and misogyny and Islamophobia and xenophobia and the terrible anti-immigrant rhetoric that Trump has engaged in. And that violence is not the answer to anything.

Roland Martin then put his finger on the key variable we have all endlessly fussed over since the election—how do you communicate to people who feel left behind by economic shifts, who genuinely don't understand how much the appalling recession economy improved over Obama's two terms, who don't have any sense of how we can turn policy around to shrink widening income and wealth inequalities in the U.S.?

> Roland: How do you make the argument that the economy is improving even though you have hardcore numbers—stock exchange is at record highs for the last eight years—recent reports that personal income is up and poverty is falling, when some people think the economy is terrible. How do you make that argument?

Clinton unfortunately—but she didn't really have a rhetorical alternative—included praising Bill Clinton's neoliberal policies in her otherwise unexceptional answer:

> Clinton: You have to make it because it's factually accurate. Barack Obama does not get the credit for pulling our economy back from the abyss. We could have had a Great Depression, not just a great recession. Yes, a lot of people were hurt. African Americans and Latinos were disproportionately hurt. So, it's my job to say, "We are standing but we're not yet running." But for heaven's sake, don't turn the economy back to the very same people who wrecked it in the first place! Trickle-down economics destroyed what was inherited from the eight years of my husband's administration. African American family income went up 33%. More people were lifted out of poverty than at any other time in recent history. We were on the right path. But along came the ideologues, and Trump wants to double down on all the wrong economic policies.

Roland then pivoted to Supreme Court issues, and Clinton responded clearly, but also cleverly hooked her answer to questions of Republican voter suppression, and the Supreme Court having gutted Section 5 of the Voting Rights Act:

> Martin: If you become President, will you ask the President to pull Merrick Garland's nomination to allow someone younger to be in his place and if you do, will the appointment be the first African American woman nominee in history?
> Clinton: I think we should stick with one president at a time. We happen to have a very good one, in my opinion, and he has nominated someone. It's a disgrace that the Senate, under Republican leadership, has failed to act on his nominee, which is why we need to elect Democrats to the Senate. I'm going to let this president serve out his term with distinction and make the decisions that he thinks are right for the country. I think he's got a pretty good track record and he's earned that right.

If I have the opportunity to make any Supreme Court appointments, I'm going to look broadly and widely for people who represent the diversity of our country and bring some commonsense, real-world experience. I'm still outraged at what the Supreme Court did to the Voting Rights Act. I was in the Senate and I voted to reauthorize it, as did ninety-eight of my colleagues, Democratic and Republican alike. George Bush signed it.

And then this Supreme Court, with this conservative majority at the time, said "Oh, we don't need the Voting Rights Act anymore." What a charade! And you can see what's happening. I see it every day. There is a concerted effort to try to shrink the franchise, make it difficult for people to vote and stop them at the polls. The only way to fix it is for a lot of people to turn out and say, "We're not going to stand for this." That's why we need a Supreme Court that actually represents the people of this country and our most fundamental values.

. . .

Late in the campaign, a curious *TJMS* listener queried:

(September 16, 2016) Will Trump be on the show?

Tom responded immediately, revealing the black component of the Trump campaign's notorious anti-press bias:

TJ: No! Because I'm on a list, with Roland. They won't appear on this show. [He goes on to explain that Trump's campaign has blacklisted anyone associated with Reach Media.]
*J then added his own comic imagining: You think that black lady in the **church** got on his ass! [if Trump were to appear on* TJMS*]*

On September 23, 2016, the *TJMS* hosted young African American activist Bree Newsome, who had been arrested the previous year for bravely shinnying up the South Carolina statehouse flagpole and removing the Confederate flag. The crew praised her, but also asked if young protesters were registering people to vote. Newsome responded that there were problems with both candidates, and that we need to change the actual structures of elections. I expected that statement— indicative of a then-popular radical youth anti-electoral mindset (which she changed soon thereafter) to receive serious *TJMS* pushback. But the crew simply thanked her for her work.[11]

The *TJMS* announced a Facebook party for the first Clinton/Trump debate on September 26, and 900,000 people signed on. The day after, the crew was gleeful over Clinton's excellent performance, and blackened her linguistic style:

J: *She straight* **low-talked** *him! Nuthin you can do!*

Tom: *A woman can always win over a man by low-talkin. Every time!*

J: *She was all up in him. There was nuthin showin but feet!*

Tom: *He was snifflin, takin sips of water . . .*

Cheryl Underwood: *She was up in there. But for the next debates, she gotta go up even further . . . I'm a Republican, but we've got to support Hillary Clinton to preserve the legacy of Barack Obama! . . . I'm voting with Hillary. . . . Let me tell you some secrets: when turnout is low, Republicans benefit! So get out and* **vote***!*

On September 28, the *TJMS* again hosted the Reverend William Barber, former state NAACP Chair and founder of the North Carolina Moral Mondays movement.[12] Roland Martin interviewed him:

Roland: *North Carolina is a huge battleground state . . . they're trying to keep blacks from voting . . .*

Reverend Barber: *We're pushin and fighting! Tomorrow night we'll have one of our tours . . . we have 1200 faith centers that we've created, Jews, Christians, Muslims . . . we're saying if you're concerned about videos not being released,* **judges** *get* **elected***. If you're concerned about cops killing people,* **prosecutors** *are* **elected***. . . . What I'm sayin to folks across North Carolina, if someone tries to take your right to vote, then they cut your healthcare, then . . . you BETTER vote now!*

Roland: *North Carolina saw huge voter turnout last time. Normal people would say good. Republicans said, Ah, hell no!*

Barber: *That's it! . . . [gives statistics, and lays out how Republicans passed the worst redistricting plan.] The courts called it apartheid redistricting. They know if* **we** *vote, they can't win. All that has to happen now is for blacks, progressive whites, and Latinos to go to the polls!*

. . .

We're calling for campuses to massively engage, the way you haven't seen since the sixties. If people are in the street protesting a police killing, they should be in the streets to vote!

About people who say they won't vote: I mean, you can survive cancer, but you might die from it. What's on the ballot? The person who will determine the Supreme Court. What's on the ballot? The person who will take away your healthcare . . .

Roland enthusiastically agrees.

Sybil adds details about down-ballot races . . .

William Barber: *This is heavy stuff!*

After Barber has signed off, Tom Joyner exclaims: *My man right there, William Barber!*

Sybil: Can he get you to church, Tom?
*Roland, drolly: He got power, but he aint got **that** much power!*

The crew was scathingly angry after Trump's performance on the October 9 debate. Guest comic Sheryl Underwood went on a stream-of-consciousness rant, pivoting between outrage and high black wit:

> *Sheryl Underwood: I have never seen so much ignorance in my life! And **praise the Lord** we aint **in** it, Sybil! I'm voting for Hillary, and tell everyone, we gotta go five deep. We gotta go in our slave names, our play names!*
> *What I don't understand, why are they so close in the polls?*
> *And what we wanta say about Hillary, Hillary gotta say to us. . . . Aint nobody talk about Ferguson, aint nobody talk about Black Lives Matter. We wanta feel safe as Americans. Aint nobody talk about jobs—and who am I gon date for the Superbowl? [laughs]*
> *We gotta make sure he does not go to the White House! You hear me sayin?*
> *Sybil: But aren't you still a Republican?*
> *S: Oh yeah I am! . . . But what I'm tellin you, when the Republicans are leavin you. . . . And runnin behind her back, like he's about to snatch her purse or sumthin . . . every drughead in the world like that, he need help, Tom! A twenty-four-step program, cause twelve aint enough! [crew loves it]*
> *Everybody get out, all the frat brothers, evahbody, we need poll-watchers! Bring your ID!*

Then it was Huggy Lowdown's turn:

> *Thank God it's the tenth of October, and last night's debate is over! We had to call an ambulance last night, cause we were playin a drinkin game. Whenever Trump sniffled, they had to take a shot!*

Then Arsenio Hall hit the theme, "going blacker" to emphasize his outrage:

> *He think he a dictator! Like Castro! He think he can put Hillary Clinton in jail! . . . They need to put him on a leash with a clothesline! Like a dog!*

Sheryl Underwood then returned, commenting on Trump's character with such brilliant comic flair that I was left laughing hysterically, no doubt along with millions of other *TJMS* listeners:

> *Hillary should've said, Sit yo little ass down on the chair! . . . He's just not **presidential**! Like JFK said, "Ask not what your country". . . or Reagan, "Tear down this wall!" You can't be the guy in the books that says, "Grab them by the va-jay-jay!" That's gon be **horrible** in granite!*

When the infamous Trump "grab'em by the pussy" videotape was released, crew and audience were beside themselves with outrage and joy, certain, as were so many of us, that this was Trump's "47% moment," the analogue to the extraordinarily damaging publicity around Mitt Romney's notorious private comments to wealthy Florida donors in 2012, that nearly half of the country was a group of takers "who are dependent on government . . . I'll never convince them that should take personal responsibility. . . ."[13] After the "pussy tape" was released, political analyst Ken Smukler began his October 10 report by gleefully singing the 1965 Tom Jones hit,

What's new pussycat, wha-oh-wa-oh-wa-oh![14]

Smukler then made the world-weary point that we already knew that Trump was a misogynist sexual harasser:

> *Tom, last night Donald Trump and Hillary Clinton took to the debate stage . . . just forty-eight hours after the release of the video . . . the tape revealed a side of Trump we've never seen before—a misogynistic sexually obsessed candidate with a libido set on warp drive! [pauses] Uh, ok, Sybil, it's **precisely** the Donald Trump we've seen before! Which is why at the Smuk Report we have no smuking clue why this videotape **matters**?!*

But the newly appointed youthful political commentator Shaun King (see Figure 7.1), a columnist for *The New York Daily News* and self-conscious male feminist, took the videotape extremely seriously, and saw nothing to joke about:

> *(October 11, 2016) What we heard was appalling . . . saying he uses his power or celebrity to force himself on women. . . . This is not ok! . . . My blood is boiling, because we are hearing how a man not only automatically degrades women, but assaults them! This is not about foul language!—What Trump describes is illegal! . . . Listen, conservatives have shown no desire or ability to stop this man. It's up to us. In twenty-seven days we're electing a new president. [He says he was a Bernie supporter, but] stopping Trump is BIGGER than our own personal preferences!*

Even the languorous nightclub habitué Huggy Lowdown, who spent most of his years on the show wittily dissing celebrities, took the election extremely seriously:

> *(October 12, 2016) That's why we've got to be prayed up and go out and vote for the only qualified candidate! Hillary Clinton! Cause the other candidate is a pumpkin-faced charlatan!*

Figure 7.1 Writer and activist Shaun King, photographed at Suffolk University. CC BY-SA 4.0.

Huggy was so motivated, alarmed, and angry that on October 6, 2016, he murdered a hit—a genre usually restricted to J Anthony Brown and Chris Paul—to underline the seriousness of this election. He sang, to the tune of Bobby McFerrin's hit, "Don't Worry, Be Happy:"[15] "Here's a little song that I wrote, What's gonna happen if you don't vote?" Huggy asserted that "Donald gonna put us in a fix, I bet the top of his head says 666!" He ended with a lounge lizard's embellishment: "Make it rain at the voting box!"

Not only Hillary Clinton, but vice presidential candidate Tim Kaine, Joe Biden, President Obama, and First Lady Michelle Obama all appeared repeatedly on the *TJMS* as Election Day approached. On October 20, Al Sharpton was on, whipped into a frenzy by Trump's untruths, and reflecting the thinking of many at the time and into the present, that Trump was campaigning solely for his own financial benefit—not expecting to win, but to monetize the publicity[16]:

> *Donald Trump has tried to poison the water, talking about how the election was rigged. . . . He has made racial references . . . like blacks are going to cheat at the polls . . . playing on the misinformation about fraudulent voting. Out of one billion votes there were 314 fraudulent ones. . . . It is clear that his hotels and casinos are on the decline . . . I predict he will have his own channel. He wants to*

build this so he can say I didn't lose legitimately . . . and he will be on the right,
keeping pressure on President Clinton. . . . It's to set up his next political scam . . .

On November 2, President Obama came on with a particularly unbuttoned tone, laying out the stakes of the race in the starkest terms—all of which were proven true after Trump took office. He "went colored" at the end to underline his dead-serious message:

> *Now I have a favor for you! I have seven days to elect someone who has pledged to continue my agenda . . . or somebody whose sole agenda is to undo everything I've done. Cause we track, we've got all kinds of metrics . . . and the Latino vote is solid, but the **black** vote is not where it should be. . . . You know what? I need people to understand that everything I've done is dependent on electing Hillary Rodham Clinton. I need you to tell your mama, your cousin . . . but if we let this thing slip, and I spend my last two months in office preparing for **Donald Trump**!? You tell everyone, Barack and Michelle asked you personally to get out the vote!*
>
> *Tom: Mr. President, what would be the worst-case scenario?*
> *President Obama: This is very straightforward: They will immediately work with Congress to pass tax cuts for the wealthiest Americans. . . . They will immediately cut Medicaid. Right away, I'll guarantee you, they'll start cutting Pell grants and support for HBCUs . . . right away they'll dig up Michelle's garden [crew laughs] and all the work we've done to make sure kids get nutritious meals. . . . The Department of Justice and all the work we've done on criminal rights, on voting rights . . . [he references the Central Park Five, who were exonerated] And today! Trump **still** insists they should be executed! . . . And so . . . if I hear any activists and young people out here sayin that there aint no difference and nuthin's gonna change . . . **NO!** . . . Tom and Sybil, you guys lifted us up mightily for so many years . . . I could not be more grateful, but I want everybody to understand we've got one more race here! Come on, let's do the work!*
> *Tom, later: Well Syb, he really **came with it**!*
> *Sybil: And you can't help but understand his passion, [because if Trump wins, all his achievements will be undone] I don't know what more you can say or do . . . I know he's not on the ticket, but he **is**!*

Crew members also sedulously and gleefully reported—and continue to report on—Trump's failure to master the most elementary material on U.S. law and governance—as Yale historian David Blight wrote, "his greatest threat to our society and to our democracy is not necessarily his authoritarianism, but his essential ignorance—of history, of policy, of political process, of the Constitution."[17] And of course veteran reporter Bob Woodward's exposé of the Trump White House, *Fear*, documented White House attorneys' and aides' misery over Trump's abysmal failure to understand, for example, the limits to his powers, the functioning of NATO, the United Nations, or of foreign aid, and his absolute inability to speak without lying.[18] And the crew and audience constantly harp on his grade-school vocabulary and deeply embarrassing grammar and spelling errors in his tweets and various White House documents, his consistent inability to speak grammatically.[19] Everyone involved with *TJMS*—crew, guests, audience—was and is hyper-aware of the grand irony of a wealthy white male upper-class product of an Ivy League education falling very far short of the literacy levels and general knowledge base of the working-class majority of black America.

On September 27, 2016, they couldn't get over Trump's characterization of "a very against-police judge" during the debate the night before. A texter wrote in dismissively that "a middle school debate team could've done better than Donald Trump!" Another texter opined that "Trump is about as smart as Jethro Bodine [from *The Beverly Hillbillies*]. Tom Joyner immediately snapped back: "Oh, Jethro is waaaay smarter!" After Trump took office, and began ordering ICE (Immigration and Customs Enforcement) sweeps of undocumented immigrants—constantly hectoring that Americans must "speak English"—Chris Paul noted scornfully on August 3, 2017: "Hell, *Trump* can barely speak English!"

The crew also rang the changes on Hillary's pantsuits, not clued in to her deliberate invocation of early-twentieth-century American suffragists in wearing white:

> (*October 20, 2016*) *Sheryl Underwood, post-debate: Donald Trump got beat down by a pantsuit, a white pantsuit, and it's not even Easter!*
> (*Same day*)
> *J: She spanked that ass so much **I'm** buyin a pantsuit, Sybil!*
> *Crew speculates she wore white because she's in Olivia Pope* (Scandal*) mode—*
>   *"She's a gladiator!"*

As Election Day approached, the crew was seriously fired up:

> (*November 8, 2016*) *Chris Paul: Over the weekend, we all set our clocks back one hour . . . and that's good practice for if Donald Trump wins the election, which will set our country back fifty years! VOTE!!!*
> (*Same day*)
> *Shaun King: Lays out Trump's exact policy statements, quotes the famous German theologian Martin Niemoller's narrative about the Nazi rise and German failures to resist: "First they came for the socialists, but I did not speak out, because I was not a socialist. . . ."[20] King enunciates: It's all about the power of speaking out for the rights of others! . . . Today we must get out and stop Donald Trump not only because his policies are dangerous . . . I promise you that **we are next**! . . . I'm embarrassed that I even have to make this statement: he's disgusting, he's dangerous, and dammit, we've got to **vote**!*

[segue to John Legend's inspiriting song "Glory" from the film Selma*]*[21]

And on the same day, a newly unrestrained, slangy Michelle Obama phoned in to beg the audience to get out the vote:

> *Michelle Obama: Man, it is o-vah!... **Please** help me sleep well at night, folks... do me that little favor!*
> *She remembers that in 2008, Malia, on the drive to the Grant Park victory celebration, said, "Daddy, there's no cars, I don't think anyone is going to come to your party!" [Crew beside themselves in joy and remembrance]*
> *She says her friends are "trippin out over Hillary's opponent... they can't really believe he exists. He represents such a throwback... this is why the country needs to move in the direction of our millennials, because otherwise we'll get left behind.... She expatiates on the improvements in the economy: "That's **my** baby! He did it!" She talks about Republican obstructionism...*
> *She finishes: "I'd like to talk with you every week, but my team wouldn't let me do it! I want to thank you for being such informed people, with a platform that not many have...*

The *TJMS* also repeatedly played a Jennifer Lewis's [star of the television show *Black-ish*] election-day song, whose refrain was: Get yo ass out and vote![22]

> *Texter: My four-year-old is jamming "Get yo ass out and vote!"*
> *Crew loves it, imagines preschool teachers dealing with toddlers singing "Yo ass!"*
> *Tom Joyner keeps interrupting the show to chant, street-protest style: VOTE! VOTE! VOTE! VOTE! VOTE!*

Trumpocalypse: The Aftermath

The morning after the presidential electoral debacle, the *TJMS* crew, like most of the country, was deeply shocked and apprehensive. All the pollsters had predicted a Clinton win, after all. But they were also beyond furious, combative, and witty with it. Huggy Lowdown maintained his politically committed persona, commenting with sardonic rage on our collective doom, and the culpability of those who deliberately didn't vote, or had thrown their votes away on a third-party candidate (and how I appreciated his fury):

> *Aint a damn thing funny in this land of milk & honey! People are still afraid to fall asleep, cause* Nightmare on Elm Street *has come to the White House!... All those mofos who voted for a third party, **thanks,** idiots! And all those who didn't vote, **thanks,** morons!*

There's two groups of people happy today! Trump supporters and the cast of
  Saturday Night Live!
*We've elected an **intoxicated racist** . . . vendors are linin up to sell red hats and*
  Confederate flags!
From Superman to Donald Duck!
From Denzel to Gomer Pyle!
*I **refuse** to call him my president, not after the president I've seen the last eight years!*
I'm about to boycott this president, yall! We need a purge!

In the days after the election, the *TJMS* remained in shock and mourning but was also wonderfully defiant. Commentators stressed the deleterious effect of the 2013 *Holder v. Shelby* Supreme Court decision, which had gutted Section 5 of the Voting Rights Act, in suppressing the black vote. Roland Martin, using the Reverend William Barber's book title, argued that we are at the end of the "Third Reconstruction," living inside a wave of historical white backlash against recent black American political mobilization.[23] The Reverend Al Sharpton added portentously—also reflecting the common black American annoyance that whites were seeing the Trump win as a sudden crisis, while African Americans have been living with crisis since they arrived here centuries ago: "This is as serious as it gets. We have to build a . . . movement of resistance. We survived George Wallace. We survived Reagan."

Comedian Chris Paul's heartbroken, deeply moving, morning-after political doggerel included a panoply—white racism, misogyny, xenophobia—of progressive coalition laments[24]:

There are no jokes to tell and no funny songs to make
Cause we're living a nightmare, with four years to wake
Last night my country 'tis of thee lost all of her majestic dignity
We elected a person whose entire campaign was built on insults and inflicting pain
He lit the fire of the angry white male, and let it burn on his campaign trail
And on election day, that angry white hate carried him to wins in majority states
What do we say to our daughters after electing a man who bragged about assault
  and doing things with his hands
And what do our Latino neighbors make of this win, and a new America that
  doesn't include them?
And where do we as black Americans go from here?
It was eight years ago we celebrated and cheered
Our first black president, a man of respect
From that we go to now facing years of neglect
My heart is broken for the country I love
No more can we pretend to be righteous and above
No more can we pretend to be a nation that's great
When on the day of our election, our people chose hate

But God remains in control, this we should always remember
And black people, be strong, we'll survive this together

Two days later, Sybil Wilkes erupted in rage (and complete accuracy) at claims by two women celebrities, Diamond and Silk (who were among the very tiny group of black Trump supporters), that Trump is not a racist and xenophobe:

> *Tell that to the people who are writing all of those really racist . . . things . . . like* **build the wall***! And scaring children to death because they might have to be taken out of this country even though they are* **United States citizens***! Tell that to the Muslims that are having their headwraps ripped off of them and telling them it's a new America! Tell that to all of the black kids who are being told that Donald Trump is in charge, you-all must* **leave this country** *now!*

TJMS Resistance: Antiracism, #MeToo, "Natural" Disasters

But the show, literally, had to go on. The *TJMS* did so by continuing its furious news coverage—essentially defaulting to its former stance, during the two long, disastrous George W. Bush terms, of consistently witty deprecation, reporting on and encouraging activism, and reaching out to experts for information. And they leavened that coverage with new and old soul music, comic hijinks, and celebrity infotainment. And their audience took up the cudgels as well, articulating my own horrified responses:

> *(November 9, 2018)*
> *Texter: I cried last night like somebody in my family had passed away.*
> *Texter: It's like waking up on a Christmas morning, and the boogeyman is sittin under your tree!*

Sherri Shepherd had a particularly thoughtful response, one that touched on the now endlessly repeated point that white Americans can drive African Americans wild with their assumption that only *now* have things gone wrong for the country:

> *(November 9, 2018) My spirit is in anguish and devastation. . . . But life still has to move on. We still have to be funny. People are openly sobbing and crying . . . that's fine. But there were a couple "clear people" [whites] at work, people who were saying "I can't work today. We're all screwed and we're gonna die." I can't be in that place, I've got an eleven-year-old. We still have to work. And I want to scream, "Well guess what's gonna happen to* **black** *folks! . . . See I still have to live, cause my landlord aint gonna take that 'we're all screwed.' . . . And black*

*people are so used to goin through crap . . . even with this **dumb booty president**. . . . Maybe we need to wake up and be more active! And march!"*

While one would imagine that protest songs would be the most memorable
music during such a national crisis, what I remember most strongly from the early
post-election shock period are, first, the *TJMS* playing Maxwell's then-new love
song "Lake by the Ocean"—which has rather abstruse lyrics—and Tom coming
on afterwards exclaiming: "Oh, I'm so messed up this morning, Maxwell's song
makes *sense* to me!"[25] And crew members and the entire black and progressive
counterpublic went wild, post-election, with the refrain from Childish Gambino's
(Donald Glover) soul hit "Redbone"— "Stay woke!"[26] While in the context of
the song, staying woke is about repelling the speaker's lover's other, threatening
suitors "creeping" her, in the broader culture, staying woke was instantly politically
repurposed as a meme of the Resistance. Finally, Ro James broke open the R&B
charts in late 2015 with his haunting, neosoul love song, "Permission," which could
be an anthem for the #MeToo movement—"Give me that green light, but only if
it feels right."[27] Moving toward two years later, "Permission" is still on constant rotation on all black radio, and with each iteration reminds me, and no doubt most
listeners, that all human sexual connections should be equally desired, and equally
consented to.

As Christmas approached, comedian Chris Paul took inspiration from the
2000 box-office smash cartoon film retelling the Dr. Seuss story, *How the Grinch
Stole Christmas*. On December 15, in a brilliant tour de force repurposing, Paul
substituted "Mr. Trump" for "Mr. Grinch" in the well-known song "You're a
Mean One, Mr. Grinch," as sung by Jim Carrey, reproducing the internal rhymes
and Carrey's growls, shouts, and swooping, condemnatory elongations, while
highlighting Trump's racism, xenophobia, Wall Street class politics, and allegiance
to a hostile foreign power[28]:

He began by singing "You're a cockroach, Mr. Trump, you're a toupee-wearing
rat," swiftly shifting to specifying that Trump was building his own swamp "with
crocodiles from Goldman Sachs." He then pivoted to Trump's racism: "You're a
bigot, Mr. Trump" . . . naming racist White House personnel. Finally, he moved to
Trump's unprecedented friendliness with the Russian dictator: "You're a puppet,
Mr. Trump, you're Putin's precious punk!" Chris Paul finished with an angry recitative: "I want to thank all you ignorant Americans who voted for the President-elect,
because thanks to you our country is sink, sank, **sunk**!"

The *TJMS* was also alive to the new problematics of race, power, and money,
given the new right-wing White House Administration. What, for example, were
HBCU bands invited to march in the Inauguration to do, given the rumors of fantastic sums being offered, and given the current financial crisis for most of those
colleges? The crew took the issue seriously, and disagreed with one another, but
they also milked it for humor:

*(January 5, 2017) They discuss the Talladega (Alabama) marching band playing at the Inauguration. Tom Joyner says he doesn't support Trump, doesn't want them to play at the Inauguration, "but if they are getting paid **millions**?—They need the money badly!"*

*Sybil: So the other side is, Sherri [Shepherd, guest comic], if you fall for this, where's the **line**? What do you **stand** for? You can't always fall for the okey-doke!*

Tom: When Dr. King was around, HCBUs weren't hurting for money. But they are now! ... I'm asking can you forgive them if they perform for the right price? And what would be the right price?

*Sherri says she wouldn't do it for **any** money. "There **is** no price." Then she starts comically equivocating: She imagines "two million dollars, a TV show, and a man—with good credit!"*

Then the texters weighed in:

*I'll perform at the Inauguration if they forgive **all** my student loan debt!*

I'm Joe in Toledo. I hate to say it, but if they gave me seven figures, I'd be the DRUM major!

Finally, a texter with actual on the ground information wrote in, bursting everyone's payday bubble:

Our local band in Tupelo was invited, but was told they had to raise their own expenses!

Before the Inauguration, the crew asked its audience on January 10, "What're we gonna miss?" And the audience instantly texted in:

Common sense and that black barbecue pit!

Class, fairness, swagger, and a great representative of mankind!

*High class! Michelle Obama will be leaving, to be replaced by **no** class!*

Definitely all the spicy food and spicy seasonings!

Then new comic contributor Lavell Crawford summed up in a single phrase the nature of the sophisticated, culturally tasteful black American administration about to exit the White House, one that certainly resonated with this baby boomer: "All the Al Green albums!"

On January 18, the crew ran a "for real for real" poll on its audience: "What's your biggest beef with President-elect Trump?"—and instantly received witty listener texts expressing withering contempt:

He's ignorant!

And absolute rejection:

He's breathin!

The *TJMS* publicized the planned Women's March, and audience members texted in their intended participation, with a self-consciously witty black women's flourish:

(January 10, 2017) I'm gonna bring a truckload of hairweave and Moscato!

The crew was beyond mirthful at the abysmally failed Inauguration, with its tiny audience—a third the size of Obama's first Inauguration crowd—and pitiful array of C-list performers.[29] Arsenio Hall claimed on January 24, 2017, that he had been "sittin in the empty part of the bleachers, watchin!" Huggy Lowdown, a DC native, said, "Syb, did you know that they still haven't broken down the bleachers from the Inauguration, and they still look the same, empty as a motherf—!" Sybil reported that Trump's Inaugural job rating was at 45%, "the lowest-ever initial rating for an American President!"

The *TJMS* lost no time in bringing in Latinx comic Carlos Mencia, on January 27, 2017, and asking him about deportation threats. Mencia reported that he had friends and relatives who were undocumented, and represented one thread of those Mexican-Americans' response to the disaster—an enduring, stoic refusal to give in:

A friend's daughter, a DACA kid, goes to UC-Irvine. She was crying after Trump was elected, and her father said [Mencia does thick Spanish accent], "Don't cry baby, I know how to get back!" And he wasn't joking! He was serious!

The *TJMS* celebrated the protests against and failure of Trump's travel ban, and tried to talk through and educate their audience on impeachment demands. Sybil pointed out trenchantly on January 31, 2017:

*But let me say this to you: Ok, you have President Trump and you don't like him, how do you feel about **President Pence**? He is more of a hardliner than Trump is, if you can believe that. Trump became a hardliner to get elected—Pence has **always** been one.*
*Tom: Talk to someone from Indiana, **they'll** tell you!*

Audience members who were already clued in on Pence's rightist, misogynist, anti-gay governance in Indiana texted in their horror with a witty, sometimes black-church embellishment—displaying their obvious knowledge of his elaborate public displays of hyper-Christian piety[30]:

Texter: Mike Pence has ties to the KKK!
Texter: Mike Pence is the Devil in disguise!

Shaun King hit the ground running, celebrating the resistance to Trump, and specifying the multiple elements of the new progressive coalition:

> *(February 2, 2017) The city of Seattle pulled all of its investments from Wells Fargo yesterday. . . . This is part of the Injustice Project, pulling money from banks that discriminate, that invest in fossil fuels, that fund the Dakota pipe-line. . . . We're fighting for equality and fairness, we're fighting for people's health-care, we're fighting for immigrants and Muslims . . . the fight may be hard, but be encouraged, everybody. We **will** win!*

By the following year, King had added an Indivisible-type electoral down-ballot focus to his activism:

> *(January 16, 2018) Our law officers are among the least trained, least educated officers than anywhere else in the world. . . . Undoing what's wrong with the cur-rent justice system will take years. But the most important thing we can do is to elect progressive, **woke,** reform-minded prosecutors! . . . No role . . . has a larger impact than the District Attorney.*
>
> *Ninety-five percent of DAs are white—it may be the whitest, male-ist [job] in America! . . . This problem with America's DAs is a ROOT problem.*

The crew, along with most of the rest of the American population, regularly mocked the dumpster fire that the Trump White House quickly revealed itself to be. With most official statements immediately exposed as untrue—examples of Du Bois's observance of the white racist "childish belief in the efficacy of lies"—personnel arriving and then leaving in disgrace at many times the pace of any other American presidential administration, the never-ending daily revelations of Russian meddling in the election, the clear financial connections among Trump family and associates and various Russian spies and oligarchs, and the endless pa-rade of racist, xenophobic, misogynist/anti-LBGTQ, and anti-environmentalist statements and policies flowing from the Executive branch and Republican Congress, the *TJMS*, like the rest of the U.S. public sphere, had no dearth of ma-terial.[31] They celebrated "friend of the show" journalist April Ryan for her hard-hitting questions at official White House press conferences. They longed for her to have been able to call out Trump openly, to "go colored," when he asked her, revealing his ignorance not only of the CBC but of proper White House protocol, if she knew members of the Congressional Black Caucus, and could she get him in touch with them?

*Tom: Wouldn't it have been nice if she could've said, "Look, **fool,** I aint your secretary!*

When Trump revealed that he had no idea who Frederick Douglass actually was, indicating that he imagined he was a contemporary, a witty texter wrote in:

(February 21, 2017) Frederick Douglass needs to tap Trump on the shoulder, and say, "What's up? I hear you know me!"

The *TJMS* treatment of Melania Trump was also fascinating. Her widely disseminated early-career nude photo was the source of much hilarity, and crew members repeatedly noted the obvious contrast to Michelle Obama's high intellectual and professional achievements, profound social conscience, and general classiness. The crew and audience are more than aware that Melania is a trophy wife—Huggy Lowdown simply calls her "Prenup 3." They know that Melania probably worked illegally in the United States while here on a tourist visa—a violation that should have led to her deportation—and regularly note Trump's extraordinary hypocrisy in railing against illegal immigrants.[32] They will not allow their audience to forget that at the Republican National Convention, Melania plagiarized parts of a First Lady Michelle Obama speech, and that again, in launching her "Be Best" project, she released a pamphlet copied from the Obama staff.[33] Huggy Lowdown cracked on May 9, 2018: "Did you know that Melania in Slovenian means *Xerox it?*"

But the *TJMS* crew are also sensitive to the temptation to slide into sexism in attacking this First Lady. Chris Paul threaded that needle quite capably, distinguishing between criticizing Melania for selling her sexuality versus parroting her husband's racist political lies:

*(January 24, 2017) Boy George has announced that people shouldn't criticize Melania Trump because of her past, because we **all** have one. . . . Well, Boy George, I'm not hating on Melania Trump because she used to be a butt-naked model, I'm hating on her because she went on Joy Behar and demanded President Obama's birth certificate!—[audio segment of Melania doing precisely that]. Chris Paul comes on again: And **that's** where she showed her ass!*

During the swift run-up to serial sexual harasser, Trump supplicant, and Fox News host Bill O'Reilly's ignominious departure, the *TJMS* followed the news, like most of the rest of us, with delight, outrage, and bated breath. As soon as word came out that he was absolutely fired, Chris Paul pulled off an extraordinarily clever murdered hit. He repurposed Sir Mix-A-Lot's highly sexist but extremely catchy, driving hip-hop manifesto, "I Like Big Butts,"[34] to opposite effect, using a sexist's music to gloat about the comedown of a racist misogynist. Chris sang: "They fired his butt and I cannot lie . . . O'Reilly is a thug, racist and smug! . . . Ooh, what a pervert, All those women you hurt!" He then pivoted to Fox News' financial concerns: "Fox thought it was funny, until it cost them **money**! Advertisers left his show, and Bill just had to go!" Paul ended the murdered hit with a bang, referencing O'Reilly's recent personal insult to senior African American California Congresswoman Maxine Waters, now affectionately nicknamed "Auntie Maxine," and imagining her feisty and powerful comeback to O'Reilly's taunting:[35] "*O'Reilly got axed! O'Reilly got axed! O'Reilly got axed!*"

Killing Obamacare and Coddling Neo-Nazis

The *TJMS* followed all of the Trump White House scandals, but perhaps the most burning issue for them and their audience was the Republicans' never-ending efforts to kill the Affordable Care Act—Obamacare—both because of its undeniable benefits to working- and middle-class Americans and because of its symbolism as the signature social-democratic achievement of the nation's first African American president.

After the Republican Congress managed to pass the second, horrifying version of Trumpcare in May 2017, Chris Paul bested his own record for creativity and withering contempt. He murdered the Geto Boys' 1991 paranoid hip-hop hit, "Mind Playing Tricks on Me"—"At night I can't sleep."[36] Paul used the well-known classic to summarize the horrors of the legislation, of the Republicans' cold-blooded disdain for suffering Americans—"You're ass-out with pre-existing conditions!" Then he focused on Trump voters' ongoing ignorance of how badly the "populist" President had suckered them—"all you Trump voters on Medicaid, congratulations, you just got played!" And he indicted voters falling for the pure racism of opposing Obamacare simply because an African American president had achieved it: "This aint about and repealin and replacing, it's about **black president** erasin!" Paul finished with the true economic populist message: "Cause healthcare all Americans deserve! What they did was unholy . . . The GOP makes me sick, homie!"

The crew also kept up the pressure, criticizing Trump for reversing President Obama's efforts to halt climate change:

> (*June 1, 2017*) *Sybil: Reports on Trump maybe pulling from Paris climate deal . . . she editorializes about catastrophic and possibly irreversible changes to the globe. Praises public-sphere black astrophysicist Neil deGrasse Tyson's tweet burning Trump for his total ignorance of and hostility to climate science.*[37]

When white supremacists marched and beat counter-protesters in Charlottesville, North Carolina on August 12, 2017, and a crazed fascist ran over and murdered progressive white protestor Heather Heyer, the *TJMS* fully covered the sickening events, treated her with honor as a civil rights martyr, named all of the injured or killed, and excoriated Trump for his failure to condemn the fascists. (The day after Heather

Heyer's funeral, Sybil played audio of her mother's heartbroken but defiantly anti-racist speech at the beginning of her news report.) And Chris Paul pulled off yet another brilliant murdered hit on August 14, 2017, transforming C-Lo Green's hilarious 2010 kiss-off song to those who had scorned him before he was successful, "Fuck You," into an indictment of Trump's coziness with neo-Nazis.[38] First he played audio of news reports on white supremacists' march and violence, underlain by the beginning of "F—You," [with the "fuck" blurred for radio play]. Chris Paul sings to the melody in C-Lo's signature style: "I see those white supremacists down in Charlottesville, and I'm like F—them! They got them little little tiki torches clenchin up their fists, and I'm like F—them and all they represent!" Paul goes on to point out that the alt-right is emboldened by "the White House and the words comin out of Trump's white mouth." Paul hilariously and accurately comments on the "out from the shadows" status of domestic white nationalist terrorists. They're "out in the open, in hush puppy shoes, drinking lattes and watching Fox News!" He adjures his audience to shout, "No! We won't let no racist intimidate us! F—them! It's time for every man and woman to stand up to hate, and tell'em, F—them!"

On August 16, Roland Martin came on, furious and loaded for bear. He was beside himself at the racism flowing from the White House down:

> Roland plays audio of the late black Democratic Texas congresswoman Barbara Jordan (1936–96) saying she won't be an idle spectator . . . he keeps repeating, rhetorically, "I will not be an idle spectator! "This president is an **immoral** leader! . . . We must do more than simply tweet or go on Facebook! This is a declaration of war! . . . Tom, for 398 years black folks have been fighting to ensure that this country lives up to its ideals! . . . It's time for people of conscience to stand up, to oppose any effort to go back to the days of Jim Crow. It means that when you come to the ballot box, I don't want to hear anyone tell me my vote doesn't matter. With a white supremacist in the White House . . . we need to say we are going to rain holy hell down on anyone who supports Donald Trump. . . . We will fight this and pick up the baton . . . [of previous generations]. 2018 will be the fiftieth anniversary of Martin Luther King's assassination. You have to decide which side you're on! . . . Heather Heyer will be buried today. . . . She is a twenty-first-century version of Viola Liuzzo, a white antiracist . . . #45, game on!"

Huggy then buttressed Martin's point, with his inimitable stylish wit:

> This mediocre mofo . . . is blamin both sides **again!** . . . . The white supremacists gave him two tiki torches up!

Even Al Sharpton, who is usually solemn when discussing national tragedies, was so aghast at Trump's narratives that he descended into ridicule:

> Meanwhile, President Can't Do It Right! . . . [He has so embarrassed the country that] the horses the Confederate soldiers are on are sayin, "**I** aint racist!"

On August 23, a texter summed up the *TJMS* audience appreciation of crew and guests speaking truth to power:

> Tom, thank you for all the education that you bring not only to black people but to white people. So many of them don't know the hell they put us through!

White comic and friend of the show Gary Owen came on to narrate a minor example of the other side—how the anti-Trump resistance can discipline racists:

> Owen describes being heckled by a Trump supporter during a comedy club set. . . ."He yelled n-word lover [Owen's wife is black] on the way out the door. I said on stage, 'My wife carries a 9! Just be careful!' . . . He left a whole Facebook rant, 'N-word lover.' [Owen then posted the rant on Instagram] People started calling his job, and him. He and his wife were both fired. They're getting overrun with calls. They're leaving town because of the rumpus. . . . What I found out: Beyoncé's got the Bey-hive. I got the G-hive! He got stung a little bit." Crew highly appreciative.

But no sooner did the renaissance of American neo-Nazis, and Trump's approval of them, register on the public transcript than the nation was engulfed with an autumn wave of climate-change-affected hurricanes: first Harvey, affecting Texas especially, then Maria and Irma, which devastated many Caribbean countries, and the Virgin Islands and Puerto Rico, which of course are part of the United States.

Harvey/Maria/Irma: Disaster Racism

The *TJMS* immediately swung into charitable action as Hurricane Harvey hit, setting up a fund for those who had taken in hurricane evacuees. By August 31, they had raised $35,000, and were about to send out $1000 gift cards. By September 25, they had taken in and were distributing $440,000. Listeners texted in on-the-ground information:

> (August 28, 2017) I'm a nurse and I can't get in to work. My neighborhood is ok but the surrounding areas are flooded.

Crew and guests tried to assess the most needy: What about Texas Southern (HBCU) students who weren't flooded out but were lacking food? What about pregnant women?

And audience members texted in their gratitude for the black community of the air:

> *(August 28, 2017) A lot of us don't have power, and we're streaming your show via phones and ipads, charging them with our car chargers! Please keep broadcasting the latest!*

The crew also warned its audience of Trump's various heinous acts perpetrated while the country was distracted by the hurricanes. On August 28, 2018, Sybil reported with anger and disgust that while we weren't looking, Trump pardoned convicted racist Arizona sheriff Joe Arpaio, and instructed the U.S. military not to induct transsexual recruits.

> *Tom: You gotta stay **woke**!*
> *Arsenio Hall: This is a **draft dodger**, telling people they can't join up!*
> *Sybil: Yeah, he had a **hangnail**! All laugh.*

Chris Paul then added his witty contribution to the horror of the Arpaio pardon:

> *Trump decided it's more important to keep his white nationalist base happy than to serve the country. . . . But it makes sense that Trump would protect Arpaio— they're from **the same hood**!*

Audience members continued to demonstrate the *TJMS's* community of the air function:

> *(August 28, 2018) Texter: Houstonians, in the past you have welcomed Detroiters. Now we welcome you back. We are dry, have good water, and can take about a million people!*

As Harvey morphed into Irma and Maria, the *TJMS* stayed on the case, accurately reporting on damage to Florida and the Caribbean, and adding those areas to their charitable fund. Sybil reported carefully on widespread Caribbean suffering over the autumn, and Tom daily read out letters from hurricane survivors being helped through the *TJMS* fund, with Stevie Wonder's poignant "Love's In Need of Love Today"[39] playing in the background. The crew were particularly incensed at Trump's cavalier and untruthful statements about suffering Puerto Ricans[40]:

> *(September 26, 2017) Tom: Trump doesn't know Puerto Ricans are Americans, does he? Trump doesn't know!*

Sybil points out that people in the White House know, so that's no excuse.

Huggy: *I know it's only Tuesday, but my favorite tweet of the week comes from (multiple Grammy-winning Nuyorican singer and actor) Marc Anthony: "Mr. President, shut the f—up and worry about Puerto Rico!" And I think it was wrong to call him* **Mr. President!**

(Later) Tom again: Syb, I think he thinks they're Mexican! He honestly doesn't know who they are! He sees them brown and speaking Spanish and he doesn't know any better!

Sybil: *Tom, you could build a* **wall** *with Trump's ignorance!*

(October 4, 2017) Sybil quotes the mayor of San Juan, Puerto Rico: "He slammed Trump again, called him Miscommunicator in Chief! Virgin Islands residents are also complaining, saying Trump should have visited them and brought basic necessities . . .

Texter: *Why do you have time to go play golf, but you don't have time to go to the U.S. Virgin Islands? I don't understand! [crew loves it]*

On October 9, they revisited Trump's appalling behavior in Puerto Rico, throwing rolls of paper towels at his audience, and imagining a Southwestern black American response to such repugnant behavior:

Tom: *Sybil, what if Trump had come to Houston and started throwin paper towels?*
Sybil, scornfully: *That would be the last we would have seen of him! . . . They don't call it Houston Strong for nuthin!*

The *TJMS* stayed on the case for hurricane victims, as did their audience:

(October 23, 2018) Blackamericaweb.com Relief Fund has organized a big black comedy benefit, "Friends with Benefits," hosted by Chris Paul and Huggy Lowdown, with proceeds to go to all hurricane victims. Everyone is donating their time and travel.

Tom: *Reports that FEMA has people waiting two to four hours just for them to pick up the phone. He's sympathetic because they receive hundreds of letters daily for the blackamericaweb relief fund, and it takes forever to verify them.*

Crew reports that they have now received more than $520,000, mostly from small donations, from all over the U.S. and the world. Thousands of people have donated.

Tom: *"Money keeps comin in, every day! Wow, that's love. It shows how black people know that we have to take care of ourselves!"*

Niger and New Trump Lows

But the autumn of 2017 was one overlapping catastrophe after another. While the nation was reeling from the news of the death and disaster wreaked on vast swathes of U.S. territory from multiple hurricanes, major California wildfires, a spate of deadly mass shootings, Trump deliberately ratcheting up nuclear war tensions with North Korea, and the aftermath of Charlottesville, four American soldiers were killed in a surprise attack in the nation of Niger.[41]

As usual, Trump dealt with the situation in the least presidential manner possible. There was no unified White House response to the tragedy, and Trump himself, after falsely claiming that President Obama had not made condolence calls to families of fallen troops, managed to be so offensive in making the mandatory presidential condolence calls to the dead troops' families that he caused yet another long-term press dumpster fire[42]:

> *(October 18, 2017) [black] Democratic Congresswoman Frederica Wilson [Florida] is on the show. She was in the car with one [black] serviceman's widow when Trump called the widow. Wilson reports that she heard the entire conversation, and that Trump was outrageously awful: He lectured the widow that her dead husband "knew what he signed up for" and didn't even remember his name. Wilson: "I'm not the only person who was in that car. This man is a sick man!"*

The following day, Chris Paul was ready with a witty, angry murdered hit on the debacle. Repurposing Naughty by Nature's ridiculous but very catchy 1991 song, "Other People's Property," [OPP], about widespread infidelity, he transformed it into an indictment of Trump as a human being[43]:

> *Audio of congresswoman on what Trump said to the widow of La David Johnson.*
> *Reporter to Congresswoman Wilson: "So when he says that you totally fabricated what he said to the wife of the soldier, and he has proof, what's your response?"*
> *Congresswoman Wilson: "Well, I don't know what kind of proof he could be talking about, I'm not the only person that was in the car ... I have proof too ... this man is a sick man, he's cold-hearted, and he feels no pity or sympathy for anyone! This is a grieving widow! And when she got off the phone she looked at me and said—He didn't even know his name!*

Chris Paul then sang to the tune of "Other People's Property: "P-O-S, abbreviation, is my final summation, of who is now the leader of this nation!" The listeners of course knew what POS means, but Chris then spells it out, summing up by using another bowdlerization of "shit:" "And if somebody asks you why the Donald is a piece of **ish.**" Paul then lays out the facts: "La David Johnson was a brave heroic Green Beret, killed in Niger, and he was left behind there for two days." He jokes about Trump golfing while the bodies were being returned to the United States, then "when he finally gave the widow a condolence call, instead of sympathy he had unmitigated gall, to twist the knife in that poor women's heart once more, by saying that he knew what he signed up for!" The song ends with a male chorus shouting that "the whole U.S." knows that "Trump is a POS!"

And the show kept up the pressure, with Sybil reporting, on October 24, 2017, on the details of the Niger disaster, and further scolding Trump: "It's so distasteful! It does not become the office!"

The following day, the Reverend Al Sharpton maintained the moral outrage:

> Let's not forget—in the middle of a Republican argument—forget that Donald Trump insulted the widow of an American officer who just gave his life for his country!

On October 26, Sybil reported that Congresswoman Wilson had received so many death threats from Trump supporters that she so far had been unable to re- turn to Washington, DC, to do her congressional work. Congressional Democrats organized a supportive group photo, in which all of them were wearing Wilson's signature red cowboy hat, but she could not be present for the photo. (She was able to return by the end of the month.)[44]

What Happened: HRC Redux

Meanwhile, Hillary Clinton published her post-election book, *What Happened.*[45] The *TJMS* brought her back on-air, as part of her book tour, on October 3, 2017, with a panel of Sybil, Jacque Reid, Al Sharpton, Roland Martin, and Shaun King:

> HRC opens by talking about gun violence and the need for gun-control legislation— more than four months before the Florida Parkland school massacre that reanimated the movement.
> Shaun King asks her about the historical fact of her approval ratings being high whenever she worked for a man, but whenever she tried to run for herself, her approval ratings sank. "I wanted to tell you that it made me check myself. . . ." [he is deliberately making a feminist point]
> Clinton is asked about Medicare for all:

I have always been for universal healthcare . . . I think there are a lot of different ways to move us toward it. . . . My personal experience was that we had to protect what was the signature achievement of President Obama . . . moving down the age scale for Medicare, offering a public option . . . Medicare for all is one aspirational important possibility. She points out that most people on Medicare also have supplemental insurance. . . . Let's have the debate based on facts, unlike the Republicans . . .

Ignored in all the mainstream media hoopla about Clinton's post-election statements, among more ordinary comments on her Electoral College loss, the *TJMS* again concentrated on precisely the issue that only they had discussed before the election. And HRC's response was crystalline:

Roland Martin: Secretary Clinton, I talked to your people about not having African American surrogates on black media, and I heard you say, "Get it done!" But your people didn't get it done?

HRC: It's just inexplicable to me . . . I have no answer for you . . . I recognize that certainly that there wasn't the level of involvement and participation that I had hoped for. . . . Anything we failed to do to change, that is on us. . . . But I want to talk about two other factors: [The first is Republican voter suppression. Then . . .] the Jim Comey letter—voters were thrown into all kinds of doubt about me, I don't blame them. And the weaponization of information on Facebook . . . Russians, Trump allies and others. The bottom line is, if we had changed 39,000 votes in three states, it wouldn't have happened.

Jacque Reid: What does the win of Donald Trump say about who we are as a nation, especially after Charlottesville?

HRC: Well, it does say that he started his campaign by dividing people . . . he continued to foment anger and frustration and resentment among the people he was aiming at . . . I tried to speak out, to tell people that it was at the very core . . . I hoped like many that he would grow, evolve . . . but he continues on that path!

. . .

*Sybil: Folks are texting in, Hillary STILL has my vote! . . . Texters are saying they've still got their **yard signs** up!*

Al Sharpton: Let me say that I've read your book and I think everyone should read it . . . and I was happy to see you spent several pages on the mothers of the movement [the mothers of innocent black men killed by police, with whom Clinton had allied during the campaign] . . . goes on to talk about gerrymandering [and thus voter suppression] . . .

HRC: Reverend Al, it could not be more important, and I appreciate you and this show and everyone who is working against it.

Roll Tide Black Radio

The alarming candidacy of multiply accused child molester and hyper-evangelist Roy Moore for Alabama Senate, and of Democrat Doug Jones's upstart effort to turn Alabama at least a bit blue, drew significant *TJMS* attention. On November 13, 2017, Sybil reported that Fox News' Sean Hannity had lost large numbers of sponsors because of his shameless Moore puffery. A texter commented in response: "Tom, if Satan was a Republican, he would win in Alabama!" On November 27, Roland Martin warned that it was the last day to register to vote in Alabama. He yelled that "there's no excuse!" for people who aren't registered: "You **know** what's at stake!" Martin went on to remind the huge *TJMS* audience that Doug Jones "prosecuted those who shot up the 16th Street Church." (He successfully prosecuted those who had not yet been charged two decades after the notorious 1963 black church bombing in Birmingham that killed four little girls.)[46] On December 4, Sybil scornfully announced that Trump had endorsed Moore. Two days later, Roland was on again, whipped into fury over black Alabama voters' "passivity," their "pathetic" historical voter turnout.

On voting day, December 12, Tom kept up the pressure:

> Tom asks audience to text him from the polls: "I know you're gonna stand up, please, **please!** Don't let me wake up to find out Roy Moore won, please!—I'm **from** Alabama and I'm voting for Doug Jones—I don't want my state represented by a pedophile! . . . Come on, black people! **It's on us!**

And black Alabamans responded in droves. One texted in that she had received a robocall for Doug Jones: "Tom, Barack Obama called my house last night! I am NEVER gonna erase that message!"

On election day, Alabama listeners reported on the local polls:

> The line is now wrapped around the church in Madison, Alabama!
> The line is long in Tuskegee!
> I'm heading to the polls in my Western hat and boots to vote for Doug Jones!
> Tom: Our girl Sheila Smoot at KISS [FM station] checked in. She says it's tight, we'll be at the polling places all day!
> Just voted in Tuscaloosa! A lot of black people are on line!

With Jones's surprise win, the *TJMS*, aware of its key role in the upset, did a series of victory laps the following morning:

> (December 13, 2017) Tom: Yes, Rev Al . . . us black people in Alabama did it!
> Sharpton points out the extraordinary fact that that black turnout exceeded that for Obama in 2008 and 2012. . . . "But we can't lose this moment getting drunk

at the victory party! We've got the tax bill [and he names numerous other is-
sues] Let's take Trumpism out!"

*Huggy Lowdown: Today is Wednesday, or as the Democrats call it, **Wins**-day!*
Sybil, I can't stop singin "Sweet Home Alabama!" [He screeches in trademark
Huggy style] Sybil, kinfolk came to vote like it was a black funeral! [crew loses
it] Sybil, people acted like it was the Essence Festival! [more appreciation]. . . .
Roy Moore said the people he wanted to come out for him had a curfew! . . . He
wanted to count the ballots himself, but he kept stopping at fourteen![crew
shouts of laughter]

Chris Paul, relishing the cliché: So we can say to Roy Moore, F—you and the horse
you rode in on!
Sybil reports gleefully, scornfully on Moore refusing to concede. She gives details . . .
Chris Paul: The Republicans should be blaming black women! Because it's the fact
that 98% of black women voted for Doug Jones and got him elected! Goes on to
milk joke by fantasizing that Doug Jones is running around buying a Girls Trip
DVD and watching Scandal and Power.

And the joyous audience metaphorically performed their own victory dances:

(December 15, 2017) Texter: Doin the wobble with the state of Alabama, cause
Doug Jones got elected!

Texter: Doin the wobble on top of Roy Moore's horse!

And black women's key electoral role was not the least bit lost on the audience:

(January 1, 2018) Texter: It's time for America to shut up and listen to the sistahs!

TJMS, DACA, Muslim Bans, Tax Bill

But the *TJMS* and its audience also maintained their broad anti-racist, anti-
xenophobic stance amidst all the horrors and distractions of the New Trump Order.
In particular, they never forgot undocumented Americans, and advocated consistently for them in this newly punitive, reflexively racist public political atmosphere:

(August 23, 2017) Chris Paul: Donald Trump held a rally in Phoenix last night.
All I'm gonna say is that, if lies were bricks, Trump would have his wall!

(September 5, 2017) Huggy goes off on Trump and DACA—explains the ac-
ronym, and defends Dreamers—"He's Freddy Kruger to the Dreamers. Hell,

*they're more American than **he** is! [Huggy mentions Trump dodging the draft, that he doesn't like the country, that he doesn't even want to live in the White House]" That Orange Anus! . . . Trump is so evil that Satan bought one of his hats!*

TJMS commentators repeatedly pointed out the broad global populations affected by DACA:

*(September 25, 2017) Al Sharpton: Many of us are looking at this whole debate that President Trump started by ending DACA—that President Obama started when they couldn't get the Dream Act passed. [gives details, points out that Trump is "all over the place."] The other misnomer is that it's just for Mexicans. I would be for it if it **was** just for Mexicans. But there are people from the Caribbean and Africa, these people are black folks! . . . This is time to come together, not a time for scapegoatin and racial profiling.*

(January 18, 2018) Roland Martin on DACA and a recent deportation. He's angry about "how callous this policy is! . . . Just last night a Haitian activist was snatched and deported. This is NOT just a Mexican thing. There are people from Haiti, from the Caribbean, from African countries. . . . Of course Democrats are embroiled in this debate. . . . The Democrats just say, We ain't voting for nuthin until there's a clean DACA bill! Republicans are scared to death that Democrats are taking over the Senate . . .

The crew was gleeful over the repeated failures of Trump's various unconstitutional Muslim bans:

(January 30, 2017) Chris Paul: As we begin week two of the Trump apocalypse . . . this bigoted action launched protests coast to coast. The only industry that's gonna boom under Trump is poster boards!

The crew was as horrified as were most Americans by the spectacle of Trump's ICE separating thousands of young children from their refugee parents, for months, often leaving them unattended, crying, in cages. Sherilynn Ifill of the NAACP Legal Defense Fund came on the show on June 19, 2018, begging listeners to call their congresspeople to protest the abomination. Sybil lamented that she was so upset about the atrocity that she was barely functioning. Then Al Sharpton phoned in, fresh from a National Action Network press conference in DC protesting ICE policy:

This must end! It should remind us of when they separated US from our parents! So you cannot sit by and say it's Mexicans, not us . . . You become a victim of the

> *normalizing of separating children from their parents ... Donald Trump has*
> *gone a bridge too far in many areas. This is one he has crossed ...*

And of course, Trump's profound hypocrisy about immigration to the U.S., given his own family's and his personal marital history, was never lost on the *TJMS* family:

> *(May 6, 2018) Tom Joyner goes off on a rant about the poor undocumented*
> *Mexican American man in Pasadena, who had lived in the U.S. for twenty-five*
> *years, who was picked up by ICE while dropping his daughter off at school.*
> *Arsenio Hall is visiting the show: "The irony is that it's being created by a president*
> *who only sleeps with immigrants!" Makes jokes about Ivanka, Melania ...*

TJMS vs. NRA

Over the last few decades, mass shootings have become an all too familiar element of American public life. Even the most progressive activists, observing dozens of scenes of carnage, and yet our abject failure after each event to effect change, had given up on achieving even the smallest move toward gun control, leaving the United States the only major industrialized nation without significant gun regulations, with the highest gun homicide rates, and the highest per-capita gun ownership.[47] But the Valentine's Day 2018 massacre at Marjory Stoneman Douglas High School in Parkland, Florida—or rather the outraged multiracial teenage student survivors' instantaneous and vehement demands for gun control, and particularly their calls for banning the AR-15 semi-automatic rifle—changed the public sphere. Frightened Florida state lawmakers actually passed a few ameliorative restrictions in the face of the teenagers' energy, media-savvy activism, and withering scorn.

Like other progressive media outlets, the *TJMS* was outraged and sorrowful, and surprised but happy with the students' rapid if very partial success. On February 15, 2018, Sybil reported the circumstances of the shooting and the names of the victims. The entire crew was in no doubt as to the NRA's responsibility for this as well as all the other mass shootings. And audience members had innovative ideas:

> *Texter: I'd support a teachers' strike until we secure better gun laws!*

On February 22, after the notorious Florida town hall meeting where students and parents ridiculed Senator Marco Rubio for his abject fealty to the NRA, the *TJMS* crew was beyond mirthful:

> *Chris Paul: For real—they tore him a new hole! Marco Rubio got booed more than*
> *at the Apollo Theater!*

Sybil plays audio of students yelling at the Capitol, then says: "Now the fake news info. Donald Trump has denied today that he called for teachers to be armed . . . he has attacked 'fake news' for twisting his words."

*Tom, aghast: I **saw** him do it! Twisted!!! . . . Marco Rubio, when's he up for re-election?*

Sybil explains. Tom is clearly panting for Rubio to be voted out. Sybil then explains that the protesting youth will be working against all the Republicans who refused to talk with them.

The following day, the audience was still gleeful about Rubio's bad press:

*(February 23, 2018) Texter: The AR 15 should be called the Marco Rubio. Because they are so **easily bought**!*

Then the crew reported that MSNBC's Joy Reid had had a guest on her MSNBC show who explained how counterproductive it would be to arm teachers. Many texters wrote in to approve.

On February 27, 2018, Sybil played audio of the Governor of Washington State, Jay Inslee, saying that arming teachers would be ridiculous. And the following day, crew, guests, and audience were all in a lather of gun control passion:

(February 28, 2018) Al Sharpton is calling for banning all weapons of war: "Let's not forget—from eighty-four to ninety-four, we had the assault weapons ban, and the number of killings went down. . . . But right now, today, there's nothing stopping them from purchasing these same armaments . . . ."

Tom: Do you think we may have the NRA on the ropes? [referring to dozens of corporations withdrawing from participation in an NRA-branded credit card]

Sharpton: Anytime you hit them in the pocket, you get their attention. . . . And that is a fool's strategy to pressure Delta . . . [referring to the Georgia State Legislature's threats to Delta Airlines]

Tom: I'm droppin my FedEx account! [to pressure them to give up their NRA-branded credit card]

Sybil: And look what light brown can do for brown! Laughs.

Sharpton, twitting Tom for his light skin tone while praising his politics: "He may be a little yella, but he's my fella!" Crew loves it.

Sybil later reports that Dick's Sporting Goods is immediately ending sales of all assault style rifles, also high capacity magazines, and will not sell to anyone under twenty-one years old. "The CEO of Dick's is making clear that the company's new policy is a direct result of the shooting. He said, 'We love those kids and their message got through to us.'"

(March 1, 2018) Texter: Imagine a black male teacher with a gun, and then they call the police about a shooter on the grounds . . .

Whole crew gets the point, comments . . .

And the crew and audience kept up the pressure against arming teachers. On March 9, 2018, Sybil reported that a teacher in Florida had finally been suspended after repeatedly using the n-word in classes, and warning white students not to have anything to do with n-words.

Texter: But they want to put guns in TEACHERS' hands?

Before the March 24, 2018 students' multiple-location March for Our Lives, *TJMS* hyped the event. The Monday after the weekend events, the crew was gleeful over their success, and particularly proud of black eleven-year-old Naomi Wadler's eloquence, and played excerpts from it.

Mellody Hobson then devoted her Monday finance briefing to laying out the appalling dollar costs of gun violence:

> *I wondered, what does all of this cost? You can't put a cost on a life. . . . But I was struck by a Johns Hopkins study last year. . . . They looked at 2006–13, 150,000 gun violence patients. There was an enormous direct cost—twenty-two billion dollars in just in-patient charges! Annually, over three billion a year. . . . The financial implication for the whole society is huge . . . Tom agonizes over just how many weapons are out there.*

> *Mellody:* **More** *than the number of Americans! She points out that the cost is about the same as "our* **entire** *Medicaid program!"*

And the *TJMS* audience reported in:

Tom, my daughter was at the march with her girlfriends in Washington, DC!

Tom: **I know** *you're proud!*

When Laura Ingraham of Fox News sneered on air at Stoneham student survivor/activist David Hogg, detailing which colleges had turned him down for admission—information that he himself had publicly disclosed—Hogg fired back, noting the effort to deflect attention from the students' gun-control demands, and inviting sponsors to boycott her show. And they did, *en masse,* and she was thrown off the air for a week. The *TJMS* crew followed the first wave of defections (on March 28, 2018) with great relish. Chris Paul chortled, Huggy Lowdown made Ingraham his Bamma of the Week, and Sybil lovingly named each sponsor that had withdrawn. It was only after the show ended that morning that I realized that the *TJMS* crew had given lengthy attention to a story with only *white* actors. The fact that Ingraham was attacking teenage survivors of a massacre, and Fox's and the NRA's overall vileness, trumped any race considerations.

Resistance on the Blackside: Waiting on Mueller

But the ongoing Special Prosecutor Mueller probe, and the Trump camp's endless clumsy efforts to duck it through threats, lies, distractions, and mass firings, remained on the *TJMS* agenda throughout. The *TJMS* played the "Russia collusion" card over and over, every single time new reporting gave them the opportunity:

During Jeff Sessions's confirmation hearings for Attorney General, the *TJMS* was utterly contemptuous:

> *(February 3, 2017) Shaun King: [discusses black people going to jail for lying under oath—Marion Jones, Lil Kim] Thirty-one years ago, Coretta Scott King warned the nation about [Jeff Sessions] . . . she questioned his commitment to . . . decency. The U.S. Senate decided the nation could not trust Jeff Sessions, and he was denied the judgeship. Now we're finding out about his communications with Russia during the campaign . . . [gives details] That is just one of the many reasons why it's so damn disturbing . . . that Jeff Sessions was caught plain as day communicating with Russian officials. . . . He said, and I quote, 'I did not have communication with the Russians.' Now we know that was a lie! . . . .It's not just wrong, it's criminal! Jeff Sessions should resign immediately. If he doesn't resign, he should be fired. . . . But this is not just about Russia. It's about honesty, it's about fairness . . . Coretta Scott King was right thirty-one years ago. He was a scoundrel then, he is a scoundrel now.*

And they repeatedly brought on knowledgeable African American politicians and newspeople to interpret the changing and horrifying scene. Representative Maxine Waters of California was a favorite:

> *(April 24, 2017) Maxine Waters says if we can follow the money, and the Russia connection is there, he should be impeached. . . . Arsenio asks, What's the oil connection? Waters explains that Rex Tillerson, formerly of Exxon, was nominated to help lift sanctions against Russia for its invasion of Crimea. . . . "The bottom line is lifting those sanctions so they can drill for oil."*
> *Sybil: Congresswoman, you were in Detroit for the NAACP dinner last night . . . asks about the changing nature of the Democratic Party.*
> *Waters mentions Kamala Harris, Corey Booker—"You've got any number of competent individuals, all of whom are very capable" . . . Sybil asks her, why not run herself?*
> *Waters: "Nonononono! I am the ranking member of the financial committee!" . . . . explains how crucial that committee is to keeping watch on Trump and his minions.*

Arsenio Hall wants to give her a minute to rip on Bill O'Reilly's hair [as O'Reilly had interrupted her on his show to make fun of hers]: "Nonononono! You cannot devote time to a sexual pervert! You cannot give him anything on this wonderful show . . . release him into the wild, with the rest of the animals!"

Sybil: Can I just say on behalf of all of us, thank you for being our voice and speaking up for all of us . . .

Texter explosions of love and respect for "Auntie Maxine."

California senator and possibly presidential hopeful Kamala Harris was on-air May 12, 2017:

You know, these are challenging times. . . . My parents met during the civil rights movement. I think this is a challenging time as well. . . . There is so much at stake. Just in the last twenty-four hours, [Attorney General] Sessions had a memo making clear that he wants to revise the war on drugs. It's outrageous. And also he wants to undo reforming the sentencing laws. It's very real, it's about turning back the clock. We have to step up and can't tire. It's going to be a long haul.

Harris inspired an audience member to text in:

Donald Trump told so many lies to Lester Holt that if he was Pinocchio, he would've been impaled!

But aside from reporting on and ridiculing the daily White House eruptions, the *TJMS* crew, like most of the American population, kept longing for closure, for the obvious charges of collusion, illegally benefiting from office (the Emoluments Clause in the Constitution), and treason finally to be brought, and for the whole poison mess to be excised from the body politic. Chris Paul, for example, on December 19 and 20, 2017, pulled off a Christmas season two-fer of murdered hits illustrating our widespread hopes for Special Prosecutor Robert Mueller's investigation. In the first, he sang to the tune of "Santa Claus is Comin to Town." He warned Trump, "Ya better lawyer up, I'm tellin you why, Robert Mueller's comin to town!" He ended dramatically: "Robert Mueller's on Trump's ass like white on rice!" Then the following day, he revisited his Christmas 2016 tour de force transformation of "You're a Mean One, Mr. Grinch," with brand-new contemptuous lyrics. "You're a monster, Mr. Trump" characterizes him as "a creature from the **white** lagoon," a "bloated wet buffoon," "the Orange Kim Jun-Un," "our nation's biggest joke," "a scrotum, a wrinkly bag of nuts." Paul ends in recitative: "Dear Santa Claus, If I could have one wish fulfilled this Christmas, it would be to Bring. Back. **Barack!**"

The crew, like the vast majority of the rest of America, found the publication of Michael Wolff's insider tell-all about the Trump White House, *Fire and Fury*,[48] a fascinating and hilarious spectacle, chock-full of further disgusting details:

(January 4, 2018) Both Chris Paul and Huggy are deeply enjoying Trump and Bannon "beefin" [likening them to rap moguls]. They discuss Wolff's White House revelations, as reported on MSNBC the night before.

Chis Paul: *Whoa, what we have here America is a good old-fashioned war between bigots!... The **sheet** has hit the fan!... Trump investigating voter fraud was like OJ swearing to find Nicole's real killer!*

Huggy: *Oh, aint nuthin like bigots beefin!* **Don't** *you enjoy it?*

Guest host Donnie Simpson: *The things in this book,* The Fire and the Fury, *are just amazing! He and Sybil enjoy themselves immensely, with remarks very similar to those on MSNBC the night before.*

Donnie: *Like he doesn't know anything! WE knew that when he got elected!*

Sybil: *I knew sumthin was up when he started tweeting "my button is bigger than yours"—he's trying to deflect! He's a major deflector.*

They discuss how frightening it is that he would push a nuclear button to deflect attention from the scandal.

Sybil: *Oh my gosh, that thing is a soap opera—if you think reality TV is crazy!?*

(January 5, 2018). Chris Paul goes on about the scandal around the Wolff book, how it details how everyone who's worked with Trump says he's unbelievably stupid, and Trump's efforts to stop publication of the book . . . Fire and Fury?! *They should have named this book* Sh—We Already Know!

Sybil then reports further on Fire and Fury. *"They are saying that they are worried about his mental state—reporters asking questions about his mental stability." Sybil notes that White House reporters were snickering during the most recent press conference as Sarah Huckabee Sanders blithely claimed Trump had no mental or psychological problems.*

*(February 15, 2018) D L Hughley reports that Trump people were in touch with Russia throughout the campaign. "That is high treason. This election was illegally stolen from the people of the U.S. If Russia was named Monica, and the red sickle was a red dress, he'd be **impeached** already!"*

The show also brought back Bernie Sanders on January 18, 2018—part of Sanders's own deliberate post-election effort to forge better bonds with African American voters[49]—to query his take on the Trump Administration and the ongoing resistance:

Bernie Sanders is on with a panel of Sybil, Jacque Reid, Roland Martin, and Al Sharpton.

Sharpton: *Senator, let me ask, one of the critical problems in our community has been gentrification. . . . We see many who call themselves progressives [who don't* recognize the crucial nature of affordable housing and invest union pension funds with developers who violate the law]—union pension funds are used to give to developers who are ruining our community..

Sanders: Reverend that's a very important point . . . it is very very hard for working people of any race to stay in the neighborhoods in which they grew up . . . that has got to be dealt with!

Then, there's an untapped resource, that is billions of dollars in pension funds. We have the potential to use those investments to create communities in which people can live with dignity.

Sybil: When you are ready to make your announcement [of 2020 candidacy], and are you prepared to come on the TJMS and make your announcement?

Second, who would be your vice presidential running mate? Sanders says it's far too early to speculate. . . . "We're talking about the future of the planet! . . . What we've got to focus on right now is significantly raising voter turnout . . . I am a little bit optimistic because of the fall 2018 elections [the possibility of taking over Congress again]. . . . That's my focus right now—creating a political revolution, getting people registered to vote . . . ."

Tom: What's ahead for our country in 2018?

Sanders: What is ahead is the absolute necessity to bring people together, to take on the racism, sexism, xenophobia, religious bigotry of the Trump Administration. . . . But we have to fight this administration—goes off on how most Americans want healthcare for all, to rebuild our infrastructure . . . a movement to make public colleges free. . . . And I want to see the minimum wage raised to fifteen bucks an hour AT LEAST. We have to fight Trump and all his divisive politics, but we have to come together around an agenda for change!

Sharpton asks him if he will campaign for whichever Democrat is nominated in 2020.

"Your point is right—no matter who the candidate is . . . we need to have a strong grassroots movement in every place in this country!"

Roland Martin: Senator Sanders, this is the fiftieth anniversary of Martin Luther King Jr.'s assassination . . . the Reverend William Barber and others have been talking to broke white folks who are voting against their own interests . . . [what do you think about that?]

Sanders: That's a very important question. I have been to . . . [lists all the states he has visited]. . . . You remember during Trump's campaign . . . [he misled American voters about his policies to improve workers' lives.] He lied in every instance! So we talk to working people in general. We say don't take out your anger on somebody because their skin color is different from yours. Stand together! . . . We cannot live in a country that is increasingly an oligarchy!

TiTi and TaTa: Evolving *TJMS* Humor

But the *TJMS* also had to keep its audience engaged, despite the daily crises with which Americans and others had to deal because of Republican governance. And filling the air with talk-show political denunciations alone could not maintain that engagement.

One entertaining shift was the institutionalization of Tuesday and Thursday mornings with comedians Sherri Shepherd and Kym Whitley, or "TiTi and TaTa." Shepherd (see Figure 7.2) is a former *The View* guest and anchor, while Whitley (see Figure 7.3) is a film and television actor. Both women are fast and funny, and connected with the *TJMS* audience through their bit, Black Moms Matter, Single Women Rule:

> *(September 28, 2017) Sherri and Kym are challenged to do a "single mom rap."*
> *They manage so beautifully that the female audience is inspired to text in their*
> *own hilarious and meaningful—note the gay rights example—"mom raps":*
> *I stole food for my kids!*
> *Go up to the school for my kids! Snatch a teacher's wig for my kids!*
> *I'm going on the TJMS cruise—for my kids!*

Figure 7.2 Actor and comic Sherri Shepherd. U.S. Navy photo by Mass Communication Specialist 3rd Class Ash Severe/Released.

Figure 7.3 Actor and comic Kym Whitley at the 2011 Comic Con in San Diego. Photo by
Gage Skidmore.

Slapped my mama—for my kids!
*Do **you** want my kids?*
Married my wife for my kids!
Drivin my car two thousand miles for my kids!
Hide my twerk for my kids!

And Kym got in perhaps the best R Kelly zinger after he appeared on Wendy
Williams's show and claimed that he was illiterate, as if that would somehow miti-
gate his alleged crimes against underage girls:

(May 10, 2018) What he meant to say was, "I don't know big words like 'un-
lawful,' or 'held against her will!'"

And Sherri and Kym definitely are audience favorites. On January 23, 2018, the
show hosted O'Shea Jackson, Jr, who starred in the just-released film *Den of Thieves*.
Sherri, Kym, and Sybil all flirted shamelessly with the actor, pronouncing him "foin."
A texter later applauded their taste, with a *TJMS* LBGTQ politics twist:

*Sherri, you're right! I'm a lesbian, and he can **git** it!*

TJMS audience members also kept the pot boiling. One text brought together excitement over the upcoming *TJMS* cruise, old-school musical taste, and LBGTQ rights:

> *(September1, 2018) My wife loves Anita Baker . . . when she heard she'll be on the cruise, she about lost it. She's goin. But I'm eight months pregnant and I can't go. I think she's gonna go without me!*

Sybil then enjoyed herself mercilessly over Tom's efforts to get the gender/sexual identities straight.

And Huggy Lowdown maintained his acerbic, angry wit over Trump&Co's white supremacist ideology throughout. As Thanksgiving 2017 approached, he announced:

> *(November 21, 2017) Today Donald Trump will take part in the American tradition of pardoning a turkey, one white, one black. And later, he'll go on twitter to attack the black one!*

As did Chris Paul:

> *Discusses his TJMS Thanksgiving: "And Jeff Sessions dropped by with a **white sheet** cake." [crew beside themselves in hysterics]*

And on January 18, 2018:

> *The ruler of American trailer trash is himself a double-wide!*

The *TJMS* enthusiastically supported the enormous global second wave of women's marches on January 20, 2018, a year after the first highly successful slapback at Trump.

> *(January 23, 2018) Tom: Sybil, Yall were **woke** this weekend at the women's march! . . . Asks why the main march was in Vegas? She explains about a specific election and gun violence. Plays Viola Davis's Vegas speech later in the show.*

The *TJMS* kept the woke flame burning throughout. On April 24, 2018, first Maxine Waters returned to the show to be feted—one listener wrote in that he had named his daughter after her, many years ago—and to predict that Trump would in the end be impeached. Then Tarana Burke, the founder of the #MeToo movement, came on to argue forcefully for a boycott of R Kelly's music, given the strong evidence of his abuse of girls and women.[50] (Her larger point was the need for the "black community" to "unlearn some things" about supporting abusive black men.) She baldly stated that she wanted the *TJMS* to boycott R Kelly's work. Tom shocked her by instantly agreeing: "Well, you got it! I won't play his songs anymore!" (Perhaps Burke did not realize that the *TJMS* had boycotted Kelly's work before, for years, during his last trial.)

As the first Trump State of the Union Address approached, the crew was beyond scornful, and noted and supported the range of protestors outside:

> *(January 28, 2018) Sybil notes that Rosie O'Donnell will be protesting outside White House just before the SOTU . . . as well as Food&Water Watch, the National Nurses Alliance, the ACLU, etc.*
>
> Tom: *Go head, Rosie!*

Then they and their guests eviscerated Trump's State of the Union performance:

> *(January 31, 2018)*
>
> Crew: *He is a trained con man—to stand there and say he did everything to bring the economy back—he did nothing! And to say he's a Dreamer! No, **we** are the Dreamers, he's a schemer!*
>
> Chris Paul: *Listening to Trump's speech last night was like listening to LaVar Ball promising that the Lakers would win the championship! . . . I hadn't seen evil white people **smile** that much since the auction scene in* Get Out! *. . . Last night Trump gave his speech, and today his staff will attempt to explain it to him!*
>
> Journalist Angela Rye visits: *"Orange-y, you need to have a seat!"*
>
> They ask her about Omarosa—*"Oh, you guys still talkin about that? We don't waste time on people who sell us out for a paycheck!"*
>
> They ask her about Trump's painfully slow SOTU performance: *"Ohmygod! It's amazing that this is the man who called for Barack Obama's Harvard transcripts, and HE CAN'T READ!"*
>
> Roland Martin then talks with Congressman Jim Clyburn of South Carolina on the SOTU:
>
> Roland: *Many of the Congressional Black Caucus members wore kente cloth items?*
>
> Clyburn: *We decided that of those who were attending, we should do so in solidarity. We wore black in solidarity with the #MeToo movement. And number two, we'd wear kente cloth to stand in solidarity with those s-hole countries in Africa the president insulted. I am very proud of what we did. People from the African diplomatic corps were elated . . .*
>
> Roland: *The speech was very long . . .*
>
> Clyburn: *What I heard was a lot of platitudes. . . . It was just laced with laudatory stories of people who've made great sacrifices. . . . Just something thrown in there to go on twitter to talk about how many standing Os he got. . . . He didn't talk about the fact that black unemployment dropped eight points*

*under Barack Obama, only one point under him. . . . He did not say **anything** of a significant nature as to the country and the economy. . . . That's the kind of foolishness this man is conducting and pretending to be President of the United States.*

Roland: He met with reporters yesterday and called for unity. What do you think?

Clyburn: The speech last night was the most divisive I've ever seen, and I've been here twenty-five years! He used the term chain migration—that has become a divisive term, why are you using it? . . . .I am really embarrassed to have had to sit there and listen to it.

[Clyburn explains that he attended because he believes we should respect the office, even if we don't respect the man who inhabits it]

Tom talks about how shockingly slowly Trump read the speech. Other crew members mimic Trump . . .

Clyburn, slyly: And there were some subject-verb agreements I took issue with as well!

As 2018 rolled on, the *TJMS* documented each alarming White House moment. On May 17, the crew was exercised over Trump openly labeling immigrants "animals." Huggy Lowdown expostulated in his inimitable style: "This antiquated pachyderm is the **worst**! Calling immigrants animals!"

Meanwhile, like many angry nonwhite Americans, the *TJMS* took to labeling racist whites "colonizers." As in, the woman who called the police on a black Oakland family peacefully barbecuing near Lake Merritt in Oakland—memed on twitter as "Barbecue Becky." As in, the man who called the Pennsylvania Highway Patrol on a group of Sigma Gamma Rho sorority sisters who had adopted a highway and were cleaning it up. He reported "black women fighting!"[51] The crew, like so many of us, openly wondered why police didn't file charges and levy fines against racist whites for wasting their time on frivolous calls.

The *TJMS* also relished the "Rosanne" debacle, after the actor self-destructed in a barrage of racist tweets, and ABC canceled her rebooted show despite its high ratings. Al Sharpton analyzed the phenomenon with the crew, focusing on the necessity of constant struggle, the irony of corporate America's discomfort with the overt racism in the Trump White House and Republican Congress, and the necessity of keeping our eyes on the prize—fighting Trump and the Republicans through active electoral participation:

(May 30, 2018) Sharpton: What happened in a matter of hours to Rosanne. . . . ***We*** *can do whatever is necessary [to make change] even in the age of Trump. . . . Even though Trump has created a poisonous atmosphere . . . remember Rosanne. If you fight, you may win, and if you don't fight, you will lose. We need to end this Trump era in a slow-walk toward 2020.*

Tom ask him, "Is it about business, not morality?"

> *Sharpton: Yes! You can't be identified with backwoods bigotry while you're trying to do a global economic deal. [he had noted the Disney Corporation's international presence] Morality is something admirable, but it's not where they live, it's where **we** live . . ..*
>
> *Sybil finds it interesting that it all happened on the same day that Starbucks closed eight thousand stores [for mandatory anti-racism training of employees]*
>
> *Sharpton: "Yes!—Congress is not discussin race, but corporate America is!"*
>
> *Sybil pivots to important primary elections coming up. Sharpton exclaims, "I'm more concerned about Stacy Abrams than about Rosanne Barr!"*

The Queen of Soul Passes

Aretha Franklin's death, on August 16, 2018, and then her lengthy, public, lying-in-state, star-studded memorial were heavily covered by news media worldwide. But Tom Joyner was a personal friend of Aretha's, so listeners learned that she was in hospice the week before she passed. Joyner couldn't reach her, as only family were getting through, and expressed his frustration and his longing to see her before the end. He recalled that she nicknamed all her friends—his was "DJ." He mimicked her calling him in the middle of the night over the years, raspily shouting, "DJ! DJ!" The *TJMS* also heavily stressed Franklin's commitment to the city of Detroit and her many local charities. Audience texters sent messages about laughing and crying, sitting in their cars, listening to the *TJMS* tribute. Others wrote in that public schools were playing Aretha hits over the public address system during class breaks, and imagined her final homegoing:

> *Texter: Aretha's not gone, because she's up in Heaven where she's taken over the choir from Luther!*

But perhaps the most adorable vignette from Aretha's passing came when the *TJMS* had her second husband (1978–84), actor Glynn Turman, on to talk about her. The veteran of *The Wire* and *House of Lies* was low-key and charming about their time together, and refreshingly honest about the nickname Aretha bestowed upon him—"Stinky." The crew, absolutely beside themselves with comedic joy, then demanded to know what *he* had called Aretha. He paused, and then said simply, as if we all should have already known, "Baby!"

This back-and-forth stimulated a witty audience member with an excellent memory to text in:

> *One day Stinky and Booger Puddin walked into a bar . . ..*

And the entire crew collapsed in wild laughter.

TJMS, *Kavanaugh*, and the 2018 Midterms

After Trump nominated Brett Kavanaugh to fill the seat on the Supreme Court vacated through Antonin Scalia's passing, the *TJMS* lost no time retailing his many lies to the Senate Judiciary Committee about his Bush-era work, and most especially focused on the multiple claims by various women that he had sexually harassed and even raped them.[52] Chris Paul was on the case, summarizing Kavanaugh's misogynist record and his potential to commit further harm:

> *(September 20, 2018) This is beyond evil! Back in high school, Kavanaugh didn't give his accuser a right to choose, and soon he'll take away **every** woman's right to choose!*

On September 21, *TJMS* brought on Sherrilyn Ifill, the head of the NAACP's Legal Defense Fund. Ifill expressed enormous compassion for Dr. Christine Blasey Ford, Kavanugh's main accuser, who had been outed by the press and received so many death threats that she and her family had had to relocate four times. Ifill, speaking as an attorney about the process, said:

> *We have some precedents [for how to handle this situation properly]. The Senate Judiciary Committee should know what **not** to do now . . . we know what happened [with the flawed hearings for Clarence Thomas, and the poor treatment Anita Hill received]. And this would be an utter embarrassment if thirty years later we repeat the same thing . . . You want a neutral investigator who is not going to talk to just the two [accusers] but to others [which we now know did not happen].*

Ifill went on to point out that Kavanaugh had lied under oath to the Senate Judiciary Committee: "We oppose his confirmation because of Kavanaugh's civil rights record. Call your senator!"

On September 24, Arsenio Hall was hosting, and wittily pointed out that there were

> *two words no man wants to hear first thing in the morning—Ronan Farrow! [the New Yorker reporter who has uncovered many violence against women cases] Oh man, they're catchin these guys, and it's good!*

Huggy Lowdown then got into the act, pleased that there was a second Kavanaugh accuser, and delighted to use his native knowledge of the DC region to make fun of Kavanaugh's claims, with the Huggy trademark screech at the end: "Now this guy is claimin to be from the mean streets of **Bethesda!**?? . . . Kava-HELL-nah!" He announced that there would be a 1pm walkout to show support for Dr. Christine Blasey Ford, and that he would be there.

As the national SCOTUS drama continued, Sybil warned on September 26 of the likelihood of Kavanaugh's accusers failing, because Senate Republicans simply refused to speak to Ford or any other accuser. After the disastrous October 6 Senate vote placed Kavanaugh on the Supreme Court, the *TJMS* was thoroughly disgusted. On October 9, Huggy Lowdown used his time to go off on Trump apologizing to Kavanaugh for having to endure women quite credibly accusing him of sexual assault, and slyly brought up the long-ago Clarence Thomas case: "How about apologizing to Dr. Christine Blasey Ford?! To Anita Hill!"

As the 2018 midterms approached, the *TJMS* crew were whipped into a frenzy, very well aware of the possibility of Democrats taking over the majority in the House, and perhaps flipping Senate seats and governorships. Tom Joyner, electrified by the charismatic Andrew Gillum's campaign for governor of Florida, actually changed his voter registration (he already owned a home in Florida) in order to be able to vote for Gillum, campaigned actively for him, and had both him and his wife R. Jai Gillum on the show repeatedly, as well as Mike Espy, running for a Senate seat from Mississippi, and Stacy Abrams, locked in a tight race for Governor of Georgia. They were also intrigued by Beto O'Roarke's highly-publicized bid to unseat Senator Ted Cruz in Texas, and brought him on as well.

On August 30, 2018, Shaun King reported that things were "on fleek in the Florida governor's race!" But he warned that, by the numbers, more Republicans had shown up in the primary, and that "black folk need to show up for the general election, because if you do, he will win!"

The *TJMS* kept up the pressure to register and vote consistently until November 6. On October 30, Huggy Lowdown lamented that "This mofo is runnin our country to the ground . . . It's Halloween and there's **nuthin** scarier than an unregistered voter!" On November 1, Tom announced that he had received so many texts from early voters reporting in that his phone had locked up.

On November 2, 5, and 6, the *TJMS* was astonishingly packed. On November 2, Richard Trumka, head of the AFL-CIO, came on to urge massive voter turnout, making it clear that union resources had been expended to defeat Republicans. Tom Joyner asked him how many AFL-CIO members there were. Trumka said about thirteen million. Tom exclaimed: "That oughta do it! I'm really encouraged!" He and Sybil then ran down the different races, and worried about the results, given how openly Republicans were trying to suppress the of color and youth vote.

And then Beto O'Roarke came on, introduced by Tom Joyner with great ceremony, to articulate his closing argument. On November 5, Mike Espy came on to talk with Roland Martin, and made it clear he was looking for a runoff.

On November 6, Stacy Abrams visited to give her campaign closer. She was delightfully personal, pointing out that she had run as herself, without going "on a crash diet. [shouts of laughter] I didn't straighten my hair!" [more shouts of laughter and approbation] All through the show, Tom read out dozens upon dozens of texts from listeners describing their poll experiences. Even though I wasn't able to listen to the full 5–9 a.m. show, I documented listeners texting in multiple times from at least twenty-two states and the District of Columbia. And many of them happily reported white support:

> *Texter: Amazing to see white people yelling* **Gillum***!*

Tom and Sybil then shared their own experiences in Florida and Texas—whites stopping Tom to tell him they loved his Gillum t-shirt, white Texans with Beto lawn signs and t-shirts.

Tom ended the show with a machine-gun delivery of dozens of voters' texts, first with Public Enemy's "Fight the Power" in the background, then the Isley Brothers' earlier "Fight the Power," then Stevie Wonder's "Love's In Need of Love Today." Then Tom announced emotionally, "Change's Gonna Come!" as Sam Cooke's signature 1964 ballad started playing, and I, along with no doubt millions of other hopelessly wound-up listeners, burst into tears.[53] Tom announced afterwards: "Now **that's** a voting carol!"

And change did come, if not all the change for which American progressives were hoping. Voter turnout increased, dramatically in some states. The Democrats took back the House, but not the Senate, as they had expected. People of color, white women, and LBGTQ candidates did well, gun-control ballot initiatives passed, and Mike Espy got the runoff he expected, which he, alas, then lost. But as of this writing, Stacy Abrams had announced she could not win but was suing the state of Georgia for its many many voting rights violations.

Tom Joyner took Gillum's defeat hard, and was quite morose at the beginning of the November 7 show. But then Shaun King came on to summarize where we were:

> [First he focused on the good news] "We retook Congress, and with people of color and women. These people will now oversee some powerful committees in Congress and will be able to check and oversee Trump . . . . [he shifts to the District Attorney races] A lot won. And Amendment 4 passed in Florida— more than one million are getting back their right to vote! All nineteen black women running for judge won!"
>
> [Now to unpack our bad news] "Our friend Gillum did lose. I'm shocked, I can't believe it. It's possibly the Bradley effect [referring to the infamous California gubernatorial loss Tom Bradley experienced despite being far ahead in the polls. The conclusion was that a significant number of whites polled were too embarrassed to admit they weren't going to vote for a black American][54] . . . it was a painful loss. He was clearly the better candidate and man. Beto lost, but was ahead til the very end. Beto's campaign electrified Democrats all over Texas and all over the U.S."

Chris Paul then contributed a murdered hit with the inspiriting chorus: "The Democrats have taken back the House!" One line happily warned: "Now we got some oversight up in there, and Donald Trump, your ass should be scared!"

Tom: *Thank you, Chris Paul! I really needed that!*

Roland Martin then came on with a lengthy analysis of the results:

> *Let's get into it. Look! A lot of people are sad today . . . but I need black people to understand that overall last night was a good night. Congresswoman Maxine Waters is now Chair of the Finance Committee . . . [He names many other new committee chairs] . . . You also potentially have black folks vying to become Speaker of the House . . . The Congressional Black Caucus got bigger last night, huge victories. And the big one: Lucy McBath is ahead in Georgia [she did win in the end]. That is shocking! If that holds, she goes to Congress . . . But also we now have a black Attorney General, Kwame Raoul, in Illinois. Proposition 4 [Florida initiative to enfranchise felons] will change the Florida vote . . . .*
> *That's seven black folks who won last night, members of Congress!*
> *What do I tell people? The bench is* **now expanding**.
> *Also with Pritzker becoming Governor in Illinois, a sister is Lieutenant Governor there. We wanted to see at least one African American governor, but the African American bench is expanding. Black America did well last night.*

Texters responded to Roland's detailed analysis and uplift variously, with hope, vengeance, and despair:

> Texter: *Thank you Roland, I feel so much better!*
> Texter: *Bull Connor [racist Alabama politician responsible for police turning dogs and fire hoses on civil rights demonstrators in the 1960s] can turn in his grave while burning in hell!*
> Texter: *I feel like a slave or a prisoner seeking freedom who's been told four more years!*

Sybil then reported the news, stressing African American "politicians living to fight another day," and giving the audience the granular details of Florida's vs. Georgia's election laws concerning recounts. She summarized the election results: "With House Democratic control, that means a lot more authority and chairmanships for our people . . . Today marks the beginning of Donald Trump's reelection campaign!"

And the huge *TJMS* audience appreciated the analysis:

> Texter: *I think Roland and Sybil are the smartest people on the planet—and not necessarily in that order!*

One would think that a committed political song would be the natural accompaniment to African American midterm Resistance activism. But during the midterm fever period, I noticed that black British/American singer Ella Mai's lively, addictive R&B love song, "Boo'd Up," had taken over the airwaves.[55] It is a bona fide nightclub and Billboard number 5 hit in the U.S., and occupied top spots all over Europe and the Commonwealth.[56] It's a candy floss piece, celebrating the singer's romantic and sexual satisfaction—"I'll never get over you until I find something new that get me high like you do . . . Ain't got to tell you what to do." Tom expressed his great enjoyment the song—happily chanting "Boo'd up, boo'd up!"—and I found myself so obsessed with it that I was serenading random strangers. At the end of this book, as at the beginning more than a half-century ago, we see the ongoing need for and function of women's public expressions of sexual pleasure in a society in which they are *still* stigmatized simply for having female bodies and sexualities.

The *TJMS* End Approaches: Prognostications

As I was finally forced to stop transcribing the show in the autumn of 2018, after fourteen and a half years of active research, I cannot report on how the *TJMS* dealt with the ongoing U.S. and global political crises of 2018–19 before their planned end of broadcasting in the fall of 2019. I cannot yet know what will happen with the dysfunctional Trump White House, especially with a new Congressional Democratic majority, with Robert Mueller's Special Prosecutor investigation and charges, the responses of the two major political parties, and the multifaceted American and global Resistance to Trump and other rightist leaders. I don't know how much Trump&Co's pro-corporate, anti-environmental policies will have harmed working-class and impoverished Americans and further degraded air, water, and soil quality globally by the time *TJMS* broadcasts its final show in 2019—and how those shifts will influence the broader electorate. I cannot know if Trump's and others' bellicose saber-rattling will have tripped us into wider war.

But I do know that the *TJMS* and their audience will have risen to the occasion, and will have been engaged, passionate, activist, and bitingly witty. The adult black working-class community of the air, until the very last hour of the show, will continue to call out official lies, share information, rage, march, and demonstrate against inequity, vote their politics, subject the universe to witty shade, sing, and dance—and report on their own states of mind and body. How I will miss them. But I have to believe that another, or multiple other media venues, will arise to serve and maintain this bulwark progressive, class-conscious, black American counterpublic.

8

"Electronic Sheets" and a New Progressive Counterpublic

> We talk, we laugh, we talk to our people, and we go out in the
> community and do good things. That's what black radio has always
> done, and we are walking in the channel that Petey Green pioneered.
> —Don Cheadle, July 10, 2007, the *TJMS* on his role as the famous
> Washington, DC, DJ Petey Greene, in *Talk to Me*

> The mainstream media is there for the *main stream*. We're there for
> black folks.
> —Tom Joyner, November 29, 2007

Over the decades, as I documented the *TJMS* and its politics, I noticed its extraordinarily high, and quite deliberate, level of connections with print and television news media, both black and mainstream. In the early years, before the internet was well-established, I would repeatedly note that Sybil was articulating analyses I'd just read in the *New York Times* or heard the previous evening on MSNBC. Callers would reference Keith Olbermann's anti-Bush, anti-war, anti-racist "special comments": "I saw it on *Countdown!*" Over time, it became clear that Sybil was rapidly reviewing news websites *during* the show in order to keep listeners as up to date as possible on breaking stories.

But the more obvious set of connections across the *TJMS* and the wider news media world was its pattern of hiring regular political commentators with connections to big, reputable television and radio news organizations—especially PBS/NPR and then CNN. Tavis Smiley represented the former, Roland Martin and then Don Lemon the latter. The 2016 arrival of younger activist Shaun King, a columnist for *The New York Daily News*, broke that pattern while maintaining it. And then there were the frequent guest appearances by a variety of American urban radio networks, PBS, CNN, and MSNBC news analysts, especially April Ryan (now also on CNN), the late Gwen Ifill, Soledad O'Brien, Van Jones, Tamron Hall, Joy Reid, Chris Matthews, and Melissa Harris-Perry. The crew would quote HBO's Bill Maher and Comedy Central's Trevor Noah—and brought Noah on the show when he published his autobiographical *Born a Crime*.[1] Clearly, the *TJMS*, after its raucous early years, aimed for a certain level of hard news *gravitas* and comprehensiveness—both to serve and to expand its audience—and equally clearly achieved it.

As well, the show inadvertently served as a "farm team" for major news channels—hosting Al Sharpton until he was picked up by MSNBC, for example. This seems to be part of a larger recent phenomenon of smaller progressive outlets acting as incubators for individuals who then move into big-time, big-money television news anchor positions—for example, Rachel Maddow and Chris Hayes moving from Air America Radio and *The Chicago Reader/In These Times/The Nation*, respectively, to MSNBC.[2] The *TJMS* has even served as a farm team for comedy shows. As we have seen, Myra J has worked as a writer on a number of Tyler Perry television vehicles, and Tom Joyner proudly noted, on October 21, 2014, that *Saturday Night Live's* Leslie Jones had worked as a writer and actor for the early-years *TJMS* soap opera "It's Your World": "That's my girl, yeah!" And, alas, J Anthony Brown left the show at the end of 2016, reportedly over programming issues, and eventually joined Steve Harvey's rival morning radio show. He was originally replaced, on varying days, by three male comics—Lavell Crawford, Arsenio Hall, and Bill Bellamy—and later by Guy Torry, with the addition of Sherri Shepherd and Kym Whitley on Tuesdays and Thursdays, as we have seen.[3]

In fact, the *TJMS* always treated MSNBC as "family." (And MSNBC's own marketing numbers indicate that African Americans watch the channel in disproportionate numbers).[4] When Keith Olbermann was suspended from MSNBC in 2010 for having made a political contribution, they took it very personally, and spent time discussing it, certain that it was due to nefarious Fox News interference:

(November 8, 2010)
Tom: Sybil, Fox is so damned bad they can go over to MSNBC and get somebody **suspended***!*
Sybil: They're so mean!
Tom is incredulous, points out that Fox anchors openly contribute to and endorse candidates.
Sybil explains difference between television personalities and news reporters— different rules apply.
Tom mimics Fox calling MSNBC and telling them to fire Olbermann. MSNBC: "Uh-ok!"
Fox is gangsta, man! Real gangsta!
J: I guess if you got all the ratings, you can do what you want.

And when the crew went to Tallahassee to march against the Stand Your Ground law, on March 10, 2014, a puzzled texter wrote in:

Why isn't the march on the news?
Crew: It **is** *on the news! Watch MSNBC for continuous coverage, or TV One for cutaways.*

And the day after the disastrous 2016 presidential election, the crew, as they laid out their own agony and analyses, anatomized the MSNBC anchors' reactions the night before as the devastating news slowly rolled in, and expressed great sympathy in particular for Rachel Maddow:

> Tom: Did you see MSNBC in the end, and Rachel bowed her head, and said "Just skip me?"

As a long-time progressive news junkie, I thus was able to document the rise of a meaningful and under-recognized public-sphere phenomenon—a new cross-medium, distinctly anti-racist, feminist, progressive counterpublic in the United States. When I first began listening to the *TJMS* in the 1990s, *The Chicago Tribune* regularly published overtly racist "underclass" stories and editorials.[5] By 2008, the same newspaper, much shrunken by internet competition and corporate greed, and still clearly Republican-owned and stuffed with right-wing columnists, was nevertheless endorsing Barack Obama for president, and running investigative stories on police, politician, and corporate abuses in minority neighborhoods. (In 2016, the editorial board could not bring themselves to endorse either Clinton or Trump, and so backed third-party candidate Gary Johnson. He received 3.8% of the Illinois vote, Trump 39.4%, and Clinton 55.4%.)[6]

Similarly, *Huffington Post*, an anti-war scandal sheet in the early 2000s, has matured into a broadly feminist, pro-LBTGQ, anti-racist, social-democratic resource today, with special "black voices" and Spanish-language sections. (Although it's still a celebrity-heavy scandal sheet.) MSNBC was broadcasting the lone anti-war radical anchor Keith Olbermann at the point we invaded Iraq in 2003, but he brought on Rachel Maddow, then Chris Hayes was hired, then Al Sharpton and Lawrence O'Donnell, then Melissa Harris-Perry, Joy Reid, and (the late) Ed Schultz. And *they* brought on a range of black, Latinx, and Asian American as well as white expert guests—among them, *Washington Post* columnist Eugene Robinson, *Chicago Tribune* columnist Clarence Page, Roosevelt Institute political scientist and *Nation* editorial board member Dorian Warren, Illinois Senator Tammy Duckworth, California Democratic Congressman Ted Lieu and California Senator Kamala Harris, *The Nation's* executive editor Richard Kim, Illinois Democratic Congressman Luis Gutiérrez, Jorge Ramos—the most famous Spanish-language newscaster in the world—and Maria Teresa Kumar of *Voto Latino*.

In parallel progression, *The Washington Post, Salon.com, Slate.com, The Atlantic, The New York Times*, CNN, and *The Guardian* have all remade themselves, if still imperfectly, into anti-racist venues. *The Atlantic* showcased formidable new talent Ta-Nehisi Coates. *The New York Times* hired the insightful, quantifying political columnist Charles Blow, *The Guardian* (and *The Nation*) Gary Younge, *Slate.com* Jamelle Bouie, *The Washington Post* (and MSNBC) added Eugene Robinson and Jonathan Capehart, *The New Yorker* Jelani Cobb, and I discovered Rutgers University professor Brittney Cooper through her columns on *Salon.com*. Non-minority reporters and writers, as well, showed more interest in and knowledge of systemic racism, and online organizing venues like Color of Change (founded 2005), TheRoot.com (founded 2008), and Democracy in Color (founded 2016) came into being.

Of course, this is the same period in which what is now being labeled the alt-right matured online.[7] The *TJMS* and its audience were hyper-aware of this phenomenon, and called out social media white supremacists quite early on:

> *(July 12, 2010) A man from Florida calls to protest hate speech against Michelle Obama—an online site labeling her a "human tarball," and saying (completely misconstruing evolutionary theory) "Darwin wasn't so wrong."*
>
> J: *That's what the internet has done, it's made it possible to be as evil as you want to and nobody knows who you are!*
>
> Tom: *And they could be workin right next to you!*
>
> Sybil, classically mordantly witty: *Yes, this is the electronic sheets over their heads!*

We could say, then, that the American niche news mediascape has shifted and is continuing to shift in pure market-choice neoliberal fashion, responding to growing aggregate consumer demand, over Clinton's two terms, through the eight long George W. Bush years, through President Obama's two terms, and now into the chaos-scape of the Trump White House. The majority of Americans have clamored for more full-scale, accurate, progressive news coverage and commentary, and a determined minority for far-right, racist, sexist, and xenophobic outlets. And they have gotten them. (I won't here get into the issue of the relative efficacy of both grotesquely wealthy U.S. rightists deliberately influencing American political apprehensions, nor of Russian troll farms doing the same.)

Indeed, since the 2016 election, commentators have been surprised to note the soaring subscription numbers for newspapers investigating and articulating fact-laden resistance to the Trump Administration's lies—*The New York Times, The Washington Post, The Guardian*—and progressive MSNBC news shows' rapid rise to number-one viewership status among the key cable news channels.[8] And we have seen the ignominious disgrace and removal of Roger Ailes, Bill O'Reilly, and others, over long-standing sexual harassment and assault claims—part of the #MeToo movement's feminist renaissance—thus greatly weakening the Fox franchise.

We now have, for the first time, an extremely strong set of *progressive* television/ radio/online ties, with similar stories being picked up simultaneously across multiple media. With far larger and faster-growing audiences than nonprofit progressive outlets like *Democracy Now!*, this entirely commercial, advertising-dependent sector is synergistically connecting print, television, radio, and the online world. They act together as a progressive public-sphere echo chamber, ensuring that their audience takes in daily outrages, triumphs, and talking points. This phenomenon, finally, parallels the much earlier, and still successful, Rush Limbaugh/Rupert Murdoch/online alt-right phenomenon.

But the ongoing irony here is the one-way mirror effect of this synergy: the *TJMS* (and its website and some other minority radio shows and websites) influenced these shifts, even providing personnel (such as Al Sharpton) and key issues (very early coverage of the Trayvon Martin case). But unless you were a member of the *TJMS* audience, you would have had no way of knowing this. The *TJMS*'s adult black working-class stylization and its primary use of radio rather than the "sexy" media of television and the internet overdetermined its mainstream U.S. public-sphere invisibility. No matter how many political issues it covered first or best, no matter how many black news analysts it trained or gave a leg up into media's major leagues, no matter how coruscatingly funny its political humor, mainstream media and nonblack Americans continued to be largely unaware of the existence of this on-air organizer of a progressive black working-class counterpublic, just as the majority of black Americans remain publicly under-represented in the ongoing "saints or sinners" mainstream media syndrome.

And this inattention has had real-world consequences. We saw multiple *TJMS* crew and analysts warning the Democratic Party, moving toward the 2016 presidential election, that its failure to advertise in black media, its failure to mobilize its minority base as the Obama organization had done—twice—could have devastating consequences. And it did. While multiple analysts, post-election, called for "us" to engage with and listen carefully to white working-class Trump voters, others have noted that real financial and labor investment in get-out-the-vote efforts in minority communities could have led, despite the Republicans' best voter-suppression efforts, to a Clinton electoral college win. Steve Phillips of *Democracy in Color*, for example, asserted in *The New York Times* that the Democrats' strategic error in 2016 was "prioritizing the pursuit of wavering whites over investing in and inspiring African-American voters, who made up 24% of Barack Obama's winning coalition in 2012. . . . In Wisconsin and Pennsylvania, the tens of thousands of African-Americans who voted in 2012 but didn't vote in 2016 far exceeded the miniscule losing margins for Hillary Clinton."[9]

And a group of political scientists in 2018 looked carefully at the data on what they labeled the 2012/2016 "Obama-to-Trump" versus "Obama to nonvoter" phenomena. They determined, again, that those who had voted for Obama but then voted for Trump "are most out of line with the Democratic coalition"—and therefore not worth the expenditure of a great deal of time and money—while the 2016 nonvoters "are quite close to the emerging Democratic consensus." In other words, Democrats should put their money into shoring up their minority and youth base, and making sure they are allowed and encouraged to vote.[10] Economist William Spriggs, as well, has written about the Democrats' long-term fatal romance with the notion of the "noble white worker who has been betrayed," and argues strongly that we instead should be "spending time helping Americans take the blinders off and see that workers, of all races, are being given the shaft by a system where corporate greed has become an elite 'entitlement.'"[11]

But an exhaustive and prestigious 2018 National Academy of Sciences study of Trump voters concluded that "pocketbook issues" had been, in any event, relatively unimportant to them. Rather, the most important factor in determining a vote for Trump was "racial and global status threat"—perceptions that white dominance was ending in the United States, and that other countries—specifically China— were threatening American global dominance. In fact, study author Diana Mutz concluded that "[p]rejudicial attitudes toward domestic minorities predict trade attitudes more strongly than the vulnerability of a person's occupation or industry of employment."[12] The *TJMS* listener who furiously exclaimed after the 2004 presidential election that "they don't care that Bush hurt them as long as he don't help us!" summed up the racist mindset that, because of the structure of the Electoral College and Russian social media dirty tricks, triumphed in 2016.

But despite the Trump-inspired financial shot in the arm for factual news media, the black radio business, and music radio in general, continued to struggle. The one-way mirror phenomenon is also clearly a factor. Right after President Obama's first inauguration, MSNBC put on a town hall in an HBCU, Texas Southern University, with Chris Matthews of MSNBC co-chairing it with Tom Joyner.[13] The crew the next morning was very hopeful about "further dialogue." But there was little mainstream coverage of the town hall, and the *TJMS* remained largely invisible in the U.S. public sphere. Similarly, the precious exclusive interview that President Obama gave the *TJMS* the day after his first, and disappointing, debate with Mitt Romney was, as we have seen, picked up everywhere, and credited to the *TJMS*. But there was no follow-up, no new mainstream media interest in the show.

I had noticed in 2017, doing my regular checks on the number of black radio stations syndicating the *TJMS*, that the stable ca. 100 number had shrunk alarmingly to ca. 80. And then the hammer fell: on October 17, 2017, Tom Joyner announced on air that he would end the show in two years. In his simultaneous blogpost on Blackamerica.web.com, "I'm putting in my two-year notice," Joyner kept the message positive, vowing that he would continue his HBCU scholarship program, and asking listeners to send in favorite show or event moments so that the crew could pull them from the vault and replay them during the years left. His blogpost garnered hundreds of responses, most of them blessing Joyner and documenting the show's benefits to their lives, from teaching them black history to "keeping us alive when we were in Ghana."

But on air and in later interviews, Tom was much more candid about the decision. He lamented: "I can see the handwriting on the wall with the radio business!" Indeed, broadcast music radio, like so many other institutions whose business model has been disrupted by internet competition, is in big trouble. Its audience overall is aging, "as Gen Z music fans . . . are embracing digital formats at the expense of radio use," using new streaming formats instead of listening to radio, as Larry Miller of New York University noted in a key 2017 report. New automobile streaming technology is eating into broadcast radio's previous position as the "bastion of AM/FM radio"—crucially important because "[t]he car is currently the number one location for listening to radio." Radio advertising revenue is stagnant, especially since 2016, the tipping point, with "streaming overtaking sales" of music in that year. Radio is now "less of a tastemaker" for new music. The large monopolistic radio chains Cumulus and iHeartMedia [formerly Clear Channel] have declared bankruptcy.[14]

Clearly, Tom Joyner had been carefully gauging the shifting radio business, and the fact that he "couldn't get a guaranteed contract" with Reach Media to maintain the show longer than two years more made the decision for him. Coverage of the retirement announcement also stressed growing competition from Steve Harvey and other black but unprogressive morning radio hosts.[15] But given the recent generational shift in music consumption because of the rise of streaming services and their deadly effect on radio shows, we can see that it never really mattered how hard the *TJMS* competed, how many different ways they tried to draw in new, younger listeners as they lost their older audience over time. They were never going to gain them. No music radio programs would.

The *TJMS* crew immediately, but of course hilariously, made their new financial anxieties clear, as well as engaging in encomia:

> *(October 17, 2017) Sybil makes jokes about doubling up her car and mortgage payments . . . the following day she suggested that she would be doing supermarket openings.*
>
> *Huggy Lowdown comes on singing a lyric from Boyz to Men, "It's so hard to say goodbye to yesterday." He then riffs on the prospect of joblessness: "Syb, I owe you a couple of dollars [on a baseball bet]. I might be able to pay you sometime in the next two years! . . . Speakin of payin, I'm takin a whole lotta stuff back today, Sybil! [he enumerates consumer goods going back to the store] Speakin of payin, Mom, you gotta wait on that hip replacement!"*
>
> *He then moves on to praise Joyner's generosity: "Who but you, brutha [would give a full two years notice]. You've been in my life more than my **real** Dad! If it wasn't for you, my passport wouldn't have stamps on it! I saw the Parthenon! I learned so much from you, brutha. First time I ever been on a private jet, it was because of Tom! I felt like a rapper! Then I had to fly commercial on my own. Oh, I had so many 'turn into a pumpkin' moments with Tom!*
>
> *Two years, man! I got to hit the lottery, add new shows, marry a **Kardashian**!"*

Then the deeply disturbed but always witty audience had their say, specifying their shock and despair, their long-term fidelity, and the show's effects on their lives:

> *Thank you for our two-year notice. I need two years to prepare!*
> *2017 just keeps getting worse and worse!*
> *When you [Tom] took that personal day, I knew sumthin was up!*
> *No more wobble!?!? [crew laughs wildly]*

I'm retiring when you do, Tom! Thirty-five years of federal government service!

*First the Obamas, now **you**!?*

*Please say it aint so, Tom! Radio will **never** be the same.*

Sybil, whatchu gon do?

Tom, I've been listenin to you since I was a freshman at Tennessee State!

Tom, I have five kids, and at least three sang the jingle to the show as their first words!

Tom, thanks not only for black radio, but for bein black ON the radio!

Miss you already, my Labor Day weekends won't be the same!

I remember when you told us where the police were hidin beside the chicken signs [when he was on-air in Dallas in his Fly Jock era].

I've been on eleven cruises, five family reunions, and every Sky Show in the DC area!

Tom you're leavin us is like losin a good woman! If she's not there, there's no reason to go home!

How will we be informed about our community and our country?

How can I be the smartest person in a family gathering if I can't listen to the TJMS?

Al Sharpton's (see Figure 8.1) reaction was the most interesting of all: he performed full-time denial, and threatened, literally *forbade* Tom from killing the show, dropping into "Southern black preacher enunciation" to underline his intensity:

Figure 8.1 Activist and broadcaster Al Sharpton. Photo courtesy of David Shankbone.

*(October18, 2018) You can't drop the mic and **ruin** the country! You **hear** me, Joyner?*

*I remembuh in the heat of Jena 6 when we couldn't get people to care about these kids, when you got on the radio and brought the crowds . . . I remembuh James Brown comin during a show, I remembuh the laughing and all, behind the scenes. You got up so early no matter what . . . But I'm not gonna **have** to remembuh—cause I know you aint goin **nowhere**! Why am I participating in this levity?*

An audience member immediately texted in: "I'm with Reverend Al! Hashtag #Don'tDroptheMic!"

The following day, the texters were even more intense:

*Tom, you can't retire til **2020**! Trump needs to be voted out of office and you need to **help** us!*

*Tom, you are selfish! How can you retire from **talkin**!*

Please say it aint so, Tom! I know I'm only one of the millions in the TJMS family!

And the next morning, October 20, 2017, Tyler Perry came on the show and tied it all up in his inimitable fashion:

Perry is on the line, loudly, theatrically crying. "I heard you were retirin, man, what'm I gonna do?" He then transforms into the character Madea: "Well actually, baby, it's Madea that's upset. Cause I hear when you retire, they cut your child support check in half!"

We might see this era of social media/streaming dominance as a technological world-historical shift, a shift that has now made it impossible for black and other minority media entities to survive. But analysis of the role of the press during the Civil Rights Movement of the 1950s and 1960s, in the study *The Race Beat*, indicates that activists then also had to be strategic and nimble in using the new and growing phenomenon of television news, in cultivating particular white print journalists, and in demanding access for minority newspeople. During Martin Luther King Jr.'s 1968 funeral, in Atlanta's Ebenezer Baptist Church, for example, Coretta Scott King noticed that all the news photographers in the church were white, and demanded that Moneta Sleet, Jr., representing *Ebony*, be allowed in, or she would banish all of them. As a result, his funeral photo won a Pulitzer Prize—the first ever won by a black photographer.[16]

And as David Karpf reminds us, in commenting on Tom Hayden's posthumous accounting of the arduous dozen-plus years of the U.S. anti-Vietnam war movement's struggle, "[a]daptation and flexibility are not new challenges for social movements."[17]

Sumanth Gopinath's analysis of the racialized ringtone industry and its music reminds us that, following literary scholar Alexander Weheliye's argument, black Americans' "digital divide" is both partial and class-based. Clearly most African Americans, and working-class and poor Americans in general, do not have the easy access to computers and computing education that middle-class and above Americans do. But black Americans were a very early and massive cellphone (and ringtone) market, not to mention their intense use of earlier technologies like boomboxes, sound systems, beepers, etc.[18] And the power and breadth of Black Twitter has been repeatedly noted. We are, after all, talking here about evolving neoliberal global capitalism, its constant Shumpeterian creative destruction of types and functions of particular technologies, and their shifting prices and thus relative availability to different class fractions of American and global consumers.

Usually when we discuss this historical and contemporary phenomenon, our focus is on the sufferings of the poor workers drawn into and then spat out of these constantly transforming and relocating industries, both at home and abroad. But production is twinned with consumption, and in this case consumption and doing politics are fused. That is, progressive black radio consumers are literally losing their outlet because the political economy of the American music industry has shifted dramatically over the past decade. Streaming is killing music radio, and it killed the *TJMS*.

It is unclear what will fill the void left when the *TJMS* does finally close up shop in 2019. But I have faith that strategic and nimble contemporary activists of color and their allies will figure out how to make best use of the shifting U.S. mediascape and its evolving technologies. As black radio historian William Barlow wrote back in 1999:

> From digital technology to demographic fragmentation, new developments
> are constantly reconfiguring the playing field for African Americans in-
> volved in the radio industry. . . . Against great odds, they have made radio
> a centerpiece of African American life. This resilience in the face of ad-
> versity offers some hope that black radio will remain an independent and
> progressive voice in the local community, the industry, and the society as
> a whole.[19]

The ongoing Black Lives Matter movement, Color of Change, Ultraviolet, #MeToo, #TimesUp, the more than 6000 local chapters of the Resistance grassroots group Indivisible, Daily Kos, Pantsuit Nation—all with inclusive progressive politics—have had various partial successes, most particularly the November 2018 midterm elections which once again brought the Democrats to power in Congress. And the sincere and thus far successful efforts of the Margery Stoneham Douglas High School shooting survivors to include all students, across class and color divides, in their anti-NRA gun control movement, are also hopeful signs.

The black counterpublic in the digital age, then, is extraordinarily multifarious. It has intermingled with the mainstream public sphere and the progressive counterpublic. But its middle-aged, working-class component will have to join other entities, and/or organize new ones for itself. More than ever, we need to attend to the lives and apprehensions of *all* Americans, and genuinely integrate our understandings of the varying specific experiences and political perspectives of Americans of color. As actor Don Cheadle described black radio's history: "We go out into the community and do good things." We all need to be doing that. And as Tom Joyner exclaimed repeatedly over the years, "We're here for black folks!" We should all be here for black folks, and for all people of color, at home and abroad. Not only is it simply the right thing to do. Our very future depends on it.

Notes

Chapter 1

1. Soyica Diggs Colbert, *Black Movements: Performance and Cultural Politics.* New Brunswick, NJ: Rutgers University Press, 2017, p. 9.
2. Zora Neale Hurston, "What White Publishers Won't Print," *Negro Digest,* 1950.
3. In her 1985, "Who's Zooming Who." See https://www.youtube.com/watch?v=f2NXv9RL1i8, accessed September 1, 2017.
4. Stephanie Anderson-Forest, "Tom Joyner: P&G's Favorite Deejay," *BusinessWeek Online,* July 12, 2004.
5. Although both the *TJMS* stream and app were beset by bugs and often "cut out." But I find that this is the case as well for a number of major music apps, like Pandora and Spotify.
6. See Stacie Williams, "Radio One Acquires Company of Nation's Top Black Radio Host," *Chicago Defender,* vol. 159, no. 142, November 23, 2004, p. 4; and no author, "Tom Joyner's Company Assumes Ownership of the *Tom Joyner Morning Show,*" *Jet,* vol. 105, no. 4, January 26, 2004, p. 64.
7. See, for example, Vern Smith, "'Fly Jock' Rides High," *Newsweek,* February 23, 1998, p. 5; Jack E. White, "Racism in Advertising? Two Radio Stars Score a Victory for black-run media," *Time,* November 1, 1999, p. 90; Katy Bachman, "When Tom Joyner Speaks, People Listen," *Mediaweek,* vol. 12, no. 26, July 1, 2002, pp. 18–22.
8. See "IMDB Biography—Tom Joyner," https://www.imdb.com/name/nm0431667/bio, accessed March 1, 2018.
9. Woodson is actually a retired rodeo cowboy with a Texas ranch, and "the man of a thousand voices"—he was also the voice of the long-defunct "Mrs. Leonard" to whom Sybil would play straight woman. See Cross Timbers Gazette Staff, "Meet the Radio Ranger," *Cross Timbers Gazette,* May 7, 2011, http://www.crosstimbersgazette.com/2011/05/07/the-radio-ranger/, accessed March 5, 2018.
10. All transcriptions are the author's, done contemporaneously with broadcasts. I monitored ten to fifteen hours of the show's twenty hours of weekly programming, more during key events/crises. Ellipses indicate gaps in transcription. At the beginning of my research, it was "transcribe or die," as there was no alternative access to show material. Later, I was able to re-play some limited archived material on blackamericaweb.com—but never the spontaneous badinage among the crew and between the crew and audience that constitutes the bulk of my research material—and also to re-listen to the day's show directly after its end, using the *TJMS* app once they adopted it in 2014. But they disbanded the replay feature in May 2016. Thus, apologies for any errors in transcription. It was simply not possible to record every

broadcast over fourteen years. I also periodically checked the "where to listen" map on the *TJMS* website to gauge listenership over time.

11. See Langston Hughes and Roy DeCarava, *The Sweet Flypaper of Life*. New York: Hill and Wang, 1955.

12. See Lucas Shaw, "'The Daily Show' Host Trevor Noah Lands New Deal After Ratings Success," *Bloomberg News*, September 14, 2017, https://www.bloomberg.com/news/articles/2017-09-14/-daily-show-host-noah-lands-new-deal-as-trump-bits-lift-ratings, accessed June 1, 2018.

13. Robert M. Entman and Andrew Rojecki, *The Black Image in the White Mind: Media and Race in America*. Chicago: University of Chicago Press, p. 207.

14. Posted on youtube: https://www.youtube.com/watch?v=PN2A50nRTY4, accessed July 1, 2017.

15. See Dolores Inés Casillas, "Sounds of Surveillance: U.S. Spanish-Language Radio Patrols La Migra." *American Quarterly*, vol. 63, no. 3, 2011, pp. 807–29, esp. p. 810.

16. See Ian Haney-Lopez, *Dog Whistle Politics: How Coded Racial Appeals Have Reinvented Racism and Wrecked the Middle Class*. New York: Oxford University Press, 2014.

17. For just one of the multitudinous accountings of the disastrous effects of NAFTA on rural Mexicans in particular, see Jeff Faux, "How NAFTA Failed Mexico," *The American Prospect*, June 16, 2003, http://prospect.org/article/how-nafta-failed-mexico.

18. On *Selma*, see A. O. Scott, "A 50-Mile March, Nearly 50 Years Later, *New York Times*, December 24, 2014, https://www.nytimes.com/2014/12/25/arts/in-selma-king-is-just-one-of-the-heroes.html, accessed May 1, 2015. What the texter actually played probably depends on her age. There are in fact *two* distinct black "Fight the Power" hits: the old-school 1975 Isley Brothers' song, and the now more well-known 1989 Public Enemy rap. See https://www.youtube.com/watch?v=wO2ebiuV3hU, and https://www.youtube.com/watch?v=8PaoLy7PHwk, respectively, accessed March 1, 2018.

19. See David Cooper, Mary Gable, and Algernon Austin, "The Public Sector Jobs Crisis: Women and African Americans Hit Hardest by Job Losses," Economic Policy Institute, Briefing Paper #339, May 2, 2012. http://www.epi.org/publication/bp339-public-sector-jobs-crisis/, accessed August 4, 2016.

20. See *The Chicago Reader* investigative reporter Ben Joravsky's many dozens of columns on Chicago mayors' siphoning of tax funds from public schools and other social goods to high-end development, through tax-increment financing (TIFs), www.chicagoreader.com/chicago/ArticleArchives?author=847359, accessed August 1, 2016.

21. See Carl Boggs, "Marxism, Prefigurative Communism, and the Problem of Workers' Control," *Radical America*, vol. 8, no. 6, November 11, 1977, pp. 99–122; Alice Echols, *Daring to Be Bad: Radical Feminism in America, 1967-75*. Minneapolis: University of Minnesota Press, 1989, p. 16. See also Wini Breines, *Community and Organization in the New Left: 1962-68*. New York: Praeger, 1982.

22. In the early 1980s, I myself belonged to national left-feminist organization, the New American Movement, that was explicitly anti-racist, and had split from a much larger group—the Democratic Socialists of America—in defense of a gay rights plank.

23. Nancy Fraser, "Rethinking the Public Sphere: A Critique of Actually Existing Democracy." In *Habermas and the Public Sphere*. Craig Calhoun, ed. Cambridge, MA: MIT Press, 1992, pp. 109–42; Michael Warner, *Publics and Counterpublics*. New York: Zone Books, 2002, pp. 118–19.

24. Benedict Anderson, *Imagined Communities: Reflections on the Origin and Spread of Nationalism*. London: Verso, 1982.

25. Nikolas Coupland, "Dialect Stylization in Radio Talk," *Language in Society*, vol. 30, 2001, pp. 345–75.

26. See Jennifer Lynn Stoever, *The Sonic Color Line: Race & The Cultural Politics of Listening*. New York: New York University Press, 2016.

27. For the 2008 song performance: https://www.youtube.com/watch?v=1xIQmFk1ok0.

28. For celebratory commentary, see, for example, Mark Anthony Neal, *What the Music Said: Black Popular Music and Black Political Culture*. New York: Routledge, 1999; Murray Forman and Mark Anthony Neal, eds., *That's the Joint: The Hip-Hop Studies Reader*. New York: Routledge, 2004. Certainly there was also, early on, both feminist hip-hop and feminist critique of misogyny in rap. See, for example, Tricia Rose, *Black Noise: Rap Music and Black Culture in Contemporary America*. Hanover, NH: University Press of New England, 1994. An example of the newer *rapprochement* between hip-hop/rap and progressive politics is Kendrick Lamar's 2015 "Alright," which has become a Black Lives Matter anthem. See https://www.youtube.com/watch?v=Z-48u_uWMHY, accessed June 1, 2017. And see also Aisha S. Durham, *Home with Hip Hop Feminism: Performances in Communication and Culture*. New York: Peter Lang, 2014, for blistering critiques of misogyny in male black popular culture, and insightful readings of the complexities of the public personae and work of major popular-cultural black female figures like Beyoncé and Queen Latifah. See also Charise Cheney's thoroughgoing analysis of the misogyny of hip-hop nation, and the roads out: Charise L. Cheney, *Brothers Gonna Work It Out: Sexual Politics in the Golden Age of Rap Nationalism*. New York: New York University Press, 2005.

For the role of music in the Civil Rights Movement, see Julie Buckner Armstrong et al., eds., *Teaching the American Civil Rights Movement: Freedom's Bittersweet Song*. New York: Routledge, 2002; Kerran L. Sanger, *"When the Spirit Says Sing!": The Role of Freedom Songs in the Civil Rights Movement*. New York: Garland, 1995; and Shana L. Redmond, *Anthem: Social Movements and the Sound of Solidarity in the African Diaspora*. New York: New York University Press, 2014.

29. See Bakari Kitwana, *Why White Kids Love Hip-Hop: Wankstas, Wiggers, Wannabes, and the New Reality of Race in America*. New York: Basic Books, 2005.

30. See, for example, Theodore Hamm, *The New Blue Media: How Michael Moore, MoveOn.org, Jon Stewart and Company Are Transforming Progressive Politics*. New York: New Press, 2008.

31. On Spanish-language U.S. radio, see for example Dan Baum, *"Arriba!* A Latino Radio Scold Gets Out the Vote," *New Yorker*, October 23, 2006; Teresa Watanabe and Hector Becerra, "The Immigration Debate: How DJs Put 500,000 Marchers in Motion," *Los Angeles Times*, March 28, 2006; and three Dolores Inés Casillas pieces: "'Puuuurrrooo MEXICO!': Listening to Transnationalism on U.S. Spanish-Language Radio." In *Beyond El Barrio: Everyday Life in Latino/a America*. Gina M. Pérez, Frank A. Gurrdy, and Adrian Burgos, Jr., eds. New York: New York University Press, 2010, pp. 44–62; "Adios El Cucuy: Immigration and Laughter Over the Airwaves." *Boom: A Journal of California*, vol. 1, no. 3, 2011, pp. 44–56; "Sounds of Surveillance: U.S. Spanish-Language Radio Patrols La Migra." *American Quarterly*, vol. 63, no. 3, 2011, pp. 807–29.

32. See "Black Radio Today 2011: How America Listens to Radio" and "Hispanic Radio Today: How America Listens to Radio," Arbitron. Nielsen recently acquired Arbitron, and no longer provides the same ethnically granular level of data.

33. See Sumanth Gopinath, *The Ringtone Dialectic: Economy and Cultural Form*. Cambridge, MA: MIT Press, 2013, pp. 241–67.

34. William Blake, "Auguries of Innocence." In *William Blake: A Selection of Poems and Letters*. Edited with an introduction by J. Bronowski. London: Penguin Books, 1965, p. 67–71.

35. See Micaela di Leonardo, *The Varieties of Ethnic Experience: Kinship, Class and Gender among Italian-Americans in Northern California*. Ithaca, NY: Cornell University Press, 1984; "White Ethnicities, Identity Politics, and Baby Bear's Chair," *Social Text* no. 41, 1994; "White Lies, Black Myths: Rape, Race, and the Myth of the Underclass," *The Village Voice*, September 22, 1992; *Exotics at Home: Anthropologies, Others, American Modernity*. Chicago: University of Chicago Press, 1998; "Gender, Race, and Class Politics: Home in New Haven." In *Companion to an Anthropology of Politics*. Joan Vincent and David Nugent, eds. New York: Blackwell, 2005.

36. The literature on these phenomena is extensive. See, minimally: William Barlow, *Voice Over: The Making of Black Radio*. Philadelphia: Temple University Press, 1999; Gilbert A. Williams, *Legendary Pioneers of Black Radio*. Westport, CT: Praeger, 1998; Melissa Harris-Lacewell, *Barbershops, Bibles, and BET: Everyday Talk and Black Political Thought*. Princeton, NJ: Princeton University Press, 2004; Mel Watkins, *On the Real Side: Laughing, Lying, and Signifying—the Underground Tradition of African American Humor that Transformed American Culture, from Slavery to Richard Pryor*. New York: Simon and Schuster, 1994.

37. The Black Great Migration from the South to the North tended to follow regional paths, and thus Chicago's African American population arrived overwhelmingly from the Mississippi Delta area. See Isabel Wilkerson, *The Warmth of Other Suns: The Epic Story of America's Black Migration*. New York: Vintage Books, 2011; and James Grossman, *Land of Hope: Chicago, Black Southerners, and the Great Migration*. Chicago: University of Chicago Press, 1989.

38. On Lamar's 2018 Pulitzer, see Joe Coscarelli, "Kendrick Lamar Wins Pulitzer in 'Big Moment' for Hip Hop," *New York Times*, April 16, 2018, https://www.nytimes.com/2018/04/16/arts/music/kendrick-lamar-pulitzer-prize-damn.html, accessed April 20, 2018.

39. The list includes documentaries such as *When We Were Kings* (1996), and films like Will Smith's portrayal in *Ali* (2001) as well as the HBO account of the Supreme Court ruling on Ali's conscientious objector status, *Muhammad Ali's Greatest Fight* (2013).

40. P. David Marshall, "Introduction." In *The Celebrity Culture Reader*. P. David Marshall, ed. New York: Routledge, 2006, 1–15, esp. pp. 2, 3, 7.

41. Karen Sternheimer, *Celebrity Culture and the American Dream: Stardom and Social Mobility*. New York: Routledge, 2011, esp. p. 236.

42. See David Harvey, *A Brief History of Neoliberalism*. New York: Oxford University Press, 2005; and Micaela di Leonardo, "Introduction: New Global and American Landscapes of Inequality." In *New Landscapes of Inequality: Neoliberalism and the Erosion of American Democracy*. Jane Collins, Micaela di Leonardo, and Brett Williams, eds. Santa Fe, NM: School of Advanced Research Press, pp. 3–19.

43. See Micaela di Leonardo, "The Neoliberalization of Minds, Space and Bodies: Rising Global Inequality and the Shifting American Public Sphere." In *New Landscapes of Inequality: Neoliberalism and the Erosion of American Democracy*. Jane Collins, Micaela di Leonardo, and Brett Williams, eds. Santa Fe, NM: School of Advanced Research Press, pp. 191–208.

44. Among a wealth of sources for these analytic points are Maude Barlow, "Donald Trump Is No Friend of a Better NAFTA," *American Prospect*, Winter 2018, pp. 10–12; Robert Kuttner, "White Nationalism and Economic Nationalism," *American Prospect*, Fall 2017, pp. 30–33; Robin Hahnel, "The Left, the Right, and Globalization," *New Politics*, vol. 16, no. 3, pp. 102–9.

45. See, for example, "The State of Working America: African Americans," Economic Policy Institute, no date, http://www.stateofworkingamerica.org/fact-sheets/african-americans/, accessed June 1, 2018.

46. A shout out to jazz musician Robert Glasper and his creative 2012 album "Black Radio," https://www.allmusic.com/album/black-radio-mw0002266610, accessed June 1, 2018.

47. See Kelly Askew and Richard Wilk, eds., *The Anthropology of Media: A Reader*. Malden, MA: Blackwell, 2002; Faye Ginsburg, Lila Abu-Lughod, and Brian Larkin, eds., *Media Worlds: Anthropology on New Terrain*. Berkeley: University of California Press, 2002; Eric W. Rothenbuhler and Mihai Coman, eds., *Media Anthropology*. Thousand Oaks, CA: Sage, 2005.

48. One exception: Marla Frederick, *Colored Television: American Religion Gone Global*. Stanford, CA: Stanford University Press, 2016. Fredericks, an anthropologist, pays careful attention to audience reception.

49. I gave interviewees the choice of their own pseudonyms. Some chose to use their actual given names.

50. See my "#MeToo is nowhere near enough," *HAU*, vol. 8, no. 3, December 2018; and my "White Lies, Black Myths: Rape, Race, and the Myth of the Underclass," *The Village Voice*, September 22, 1992. Reprinted in Roger Lancaster and Micaela di Leonardo, eds., *The Gender/Sexuality Reader*. New York: Routledge, 1997, pp. 52–68.

51. See Adolph L. Reed, Jr., *W.E.B. Du Bois and American Political Thought*. New York: Oxford University Press, pp. 4ff, for a discussion of racial vindicationism.

52. "Radio texture" is Jo Tacchi's term. See her "Radio Texture: Between Self and Others." In *The Anthropology of Media: A Reader.* Kelly Askew and Richard Wilk, eds. Malden, MA: Blackwell, 2002, pp. 241–57.

53. A note on transcription and language: I am well aware of the dangers of engaging in minstrelsy in accurately representing various forms of working-class/regional black American speech. But I have chosen to represent them because the very nature of the show involves extensively *play* with and *signifying* across the broad varieties of African American speech, and the crew are not above teasing audience members over regional accents and grammatical and other errors. Only through accurate transcription could I give the reader access to that play, that signification. I also accurately transcribe *white* speakers' accents and pronunciations here, and have done so since my first ethnographic publications in the 1980s.

Chapter 2

1. Herb Kent and David Smallwood, *The Cool Gent: The Nine Lives of Radio Legend Herb Kent*. Chicago: Lawrence Hill Books, 2009, p. 11.

2. W. E. B. Du Bois, *Dusk of Dawn: An Essay towards an Autobiography of a Race Concept*. New York: Harcourt, Brace and Co., 1940, p. 148.

3. See https://www.youtube.com/watch?v=JClnWuutF5I; https://www.youtube.com/watch?v=b4gQ6xwISRs, accessed August 16, 2016.

4. Susan Douglas, *Listening In: Radio and the American Imagination*. Minneapolis: University of Minnesota Press, 2004 [1999], p. 5.

5. In her 1979 "On the Radio." See https://www.youtube.com/watch?v=PYm0tAvmG9k, accessed September 1, 2017.

6. See https://www.youtube.com/watch?v=fw9j2EN4TU4, accessed September 8, 2016.

7. See John Storm Roberts, *The Latin Tinge: The Impact of Latin American Music on the United States*. New York: Oxford University Press, 1979; and https://www.youtube.com/watch?v=xn50JSI0W-E; https://www.youtube.com/watch?v=MSDyiUBrUSk, accessed September 8, 2016.

8. See Ken Emerson, *Always Magic in the Air: The Bomp and Brilliance of the Brill Building Era*. New York: Viking, 2005.

9. See https://www.youtube.com/watch?v=425GpjTSlS4, accessed September 1, 2017.

10. See https://www.youtube.com/watch?v=H1z45jVlM34 for Fats Domino's performance.

11. See https://www.youtube.com/watch?v=AbBr2bgAbcM, accessed August 4, 2016. See also music journalist David Hajdu, *Love for Sale: Pop Music in America*. New York: Farrar, Straus and Giroux, 2016, pp. 3–12, for a lyrical autobiographical description of the profound role of a different technology—diner jukeboxes—in his own musical coming of age.

12. Quoted in Douglas, *Listening In*, p. 227. See "The Bleatniks," *Time*, August 11, 1961, p. 48. For "Tossin and Turnin," see https://www.youtube.com/watch?v=ghFBvB accessed September 8, 2016.

13. See http://www.beatlesbible.com/1964/08/19/live-cow-palace-san-francisco/, accessed August 5, 2014.

14. For one of many treatments of this phenomenon, see James Maycock, "White Men Sing the Blues," *Independent*, June 3, 1999. http://www.independent.co.uk/arts-entertainment/music-white-men-sing-the-blues-1097966.html, accessed June 2, 2016. Craig Werner also notes also that many black musicians were directly hired by flush white bands, as the Beatles

hired Billy Preston. See also his treatment of British Invasion groups' varying relations with blues and soul musicians. Craig Werner, *A Change Is Gonna Come: Music, Race, and the Soul of America*. Revised. Ann Arbor: University of Michigan Press, 2006, p. 43, pp. 81ff.

15. See http://www.latimes.com/local/obituaries/la-me-b-b-king-20150515-story.html, accessed August 16, 2016.

16. For Malvina Reynolds' performance of "Little Boxes," see https://www.youtube.com/watch?v=2_2lGkEU4Xs; for Dylan's performance of "Blowing in the Wind, see https://www.youtube.com/watch?v=3l4nVByCL44; for Peter, Paul & Mary's cover, see https://www.youtube.com/watch?v=Ld6fAO4idaI ; for the Byrds' version of "Turn! Turn! Turn!," see https://www.youtube.com/watch?v=W4ga_M5Zdn4, accessed August 5, 2014.

17. See http://www.singout.org/sohistry.html, accessed August 5, 2014, for the history of *Sing Out!*

18. See Allen Ginsberg, *Howl and Other Poems*. San Francisco: City Lights Books, 1965 [1956]; John Cohen and Mike Seeger, *New Lost City Ramblers Song Book*. New York: Oak Publications, 1964; and http://history1900s.about.com/od/1950s/qt/peacesymbol.html, accessed August 2, 2014, and http://www.cnduk.org/information/info-sheets/item/437-the-history-of-cnd, accessed August 2, 2014, for histories of the peace symbol and the CND. I also discovered, researching this book, that the Bay Area anti-war left was so small in those years that there were close ties between the KPFA founders and Roy Kepler, founder of Kepler's Books. See Matthew Lasar, *Pacifica Radio: The Rise of an Alternative Network*. Philadelphia: Temple University Press, 1999, p. 99.

19. On *Sing Out!*'s, history, see their website, http://www.singout.org/sohistry.html, accessed August 25, 2014. See *Blues Classics by Memphis Minnie* and *Memphis Minnie, Volume 2*, Blues Classics 1 & 13, 1964 and 1967. Berkeley: Blues Classics Records. Liner notes by Chris Strachwitz. On Memphis Minnie's life and music, see also http://memphismusichalloffame.com/inductee/memphisminnie/, accessed August 5, 2014.

20. Memphis Minnie's "Chauffeur Blues" can be heard at https://www.youtube.com/watch?v=KiRoNuw5x4M; John Hurt's "Candy Man" at https://www.youtube.com/watch?v=bMG_6xa0qRA, both accessed August 2, 2014.

21. See the classic study, Eric Lott, *Love and Theft: Blackface Minstrelsy and the American Working Class*. New York: Oxford University Press, 1993.

22. For Dylan's performance of "Masters of War," see https://www.youtube.com/watch?v=exm7FN-t3PY; "Blowing in the Wind," https://www.youtube.com/watch?v=3l4nVByCL44; "Times They Are A-Changin'," https://www.youtube.com/watch?v=e7qQ6_RV4VQ; "With God on Our Side," https://www.youtube.com/watch?v=cAgAvnvXF9U; "Hard Rain's Gonna Fall," https://www.youtube.com/watch?v=T5al0HmR4to; "Lonesome Death of Hattie Carroll," see https://www.youtube.com/watch?v=1jiYVUU1RXQ; "Only a Pawn in Their Game," https://www.youtube.com/watch?v=pbL2PpBwQmY. For Baez's performance of "Birmingham Sunday," see https://www.youtube.com/watch?v=WQ0y-vO9QLE, all accessed August 5, 2014.

23. Martin Luther King, Jr., *Why We Can't Wait*. New York: Harper and Row, 1964.

24. See Matthew Lasar, *Pacifica Radio: The Rise of an Alternative Network*. Philadelphia: Temple University Press, 1999.

25. See Lasar, *Pacifica*, pp. 99ff. Also see http://thankyouoneandall.co.uk/letters/grateful_dead.htm, accessed August 5, 2014.

26. Douglas, *Listening In*, p. 258.

27. Hajdu, *Love for Sale*, p. 163.

28. See Douglas, *Listening In*, pp. 256–83.

29. See https://www.youtube.com/watch?v=3W7-ngmO_p8, accessed August 16, 2016.

30. See Douglas, *Listening In*, pp. 278–83, esp. p 280.

31. Douglas, *Listening In*, p. 280.

32. Douglas, *Listening In*, pp. 284–70; Robert W. McChesney, *The Problem of the Media: Communication Politics in the 21st Century*. New York: Monthly Review Press, p. 197.

33. A Berkeley Greek-American who married black, Otis had an extraordinarily long career, spanning swing jazz, hard bop, blues, and R&B. See his memoir, *Upside Your Head: Rhythm and Blues on Central Avenue*. Hanover, CT: Wesleyan University Press, 1993.

34. See Werner, *A Change Is Gonna Come*, p. 168.

35. See https://www.youtube.com/watch?v=rc0XEw4m-3w, accessed August 2, 2014.

36. See http://bayarearadio.org/schneider/kdia.shtml, http://bayarearadio.org/audio/kdia/, accessed September 2, 2014; Episode 9, "Civil Rights," in *Black Radio*, National Public Radio/The Smithsonian Institution, 1995; and Louis Cantor, *Wheelin' on Beale: How WDIA-Memphis Became the Nation's First All-Black Radio Station and Created the Sound That Changed America*. New York: Pharos Books, 1992. In addition, Craig Werner notes that WDIA DJs estimated that half of their audience was white, especially for the evening shows. See Werner, *A Change Is Gonna Come*, p. 76.

37. B. B. King, taped interview, aired on WDUQ, Pittsburgh, February 15, 1998, quoted in Kathy M. Newman, "The Forgotten Fifteen Million: Black Radio, Radicalism, and the Construction of the 'Negro Market.'" In *Communities of the Air: Radio Century, Radio Culture*. Susan Merrill Squier, ed. Durham, NC: Duke University Press, 2003, pp. 109–33, esp. p. 119.

38. Steven Walsh, "Black-Oriented Radio and the Civil Rights Movement." In *Media, Culture, and the African American Freedom Struggle*. Brian Ward, ed. Gainesville: University of Florida Press, 2001, pp. 67–81.

39. See, for example, William Barlow, *Voice Over: The Making of Black Radio*. Philadelphia: Temple University Press, 1999; Gilbert A. Williams, *Legendary Pioneers of Black Radio*. Westport, CT: Praeger, 1998; Mark Newman, *Entrepreneurs of Profit and Pride: From Black-Appeal to Radio Soul*. Westport, CT: Praeger, 1988; Jannette Dates and William Barlow, eds., *Split Image: African Americans in the Mass Media*. Washington, DC: Howard University Press, 1993; Kathy M. Newman, "The Forgotten 15 Million: Black Radio, Radicalism, and the Construction of the 'Negro Market.'" In *The Race and Media Reader*. Gilbert B. Rodman ed. New York: Routledge, 2014, pp. 94–107; Catherine Squires, "Black Talk Radio: Community Needs and Identity," *Harvard International Journal of Press/Politics*, vol.5, no. 22, 2000, pp. 73–95; Sonja D. Williams, *Word Warrior: Richard Durham, Radio, and Freedom*. Urbana: University of Illinois Press, 2015; Cantor, *Wheelin' on Beale*. Steven Walsh, in "Black-Oriented Radio," pp. 68ff., points out that the notion of "white captivity"—the frequent white ownership of black stations—may have soured black commentators' vision of black radio's contribution to the freedom struggle, thus dampening historical research on black radio politics.

40. See Peter Guaralnick, *Sweet Soul Music: Rhythm and Blues and the Southern Dream of Freedom*. New York: Harper and Row, 1986; Rob Bowman, *Soulsville, USA: The Story of Stax Records*. New York: Shirmer Books, 1997; Robert Gordon, *Respect Yourself: Stax Records and the Soul Explosion*. New York: Bloomsbury, 2013.

41. John A. Jackson, *A House on Fire: The Rise and Fall of Philadelphia Soul*. Oxford, UK: Oxford University Press, 2004, p. ix. See also Tony Cummings, *The Sound of Philadelphia*. London: Methuen, 1975.

42. See https://www.youtube.com/watch?v=9-LuNJXFGTU; http://www.azlyrics.com/lyrics/ojays/shipahoy.html, accessed August 10, 2016.

43. Alex Haley, *Roots*. Garden City: Doubleday, 1976; *Roots*, directed by Marvin J. Chomsky, ABC Studios, 1977.

44. See http://rockhall.com/inductees/sly-and-the-family-stone/bio/, accessed August 5, 2014. See also Greil Marcus's treatment of Sly Stone in his early example of rock journalism meets American studies, *Mystery Train: Images of America in Rock 'n' Roll Music*. New York: E.P. Dutton, 1975, pp. 75–111.

45. See https://www.allmusic.com/artist/sly-the-family-stone-mn0000033161/biography, accessed August 5, 2014.

46. For "Everyday People," see https://www.youtube.com/watch?v=3JvkaUvB-ec; Craig Werner, *A Change Is Gonna Come: Music, Race and the Soul of America*. Revised. Ann Arbor: University of Michigan Press, 2006, pp. 104–5..

47. See https://www.allmusic.com/style/blue-eyed-soul-ma0000012036, accessed September 5, 2014.

48. See https://www.youtube.com/watch?v=t9BRqGpppJw; https://www.youtube.com/watch?v=QbzkwLWK-Ps; for a live version, see https://www.youtube.com/watch?v=1rb5F8y5Mhw; all accessed July 1, 2017.

49. See *The Original Kings of Comedy*, directed by Spike Lee, MTV Productions, 2000; and the official trailer, https://www.youtube.com/watch?v=7g7MDO011go, accessed July 1, 2017.

50. Just to underline the depth of my post-1970s white rock-musical ignorance: In 2018, I narrated this old story to two female graduate students, one Chinese, one Turkish. Unlike me, they both immediately caught the reference to Kurt Cobain.

51. See the film *Muscle Shoals*, directed by Greg Camalier, Magnolia Pictures, 2013. Also see C. S. Fuqua, *Music Fell on Alabama: The Muscle Shoals Sound that Shook the World*. Montgomery, AL: NewSouth Books, 2005. Peter Guralnick, *Sweet Soul Music: Rhythm and Blues and the Dream of Freedom*. New York: Harper and Row, 1986, p. 198.

52. Werner, *A Change Is Gonna Come*, p.72.

53. Werner, *Change Is Gonna Come*, p. 86.

54. Gayle Wald, "Soul's Revival: White Soul, Nostalgia and the Culturally Constructed Past." In *Soul: Black Power, Politics and Pleasure*. Monique Guillory and Richard C. Green, eds. New York: New York University Press, 1998, p. 151.

55. Werner, *Change Is Gonna Come*, p. 22.

56. See Mark Ribowsky, *Dreams to Remember: Otis Redding, Stax Records, and the Transformation of Southern Soul*. New York: Liveright Publications, 2015, p. 85; Guralnick, *Sweet Soul Music*, pp. 11, 263–64; Charles L. Hughes, *Country Soul: Making Music and Making Race in the American South*. Chapel Hill: University of North Carolina Press, p. 28.

57. Hughes, *Country Soul*, p. 126.

58. *Standing in the Shadows of Motown*, directed by Paul Justman, Artisan Home Entertainment, 2002. The original book on the topic is Dr. Licks and James Jamerson, *Standing in the Shadows of Motown: The Life and Music of Legendary Bassist James Jamerson*. Milwaukee, WI: Hal Leonard Corporation, 1989.

59. See http://twentyfeetfromstardom.com, accessed August 5, 2014.

60. See Craig Werner on black American audience appreciation of the Righteous Brothers. Werner, *Change Is Gonna Come*, p. 84.

61. See http://www.v103.com/onair/herb-kent-3680/, accessed August 20, 2014, for a summary of Herb Kent's career. See https://www.youtube.com/watch?v=I-hKBmTAADo, accessed August 20, 2014.

62. See http://www.bostonglobe.com/ideas/2013/06/01/how-boston-powered-gay-rights-movement/wEsPZOdHhByHpjeXrJ6GbN/story.html, for an accounting of *Gay Community News*, a professionally run, well-researched and well-written paper, which was also one of the earliest periodicals to cover the HIV/AIDs crisis.

63. In deep debt, UDC sold the station, despite widespread protests, in 1997. See Barlow, *Voice Over*, p. 290.

64. See https://www.youtube.com/watch?v=qGaoXAwl9kw; and Mike Power, "Gil Scott-Heron Obituary," *The Guardian*, May 29, 2011, https://www.theguardian.com/music/2011/may/28/gil-scott-heron-obituary, accessed July 1, 2017. On Nina Simone, see http://www.ninasimone.com, accessed November 27, 2018.

65. See Barlow, *Voice Over*, pp. 236–41, esp. p. 239.

66. See https://www.youtube.com/watch?v=iCZ22D2SRD0, accessed July 1, 2017.

67. See Barlow, *Voice Over*, pp. 271–78.

68. Cathy Hughes in episode 7, "The Woman's Touch," *Black Radio* series, National Public Radio/The Smithsonian Institution, 1995, including a larger discussion of the growth of Quiet Storm programming.

69. Barlow, *Voice Over,* pp. 274–75, esp. p. 275. See also *Black Radio* series, National Public Radio/The Smithsonian Institution, 1995. For Luther's "Never Too Much," see https://www.youtube.com/watch?v=pNj9bXKGOiI, accessed September 9, 2014.

70. See Craig Werner's discussion of Wonder's contribution in *Change Is Gonna Come,* pp. 187ff.

71. On WPFW's history and current functioning, see Barlow, *Voice Over,* pp. 290–91; http://pacificanetwork.org/?p=700; http://forums.allaboutjazz.com/showthread.php?3284-WPFW-in-Washington-in-Trouble; and http://www.washingtoncitypaper.com/articles/43566/the-airing-of-grievances-can-wpfw-modernize-while-remaining-dcs/, all accessed September 2, 2014.

72. On Carter's campaign's and domestic policies, see Martin Schram, *Running for President 1976: The Carter Campaign.* New York: Stein and Day, 1977; Lawrence H. Shoup, *The Carter Presidency and Beyond: Power and Politics in the 1980s.* Palo Alto, CA: Ramparts Press, 1980; Judith Stein, *Pivotal Decade: How the United States Traded Factories for Finance in the Seventies.* New Haven, CT: Yale University Press, 2010, chaps. 7–10. For Carter and the Hyde amendment, see Rosalind Petchesky, *Abortion and Women's Choice.* Revised ed. Boston: Northeastern University Press, 1990, p. 287.

73. On Carter foreign policy, see Gaddis Smith, *Morality, Reason, and Power: American Diplomacy in the Carter Years.* New York: Hill and Wang, 1986; and Haynes Johnson, *Sleepwalking Through History: America in the Reagan Years.* New York: Anchor Books, 1991, chaps. 1 and 2. On the hostage crisis and Reagan's election, see Gary Sick, *October Surprise: America's Hostages in Iran and the Election of Ronald Reagan.* New York: Times Books, 1991. On Carter and South Africa, see William Minter, "Destructive Engagement: United States and South Africa in the Reagan era." In *Destructive Engagement: Southern Africa at War.* Phyllis Johnson and David Martin, eds. Harare: Zimbabwe Publishing House, 1986, pp. 281–320.

74. See Maria Odum, "The 'Bama: Talking and Living Blues on Radio," *New York Times,* April 5, 1992; Jonathan Rowe, "Welcome to Wobegon . . . Er, 'Bama," *Christian Science Monitor,* July 13, 1987; and "Jerry Washington, disk Jockey, 64," unsigned *New York Times* obituary, October 6, 1994, for profiles of Washington's life and the Bama Hour; and Matthew Lasar, *Uneasy Listening: Pacifica Radio's Civil War.* Black Apollo Press, 2006, pp. 132–33.

75. See Bart Barnes, "Disc Jockey Jerry 'The Bama' Washington Dies," *The Washington Post,* October 5, 1994; Odum, "The 'Bama' "; Rowe, "Welcome to Wobegon."

76. Rowe, "Welcome to Wobegon."

77. See Peter Guaralnick's account of O. V. Wright's and Z. Z. Hill's careers in his *Sweet Soul Music,* pp. 280–86 and p. 295, respectively.

78. See https://www.youtube.com/watch?v=6SP5JHLqXM8, accessed August 23, 2016.

79. For her performance, see https://www.youtube.com/watch?v=emkqc3PIw8E, accessed November 7, 2018.

80. See Andre Gunder Frank, "A Third-World War: A Political Economy of the Persian Gulf War and the New World Order." In *Triumph of the Image: The Media's War in the Persian Gulf—A Global Perspective.* Hamid Mowlana, George Gerbner, and Herbert Schiller, eds. Boulder, CO: Westview Press, 1992, 3–21.

81. For WPKN, see https://www.wpkn.org, accessed August 12, 2014.

82. See http://radiobilingue.org/en/, accessed November 5, 2018.

83. See Williams, *Legendary Pioneers,* p. 133.

84. See Claudia Puig, "Tom Joyner: The Work Ethic Works," *Los Angeles Times,* April 21, 1994, http://articles.latimes.com/1994-04-21/entertainment/ca-48749_1_tom-joyner-morning-show, accessed March 15, 2018.

85. Tom Joyner, *Clearing the Air: The Making of a Radio Personality.* Self-published, 1995, p. 45. To my knowledge, even of the only half-dozen scholars who have written about the *TJMS,* only one, besides myself, seems to have read Joyner's book—but that scholar seems both unaware of Joyner's early neoconservatism, and also unaware of the show's overall pro-gay

and pro-single mother stances. See Terance Leonardo Wooten, "Towards a New Black Nation: Space, Place, Citizenship, and Imagination." MA Thesis, Ohio State University, 2011.

86. *Clearing the Air*, p. 68.
87. *Clearing the Air*, pp. 145, 147.
88. *Clearing the Air*, pp. 150, 156.
89. See Williams, *Legendary Pioneers*, p. 139. See Richard Rothstein, "The Making of Ferguson," *The American Prospect*, October 14, 2014. http://prospect.org/article/making-ferguson-how-decades-hostile-policy-created-powder-keg, accessed August 10, 2016.
90. See Melissa Harris-Lacewell, *Barbershops, Bibles, and BET: Everyday Talk and Black Political Thought*. Princeton, NJ: Princeton University Press, 2004, p. 243.
91. See Todd Steven Burroughs, *Drums in the Global Village: Toward an Ideological History of Black Media*. Ph.D. Diss., University of Maryland, College Park, 2001, pp. 213–15.
92. See *Drums in the Global Village*, p. 213; and Adolph L. Reed, Jr., *The Jesse Jackson Phenomenon: The Crisis of Purpose in Afro-American Politics*. New Haven, CT: Yale University Press, 1986.
93. Shonda McClain, "Listeners Have Mixed Views of New WDAS Morning Show," *The Philadelphia Tribune*, vol. 113, no. 78, October 26, 1996.
94. Esther Iverem, "Nice guy. great show. Uh-oh. Joyner Is a National Hit. Local Radio Says That Hurts," *Washington Post*, May 14, 1996, https://www.washingtonpost.com/archive/lifestyle/1996/05/14/nice-guy-great-show-uh-oh-joyner-is-a-national-hit-local-radio-says-that-hurts/f877919c-44f4-441c-a676-6963cf43b5e0/?utm_term=.989c41b50a92, accessed March 5, 2018.
95. See *Drums in the Global Village*, p. 207.
96. Dwight E. Brooks and George L. Daniels, "The Tom Joyner Morning Show: Activist Radio in an Age of Consolidation," *Journal of Radio Studies*, vol. 9, no. 1, 2001, pp. 8–32, esp. pp. 20–22.
97. *Listening In*, p. 230.
98. Dates and Barlow, *Split Image*, p. 215.
99. See also Douglas, *Listening In*, pp. 248–51.
100. Dates and Barlow, *Split Image*, p. 223; see also Douglas, *Listening In*, pp. 250–53.
101. Although V103, where the *TJMS* was syndicated from its 1994 founding until Clear Channel threw them off the air a few months after President Obama was first elected in 2008, was and is owned by a classic white conservative corporation (now merged with iHeartMedia, Inc.).
102. Douglas, *Listening In*, pp. 234ff.; Barlow, *Voice Over*, p. 228; "Black Radio," NPR/Smithsonian series, 1995, episode 6, "Sounding Black," episode one, "In the Beginning."
103. Kent, *The Cool Gent*, p. 45.
104. See Robert W. McChesney, *The Problem of the Media: Communication Politics in the 21st Century*. New York: Monthly Review Press, 2004; Edward Herman and Noam Chomsky, *Manufacturing Consent: The Political Economy of Mass Media*. New York: Pantheon, 1988.
105. William Greider, "All the King's Media," *The Nation*, November 2, 2005. http://www.thenation.com/doc/20051121/greider, accessed May 3, 2006.
106. See Douglas, *Listening In*, p. 299, McChesney, *The Problem of the Media*, pp. 98–132.
107. See Micaela di Leonardo, *Exotics at Home: Anthropologies, Others, American Modernity*. Chicago: University of Chicago Press, 1989, pp. 271–72.
108. Douglas, *Listening In;*, *Voice Over*; McChesney, *The Problem of the Media*.
109. Douglas, *Listening In*, pp. 90, 103.
110. Douglas, *Listening In*, pp. 270–80.
111. C. Riley Snorton, "New Beginnings: Racing Histories, Democracy, and Media Reform," *International Journal of Communication*, vol. 2, 2008, pp. 23–41.
112. Mark Anthony Neal, *What the Music Said: Black Popular Music and Black Popular Culture*. New York: Routledge, 1999, pp. 125–29, esp. p. 126.

113. See di Leonardo, *Exotics at Home*, pp. 112–34; and "Black Myths, White Lies: Rape, Race, and the Myth of the 'Underclass.'" In *The Gender/Sexuality Reader: Culture, History, Political Economy*. Roger J. Lancaster and Micaela di Leonardo, eds. New York: Routledge, 1997, pp. 53–68.

114. *What the Music Said*, pp. 128–29.

115. *What the Music Said*, p. 127.

116. *What the Music Said*, p. 128.

117. For lyrics, see http://www.metrolyrics.com/music-lyrics-leela-james.html; official video: https://www.youtube.com/watch?v=3qQqkzq3Xo8, accessed August 2, 2104.

118. Barlow, *Voice Over*, p. 260.

119. Mark Anthony Neal, *Songs in the Key of Black Life: A Rhythm and Blues Nation*. New York: Routledge, 2003, pp. 159, 156.

120. I have done repeated searches to document this extraordinary lack (or merely *en passant* mention) of media and scholarly attention to the *TJMS* powerhouse. See Micaela di Leonardo, "Neoliberalism, Nostalgia, Race Politics, and the American Public Sphere: A Case Study of the Tom Joyner Morning Show," *Cultural Studies*, vol. 22, no. 1, 2008, pp. 1–34, esp. pp. 4 and 31, n 7. Aside from the very early *Washington Post* and *Los Angeles Times* articles, the only substantive major newspaper piece is Felicia R. Lee, "Building a Conversation, One Radio Show at a Time," *New York Times*, February 13, 2007. See Dwight E. Brooks and George L. Daniels, "The Tom Joyner Morning Show: Activist Radio in an Age of Consolidation," *Journal of Radio Studies*, vol. 9, no. 1, 2001, pp. 8–32; Neal, *Songs in the Key of Black Life*, p. 140; Harris-Lacewell, *Barbershops*, pp. 237–49, esp. p. 237. There is also a short positive article on the show from the defunct magazine *Emerge*: Sandra Gregg, "Tom Joyner." In *The Best of Emerge Magazine*. George Curry, ed. New York: Ballantine, 2003 [1998], pp. 114–20. See also the short treatment of *TJMS* in Catherine Squires, *African Americans and the Media*. New York: Polity, 2009, pp. 194–96.

121. Harris-Lacewell, *Barbershops*, p. 241.

122. See Dean Robinson, *Black Nationalism in American Politics and Thought*. Cambridge: Cambridge University Press, 2001.

Chapter 3

1. Fred Moten, "The Case of Blackness," *Criticism*, vol. 50, no. 2, Spring 2008, pp. 177–218, esp. p. 177.

2. Dorothy Roberts, *Killing the Black Body: Race, Reproduction, and the Meaning of Liberty*. New York: Vintage Books, 1997, p. 21.

3. See http://v103.iheart.com/features/remembering-herb-kent-2608/; http://www.chicagotribune .com/news/local/breaking/ct-herb-kent-obit-20161023-story.html, both accessed October 25, 2016.

4. See Herb Kent's page on WVAZ's website, http://www.v103.com/onair/herb-kent-3680/, accessed October 14, 2014.

5. Muhammed moved to 106.3 soon thereafter. He died July 16, 2015, and I learned more about him as V103 DJs eulogized him. He was a grandson of Elijah Muhammed, the founder of the Black Muslims. See http://www.radiofacts.com/chicago-radio-dj-wali-muhammad-dies/, accessed July 24, 2015.

6. July 31, 2004 broadcast, my notes. I'm not sure how Kent picked up this fact in 2004, but see Brent Staples' 2014 *New York Times* column, http://www.nytimes.com/2014/05/31/opinion/x-men-not-all-fiction.html, accessed October 6, 2014.

7. The conversation happened on November 14, 1996.

8. Stephen Steinberg, *Turning Back: The Retreat from Racial Justice in American Thought and Policy*. Boston: Beacon Press, pp. 107–36.

9. Micaela di Leonardo, *Exotics at Home: Anthropologies, Others, American Modernity.* Chicago: University of Chicago Press, 1998, pp. 112–27.

10. di Leonardo, *Exotics*, pp. 269–71.

11. See the full Dan Quayle "Murphy Brown" speech, Michael A. Cohen, "Live From the Campaign Trail," http://livefromthetrail.com/about-the-book/speeches/chapter-18/vice-president-dan-quayle, accessed July 31, 2015.

12. See Judith Stacey, *In the Name of the Family: Rethinking Family Values in the Postmodern Age.* Boston: Beacon Press, 1996, pp. 98–102.

13. For PROWRA details and consequences, see Jane Collins with Victoria Mayer, *Both Hands Tied: Welfare Reform and the Race to the Bottom of the Labor Market.* Chicago: University of Chicago Press, 2010.

14. Judith Stacey, "The Neo-Family Values Campaign." In *The Gender/Sexuality Reader.* Roger Lancaster and Micaela di Leonardo, eds. New York: Routledge, pp. 453–70.

15. Stacey, "Neo-Family," p. 458.

16. See Katherine Q. Seelye, "Moral Values Cited as a Defining Issue of the Election," *New York Times,* November 4, 2004.

17. Allan J. Lichtman, *White Protestant Nation: The Rise of the American Conservative Movement.* New York: Atlantic Monthly Press, 2008, pp. 2,3.

18. Lichtman, *White Protestant Nation*, p. 322.

19. See Micaela di Leonardo, "Habits of the Cumbered Heart: Ethnic Communities and Women's Culture as American Invented Traditions." In *Golden Ages, Dark Ages: Imagining the Past in Anthropology and History.* Jay O'Brien and William Roseberry, eds. Berkeley: University of California Press, pp. 234–52.

20. Susan Faludi, *Backlash: The Undeclared War Against American Women.* New York: Crown, 1991, p. 14.

21. Lichtman, *White Protestant Nation*, p. 320.

22. Lichtman, *White Protestant Nation*, p. 6.

23. Dorothy Roberts, *Killing the Black Body: Race, Reproduction, and the Meaning of Liberty.* New York: Vintage, 1997, p. 10

24. Stephanie Coontz, *The Way We Never Were: American Families and the Nostalgia Trap.* New York: Basic Books, 1992, p. 235.

25. See John Demos, *A Little Commonwealth: Family and Life in Plymouth Colony.* New York: Oxford University Press, pp. 120ff.; Steven Mintz and Susan Kellogg, *Domestic Revolutions: A Social History of American Life.* New York: Free Press, 1988, pp. 1–23, esp. p. 15.

26. Sara M. Evans, *Born for Liberty: A History of Women in America.* New York: Free Press, 1989, 147ff.; Virginia Yans-McLaughlin, "Patterns of Work and Family Organization: Buffalo's Italians." In *The American Family in Social-Historical Perspective.* Michael Gordon, ed. New York: St. Martin's Press, pp. 136–51, esp. p. 142. Mintz and Kellogg, *Domestic Revolutions*, p. 84; Evans, *Born for Liberty*, pp. 130ff.

27. See Herbert Gutman, *The Black Family in Slavery and Freedom, 1720-1925.* New York: Vintage Books, 1976; Jacqueline Jones, *Labor of Love, Labor of Sorrow: Black Women, Work, and Family from Slavery to the Present.* New York: Vintage, 1985, pp. 46ff.; Mintz and Kellogg, *Domestic Revolutions*, pp. 77ff.

28. Coontz, *The Way We Never Were*, p. 5.

29. Jane Collins and Victoria Mayer, *Both Hands Tied: Welfare Reform and the Race to the Bottom of the Low-Wage Labor Market.* Chicago: University of Chicago Press, 2010, p. 21.

30. See Jones, *Labor of Love*, p. 305.

31. See Collins and Mayer, *Both Hands*, pp. 26–54 for a detailed historical account of these political-economic shifts in Milwaukee-Racine.

32. Indeed, Tom Joyner declared on-air on May 4, 2018, that 70% of his audience was comprised of black women.

33. See Dolores Inés Casillas, "Sounds of Surveillance: US Spanish-Language Radio Patrols La Migra," *American Quarterly,* vol. 53, no. 3, September 2011, https://muse.jhu.edu/article/450017/pdf, accessed July 30, 2015.

34. See Lisa Lee, "Myra J Live. Love. Laugh," *Diesel Magazine,* 2014, http://www.diezelmagazine. com/myra-j-live-love-laugh/, accessed July 30, 2015.

35. I actually missed this original performance, so do not know the date. The *TJMS* replayed it on February 16, 2018, as an example of "how Sybil jams folks up!"

36. See https://www.youtube.com/watch?v=8tj-FuuzBZk, accessed July 1, 2017.

37. Over the course of the *TJMS*'s history, the Reverend Al Sharpton's reputation in the wider public sphere has risen significantly. He was treated for years as a mere race-huckster buffoon but has now gained a measure of reportorial respect. See Greg Howard, "Al Sharpton, Reconsidered," *New York Times,* March 11, 2018, "New York" section, p. 24.

38. See Manu Raj, Edward Isaac-Rovere, and John Bresnahan, "How the Democrats Lost the Senate," *Politico,* November 5, 2014, http://www.politico.com/story/2014/11/democrats-lose-2014-midterms-112581, accessed July 1, 2017.

39. The girl who stole the watch was 17, but the other girl involved may have been as young as 12. See David Streitfeld, "R. Kelly Is Acquitted in Child Pornography Case," *New York Times,* June 14, 2008, http://www.nytimes.com/2008/06/14/arts/music/14kell.html, accessed August 17, 2015.

40. See https://www.youtube.com/watch?v=nRuH-6L5RrA, accessed July 1, 2017.

41. Adam Liptak, "Supreme Court Rejects Contraceptives Mandate for Some Corporations, *New York Times,* June 30, 2014, https://www.nytimes.com/2014/07/01/us/hobby-lobby-case-supreme-court-contraception.html?_r=0, accessed July 1, 2017.

42. On Dr. Drai, see https://drdrai.com/about-dr-drai, accessed April 20, 2018.

43. See Amy Chozick and Patrick Healey, "Anthony Weiner and Human Abedin to Separate after His Latest Sexting Scandal," *New York Times,* August 29, 2016, https://www.nytimes.com/2016/08/30/nyregion/anthony-weiner-sexting-huma-abedin.html, accessed March 15, 2018, for an accounting of the congressman's multiple sexting scandals.

44. See https://www.youtube.com/watch?v=z-0VH-0D6NY for Durant's speech; and "A Song for Mama," https://www.youtube.com/watch?v=NFRW4_46dJg, both accessed July 1, 2017.

45. Actually, Swoopes is bisexual. At the time of this show, she had announced she was gay after having been married to a man and had a child. Later she and her woman partner broke up, and she and a long-time male friend married. See https://www.biography.com/people/sheryl-swoopes-9542142, accessed March 5, 2018.

46. https://www.youtube.com/watch?v=CDhdv2wQL0E, accessed July 1, 2017.

47. https://www.youtube.com/watch?v=y6Sxv-sUYtM; J's murdered hit is on YouTube: https://www.youtube.com/watch?v=JI3PYoe67Ws, both accessed July 1, 2017.

48. For "Street Life," see https://www.youtube.com/watch?v=-iVR7WLsvAg, accessed July 1, 2017; Blackamericaweb posted the entire song: https://blackamericaweb.com/2014/09/19/j-anthony-browns-murdered-hit-league-life-listen/, accessed July 1, 2017.

49. "Recitative" is a musical term describing singers "speaking" rather than singing particular lines. That is what J does here.

50. See https://www.youtube.com/watch?v=7lp7FtJXp7k, accessed July 1, 2017; Brown's entire song is posted on YouTube: https://www.youtube.com/watch?v=llU3DiFr8Ww, accessed July 1, 2017.

51. Evelyn Brooks Higginbotham, *Righteous Discontent: The Women's Movement in the Black Baptist Church, 1880-1920.* Cambridge, MA: Harvard University Press, 1993, esp. pp. 14–15.

52. Higginbotham, *Righteous Discontent,* p. 186.

53. *Righteous Discontent,* p. 187.

54. *Righteous Discontent,* p. 199.

55. *Righteous Discontent,* p. 202.

56. See the special issue on the politics of respectability in *Souls: A Critical Journal of Black Politics, Culture, and Society,* vol. 18, nos. 2-4, 2016; and Brittney Cooper's recent intellectual genealogy of black women theorists' dissent from respectability politics, *Beyond Respectability: The Intellectual Thought of Race Women.* Champaign-Urbana: University of Illinois Press, 2017.

57. Although an internet search indicates that some commentators have associated the show, both positively and negatively, with respectability politics. See, for example, Maya K. Francis, "Former NBC Reporter Don Lemon a Hypocrite on Stop and Frisk," *Philadelphia News & Opinion*, November 6, 2013, http://www.phillymag.com/news/2013/11/06/don-lemon-hypocrite-stop-and-frisk/, accessed September 17, 2016; Kevin Cokley, "We Let Bill Cosby into Our Homes, So He Owes Us an Explanation," *American Prospect*, November 20, 2104, http://prospect.org/article/we-let-bill-cosby-our-homes-so-he-owes-us-explanation, accessed September 17, 2016.

Chapter 4

1. See http://www.urbandictionary.com/define.php?term=GROWN%20AND%20SEXY, signed by L. Martin, December 5, 2005. Accessed September 30, 2016.
2. See https://www.youtube.com/watch?v=osI2MUBLoeU, accessed September 1, 2017.
3. Fredrick C. Harris, "The Rise of Respectability Politics," *Dissent*, Winter 2014, pp. 1–8, esp. p. 2.
4. See my accounting of the histories of culture of poverty and underclass ideology in *Exotics at Home: Anthropologies, Others, American Modernity*. Chicago: University of Chicago Press, 1998, pp. 112–27.
5. Michael J. Katz, *In the Shadow of the Poorhouse: A Social History of Welfare in America*. New York: Basic Books, 1986.
6. Quoted in Michael Eric Dyson, *Is Bill Cosby Right? Or Has the Black Middle Class Lost Its Mind?* New York: Basic Civitas Books, 2005, pp. xi–xii.
7. E. Frances White, *Dark Continent of Our Bodies: Black Feminism and the Politics of Respectability*. Philadelphia: Temple University Press, 2001.
8. Darlene Clark Hine, "Rape and the Inner Lives of Black Women in the Middle West: Preliminary Thoughts on the Culture of Dissemblance." In *The Gender/Sexuality Reader*. Roger Lancaster and Micaela di Leonardo, eds. New York: Routledge, 1997, pp. 434–39.
9. Evelynn M. Hammonds, "Toward a Genealogy of Black Female Sexuality: The Problematic of Silence." In *Feminist Theory and the Body*. Janet Price and Margrit Shildrick, eds. Edinburgh: Edinburgh University Press, 1999, pp. 93–104.
10. See also Miriam Petty's insightful analysis of Tyler Perry's use of Atlanta staging and the politics of class in her "'Old Folks at Home:' Tyler Perry and the Dialectics of Nostalgia," *Quarterly Review of Film and Video*, May 19, 2017, pp. 1–19.
11. Robert J. Patterson, "'Do You Want to Be Well?' The Gospel Play, Womanist Theology, and Tyler Perry's Artistic Project." In *Womanist and Black Feminist Responses to Tyler Perry's Productions*. LaRhonda S. Manigault-Bryant, Tamura A. Lomax, and Carol B. Duncan, eds. New York: Palgrave Macmillan, 2014, pp. 217–33, esp. p. 224.
12. Brittney Cooper, "Talking Back and Taking My 'Amens' with Me: Tyler Perry and the Narrative Colonization of Black Women's Stories." In *Womanist and Black Feminist Responses to Tyler Perry's Productions*. LaRhonda S. Manigault-Bryant, Tamura A. Lomax, and Carol B. Duncan, eds. New York: Palgrave Macmillan, 2014, pp. 237–49, esp. p. 237.
13. Brittney Cooper, "Talking Back," p. 237.
14. Brittney Cooper, "Talking Back," p. 248. See also her historical accounting of black women activists' anti-respectability politics activism: Brittney C. Cooper, *Beyond Respectability: The Intellectual Thought of Race Women*. Champaign-Urbana: University of Illinois Press, 2017.
15. Adolph Reed, Jr, "Romancing Jim Crow," originally appeared in *The Village Voice*, April 6, 1996. It was reprinted in his *Class Notes: Posing as Politics and Other Thoughts on the American Scene*. New York: New Press, 2000, pp. 14–24.
16. *Romancing Jim Crow*, pp. 14, 15.
17. *Romancing Jim Crow*, pp. 19–20.

18. Harris, "Rise," pp. 1–2.

19. See, for example, Signithia Fordham, *Blacked Out: Dilemmas of Race, Identity, and Success at Capital High*. Chicago: University of Chicago Press, 1996.

20. This black-music meme, "Throw your hands in the air like you just don't care!" has been in broad use since at least the hip-hop 1980s. It shows up in lyrics by The Sugar Hill Gang, Grandmaster Flash and the Furious Five, The Pharcyde, and Outkast, among many others.

21. "Wobble Baby" by VIC, came out in 2012. Official video https://www.youtube.com/watch?v=qd6UI6wEIsU, accessed September 25, 2015.

22. The Dougie took off in 2008. See https://www.wsj.com/video/oculus-go-vr-made-easy-and-cheap/079F519D-BB1A-460B-B516-0FA66ABA161E.html, accessed September 25, 2015.

23. For "Hooks," see https://www.youtube.com/watch?v=3Cau-MFQFo8, accessed July 1, 2017.

24. See Elizabeth Hartman, "Hearing Sex: An Ethnographic and Ethnomusicological Study of Striptease in the Midwestern U.S." Ph.D. Diss., Northwestern University, 2016.

25. See Delta Sigma Theta website, http://www.deltasigmatheta.org.

26. For J's performance, see https://www.youtube.com/watch?v=IRPM72nb4Cc, accessed March 5, 2018.

27. See Bethany McLean, "Why Sheryl Sandberg, Bill Bradley, and Oprah Love Mellody Hobson," *Vanity* Fair, March 30, 2015, https://www.vanityfair.com/news/2015/03/mellody-hobson-ariel-investments-fighting-stereotype, accessed July 1, 2017.

28. See Reuben Fischer-Baum, Kim Soffen, and Heather Long, "Republicans Say It's a Tax Cut for the Middle Class. The Biggest Winners Are the Rich," *Washington Post*, January 30, 2018, https://www.washingtonpost.com/graphics/2017/business/what-republican-tax-plans-could-mean-for-you/?utm_term=.5a48797cad29, accessed May 1, 2018.

29. Which only become common on the *TJMS* in 2017, but goes back to at least 2004. See http://www.urbandictionary.com/define.php?term=ride%20or%20die, accessed July 1, 2017.

30. George Lipsitz, *The Possessive Investment in Whiteness: How White People Profit from Identity Politics*. Philadelphia: Temple University Press, 2006.

31. Actually, up until the treaty of Guadalupe Hidalgo in 1848, at the end of the Mexican-American war.

32. See, for example, Melanie McAlister, *Epic Encounters: Culture, Media, and U.S. Interests in the Middle East Since 1945*. Berkeley: University of California Press, 2001, pp. 84–124, and pp. 198 ff. in Carolyn Moxley Rouse, John L. Jackson, Jr., and Marla F. Frederick, *Televised Redemption: Black Religious Media and Racial Empowerment*. New York: New York University Press, 2016.

33. See "Attacks in Paris," *New York Times*, https://www.nytimes.com/news-event/attacks-in-paris, accessed July 1, 2017, accessed March 15, 2018.

34. For a crisp, accurate narrative of that backdrop, See Mahmood Mamdani, *Good Muslim, Bad Muslim: American, the Cold War, and the Roots of Terror*. New York: Pantheon, 2004.

35. See Richard Pollack, "The Cost of Doing Business on the Open Sea," *The Nation*, May 11, 2009, https://www.thenation.com/article/cost-doing-business-open-sea/, accessed April 27, 2018, for an indictment of wealthy shipping companies deliberately endangering their crews through failure to pay for decent ship security. See Jeffrey Gettelman, "The Pirates Are Winning!" *New York Review of Books*, October 14, 2010, http://www.nybooks.com/articles/2010/10/14/pirates-are-winning/ for an account of the rise of piracy in lawless, abandoned Somalia.

36. See Kevin Sack and Gardiner Harris, "President Obama Eulogizes Charleston Pastor as One Who Understood Grace," *New York Times*, June 26, 2015, https://www.nytimes.com/2015/06/27/us/thousands-gather-for-funeral-of-clementa-pinckney-in-charleston.html?_r=0, accessed July 1, 2017.

37. Tank's lyrics: http://www.metrolyrics.com/when-we-lyrics-tank.html, accessed August 15, 2018.

38. For her performance of the song, see https://www.youtube.com/watch?v=qB_IvRcr04E, accessed September 1, 2018.

39. See https://www.youtube.com/watch?v=tnDh0JhmaFwaccessed September 30, 2016.

40. See https://www.allmusic.com/album/grown-sexy-mw0000346899, accessed October 4, 2016.

41. See http://www.urbandictionary.com/define.php?term=GROWN%20AND%20SEXY, signed by L. Martin, December 5, 2005. Accessed September 30, 2016.

42. He also published a collection of these "church announcements." See J. Anthony Brown, *Reverend Adenoids' Church Announcements*. N.p.: KKT Publishing, 2000.

43. The *TJMS* crew did not coin the phrase "church mess," which has apparently had black-church currency for some decades. See Guthrie P. Ramsey, Jr., *Race Music: Black Cultures from Bebop to Hip-Hop*. Berkeley: University of California Press, 2003, p. 13.

44. See, for up-to-date analyses of black religion in the U.S. and abroad, Marla F. Frederick, *Colored Television: American Religion Gone Global*. Stanford, CA: Stanford University Press, 2016; and Carolyn Moxley Rouse, John L. Jackson, Jr., and Marla F. Frederick, *Televised Redemption: Black Religious Media and Racial Empowerment*. New York: New York University Press, 2016.

45. https://www.youtube.com/watch?v=mOzdfaEPaR0https://www.youtube.com/watch?v=mOzdfaEPaR 0, accessed July 1, 2017.

46. See Drew DeSilver, "Black Unemployment is Consistently Twice That of Whites," Pew Research Report, FactTank, News in the Numbers, August 21, 2013. http://www.pewresearch.org/fact-tank/2013/08/21/through-good-times-and-bad-black-unemployment-is-consistently-double-that-of-whites/, accessed September 16, 2015.

47. See James Grossman, *Land of Hope: Chicago, Black Southerners, and the Great Migration*. Chicago: University of Chicago Press, 1991; Isabel Wilkerson, *The Warmth of Other Suns: The Epic Story of America's Great Migration*. New York: Random House, 2010.

48. Farah Jasmine Griffin, *Who Set You Flowin': The African American Migration Experience*. New York: Oxford University Press, 1995, p. 182. See also Zandria F. Robinson, *This Ain't Chicago: Race, Class, and Regional Identity in the Post-Soul South*. Chapel Hill: University of North Carolina Press, 2014.

49. https://www.youtube.com/watch?v=l93wAqnPQwk, accessed October 8, 2015.

50. See Jamiles Lartey, "Louisiana Teacher Handcuffed Forcibly after Asking Questions at Board Meeting," *The Guardian*, January 9, 2018 https://www.theguardian.com/us-news/2018/jan/09/louisiana-teacher-handcuffed-forcibly-after-asking-questions-at-board-meeting, accessed March 1, 2018.

51. For scholarly sleuthing on proof of Brown's claim that he wrote as well as sang the song, see William Browning, "Who Really Wrote 'Merry Christmas Baby'"? *Smithsonian Magazine*, November 2017, https://www.smithsonianmag.com/arts-culture/who-wrote-merry-christmas-baby-180965207/, accessed March 1, 2018.

52. https://www.youtube.com/watch?v=1cs_LtUuXv0, accessed July 1, 2017.

53. For Little Milton, see Tony Russell, "Little Milton," *The Guardian*, August 5, 2005, https://www.theguardian.com/news/2005/aug/06/guardianobituaries; For The Meters, see no author, "The Meters Bio," *Rolling Stone*, n.d., https://www.rollingstone.com/music/artists/the-meters/biography, both accessed May 1, 2018.

54. On Johnnie Taylor, see https://www.allmusic.com/artist/johnnie-taylor-mn0000198162. For Tyrone Davis, see https://www.allmusic.com/artist/tyrone-davis-mn0000806507/biography, both sites accessed September 1, 2017. Sybil's ignorance of Tyrone Davis's work is most surprising, as he was a native Chicagoan.

55. See Sydney Scott, "Do You Know These 10 Things about Bad Boy Records?" *Essence*, June 26, 2017, accessed May 1, 2018.

56. See https://www.youtube.com/watch?v=0d27679i-X4, accessed September 20, 2016.

57. See https://www.youtube.com/watch?v=PIksbyVq5jA, accessed September 20, 2016.

58. See   http://www.idolator.com/6942561/whitney-houston-r-kelly-i-look-to-you?safari=1, accessed October 3, 2016.

59. See "Famed Attorney Johnnie Cochran dead," CNN, March 30, 2005, http://www.cnn.com/2005/US/03/29/cochran.obit/, accessed September 23, 2016.

60. See "Rice Spars with Democrats in Hearing," CNN, January 19, 2005, http://www.cnn.com/2005/ALLPOLITICS/01/18/rice.confirmation/, accessed June 14, 2008.

61. See David Streitfeld, R. Kelly is Acquitted in Child Pornography Case," *New York Times,* June 14, 2008, accessed September 21, 2016.

62. See her report: https://www.youtube.com/watch?v=kjK09Ti7MCM, accessed December 13, 2017.

63. See Glenn Thrush, "Under Ben Carson, HUD Scales Back Fair Housing Enforcement," *New York Times*, March 28, 2018, https://www.nytimes.com/2018/03/28/us/ben-carson-hud-fair-housing-discrimination.html, accessed November 6, 2018.

64. See https://www.youtube.com/watch?v=RTtc2pM1boE for Feliciano's performance, accessed May 1, 2018.

65. See "Ten Reasons Vice President Joe Biden Is Hip Hop," KISS FM, https://kissrichmond.com/906691/10-reasons-vice-president-joe-biden-is-hip-hop/, accessed March 5, 2018.

66. For a review of the book, see https://www.nytimes.com/2008/05/05/books/05masl.html, accessed September 21, 2016.

67. See Dave Laing, "Teena Marie Obituary," *Guardian*, December 27, 2010, https://www.theguardian.com/music/2010/dec/27/teena-marie-obituary,   accessed   September 22, 2016.

68. See Jessica Schladeback, "New Jersey Court Tosses Order Requiring Divorced Parents to Pay for Daughter's Tuition," *New York Daily News,* February 11, 2017, http://www.nydailynews.com/news/national/court-tosses-order-forcing-parents-pay-daughter-tuition-article-1.2970019, accessed July 1, 2017.

69. Nicole R. Fleetwood, *Racial Icons: Blackness and the Public Imagination.* New Brunswick, NJ: Rutgers University Press, 2015, p. 109.

70. See http://m.mlb.com/news/article/1016357//, accessed September 23, 2016.

71. See Tom Roody, "Boxer Wearing America First Shorts Beaten in Six Rounds by Mexican Rival," *Newsweek*, April 13, 2018, http://www.newsweek.com/boxing-america-first-mexico-885474, accessed April 16, 2018.

72. See Christine Hauser, "Men Arrested at Starbucks Hope to Ensure 'This Situation Doesn't Happen Again,'" *New York Times,* April 19, 2018, https://www.nytimes.com/2018/04/19/us/starbucks-black-men-arrests-gma.html, accessed April 25, 2018.

73. For the history of James Weldon Johnson's "Lift Up Ev'ry Voice and Sing," see Samantha Schmidt, "'Lift Ev'ry Voice and Sing:' the story behind the 'black national anthem' that Beyoncé sang," *Washington Post*, reprinted in *The Chicago Tribune,* April 16, 2018, http://www.chicagotribune.com/entertainment/music/ct-lift-every-voice-and-sing-beyonce-coachella-20180416-story.html, accessed April 20, 2018.

74. For his performance of that song, see https://www.youtube.com/watch?v=pB-5XG-DbAA.

75. See https://www.imdb.com/name/nm0680983/awards, accessed July 1, 2017.

76. See David Freeland, "Behind the Song: "Abraham, Martin, and John," *American Songwriter*, December 9, 2011, http://americansongwriter.com/2009/12/behind-the-song-abraham-martin-and-john/, accessed October 11, 2016. The segment aired on July 20, 2009.

77. See Bruce Weber, "James Garner, Witty, Handsome Leading Man, Dies at 86," *New York Times*, July 20, 2014, https://www.nytimes.com/2014/07/21/movies/james-garner-actor-dies-at-86.html, accessed July 1, 2017. Note that while this obituary states that Garner "was active on behalf of civil rights and environmental issues," it does not mention his funding help and presence at the March on Washington.

78. Virginia Woolf, *Three Guineas*. London: Hogarth Press, 1938.

79. See "Timeline: Lance Armstrong's Journey from Deity to Disgrace," *The Guardian*, March 18, 2015, https://www.theguardian.com/sport/2015/mar/09/lance-armstrong-cycling-doping-scandal, accessed July 1, 2017.

80. Although his strategic moves did not save him from doing prison time, and being banned for life from holding a CFO appointment, for defrauding the company. See https://www.reuters.com/article/us-healthsouth-scrushy/out-of-prison-former-healthsouth-ceo-scrushy-seeks-redemption-idUSBRE96K04D20130721, accessed March 5, 2018.

81. See "Key Players in the CIA Leak Investigation," *Washington Post,* July 3, 2007, http://www.washingtonpost.com/wp-srv/politics/special/plame/Plame_KeyPlayers.html, accessed March 5, 2018.

82. See Gary Owen's official website, http://garyowen.com, accessed July 1, 2017.

Chapter 5

1. Chuck Todd and Sheldon Gawiser, *How Barack Obama Won.* New York: Penguin, 2009, p. 26.

2. Jennifer Lynn Stoever, *The Sonic Color Line: Race & The Cultural Politics of Listening.* New York: New York University Press, 2016, p. 232.

3. See https://www.youtube.com/watch?v=nwi37EjbuIE, accessed September 1, 2017.

4. See J. W. Carmichael Jr., and others, "Project Soar (Stress on Analytical Reasoning), Classroom Guide 1981, http://eric.ed.gov/?id=ED204103, accessed October 12, 2016; Pearl Stewart, "Why Xavier Remains No. 1," *Black Issues in Higher Education,* vol. 18, no. 11, 2001, http://search.proquest.com/openview/92563bf4ff99850b3949b668fa70a0cf/1?pq-origsite=gscholar, accessed October 12, 2016. Disclosure: my beloved late mother-in-law, Clarita MacDonald Reed, ran the reading and testing labs at Xavier for more than a quarter-century. See also, on contemporary HBCU funding problems and the historical role of Howard University, Jelani Cobb, "Hard Tests: A Historically Black University in the Age of Trump," *New Yorker,* January 15, 2018, pp. 44–51; and a panel of social scientists on HBCUs' legacy, Darrick Hamilton et al., "The Continuing Case for America's Historically Black Colleges and Universities," *American Prospect,* Fall 2015, pp. 54–61.

5. See http://www.firehero.org/fallen-firefighter/vernon-a-richard/, accessed November 7, 2016.

6. See Mark Landler, "American POWs Await Return Home," *New York Times,* April 8, 2003, https://www.nytimes.com/2003/04/18/international/worldspecial/american-pows-await-return-home.html, accessed March 1, 2018.

7. Curtis Mayfield, "If There's a Hell Below," https://www.youtube.com/watch?v=x1xmXOP3lhM, accessed March 1, 2018.

8. See https://www.youtube.com/watch?v=QFUSP9_IOkM; and https://www.youtube.com/watch?v=8ShXwamvksQ, accessed November 7, 2016.

9. See https://georgewbush-whitehouse.archives.gov/news/releases/2002/03/20020313-8.html, accessed November 7, 2016.

10. See https://www.youtube.com/watch?v=4C3wsTTatRY, accessed October 11, 2016.

11. See, for example, David Gonzalez, "From the Margins of Society to Center of a Tragedy," *New York Times,* September 2, 2005; Michael Lewis, "Wading Toward Home," *New York Times Sunday Magazine,* October 9, 2005; David Remnick, "High Water: How President and Citizens React to Disaster," *The New Yorker,* October 3, 2005, pp. 48–57.

12. See Suzanne Perry, "Shell-Shocked into Action: Black Groups, Critical of Slow Response to Katrina, Vow to Strengthen Their Own Charitable Efforts," *The Chronicle of Philanthropy* September 29, 2005, p. 29; Peter Applebome, "Storms Stretch Thin Safety Net for 2 Colleges," *New York Times,* September 25, 2005; Judith Dobrzynski, "Shock of Katrina Pushes Black Charities to New Fundraising," *New York Times,* November 14, 2005. The latter piece mentions the *TJMS* only *en passant*. Perry covers a number of black charity efforts

whose fundraising results are pitiful compared to the *TJMS* numbers but never mentions the show. Only Bryan Curtis, in *Slate*, actually notes that the *TJMS* was "the voice of Hurricane Katrina," but he identifies it as black-nationalist and entirely altruistic, missing the show's progressive politics. See "TJMS: The Voice of Hurricane Katrina," *Slate*, September 21, 2005, https://slate.com/news-and-politics/2005/09/tom-joyner-voice-of-the-hurricane.html, accessed October 1, 2005.

13. http://www.hbo.com/documentaries/when-the-levees-broke-a-requiem-in-four-acts. See also Soyica Diggs Colbert, *Black Movements: Performance and Cultural Politics*. New Brunswick, NJ: Rutgers University Press, 2017, pp. 161–67, for an insightful analysis of the staging of the jazz funeral in the film.

14. See coverage of the march and rally in Krissah Thompson and Spencer Hsu "Tens of Thousands Attend Progressive 'One Nation Working Together' Rally in Washington," *Washington Post*, October 2, 2010, http://www.washingtonpost.com/wp-dyn/content/article/2010/10/01/AR2010100104440_2.html?sid=ST2010100104461, accessed July 1, 2017. C-SPAN documents Joyner's role: https://www.c-span.org/organization/?102610/one-nation-working-together, accessed July 1, 2017.

15. See Richard Adams, "Joe Barton: the Republican Who Apologized to BP," *The Guardian*, June 17, 2010, https://www.theguardian.com/world/richard-adams-blog/2010/jun/17/joe-barton-bp-apology-oil-spill-republican, accessed July 25, 2017.

16. See Gregg, "Tom Joyner," https://books.google.com/books?id=bVR9Fq7f2-wC&pg=PA114&lpg=PA114&dq=%22sandra+gregg%22+%22emerge+magazine%22&source=bl&ots=Pn8HpnmH2E&sig=D3bYaXNEAFG_q9QpvZZzhPS4kJ0&hl=en&sa=X&ved=0ahUKEwio8KSl6rraAhUBMqwKHaVRAbwQ6AEILDAB#v=onepage&q=%22sandra%20gregg%22%20%22emerge%20magazine%22&f=false, accessed March 5, 2018.

17. See David Stout, "Judge Opposed by Democrats Confirmed," *New York Times*, October 24, 2007, https://www.nytimes.com/2007/10/24/washington/24cnd-southwick.html, accessed October 21, 2016.

18. Biz Markie video: https://www.youtube.com/watch?v=9aofoBrFNdg; Chris Paul posted his full song: https://www.youtube.com/watch?v=DBTLGDuRzyE, both accessed July 1, 2017.

19. See, for example, David Bacon, *Children of NAFTA: Labor Wars on the US/Mexico Border*. Berkeley: University of California Press, 2005.

20. Among many other sources, for PROWRA's (Personal Responsibility and Work Opportunity Act) effects, see Jane Collins and Victoria Mayer, *Both Hands Tied: Welfare Reform and the Race to the Bottom of the Low-Wage Labor Market*. Chicago: University of Chicago Press, 2010. Re the 1994 crime bill, see Michelle Alexander, *The New Jim Crow: Mass Incarceration in the Age of Colorblindness*. New York: New Press, 2012, pp. 56ff. On deregulation, see Jeff Madrick, *The Age of Greed: The Triumph of Finance and the Decline of America, 1970–the Present*. New York: Alfred Knopf, 2011.

21. For an accounting of the normalization of underclass ideology across the 1980s and 1990s, see Micaela di Leonardo, "Black Myths, White Lies: Rape, Race, and the Black 'Underclass.'" In Roger Lancaster and Micaela di Leonardo, eds. *The Gender/Sexuality Reader*. New York: Routledge, 1997, pp. 53–68.

22. Toni Morrison, "Comment," *The New Yorker*, October 5, 1998, http://www.newyorker.com/magazine/1998/10/05/comment-6543, accessed October 21, 2016.

23. See videos: https://www.youtube.com/watch?v=dpWmlRNfLck; https://www.youtube.com/watch?v=bRdw2romPII; https://www.youtube.com/watch?v=AlsRWxC55I4; https://www.youtube.com/watch?v=yh1E6yl9Wk8; https://www.youtube.com/watch?v=MYl6_bNv7as; https://www.youtube.com/watch?v=Hh7ANTOQ2Rs, all accessed July 1, 2017.

24. There *was* a rightist attack on the event. See Washington Times staff, "Blacks, Latinos Rocking the Vote," *Washington Times*, October 30, 2004, http://m.washingtontimes.com/news/2004/oct/30/20041030-120752-7406r/, accessed November 7, 2016.

25. Video: https://www.youtube.com/watch?v=0rEsVp5tiDQ, accessed July 1, 2017.

26. Northwestern University's library website listed 59 books and films and 7,148 articles on the subject less than two years after the election. See, for example, Gwen Ifill, *The Breakthrough: Politics and Race in the Age of Obama.* New York: Doubleday, 2009; David Remnick, *Bridge: The Life and Rise of Barack Obama.* New York: Alfred Knopf, 2010; Amy Rice and Alicia Sams, "By the People: The Election of Barack Obama." HBO Documentary Films, 2009; Chuck Todd and Sheldon Gawiser, *How Barack Obama Won: a State-by-State Guide to the Historic 2008 Presidential Election.* New York: Vintage, 2009; Richard Wolffe, *Renegade: The Making of a President.* New York: Crown, 2009.

27. *How Barack Obama Won*, p. 31.

28. See *How Barack Obama Won*, p. 32.

29. David Bositis, "Blacks and the 2008 Elections: A Preliminary Analysis." Joint Center for Political and Economic Studies, vol. 36, no. 5, December 2008, pp. 12–16.

30. *How Barack Obama Won*, p. 30.

31. See Michael S. Lewis-Beck, Charles Tien, and Richard Nadeau, "Obama's Missed Landslide: A Racial Cost?" *Political Science and Politics*, vol. 43, no. 1, pp. 69–76. (David Bositis, of the Joint Center, comes closest in his statement that "black voters were key" to Obama's wins in Florida, North Carolina, Ohio, and Virginia. See "Blacks and the 2008 Elections," p. 15.)

32. Mark Hugo Lopez and Paul Taylor, "Dissecting the 2008 Electorate: Most Diverse in US History," Pew Research Center Publications, April 30, 2009, pp. 1–2.

33. But in fact, as we saw in chapter 2, Joyner began his career in the Reagan era, and in those early years identified as a conservative.

34. See Julie Bosman, "Edwards Attacks Obama for View of Reagan," *New York Times*, January 18, 2008.

35. See Taylor Branch, *At Canaan's Edge: America in the King Years, 1965-68.* New York: Simon and Schuster, 1988, pp. 210–11.

36. Video: https://www.youtube.com/watch?v=3gOHvDP_vCs, accessed July 1, 2017.

37. See, for example, Patrick Healey and Katherine Q. Seelye, "Clinton Says She 'Misspoke' about Dodging Sniper Fire," *New York Times*, March 25, 2008.

38. See Micaela di Leonardo, *Exotics at Home: Anthropologies, Others, American Modernity.* Chicago: University of Chicago Press, 1998, pp. 40ff.

39. Pat Buchanan, "A Brief for Whitey." March 21, 2008, http://buchanan.org/blog/pjb-a-brief-for-whitey-969, accessed September 20, 2010.

40. For the story of that firing, see Tim Mak, "Pat Buchanan Axed by MSNBC," *Politico*, February 17, 2012, https://www.politico.com/story/2012/02/msnbc-axes-pat-buchanan-073014, accessed March 5, 2018.

41. For his performance, see https://www.youtube.com/watch?v=FvJj7SN9EWI, accessed March 1, 2018.

42. https://www.youtube.com/watch?v=QsiSRSgqE4E, accessed November 7, 2016.

43. See Smukler's own publishing page, http://www.libertycitypress.com/11-Main/12-Front-Page/author/74-Ken-Smukler.html, accessed November 7, 2016.

44. Video: https://www.youtube.com/watch?v=TZtiJN6yiik, accessed July 1, 2017.

45. Videos: https://www.youtube.com/watch?v=3jeMvJoQGtQ; https://www.youtube.com/watch?v=Dxl4lQ8tmdM, accessed July 1, 2017.

46. Videos: https://www.youtube.com/watch?v=YnhI_ECOAK4; https://www.youtube.com/watch?v=4C3wsTTatRY; https://www.youtube.com/watch?v=kVpWes8MFm4.

47. For performances of these songs, see https://www.youtube.com/watch?v=Pq-XKuzVgCM; https://www.youtube.com/watch?v=jjXyqcx-mYY; https://www.youtube.com/watch?v=Wai6OM3YKTk; https://www.youtube.com/watch?v=DgtMHdir_7A, all accessed March 5, 2018.

48. See https://www.youtube.com/watch?v=YNyVq-K3x18, accessed July 1, 2017.

49. See http://www.thedailyshow.com/watch/mon-may-2-2011/to-kill-a-mockingturd, accessed July 1, 2012.

50. See Adam Liptak, "Supreme Court Finds Bias Against White Firefighters," *New York Times*, June 29, 2009, http://www.nytimes.com/2009/06/30/us/30scotus.html, accessed July 1, 2017.

51. See, for example, her attempts to benefit private, for-profit schools to the detriment of public schools, to muzzle sexual assault investigations in schools, and to use federal funds to arm schools. See, among many sources, Sharon Otterman, "De Vos Visits New York Schools, but Not One Run by the City," *New York Times*, May 16, 2018, https://www.nytimes.com/2018/05/16/nyregion/devos-visits-new-york-jewish-schools-not-public.html; Erica Green, "Education Secretary Considers Using Federal Funds to Arm Schools," *New York Times*, August 22, 2018, https://www.nytimes.com/2018/08/22/us/politics/betsy-devos-guns.html; Erica Green, "Education Secretary Besty De Vos Is Sued Over Sexual Assault Guidance," *New York Times*, January 25, 2018, https://www.nytimes.com/2018/01/25/us/politics/betsy-devos-sexual-assault-guidelines-lawsuit.html, all accessed November 15, 2018.

52. See, for example, Boyce Watkins, "Tavis Smiley Can't Win with Anti-Obama Talk," *The Grio*, March 20, 2010, http://thegrio.com/2010/03/20/httpwwwthegriocomopinionwhy-tavis-smiley-cant-win-when-it-comes-to-obama/, accessed July 1, 2017; Brennan Williams, *Huffpost*, "Tavis Smiley: Black Americans Have Lost Ground under Obama," September 12, 2014, http://www.huffingtonpost.com/2014/09/12/tavis-smiley-black-americans-obama_n_5812020.html, accessed July 1, 2017.

53. See https://www.youtube.com/watch?v=5DmYLrxR0Y8, accessed July 1, 2017.

54. See Aisha S. Durham, *Home with Hip Hop Feminism*. New York: Peter Lang, 2014, pp. 99–100 for a blistering account of Steve Harvey's misogyny. And re political motives for Clear Channel's action: On March 25, 2009, Tom Joyner explained on-air that Clear Channel "were so eager to fire me [but] the contract doesn't run out til the end of the year. So the money's good!"

55. See Mike McIntire, "Conservative Nonprofit Acts as a Stealth Business Lobbyist," *New York Times*, April 21, 2012, http://www.nytimes.com/2012/04/22/us/alec-a-tax-exempt-group-mixes-legislators-and-lobbyists.html.

56. West mixed his personal grievances—that he wasn't invited to the Inauguration or the White House, etc.—with progressive policy disappointments, for example, Obama's Wall Street-oriented economic team. He called for third-party presidential candidates. See Chris Hedges, "The Obama Deception: Why Cornel West Went Ballistic." Truthdig, May 16, 2011, http://www.truthdig.com/report/ page2/the obama deception why cornel west went ballistic 20110516/, accessed June 1, 2012; Melissa Harris-Perry, "Breaking News: Not All Black Intellectuals Think Alike." *The Nation*, June 13, 2011, p. 10.

57. Of course, the following year, the Supreme Court invalidated section five, tying the hands of the Department of Justice in its efforts to fight voter suppression. See Adam Liptak, "Supreme Court Invalidates Key Part of Voting Rights Act," *New York Times*, June 25, 2013, http://www.nytimes.com/2013/06/26/us/supreme-court-ruling.html, accessed June 1, 2015.

58. Video: https://www.youtube.com/watch?v=3Fmo8I_XSCI, accessed July 1, 2017.

59. Chris Paul posted the entire song. See http://www.youtube.com/watch?v=jVhVZlnRmw0, accessed July 1, 2017.

60. See, for example, Frank James, "'I Was Just Too Polite,' Says Obama, Vowing to Hit Hard at Next Debate," NPR, October 10, 2012, http://www.npr.org/sections/itsallpolitics/2012/10/10/162658971/i-was-just-too-polite-says-obama-vowing-to-hit-hard-at-next-debate; Lucy Madison, "Obama: I Was 'Too Polite' in Debate," CBS News, October 10, 2012, http://www.cbsnews.com/news/obama-i-was-too-polite-in-debate/; CNN political unit, "Obama on Debate: 'I Was Just Too Polite,'" CNN, October 10, 2012, http://politicalticker.blogs.cnn.com/2012/10/10/obama-on-debate-i-was-just-too-polite/, all accessed July 12, 2017.

61. See Roger Simons, "Joltin' Joe Biden Wins the Bout," *Politico*, October 10, 2012, https://www.politico.com/news/stories/1012/82323_Page2.html#; A local Philadelphia black station, WRNB 100.3, still has the excerpt up online. See https://rnbphilly.com/2378850/

tjms-vice-presidential-debate-2012-mini-mix-10-12-12-audio/, accessed April 3, 2018. Re Biden's role in the Clarence Thomas/Anita Hill hearings, see Kate Phillips, "Biden and Anita Hill, Revisited," *New York Times,* August 23, 2008, https://thecaucus.blogs.nytimes.com/ 2008/08/23/biden-and-anita-hill-revisited/, accessed June 15, 2018.

62. See, for example, Jane Mayer, "In the Withdrawal from the Paris Climate Agreement, the Koch Brothers' Campaign Becomes Overt," *The New Yorker,* June 5, 2017, https://www. newyorker.com/news/news-desk/in-the-withdrawal-from-the-paris-climate-agreement-the-koch-brothers-campaign-becomes-overt, accessed May 12, 2018.

63. See https://www.youtube.com/watch?v=p9DIN0nFHvs, accessed May 5, 2018. For the making of the "Whoop That Trick" chant, see this excerpt from *Hustle & Flow,* https://www. youtube.com/watch?v=R4Yu5TIgnTI, accessed March 5, 2018.

64. A popular teddy bear. See Bridget Carey, "The Life, Death, and Resurrection of Teddy Ruxpin," CNET, September 21, 2017, https://www.cnet.com/features/teddy-ruxpin-history-disney-atari-2017-return/, accessed March 15, 2018.

65. For song audios, see https://www.youtube.com/watch?v=FHDwRECFL8M; https://www. youtube.com/watch?v=CJTxnxXUMA0; https://www.youtube.com/watch?v=xz4YQZ01Q_ A; https://www.youtube.com/watch?v=3GwjfUFyY6M; https://www.youtube.com/watch? v=cBDqgSOwxkc; https://www.youtube.com/watch?v=zbYcte4ZEgQ, all accessed March 5, 2018.

66. For performances of the songs, see https://www.youtube.com/watch?v=8dM5QYdTo08; https://www.youtube.com/watch?v=eLWJSFJ7D1Y, both accessed March 5, 2018.

67. William Frey, "Minority Turnout Determined the 2012 Election," Brookings, May 10, 2013, https://www.brookings.edu/research/minority-turnout-determined-the-2012-election/, accessed June 1, 2015.

Chapter 6

1. Guthrie Ramsay, Jr., *Race Music: Black Cultures from Bebop to Hip-Hop.* Berkeley: University of California Press, 2003, p. 41.

2. Frederick Douglass, "West India Emancipation" speech, Canandaigua, New York, August 3, 1857, http://www.blackpast.org/1857-frederick-douglass-if-there-no-struggle-there-no-progress, accessed May 1, 2018.

3. See Robert Gooding-Williams, ed., *Reading Rodney King, Reading Urban Uprisings.* New York: Routledge, 1993.

4. Video: https://www.youtube.com/watch?v=4Gd6EhRRNJc, accessed July 1, 2017.

5. See, among a wealth of sources: Angela Davis, *Arbitrary Justice: The Power of the American Prosecutor.* New York: Oxford University Press, 2007; Ruth Wilson Gilmore, *Golden Gulag: Prison, Surplus, Crisis, and Opposition in Globalizing California.* Berkeley: University of California Press, 2007; Michelle Alexander, *The New Jim Crow: Mass Incarceration in the Age of Colorblindness.* Rev. ed. New York: New Press, 2012; Jeffrey Toobin, "Rights and Wrongs: A Judge Takes on Stop-and-Frisk," *The New* Yorker, May 27, 2013, http://www.newyorker. com/magazine/2013/05/27/rights-and-wrongs-2; Ta-Nehisi Coates, "The Black Family in the Age of Mass Incarceration." *The Atlantic,* October 2015. http://www.theatlantic.com/ magazine/archive/2015/10/the-black-family-in-the-age-of-mass-incarceration/403246/; Sharon LaFraniere and Andrew Lehren, "The Disproportionate Risk of Driving While Black," *New York Times,* October 25, 2015; ACLU, "School to Prison Pipeline Infographic," https://www.aclu.org/infographic/school-prison-pipeline-infographic, accessed July 1, 2017; Jessica Silver-Greenberg and Robert. Gebeloff, "Arbitration Everywhere, Stacking the Deck of Justice," *New York Times,* October 31, 2015, https://www.nytimes.com/2015/ 11/01/business/dealbook/arbitration-everywhere-stacking-the-deck-of-justice.html?_ r=0; David Cole, "The Truth about Our Prison Crisis, *New York Review of Books,* June 22, 2017,   http://www.nybooks.com/articles/2017/06/22/truth-about-our-prison-crisis/;

Bryan Stevenson, "The Presumption of Guilt, *New York Times,* June 13, 2017, http://www.nybooks.com/articles/2017/07/13/presumption-of-guilt/; Chandra Bozel, "The Prison-Industrial Complex," *New York Times,* March 21, 2016. http://www.nytimes.com/2016/03/21/opinion/the-prison-commercial-complex.html?action=click&pgtype=Homepage&clickSource=story-heading&module=opinion-c-col-right-region&region=opinion-c-col-right-region&WT.nav=opinion-c-col-right-region, all accessed July 1, 2017; Angela Davis, ed. *Policing the Black Man: Arrest, Prosecution, and Imprisonment.* New York: Pantheon, 2017; Paul Butler, *Chokehold: Policing Black Men.* New York: New Press, 2017.

6. See Timothy Williams, "Study Supports Suspicion That Police Are More Likely to Use Force on Blacks," *New York Times,* July 7, 2016, https://www.nytimes.com/2016/07/08/us/study-supports-suspicion-that-police-use-of-force-is-more-likely-for-blacks.html, accessed July 17, 2017.

7. See "Rod Blagojevich," *Chicago Tribune,* http://www.chicagotribune.com/topic/politics-government/government/rod-blagojevich-PEPLT007479-topic.html, accessed July 1, 2017.

8. For details, see the *Chicago Tribune* site: "Jon Burge: Latest Stories, Archives, Photos," https://www.chicagotribune.com/news/ct-jon-burge-chicago-police-torture-timeline-20180919-htmlstory.html, accessed July 1, 2017.

9. See Mark Potok, "The Trump Effect," Southern Poverty Law Center, February 15, 2017, https://www.splcenter.org/fighting-hate/intelligence-report/2017/trump-effect, accessed July 1, 2017.

10. See Kevin Quealy and Margot Sanger-Katz, "Compare These Gun Death Rates: The U.S. Is in a Different World," *New York Times,* June 13, 2016, https://www.nytimes.com/2016/06/14/upshot/compare-these-gun-death-rates-the-us-is-in-a-different-world.html, accessed July 17, 2017.

11. See Ezra Klein, "Twelve Facts about Guns and Mass Shootings in the United States, *Washington Post,* December 14, 2012, https://www.washingtonpost.com/news/wonk/wp/2012/12/14/nine-facts-about-guns-and-mass-shootings-in-the-united-states/?utm_term=.70f7e27e0c7a, accessed July 17, 2017.

12. See Richard Fausset, Alan Blinder and Michael S. Schmidt, "Gunman Kills 4 Marines at Military Site in Chattanooga," *New York Times,* July 16, 2015, https://www.nytimes.com/2015/07/17/us/chattanooga-tennessee-shooting.html?_r=0, accessed July 17, 2017.

13. See Julia Preston, "Li'l Kim Gets One Year in Prison," *New York Times,* July 7, 2005, http://www.nytimes.com/2005/07/07/nyregion/lil-kim-gets-one-year-in-prison.html?_r=0, accessed July 6, 2017.

14. See a summary of the case in Tara Kadlioglu, "Trial of Brothers Starts in Burr Oak Cemetery Scandal," *Chicago Tribune,* January 29, 2015, http://www.chicagotribune.com/suburbs/daily-southtown/chi-sta-burr-oak-cemetery-scandal-20150129-story.html, accessed April 20, 2018.

15. See Niraj Chokshi, "False Confessions, Mistaken Witnesses, Corrupt Officials: Putting the Innocent in Jail," *New York Times,* March 15, 2018, first section, p. 22.

16. See Abby Phillip, "Alabama Inmate Free after Three Decades on Death Row. How the Case against Him Unraveled," *Washington Post,* April 3, 2015, https://www.washingtonpost.com/news/morning-mix/wp/2015/04/03/how-the-case-against-anthony-hinton-on-death-row-for-30-years-unraveled/?utm_term=.54e511af919e, accessed July 1, 2017.

17. See Chester Sori, "Anthony Graves and the Long Struggle to Freedom," The Innocence Project November 19, 2010, https://www.innocenceproject.org/anthony-graves-and-the-long-struggle-to-freedom/, accessed March 1, 2018.

18. This event is one of the very few times multiple mainstream outlets—CNN, CBS, NBC, NPR, PBS, *New York Times*—covered a Tom Joyner story. PBS, in its written coverage, even saluted him as "one of radio's best known voices." See Frank James, "Tom Joyner's Wrongly Executed Relatives Exonerated—94 Years Too Late," NPR, October 14, 2009, https://www.npr.org/sections/thetwo-way/2009/10/tom_joyners_falsely_executed_r.html, accessed April 20, 2018.

19. See "Plea Agreement Reached in Jena Six Case," Southern Poverty Law Center, June 26, 2009, https://www.splcenter.org/news/2009/06/26/plea-agreement-reached-jena-six-case, accessed June 29, 2017.

20. See https://www.youtube.com/watch?v=HqYnevHibaI, accessed July 1, 2017.

21. See Michael Wilson, "3 Detectives Acquitted in Bell Shooting," *New York Times*, April 26, 2008, https://www.nytimes.com/2008/04/26/nyregion/26BELL.html, accessed June 1, 2017.

22. See Brian Stelter, "In Slain Teenager's Case, a Long Route to National Attention," *New York Times*, March 25, 2012, http://www.nytimes.com/2012/03/26/business/media/for-martins-case-a-long-route-to-national-attention.html, accessed June 30, 2017. Stelter does refer to the role of "black radio hosts" and Al Sharpton's own radio show, but misses *TJMS* coverage altogether.

23. See https://thelede.blogs.nytimes.com/2012/03/23/if-i-had-a-son-hed-look-like-trayvon-obama-says/, accessed June 30, 2017.

24. "Wide Racial, Partisan Gaps in Reactions to Trayvon Martin Coverage," Pew Research Center, April 3, 2012, http://www.people-press.org/2012/04/03/wide-racial-partisan-gaps-in-reactions-to-trayvon-martin-coverage/, accessed July 1, 2017.

25. See John Nichols, "ALEC Exposed," *The Nation*, August 1–8, 2011, https://www.thenation.com/article/alec-exposed/, accessed July 1, 2017.

26. Krissah Thompson and Lonnae O'Neal Parker, "For Trayvon Martin's Friend Rachel Jeantel, a 'Village' of Mentors Trying to Keep Her on Track," *Washington Post*, June 4, 2014, https://www.washingtonpost.com/lifestyle/style/for-rachel-jeantel-travyon-martins-friend-the-journey-continues/2014/06/04/0135d5a2-ec11-11e3-93d2-edd4be1f5d9e_story.html?utm_term=.bb637a1dcb69, accessed July 4, 2017.

27. Tom Joyner paid for a psychologist, for tutors and mentors, a makeover, and tuition at an alternative high school from which she graduated in 2014. And this particular *TJMS* act of charity received more mainstream press attention than had all of its HBCU work over decades, combined. See, for example, Alana Abramson, "Radio Host Tom Joyner Offers Rachel Jeantel Full College Scholarship," ABC News, July 17, 2013, http://abcnews.go.com/blogs/headlines/2013/07/radio-host-tom-joyner-offers-rachel-jeantel-full-college-scholarship/; Dana Ford, "Radio Host Offers Rachel Jeantel a Full Ride to College, CNN, July 17, 2013, http://www.cnn.com/2013/07/16/us/zimmerman-trial-witness-scholarship/index.html; Danielle Young, "Rachel Jeantel Accepts Tom Joyner's Scholarship," *HELLOBEAUTIFUL*, July 17, 2013, https://hellobeautiful.com/2657998/rachel-jeantel-accepts-tom-joyners-scholarship/; Danielle Cadet, "Rachel Jeantel Graduates High School," *Huffington Post*, June 5, 2014, http://www.huffingtonpost.com/2014/06/05/rachel-jeantel-graduates-high-school_n_5454330.html; David Boroff, "Trayvon Martin Friend Rachel Jeantel, Who Was Humiliated during George Zimmerman Trial, Turns Life Around," *New York Daily News*, July 14, 2014, http://www.nydailynews.com/news/national/trayvon-martin-friend-rachel-jeantel-turns-life-article-1.1866446, all accessed July 4, 2017.

28. Video: https://www.youtube.com/watch?v=yrotsEzgEpg, accessed July 1, 2017.

29. See Steven Nelson, "Angela Corey Wants to Throw Marissa Alexander Back in Jail, Allegedly Without Cause," *U.S. News*, January 8, 2014, https://www.usnews.com/news/articles/2014/01/08/angela-corey-wants-to-throw-marissa-alexander-back-in-jail?page=2, accessed July 1, 2017.

30. See Wesley Lowery, "In Ferguson, Reporter Gives Account of His Arrest, *New York Times*, August 14, 2014, https://www.washingtonpost.com/politics/in-ferguson-washington-post-reporter-wesley-lowery-gives-account-of-his-arrest/2014/08/13/0fe25c0e-2359-11e4-86ca-6f03cbd15c1a_story.html?utm_term=.98a9759d3bf9, accessed July 1, 2017.

31. The *TJMS* Ferguson coverage overlapped a great deal with MSNBC's—anchor Chris Hayes went to Ferguson and stayed there, reporting from the streets, for many days, and talked to many of the same activists and politicians.

32. See, for example, Tauhid Chappell, "Parents Are Having 'the Talk' with Their Children. What Did Yours Say?, *Washington Post*, July 11, 2016, https://www.washingtonpost.com/posteverything/wp/2016/07/11/parents-are-having-the-talk-with-their-children-about-police-what-did-yours-say/?utm_term=.74f7d0910dbb; Taylor Pittman, "Inside the Heartbreaking Talk Black Parents Must Have with Their Kids, *Huffington Post*, November 4, 2016, http://www.huffingtonpost.com/entry/inside-the-heartbreaking-talk-black-parents-must-have-with-their-kids_us_581ca092e4b0d9ce6fbb465b; Gita Ghandbhir and Blair Foster, "A Conversation with My Black Son," *New York Times*, March 17, 2015, https://www.nytimes.com/2015/03/17/opinion/a-conversation-with-my-black-son.html, all accessed July 1, 2017.

33. This information directly mirrors that offered in a *Washington Post* story published the same day, so I assume that was Joyner's source. See Abby Ohlheiser, "Here's what we know about Darren Wilson, the Officer Who Shot Michael Brown," *Washington Post*, August 25, 2017, https://www.washingtonpost.com/news/post-nation/wp/2014/08/25/heres-what-we-know-now-about-darren-wilson-the-officer-who-shot-michael-brown/?utm_term=.bf6640eaa284, accessed July 1, 2017.

34. Richard Rothstein, "The Making of Ferguson: Public Policies at the Root of Its Troubles," Economic Policy Institute Report, October 14, 2014, http://www.epi.org/publication/making-ferguson/, accessed June 1, 2017. See also his later, book-length treatment of the issue in *The Color of Law: A Forgotten History of How the Government Segregated America*. New York: W. W. Norton, 2017.

35. Video: https://www.youtube.com/watch?v=Wb9By-lODgk, accessed July 1, 2017.

36. Video: https://www.youtube.com/watch?v=Oq6qjYcx7VU, accessed July 1, 2017.

37. See https://www.youtube.com/watch?v=JXRN_LkCa_o, accessed July 1, 2017.

38. See https://www.youtube.com/watch?v=nDMoCUC4Mro, accessed July 1, 2017.

39. See https://www.youtube.com/watch?v=KDBF_KNx96o, accessed July 1, 2017.

40. From her "Love Is Found." See https://www.youtube.com/watch?v=KDBF_KNx96o, accessed July 1, 2017.

Chapter 7

1. Charles Blow, "A Rebel, a Warrior, and a Race Fiend," *New York Times*, September 25, 2017, https://www.nytimes.com/2017/09/25/opinion/columnists/trump-race-nfl-nba.html?rref=collection%2Fsectioncollection%2Fopinion&action=click&contentCollection=opinion&region=rank&module=package&version=highlights&contentPlacement=3&pgtype=sectionfront&_r=0, accessed September 25, 2017.

2. W. E. B. Du Bois, *Dusk of Dawn: An Essay towards an Autobiography of a Race Concept*. New York: Harcourt, Brace and Co, 1940, p. 151.

3. For an account of Joy Reid's Congolese/Guinean immigrant background, career, and politics, see Laura M. Holson, "How Joy Reid of MSNBC Became a Heroine of the Resistance," *New York Times*, February 10, 2018, https://www.nytimes.com/2018/02/10/style/joy-reid-msnbc.html, accessed May 1, 2018.

4. See David Hinckley, "New York City's Newest Urban Radio Station Set to Launch in July," *New York Daily News*, June 26, 2014, http://www.nydailynews.com/entertainment/new-york-city-new-urban-radio-station-article-1.1845044, accessed July 15, 2017.

5. For those who are puzzled by the reference—it's a play on rapper Lupe Fiasco.

6. See Luke Harding, "How Trump's Campaign Chief Got a Strongman Elected in Ukraine," *The Guardian*, August 16, 2010, https://www.theguardian.com/us-news/2016/aug/16/donald-trump-campaign-paul-manafort-ukraine-yanukovich, accessed March 1, 2018.

7. See Manuel Roig-Franzia, Scott Higham, Paul Fahi, and Chrissa Thompson, "The Fall of Roger Ailes," *Washington Post*, July 22, 2016, https://www.washingtonpost.com/lifestyle/style/the-fall-of-roger-ailes-he-made-fox-his-locker-room-and-now-women-are-telling-

their-stories/2016/07/22/5eff9024-5014-11e6-aa14-e0c1087f7583_story.html?utm_term=.0db7189b27b3, accessed March 1, 2018.

8. See Glenn Kessler and Meg Kelly, "President Trump Made 2140 False or Misleading Claims in His First Year," *Washington Post*, January 20, 2018, https://www.washingtonpost.com/news/fact-checker/wp/2018/01/20/president-trump-made-2140-false-or-misleading-claims-in-his-first-year/?utm_term=.e30e3c128096, accessed May 1, 2018.

9. Billy Paul's 1972 hit. See https://www.youtube.com/watch?v=n2v98PGBZH4, accessed July 1, 2017.

10. Almita Miranda pointed out to me that Erik Estrada, Freddy Prince, and Jose Feliciano are all actually Puerto Rican, not Mexican. It is not clear whether or not Ken Smukler was aware of that fact.

11. BLM and other youth civil rights organizations have had varied and shifting stances on electoral politics. See Nathalie Baptiste, "Origins of a Movement," *The Nation*, February 9, 2017, https://www.thenation.com/article/origins-of-a-movement/, accessed March 1, 2018.

12. On Moral Mondays and the Reverend William Barber, see Jedediah Purdy, "North Carolina's Long Moral March and Its Lessons for the Trump Resistance, *The New Yorker,* February 17, 2017, https://www.newyorker.com/news/news-desk/north-carolinas-long-moral-march-and-its-lessons-for-the-trump-resistance, accessed March 1, 2018.

13. See David Corn, "Secret Video: Romney Tells Republican Donors What He REALLY Thinks of Obama Voters," *Mother Jones* September 17, 2012, https://www.motherjones.com/politics/2012/09/secret-video-romney-private-fundraiser/, accessed March 1, 2018.

14. Video: https://www.youtube.com/watch?v=Ga3I5DTIA-E, accessed July 1, 2017.

15. See https://www.youtube.com/watch?v=d-diB65scQU, accessed May 1, 2018.

16. See, for example, Sally Persons, "Trump Did Not Expect, Want to Win the Presidency, *Washington Times*, January 3, 2018, https://www.washingtontimes.com/news/2018/jan/3/president-trump-did-not-expect-want-win-presidency/, accessed March 1, 2018.

17. David Blight, "Trump and History—Ignorance and Denial," National Underground Railroad Freedom Center, n.d, https://freedomcenter.org/voice/trump-and-history-ignorance-and-denial, accessed November 7, 2018.

18. Bob Woodward, *Fear: Trump in the White House.* New York: Simon and Schuster, 2018.

19. See, among many sources noting these errors, Mark Abadi, "Trump and His White House Have Made Some Embarrassing Spelling Mistakes—Here Are the Worst Ones," *Business Insider*, July 19, 2017, https://itunes.apple.com/us/app/adblock-for-safari/id1402042596?mt=12, accessed November 7, 2018.

20. See Martin Niemoller, "First They Came for the Socialists," *Holocaust Encyclopedia*, https://www.ushmm.org/wlc/en/article.php?ModuleId=10007392, accessed July 1, 2017.

21. Video: https://www.youtube.com/watch?v=HEFRPLM0nEA, accessed July 1, 2017.

22. Video in Adam Salandra, "Jennifer Lewis Wants You to Get Yo Ass Out and Vote," Logo, November 8, 2016, http://www.newnownext.com/jenifer-lewis-vote/11/2016/, accessed March 1, 2018.

23. The Reverend J. William Barber II, *The Third Reconstruction: Moral Mondays, Fusion Politics, and the Rise of a New Justice Movement.* Boston: Beacon Press, 2016.

24. Reprinted in full with permission of the author.

25. See https://www.youtube.com/watch?v=BsSu0bRZEHM, accessed March 5, 2018.

26. For performance, see https://www.youtube.com/watch?v=Kp7eSUU9oy8, accessed June 15, 2018.

27. See https://www.youtube.com/watch?v=qp1Pq2Fuw30, accessed March 5, 2018.

28. The original song is on YouTube: https://www.youtube.com/watch?v=Aga1BOSu7yY, accessed July 1, 2017.

29. Linda Qiu, "Donald Trump Had Biggest Inaugural Crowd Ever? Metrics Don't Show It," *Politifact,* January 21, 2017, https://www.politifact.com/truth-o-meter/statements/2017/jan/21/sean-spicer/trump-had-biggest-inaugural-crowd-ever-metrics-don/, accessed June 1, 2018.

30. On Pence's record on women's LBGTQ, and race issues, see Rachael Revesz, "Mike Pence Poses Biggest Threat to Women in a Generation, Say Campaigners," *Independent*, January 17, 2017, https://www.independent.co.uk/news/world/americas/mike-pence-vice-president-womens-rights-opponent-abortion-roe-v-wade-indiana-governor-purvi-patel-a7529801.html; Charlotte Clymer, "HRC Exposes 'The Real Mike Pence'—from Anti-LBGTQ Fanaticism to Assault on American Institutions," Human Rights Campaign, April 19, 2018, https://www.hrc.org/blog/hrc-exposes-real-mike-pence-from-anti-lgbtq-fanaticism-to-assault-on-am; Chris Walker, "Here are some of Mike Pence's Most Controversial Stances on Gay Rights, Abortion, and Smoking," *Business Insider*, November 14, 2016, https://www.businessinsider.com/mike-pences-most-controversial-stances-on-gay-rights-abortion-and-smoking-2016-11, all accessed November 7, 2018.

31. Considering falsehoods, the *New York Times* carefully compared Trump to President Obama. They concluded that in his first 10 months alone, Trump had told six times the number of falsehoods than President Obama had during his entire eight years in office. See David Leonhardt, Ian Prasad Philbrick, and Stuart A. Thompson, "Trump's Lies vs. Obama's," *New York Times*, December 14, 2017, https://www.nytimes.com/interactive/2017/12/14/opinion/sunday/trump-lies-obama-who-is-worse.html. On Trump's ignorance of American history, see Colbert I. King, "Trump's Astounding Ignorance about History," *Washington Post*, July 1, 2018, https://www.washingtonpost.com/blogs/post-partisan/wp/2018/07/16/trumps-astounding-ignorance-about-history/?noredirect=on&utm_term=.f03b214d99ca, both accessed November 7, 2018.

32. See Rosalind S. Helderman and Mary Jordan, "Many Questions and Few Answers about How Melania Trump Immigrated to the U.S.," *Washington Post*, August 4, 2016, https://www.washingtonpost.com/politics/many-questions-and-few-answers-about-how-melania-trump-immigrated-to-the-us/2016/08/04/0c13cc1a-5a3f-11e6-831d-0324760ca856_story.html?utm_term=.6b1b48f662dd, accessed July 1, 2017.

33. See Katie Rogers, "As Melania Trump Faces Plagiarism Charges, Her Staff Lashes Out at News Media," *New York Times*, May 8, 2018, https://www.nytimes.com/2018/05/08/us/politics/melania-trump-plagiarism-be-best-initiative.html, accessed May 10, 2018.

34. Video: https://www.youtube.com/watch?v=reTx5sqvVJ4, accessed July 1, 2017.

35. See Amy B. Wang, "Maxine Waters Swings Back at Bill O'Reilly, *Washington Post*, March 9, 2017, https://www.washingtonpost.com/news/the-fix/wp/2017/03/28/bill-oreilly-compared-a-black-congresswomans-hair-to-a-james-brown-wig/?utm_term=.9accb5b306f6, accessed March 1, 2018.

36. See https://www.youtube.com/watch?v=KutXyPEEbQs, accessed May 1, 2018.

37. See Lee Moran, "Neil deGrasse Tyson Burns Donald Trump over Possible Paris Climate Deal Withdrawal," *Huffpost*, June 1, 2017, https://www.huffingtonpost.com/entry/neil-degrasse-tyson_us_592fdff0e4b0e09b11edbf7e, accessed November 5, 2018.

38. For his performance, see https://www.youtube.com/watch?v=CAV0XrbEwNc&oref=https%3A%2F%2Fwww.youtube.com%2Fwatch%3Fv%3DCAV0XrbEwNc&has_verified=1, accessed March 1, 2018.

39. For his performance, see https://www.youtube.com/watch?v=FGZYWSfiYbM, accessed May 1, 2018.

40. See Frances Robles, "Trump calls Storm Response in Puerto Rico, Where 3,000 Died, 'One of the Best,'" *New York Times*, September 11, 2018, https://www.nytimes.com/2018/09/11/us/trump-puerto-rico-maria-response.html, accessed November 7, 2018.

41. See Rukmini Callimachi, Helene Cooper, Eric Schmitt, Alan Blinder, and Thomas Gibbons-Neff, "An Endless War: Why 4 US Soldiers Died in a Remote African Desert," *New York Times*, February 20, 2018, https://www.nytimes.com/interactive/2018/02/17/world/africa/niger-ambush-american-soldiers.html, accessed March 1, 2018.

42. See Mark Landler, "Trump Falsely Claims Obama Didn't Contact Families of Fallen Troops," *New York Times*, October 16, 2017, https://www.nytimes.com/2017/10/16/us/politics/trump-obama-killed-soldiers.html; Mark Landler and Yamiche Alcindor, "Trump's

Condolence Call to Soldier's Widow Ignites an Imbroglio," *New York Times*, October 18, 2017, https://www.nytimes.com/2017/10/18/us/politics/trump-widow-johnson-call.html, accessed November 7, 2018.

43. For their performance, see https://www.youtube.com/watch?v=fHLTGc29PBk, accessed March 1, 2018.

44. See Heather Caygle, "Rep. Wilson returns to Capitol after Facing Death Threats," *Politico*, November 1, 2017, https://www.politico.com/story/2017/11/01/frederica-wilson-congress-threats-kelly-244434, accessed November 5, 2018.

45. Hillary Rodham Clinton, *What Happened*. New York: Simon and Schuster, 2017.

46. See Deneen L. Brown, "Doug Jones Triumphs in an Alabama Senate Race That Conjured a Deadly Church Bombing," *Washington Post*, November 9, 2017, https://www.washingtonpost.com/news/retropolis/wp/2017/11/09/an-alabama-senate-race-conjures-the-awful-1963-church-bombing-that-killed-4-black-girls/?utm_term=.f49eef010100, accessed March 1, 2018.

47. See John Donohue, "How Does US Gun Control Compare to the Rest of the World?" *Newsweek*, June 19, 2017, http://www.newsweek.com/us-gun-control-compare-rest-world-627184, accessed March 1, 2018.

48. Michael Wolff, *Fire and Fury: Inside the Trump White House*. New York: Henry Holt, 2018.

49. See Jonathan Martin, "Sanders, in Courting Blacks, Is Tripped Up by Notion He Slighted Obama," *New York Times*, April 7, 2018, A13.

50. See Sandra E. Garcia, "The Woman Who Created #MeToo Long Before Hashtags," *New York Times*, October 31, 2107, https://www.nytimes.com/2017/10/20/us/me-too-movement-tarana-burke.html, accessed April 24, 2018.

51. The barbecue story had a lovely sequel: black community members showed up at the same site for a grand party. They played Frankie Beverly and Maze and did the electric slide. The videos of the defiantly celebrating neighbors went viral. See Alyssa Pereira, "Oakland Locals Have Massive Party Where Woman Called Police on Black Men's Barbecue," *SFGate*, May 14, 2018, https://www.sfgate.com/local/article/lake-merritt-racist-incident-police-barbecue-video-12914095.php; and see Cleve R. Wootson Jr, "Add 'Performing Community Service While Black' to the List of Things That Make You Suspicious," *Washington Post*, May 15, 2018, https://www.washingtonpost.com/news/grade-point/wp/2018/05/15/add-performing-community-service-while-black-to-the-list-of-things-that-make-you-suspicious/?noredirect=on&utm_term=.0c257af2a67a, all accessed May 18, 2018.

52. On lying to the Judiciary Committee, see Charlie Savage, "Kavanaugh is Pressed on Knowledge of Some Bush-Era Disputes," *New York Times*, September 5, 2018, https://www.nytimes.com/2018/09/05/us/politics/kavanaugh-leahy-bush-disputes.html; on the various women's claims and the FBI's failure to investigate them thoroughly, see Michael D. Shear, Michael S. Schmidt, and Adam Goldman, "FBI Review of Kavanaugh Was Limited from the Start," *New York Times*, October 5, 2018.

53. For Sam Cooke's performance of his last song, with a beautiful, time-defying montage of global progressive photos, see https://www.youtube.com/watch?v=wEBlaMOmKV4, accessed November 5, 2018.

54. See Collins' English Dictionary, "Bradley effect," n.d., https://www.collinsdictionary.com/us/dictionary/english/bradley-effect, accessed November 5, 2018.

55. See https://www.youtube.com/watch?v=6YNZlXfW6Ho for her performance, accessed November 10, 2018.

56. See Patrick Ryan, "'Boo'd Up': How Newcomer Ella Mai Made the Most Swoon-Worthy Song of the Summer," *USA Today*, July 30, 2018, https://www.usatoday.com/story/life/music/2018/07/30/bood-up-how-ella-mai-made-most-romantic-summer-song/837810002/; and Brittany Spanos, "Ella Mai's Surprise Smash," *Rolling* Stone, October 5, 2018, https://www.rollingstone.com/music/music-features/ella-mai-interview-bood-up-trip-album-732451/, both accessed November 10, 2018.

Chapter 8

1. Trevor Noah, *Born a Crime: Stories From a South African Childhood.* New York: Spiegel and Grau, 2016.

2. See Rachel Maddow Biography, MSNBC, http://www.msnbc.com/the-rachel-maddow-show/rachel-maddow-biography; and Chris Hayes Biography, http://www.msnbc.com/all-chris-hayes/chris-hayes-biography, both accessed July 1, 2017.

3. See Rodney Ho, "J Anthony Brown on his Tom Joyner Departure," *AJC.com,* April 24, 2017, http://radiotvtalk.blog.ajc.com/2016/12/01/j-anthony-brown-on-his-tom-joyner-departure-it-was-not-a-salary-dispute/, accessed July 1, 2017.

4. See https://www.quantcast.com/msnbc.com#trafficCard, accessed April 28, 2018. Thanks to journalism graduate student Yuyi Chen for this citation.

5. I wrote about and cited these stories, as well as alarming readers' letters, in my *Exotics at Home: Anthropologies, Others, American Modernity.* Chicago: University of Chicago Press, p. 396.

6. See https://www.politico.com/mapdata-2016/2016-election/results/map/president/, accessed March 5, 2018.

7. See Christopher Caldwell, "What the Alt-Right Really Means, *New York Times,* December 2, 2016, https://www.nytimes.com/2016/12/02/opinion/sunday/what-the-alt-right-really-means.html, accessed March 1, 2018.

8. See Callum Borchers, "Is Donald Trump Saving the News Media? *Washington Post,* February 6, 2017; Ken Doctor, "Trump Bump Grows into Subscription Surge—and Not Just for the *New York Times,*" *TheStreet,* March 3, 2017, https://www.thestreet.com/story/14024114/1/trump-bump-grows-into-subscription-surge.html; A. J. Katz, "Q2 2017 Ratings: Rachel Maddow Has the No. 1 Cable News Show Among Adults 25-54," *AdWeekTVNewser,* June 27, 2017, http://www.adweek.com/tvnewser/q2-2017-ratings-rachel-maddow-has-the-no-1-cable-news-show-among-adults-25-54/333372, accessed July 1, 2017.

9. Steve Phillips, "The Democratic Party's Billion-Dollar Mistake," *New York Times,* July 20, 2017. See also Ari Berman, "Rigged: How Voter Suppression Threw Wisconsin to Trump and Changed the Election," *Mother Jones,* November/December 2017, pp. 24–31. See also Micaela di Leonardo, "The Trumpocalypse and Black Radio," *Cultural Anthropology* "Hotspots" website, January 18, 2017, https://culanth.org/fieldsights/1033-the-trumpocalypse-and-black-radio.

10. See Sean McElwee, Jesse H. Rhodes, Brian F. Schaffner, and Bernard L. Fraga, "The Missing Obama Millions," *New York Times* March 11, 2018, Sunday review section, p. 3.

11. William E. Spriggs, "Why the White Worker Theme Is Harmful," *American Prospect,* Summer 2017, pp. 43–45, esp. pp. 43, 45.

12. Diana C. Mutz, "Status Threat, Not Economic Hardship, Explains the 2016 Presidential Vote," *Proceedings of the National Academy of Sciences,* April 23, 2018, http://www.pnas.org/content/early/2018/04/18/1718155115, accessed April 27, 2018.

13. See Tom Joyner, "Obama's American Town Hall Live Blog," Blackamericaweb.com, January 18, 2010, https://blackamericaweb.com/2012/03/10/obamas-america-town-hall-live-blog/, accessed March 1, 2018.

14. See Larry S. Miller, "Paradigm Shift: Why Radio Must Adapt to the Rise of Digital," *Entertainment and Sport Lawyer,* vol. 34, Fall 2017, https://www.americanbar.org/groups/entertainment_sports/publications/entertainment-sports-lawyer/2017/fall2017/paradigm-shift.html, accessed March 11, 2018. Also see an outtake press report on this study, Robert Channick, "Digital Audio Factors in Swan Song to Rock," *The Chicago Tribune,* March 11, 2018, business section. See also Ben Sisario, "Bankrupt, IHeartMedia Has Deals to Cut Debt," *New York Times,* March 16, 2018, B3.

15. See Rodney Ho, "Exclusive—Tom Joyner on Retirement," *Atlanta Journal-Constitution,* January 30, 2018, http://radiotvtalk.blog.ajc.com/2018/01/30/exclusive-tom-joyner-on-2019-retirement-couldnt-get-a-guaranteed-contract-after-two-years/; and no author, "Lack

of Long-Term Deal Behind Joyner's Retirement," InsideRadio, January 31, 2018, http://www.insideradio.com/free/lack-of-long-term-deal-behind-tom-joyner-s-retirement/article_671c01fa-06d1-11e8-a550-a3f974a38708.html accessed March 15, 2018. See also wildly positive Detroit television coverage of the show's functions—"the voice of millions"— and interview with Joyner by journalist Paul Tutman, ClickonDetroit, https://www.clickondetroit.com/entertainment/iconic-morning-radio-host-tom-joyner-prepares-to-retire-reflects-on-legacy, accessed April 25, 2018.

16. Gene Roberts and Hank Klibanoff, *The Race Beat*. New York: Knopf, p. 404.

17. See David Karpf, "The Long Arc of Protest," *American Prospect*, August 16, 2017, http://prospect.org/article/long-arc-protest, accessed March 15, 2018.

18. Sumanth Gopinath, *The Ringtone Dialectic: Economy and Cultural Form*. Cambridge, MA: MIT Press, 2013, pp. 241–67; Alexander Weheliye, *Phonographies: Grooves in Sonic Afro-Modernity*. Durham, NC: Duke University Press, 2005.

19. William Barlow, *Voice Over: The Making of Black Radio*. Philadelphia: Temple University Press, 1999, p. 298.

Permissions

The author is grateful to the following publishers for their agreement to republish work in this book:

American Anthropological Association, for permission to publish Micaela di Leonardo, "Grown Folks Radio: U.S. Election Politics and a 'Hidden' Black Counterpublic" as published in *American Ethnologist*, vol. 39, no. 4, November 2012, pp. 661–72.

Cultural Anthropology, for permission to publish Micaela di Leonardo, "The Trumpocalypse and Black Radio," *Cultural Anthropology*, "Hotspots" website, January 18, 2017. https://culanth.org/fieldsights/1033-the-trumpocalypse-and-black-radio.

Taylor & Francis, for permission to publish Micaela di Leonardo, "Neoliberalism, Nostalgia, Race Politics, and the American Public Sphere," *Cultural Studies*, vol. 22, no. 1, 2008, pp. 1–34.

Taylor & Francis, for permission to publish Micaela di Leonardo, "Partyin' with a Purpose: Black Respectability Politics and the Tom Joyner Morning Show," *Souls*, vol. 18, no. 2-4, 2016, pp. 358–78.

Index

Note: Figures are indicated by an italic *f* following the page number.